IDEAS IN CONTEXT

MILTON AND REPUBLICANISM

MILTON
AND REPUBLICANISM

EDITED BY

DAVID ARMITAGE
Columbia University

ARMAND HIMY
Université de Paris X-Nanterre

QUENTIN SKINNER
University of Cambridge

CAMBRIDGE
UNIVERSITY PRESS

Published by the Press Syndicate of the University of Cambridge
The Pitt Building, Trumpington Street, Cambridge CB2 1RP

40 West 20th Street, New York, NY 10011-4211, USA
10 Stamford Road, Oakleigh, Melbourne 3166, Australia

© Cambridge University Press 1995

First published 1995

Printed in Great Britain at the University Press, Cambridge

A catalogue record for this book is available from the British Library

Library of Congress cataloguing in publication data applied for

ISBN 0 521 55178 1 hardback

Contents

Notes on contributors

DAVID ARMITAGE is Assistant Professor of History at Columbia University. He has edited Bolingbroke's *Political Writings* for Cambridge Texts in the History of Political Thought and *Theories of Empire 1450–1800*, both of which are in press. He is now working on a study of the ideological origins of the British Empire.

CEDRIC C. BROWN is Senior Lecturer in English at the University of Reading. He is the author of *John Milton's Aristocratic Entertainments* (1985) and *John Milton: a Literary Life* (1995). He has also edited *The Poems and Masques of Aurelian Townshend* (1983) and *Patronage, Politics, and Literary Traditions in England, 1558–1658* (1993).

THOMAS N. CORNS is Professor of English at the University of Wales, Bangor. He is the author of *The Development of Milton's Prose Style* (1982), *Milton's Language* (1990), *Uncloistered Virtue: English Political Literature, 1640–1660* (1992) and *Regaining 'Paradise Lost'* (1994). He is currently co-editing the complete works of Gerrard Winstanley.

TONY DAVIES is Senior Lecturer in English at the University of Birmingham. He has edited two collections of Milton's poetry and prose and is co-author of *Rewriting English* (1985).

MARTIN DZELZAINIS is Lecturer in English at Royal Holloway, University of London. He has edited Milton's *Political Writings* (1991) for Cambridge Texts in the History of Political Thought. He is currently working on the ideological origins of the English Revolution and on a study of Spenser's *Færie Queene*.

ARMAND HIMY is Professor of English at the Université de Paris X-Nanterre. He is the author of *Pensée, Mythe et Structure dans 'Paradise Lost'* (1977) and *Le Puritanisme* (1987), and the editor of volumes of essays on *Comus*, Donne, and Vaughan. He is completing a bilingual edition and translation of *Paradise Lost* into French.

VICTORIA KAHN is Professor of English and Comparative Literature at Princeton University. She is the author of *Rhetoric, Prudence and Skepticism in the Renaissance* (1985) and *Machiavellian Rhetoric: From the Counter-Reformation to Milton* (1994). She also co-edited *Machiavelli and the Discourse of Literature* (1994).

ROGER LEJOSNE is Emeritus Professor of English Language and Literature at the Université de Picardie at Amiens. He is the author of *La Raison dans l'Œuvre de John Milton* (1981), and recently collaborated on the French translation of Samuel Pepys's *Diary*.

QUENTIN SKINNER is Professor of Political Science in the University of Cambridge and a Fellow of Christ's College. He is the author of *The Foundations of Modern Political Thought* (2 volumes, 1978) and *Reason and Rhetoric in the Philosophy of Hobbes* (forthcoming). His previous publications on republicanism include *Machiavelli* (1981) and, as co-editor, *Machiavelli and Republicanism* (1988).

NIGEL SMITH is Lecturer in English at Oxford University and a Fellow of Keble College. He has edited the Ranter pamphlets and is the author of *Perfection Proclaimed: Language and Literature in English Radical Religion, 1640–1660* (1989) and *Literature and Revolution in England, 1640–1660* (1994).

ELIZABETH TUTTLE is Senior Lecturer in Anglo-American Studies at the Université de Paris X-Nanterre. She is the author of *Religion et Idéologie dans la Révolution Anglaise 1647–1649: Salut du Peuple et Pouvoir des Saints* (1989), and she is now working on a study of politics, religion and iconography in England, 1620–1660.

NICHOLAS VON MALTZAHN is Associate Professor of English at the University of Ottawa. His publications include *Milton's 'History of Britain': Republican Historiography in the English Revolution* (1991). He is completing a book on Milton and his readers, 1650–1750.

BLAIR WORDEN is Fellow and Tutor in Modern History at St Edmund Hall, Oxford. He is the author of *The Rump Parliament, 1648–1653* (1974) and a series of studies on the politics, religion and literature of early modern England, and has edited Edmund Ludlow's *A Voyce from the Watch Tower* (1978). He is now writing on Sidney's *Arcadia*.

Preface

The Colloquium on 'Milton and Republicanism' which gave rise to this volume was held at the Université de Paris X-Nanterre, in April 1992. Armand Himy, in consultation with Quentin Skinner, drew up the original list of participants and issued invitations to the speakers, among whom were myself, Cedric Brown, Tony Davies, Martin Dzelzainis, Roger Lejosne, Elizabeth Tuttle and Blair Worden, as well as Armand Himy and Quentin Skinner themselves. The organizers are grateful to the speakers, as well as to the other scholars who presented papers, those who chaired sessions, and the audience in Nanterre for the effort they put into making the Colloquium such a success.

The responsibility for turning the papers from the Colloquium into the present volume has been divided between myself and Quentin Skinner. While the final organization of the volume has been my responsibility, I discussed it with Quentin Skinner at every stage. We selected the initial group of papers for inclusion in consultation with Armand Himy and representatives of the Cambridge University Press. I then approached further prospective contributors and commissioned the remaining essays. Quentin Skinner conducted the negotiations between the editors and the Press, and he and I read and commented on the completed essays before publication. We are grateful to those of our contributors who were present in Nanterre for the speed with which they undertook revisions – sometimes substantial – to their papers, as well as to those who joined the project at a later stage, for producing original and appropriate essays under the constraints of a tight deadline. I should also like particularly to thank Martin Dzelzainis, Quentin Skinner, Nigel Smith and the anonymous reader for the Press for their advice regarding the volume and its contents, as well as the Master and Fellows of Emmanuel College,

Cambridge, for their support and hospitality at all stages of my work on the book.

The editors wish to thank the Université de Paris X-Nanterre, and the Centre de Recherches sur les Origines de la Modernité et les Pays Anglophones, for placing their facilities at our disposal for the original Colloquium. That a volume has resulted so quickly from that Colloquium is thanks to Quentin Skinner, who has propelled the project with exemplary efficiency and courtesy, and to Richard Fisher, who has put his own energy and skill, as well as the heartening faith of the Press, behind the volume at every stage of its gestation. Frances Brown copy-edited the manuscript swiftly and exactly, and David Atkins compiled the index. Our thanks to both of them for their careful work.

The frontispiece and cover show the clay bust of Milton in the Senior Combination Room of Christ's College, Cambridge. College tradition holds that the bust is a life-study of Milton executed either by Edward Pierce or by Abraham Simon, though its provenance is unknown before 1738 when it was in the possession of the antiquarian and engraver George Vertue. After Vertue's death, the bust was acquired by the radical whig Miltonian and republican Thomas Hollis, who later presented it to 'the College in which my hero Milton, and the guide of my paths, was bred'. It was engraved twice in the eighteenth century, and was the model for the nineteenth-century marble bust in the College Hall. We are very grateful to the Master and Fellows of Christ's College for permission to reproduce this striking and tangible link between Milton and later English republicanism.

David Armitage

ABBREVIATIONS

CPW *Complete Prose Works of John Milton*, general ed. Don M. Wolfe (8 vols., New Haven, 1953–82)

PL Milton, *Paradise Lost*, ed. Alastair Fowler (London, 1971). All references to *Paradise Lost* are to this edition; all other references to Milton's poetry are to Milton, *Complete Shorter Poems*, ed. John Carey (London, 1971)

PART ONE

Defining Milton's republicanism

CHAPTER I

Milton's classical republicanism

Martin Dzelzainis

I

In *Behemoth, or The Long Parliament*, Thomas Hobbes laid much of the blame for the Civil War at the door of the universities which, he said, 'have been to this nation, as the wooden horse was to the Trojans'.[1] This was also a warning because until the universities were reformed they would continue to pose the same threat: 'The core of rebellion, as you have seen by this ... are the Universities.'[2] Their potential for causing rebellion arose from a single source: the prominence of the ancient languages in the curriculum. For Hobbes believed that anyone acquiring a mastery of these languages was in effect being handed the keys to an ideological arsenal.

Two groups especially had exploited the opportunity presented to them. One was the clergy who were able to 'pretend' that linguistic expertise endowed them with 'greater skill in Scriptures than other men have'.[3] This meant they could 'impose' their 'own sense' of Scripture on their 'fellow-subjects' despite the fact that the Bible was available in English.[4] They could also invoke the same 'skill' whenever they sought to 'publish or teach ... private interpretations' which brought the king's authority into question – something which Hobbes regarded as a matter of the utmost consequence since 'the interpretation of a verse in the Hebrew, Greek, or Latin Bible, is oftentimes the cause of civil war and the deposing and assassinating of God's anointed'.[5]

The other group armed in this fashion was the gentry – the 'men of the better sort', 'democratical gentlemen' or simply 'democraticals' as

I am greatly indebted to David Armitage and Quentin Skinner for their prompt and perceptive comments on a draft of this essay.

[1] Thomas Hobbes, *Behemoth or the Long Parliament*, ed. Ferdinand Tönnies, intro. Stephen Holmes (Chicago, 1990), p. 40.   [2] *Ibid.*, p. 58.   [3] *Ibid.*, p. 90.   [4] *Ibid.*, p. 53.
[5] *Ibid.*, pp. 55, 144.

3

Hobbes often called them.[6] They had gained access to the reserves of classical history and moral philosophy which 'furnished' them 'with arguments for liberty out of the works of Aristotle, Plato, Cicero, Seneca, and out of the histories of Rome and Greece, for their disputation against the necessary power of kings'.[7] The effect on the 'exceeding great number' who were 'so educated' had been calamitous. It was impossible to persuade those who had 'acquired the learning of a university', and 'especially' those who had 'read the glorious histories and the sententious politics of the ancient popular governments', that they might conceivably lack 'any ability requisite for the government of a commonwealth'. For once they 'read the books written by famous men of the ancient Grecian and Roman commonwealths', in which 'popular government was extolled by the glorious name of liberty, and monarchy disgraced by the name of tyranny', they quite simply fell 'in love with their forms of government'.[8]

Hobbes then clears a path connecting these claims to his account of the fall of the monarchy. When asked to explain how such a seemingly powerful monarch as Charles I could 'miscarry', Hobbes replies that this was because the people had been 'corrupted'. Asked 'what kind of people were they that could so seduce them?', he responds by singling out the 'ministers' and 'men of the better sort'.[9] It was the 'seditious Presbyterian ministers' and 'ambitious ignorant orators' who between them 'reduced this government into anarchy'.[10] The former, 'by a long practised histrionic faculty', had 'preached up the rebellion powerfully', while the latter, 'by advantage of their eloquence', had been able to 'sway' the Commons.[11] As for the origin of the seditious doctrines which these audiences were seduced into embracing, the answer is simple: 'as the Presbyterians brought with them into their churches their divinity from the universities, so did many of the gentlemen bring their politics from thence into the Parliament'.[12]

While Hobbes does not hide his contempt for these doctrines, he offers little by way of rebuttal. That he was restraining himself primarily out of a sense of literary decorum is shown by his tart response when invited to explicate the concept of transubstantiation: 'I am now in a narration, not in a disputation; and therefore I would have you consider at this time nothing else, but what effect this doctrine would work upon kings and their subjects.'[13] Disputation was not the province of the historian, to whom the content of ideas

[6] *Ibid.*, pp. 3, 26, 30.   [7] *Ibid.*, p. 56.   [8] *Ibid.*, pp. 3, 23.   [9] *Ibid.*, pp. 2–3.
[10] *Ibid.*, p. 109.   [11] *Ibid.*, pp. 3, 159.   [12] *Ibid.*, p. 23.   [13] *Ibid.*, p. 15.

mattered less than the uses to which they had been put. *Behemoth* is in fact a history of such usages, written, as Deborah Baumgold puts it, in order 'to expose ideas as no more than pretences masking ambition'.[14] Hobbes's prose is saturated with the language of deceit – 'design', 'end', 'trick', 'imposture', 'show', 'fraud', 'gull' and 'abuse'.[15] In unmasking these deceits, however, Hobbes never claims to be privy to inner counsels like some latter-day Tacitus or Procopius. Still less does he claim to know what went on in individuals' minds: 'I cannot enter into other men's thoughts, farther than I am led by the consideration of human nature.'[16] What he does attempt is a rational reconstruction of their thinking. Faced with some or other ideological assertion, his response is to follow the 'rule' adopted in the concluding chapter of *Leviathan*: when examining 'Doctrines', the thing to do is, like Cicero, to ask *cui bono*?[17]

One can see how the republican dogma acquired at university by the 'democraticals' might have served to further their ambitions. But who stood to benefit from having the classical texts taught there? How had they come to feature in the curriculum in the first place, or, to extend Hobbes's simile, how did the Greeks get into this particular Trojan horse? Hobbes's answer emerges during a discussion which begins when he is asked to explain 'the Pope's design in setting up the Universities'.[18] His reply is that the 'profit [i.e., *bonus*] that the Church of Rome expected from them, and in effect received, was the maintenance of the Pope's doctrine, and of his authority over kings and their subjects, by school-divines'.[19] The schoolmen met their part of the bargain by creating an ideology which succeeded in and by drawing attention to itself; that is, by fashioning 'unintelligible distinctions to blind men's eyes, whilst they encroached upon the right of kings'. In a self-conscious departure from the usual humanist view, Hobbes credits Peter Lombard and Duns Scotus with the deepest cunning even though anyone who did not know 'it was the design' would consider them 'the most egregious blockheads in the world, so obscure and senseless are their writings'.[20]

In contriving these 'impostures', the schoolmen turned first to Aristotle precisely because his writings were unrivalled 'for their

[14] Deborah Baumgold, 'Hobbes's Political Sensibility: The Menace of Political Ambition', in Mary G. Dietz (ed.), *Thomas Hobbes and Political Theory* (Lawrence, Kansas, 1990), p. 84.
[15] See Hobbes, *Behemoth*, pp. 16, 26, 40, 41, 75, 85, 90, 98, 113, 158.   [16] *Ibid.*, p. 29.
[17] Thomas Hobbes, *Leviathan*, ed. Richard Tuck (Cambridge, 1991), p. 474.
[18] Hobbes, *Behemoth*, p. 40.   [19] *Ibid.*, p. 17.   [20] *Ibid.*, pp. 40–1.

aptness to puzzle and entangle men with words'.[21] But if 'advantage' explained how Aristotle's 'logic, physics and metaphysics' had infiltrated the universities, Hobbes admits that the success of his 'politics' cannot be accounted for in the same way:

> It has, I think, done them no good, though it has done us here much hurt by accident. For men, grown weary at last of the insolence of the priests, and examining the truth of those doctrines that were put upon them, began to search the sense of the Scriptures, as they are in the learned languages; and consequently (studying Greek and Latin) became acquainted with the democratical principles of Aristotle and Cicero, and from the love of their eloquence fell in love with their politics, and that more and more, till it grew into the rebellion we now talk of, without any other advantage to the Roman Church but that it was a weakening to us.[22]

Significantly, Hobbes switches from the language of interests to that of the passions. All he had to do was show how the first generation of classical scholars might have introduced themselves to Aristotle and Cicero, at which point the parties could be left to their own devices. From the scholars' becoming 'acquainted' with their principles it was a short step to 'love' of their eloquence and finally infatuation with their politics. Hobbes is thus driven to a surprising conclusion: to the extent that this chain of events – the rediscovery of the ancient texts and their subsequent entrenchment in the curriculum which in turn made possible a recrudescence of classical republicanism – was not anchored in any design or of benefit to anyone, the Civil War could be said to have happened 'by accident'.

Hobbes sets the seal on this 'ideological explanation of the war'[23] with his observations on Milton and Salmasius. His preference for discussing public documents and forms of discourse rather than specific texts makes it all the more striking when he interrupts his narrative to volunteer his opinion of Salmasius' *Defensio Regia* (1649) and Milton's *Pro Populo Anglicano Defensio* (1651):

> I have seen them both. They are very good Latin both, and hardly to be judged which is better; and both very ill reasoning, hardly to be judged which is worse; like two declamations, *pro* and *con*, made for exercise only in a rhetoric school by one and the same man. So like is a Presbyterian to an Independent.[24]

Hobbes's lumping together of these bitter rivals was meant to shock.

[21] *Ibid.*, pp. 41–2.   [22] *Ibid.*, p. 43.
[23] The phrase is Baumgold's, 'Hobbes's Political Sensibility', p. 82.
[24] Hobbes, *Behemoth*, pp. 163–4.

Where Europe thought it had witnessed the sharpest possible contest of principle between an opponent of regicide on one side and a defender of it on the other, Hobbes saw unwitting collusion between twin offspring of the Reformation (a view subtly underscored by the studied symmetry of Hobbes's prose at this point). Nor is the remark about the excellence of their Latin offered in mitigation. On the contrary, it is intended to aggravate their offence. Twice before, in his early political works, Hobbes had quoted Sallust's verdict on Catiline – 'a man of considerable eloquence but small wisdom' – by way of illustrating the qualities typical of promoters of sedition.[25] Now, more than twenty years later, Milton and Salmasius are condemned for exhibiting the same lethal combination of attributes: eloquence and 'ill reasoning'. For all their prestige, they were really modern Catilines and therefore no different from the seditious preachers and 'haranguers' who had brought the country to ruin.

II

Hobbes's verdict on Milton was delivered from a unique perspective. However, there is some evidence that it was accepted by others. John Aubrey's comment, to the effect that it was Milton's 'being so conversant in Livy and the Roman authors, and the greatness he saw donne by the Roman commonwealth, and the vertue of their great Commanders' which had 'induc't' him to write 'against Monarchie', is sometimes quoted as offering independent corroboration of what Hobbes had claimed.[26] In fact, it may only echo conversations about Milton with Hobbes, who was Aubrey's close friend. Alternatively, it may have been prompted by reading the manuscript of *Behemoth*, to which Aubrey had access well before it was published.[27]

Even though Hobbes and Aubrey are hostile witnesses, they do raise an important question. If to be a republican at all was to be a classical republican, then what exactly was the classical element in Milton's republicanism? The standard answer to this question is that supplied by Zera S. Fink in *The Classical Republicans*. In the chapter he

---

[25] Sallust, *Bellum Catilinae*, in *Sallust*, trans. and ed. J. C. Rolfe (London, 1965), p. 8 (v.5): 'satis eloquentiae, sapientiae parum'. For this point, see Quentin Skinner, '"*Scientia civilis*" in Classical Rhetoric and in the Early Hobbes', in Nicholas Phillipson and Quentin Skinner (eds.), *Political Discourse in Early Modern Britain* (Cambridge, 1993), pp. 90–1.

[26] John Aubrey, *Brief Lives*, ed. Oliver Lawson Dick (London, 1960), p. 203.

[27] See the letter from Aubrey to John Locke, 11 February 1673, quoted by Richard Tuck, 'Hobbes and Locke on Toleration', in Dietz, *Hobbes and Political Theory*, p. 154.

devotes to the development of Milton's political thought, Fink (as he
does throughout the book as a whole) gives pride of place to Polybius,
the Greek historian who was more responsible than any other ancient
writer for popularizing the theory that the only stable and therefore
durable form of constitution was one consisting of a mixture of
monarchy, aristocracy and democracy.[28] As Fink points out, Milton
rehearsed this theory – explicitly citing Polybius – in the very first
prose work he published, *Of Reformation* (May 1641).[29] But Fink also
goes on to argue that the Polybian theory of the mixed state remained
a constant and unchanging feature in Milton's thinking between
1641 and 1660.[30] No matter how the political landscape altered
during the Civil War and Interregnum, Milton always sought to
discern in it the contours of the mixed state. All regimes were to be
assessed first and foremost in terms of how they instantiated the
requisite mixture of monarchical, aristocratic and democratic elements.
Thus whenever it was that Milton finally made the 'transition to
republicanism', Fink maintains, it was solely because he now thought
that a republic was 'superior to a monarchy as a means of realizing
the ideal of a mixed state'.[31]

My contention is that Fink has misrepresented the sources and, as a
result, the nature of Milton's classical republicanism. Fink's inflated
claim on behalf of Polybius is prima facie implausible, given that
Milton cites a panoply of classical sources in his published work of the
1640s and 1650s while only mentioning Polybius twice.[32] To insist on
the theoretical primacy at all times of the mixed state in Milton's
thinking is also to obscure the direct nature of his engagement with
the failings of monarchy and the merits of a republic. It is also
mistaken in point of fact. As we shall see, the arguments which Milton
advanced on behalf of a republic and against monarchy, especially in
1649, are almost impossible to reconcile with the notion of a mixed
constitution (in which, by definition, an element of monarchy
subsists), except at the cost of some violence to the texts in which they
are presented. In a less polemical and more constructive vein, I shall
seek to demonstrate that it is instead Aristotle, Sallust and, above all,
Cicero who must be regarded as the main authorities from whom
Milton derived his republican principles. Hobbes was right to this

[28] See Zera S. Fink, *The Classical Republicans*, 2nd edn (Evanston, 1962), pp. 1–10, 90–122.
[29] See Fink, *Classical Republicans*, pp. 95–6; *CPW*, I, 599.
[30] See Fink, *Classical Republicans*, pp. 97, 109, 120, 122.
[31] Fink, *Classical Republicans*, p. 103 and n.   [32] See *CPW*, IVi, 439 for his second citation.

extent at least: when examining the political consequences of a classical education, one should cast the net as widely as possible.

III

The best place to begin therefore is where Hobbes suggested: the universities. As it happens, Milton too thought that they were the *fons et origo* of a pernicious ideology and therefore in need of reform. However, his critique of their failings was based on altogether different assumptions from those of Hobbes, and it issued in a diametrically opposed set of prescriptions.

When the bishops came under attack in the early stages of the Long Parliament, one argument used in their defence was that they were indispensable by virtue of their importance as patrons of learning. As a committed Presbyterian, who regarded episcopacy as 'a natural tyrant in religion, & in state the agent & minister of tyranny', Milton poured scorn on this claim.[33] Far from promoting learning, 'learning could not readily be at a worse passe in the Universities then it was now under their government'.[34] Institutions which 'should be fountaines of learning and knowledge' had actually been 'poyson'd and choak'd' by the system of patronage. Holding out the prospect of 'honour and preferment' only attracted the wrong type of student and was 'the root of all our mischiefe'. Accordingly, Milton urged, 'that which they alleage for the incouragement of their studies, should be cut away forthwith as the very bait of pride and ambition'.[35]

The idea that the universities were forcing-houses of Presbyterianism and classical republicanism would have struck Milton (rightly) as absurd. On the contrary, their greatest service to the Anglican hierarchy was to stifle such initiatives. The clergy had little or no linguistic expertise. Their Latin was 'barbarous' and their literary taste – 'preferring the gay ranknesse of *Apuleius*, *Arnobius*, or any moderne fustianist, before the native *Latinisms* of *Cicero*' – even worse. Most failed to grasp the rudiments of Greek and therefore lacked 'any sound proficiency in those *Attick* maisters of morall wisdome and eloquence'. As for Hebrew, Milton declared, 'their lips are utterly uncircumcis'd'.[36] The same could be said of 'many of the Gentry'. Being 'honest and ingenuous', they naturally assumed that by 'comming to the Universities' they would 'store themselves with good

---

[33] *CPW*, I, 853.   [34] *Ibid.*, 945–6.   [35] *Ibid.*, 718.   [36] *Ibid.*, 934.

and solid learning'. But since their intellectual diet consisted solely of 'monkish and miserable sophistry' and 'metaphysical gargarisms' they were 'sent home' without having read any 'true and generous philosophy'.[37] This was true even of the parliamentarians who are the subject of Milton's panegyric in *An Apology against a Pamphlet* (April 1642). Indeed Milton can think of no greater testament to their 'mature wisdom, deliberat virtue, and deere affection to the publick good' than their having overcome the setback of attending university. The experience of being 'sent to those places, which were intended to be the seed plots of piety and the Liberall Arts, but were become the nurseries of superstition, and empty speculation' would have proved the undoing of lesser men.[38]

This irony soon recoiled upon Milton. Once the parliamentary armies had failed to secure a breakthrough at the start of the war, the military situation deteriorated. Defeat was only narrowly staved off in 1643, while Parliament saw its armies decimated in 1644. The leadership's solution was to enter into an alliance with the Scots, enshrined in the Solemn League and Covenant of September 1643, whereby the Scots agreed to commit their forces in return for an undertaking that the English would introduce a Presbyterian form of church government. Milton's response to the mismanagement of the war and also, by this time, to the prospect of an imposed Presbyterian church (his views on divorce had been denounced by Presbyterian ministers), was to revise his complacent assessment of the parliamentary leadership. It now appeared that they had not after all succeeded in 'correcting' their 'mis-instruction' at university.[39]

This reassessment bore fruit in Milton's *Of Education*, a pamphlet addressed to Samuel Hartlib and published in June 1644. Although the exordium rehearses the topos of a reluctance to write, there is no doubting the urgency and importance of the subject for Milton. When he told Hartlib that his 'minde' was 'for the present halfe diverted in the persuance of some other assertions', it was no exaggeration.[40] He had just seen the much-enlarged second edition of *The Doctrine and Discipline of Divorce* through the press in February, was almost certainly at work on *The Judgement of Martin Bucer, Concerning Divorce* which appeared in August and may already have been contemplating his *Areopagitica* (November). Nevertheless he put all this to one side. Behind the diffident pose – Milton hopes Hartlib

[37] *Ibid.*, 854.   [38] *Ibid.*, 922–3.   [39] *Ibid.*, 923.   [40] *CPW*, II, 363.

'can accept of these few observations which have flowr'd off'[41] – lay a deep anxiety about the malaise afflicting the parliamentary cause and a conviction that the only cure for it was, in effect, a New Model education.

As a 'demonstration of what we should not doe', Milton then mounts a renewed assault on the universities.[42] Once again, he roundly criticizes them for failing to give students a proper grounding in the classical languages. This is not simply a matter of 'words and lexicons', important though Milton thinks these are – witness his own manual, *Accedence Commenc't Grammar* (1669), and the vast Latin Thesaurus left incomplete at his death.[43] Since a 'language is but the instrument convaying to us things usefull to be known', what really counts is the reading which it makes accessible. But the students never get this far. No sooner have they left the 'Grammatick flats & shallows' than they are plunged into the 'most intellective abstractions of Logick & Metaphysicks'. The result is to instill them with a 'hatred and contempt of learning'.[44] Far from handing over the keys to the arsenal, the universities were confiscating them.

One of Milton's arguments for divorce in 1643 had been that to deny this form of relief to those who were unhappily married was to render them 'unserviceable and spiritles to the Common-wealth' – or, as he was to put it more trenchantly still in *Tetrachordon* (1645), 'unactive to all public service, dead to the Common-wealth'.[45] This expresses precisely the burden of the charge that he now levels against the graduates of his day. When choosing their careers, he alleges, they are motivated solely by personal gain. Those who enter the church do so because they are 'ambitious and mercenary'. Those going in for the 'trade of Law' are enticed by 'pleasing thoughts' of 'flowing fees'. While those who 'betake them to State affairs' do so 'with souls so unprincipl'd in vertue, and true generous breeding, that flattery, and court shifts and tyrannous aphorismes appear to them the highest points of wisdom; instilling their barren hearts with a conscientious slavery'. In view of the alternatives, Milton is even prepared to concede that those 'of a more delicious and airie spirit' who simply 'retire' and devote themselves 'to the enjoyments of ease and luxury'

---

[41] *Ibid.*, 366.   [42] *Ibid.*, 376.
[43] *Ibid.*, 369. For the date of *Accedence Commenc't Grammar*, see *CPW*, VIII, 32–6; for what is known of the Latin Thesaurus, see Helen Darbishire, *The Early Lives of Milton* (London, 1932), pp. 4, 29, 45–6, 47, 72, 166, 192, 339–40, and especially the prefatory note to *Linguae Romanae Dictionarium Luculentum Novum* (Cambridge, 1693), sig. A2ᵛ. See further below, p. 200 n. 93.
[44] *CPW*, II, 369, 374–5.   [45] *Ibid.*, 347, 632.

may actually be adopting the 'wisest and safest course'.[46] In short, nothing could be further removed from Hobbes's vision of gentlemen 'in love' with republican forms of government than this portrait of a generation interested only in themselves and 'dead to the Commonwealth'.

Milton then sets about the task of showing how this dire state of affairs can be transformed. He begins with a grandiloquent statement of his ideal: 'I call therefore a compleate and generous Education that which fits a man to perform justly, skilfully and magnanimously all the offices both private and publike of peace and war.'[47] Milton's terminology is nevertheless precise and reveals much about the assumptions which underpin his argument as a whole. 'Magnanimously', for example, certainly bears the sense of acting with the *magnanimitas* defined by Seneca as a readiness to disdain the preoccupations of the small-minded.[48] Milton himself displays *magnanimitas* in censuring the graduates, while what they are being censured for is lacking *magnanimitas* in their narrow pursuit of professional gain. 'Offices', however, points us firmly in the direction of the single most influential classical work of moral philosophy, Cicero's *De Officiis*, and 'magnanimously' to just those sections in Book I where Cicero analyses the virtue of fortitude, the key elements of which are courage and greatness of spirit (*magnitudo animi*).[49] Cicero too thinks that greatness of spirit is utterly inconsistent with a desire for money since 'nothing is more the mark of a mean and petty spirit than to love riches'.[50] But this remark is merely part of the preliminaries to a discussion which is wholly taken up with questions of the duties (*officia*) to which those possessed of fortitude are peculiarly fitted. Cicero's belief is that it is those engaged in public life, and especially those discharging the highest military and civic duties, who will need greatness of spirit the most. This leads into a debate about the respective merits of the offices of peace and war where Cicero questions the opinion held by many that 'military affairs are of greater significance than civic'.[51] Without much difficulty, Cicero

---

[46] *Ibid.*, 375–6.   [47] *Ibid.*, 377–9.

[48] On Seneca's concept of magnanimity, see Quentin Skinner, 'Ambrogio Lorenzetti: The Artist as Political Philosopher', *Proceedings of the British Academy*, 72 (1986), 28–9.

[49] See Cicero, *De Officiis*, trans. and ed. Walter Miller (London, 1975), pp. 62–94 (1.18.61 to 1.26.92). However, the translation I have used is that made by Margaret Atkins in Cicero, *On Duties*, ed. M. T. Griffin and E. M. Atkins (Cambridge, 1991).

[50] Cicero, *On Duties*, p. 27; *De Officiis*, 1.20.68, p. 70: 'nihil enim est tam angusti animi tamque parvi quam amare divitias'.

[51] Cicero, *On Duties*, p. 29; *De Officiis*, 1.22.74, p. 74: 'res bellicas maiores esse quam urbanas'.

arrives at the conclusion that it is not the soldiers but the 'civilians who are in charge of public affairs'[52] and determine policy by their speeches in the Senate who deserve the highest praise – a view he sums up by ostentatiously quoting one of his own verses: 'Let arms yield to the toga, and laurels to laudation.'[53]

It would hardly be an overstatement to say that Cicero's analysis of fortitude in *De Officiis* served as the blueprint for *Of Education*, This was because Milton had concluded that fortitude was precisely the virtue which the parliamentary leadership lacked most. For in this 'dangerous fit of the common-wealth', as Milton describes the situation in 1644, many 'great counsellers' had 'shewn themselves' to be nothing but 'poor, shaken, uncertain reeds' with 'a tottering conscience'.[54] Everything Milton proposes is therefore directed towards ensuring that his students will be 'enflam'd with the study of learning, and the admiration of vertue', and as a result 'stirr'd up with high hopes of living to be brave men, and worthy Patriots'.[55] Unlike the academies and schools of the ancient Greeks, Milton's will be 'equally good both for peace and war'.[56] Accordingly, a section of the work is entirely devoted to a programme of military exercises and instruction – including 'seasonable lectures and precepts' on the subject of 'true fortitude' – the outcome of which will be that graduates 'come forth renowned and perfect Commanders in the service of their country'.[57] But Milton, in keeping with Cicero's sense of priorities, is even more concerned to guarantee a supply of able statesmen and orators. Accordingly, students are required to master 'the beginning, end, and reason of politicall societies' in the expectation that they will prove to be 'stedfast pillars of the State'.[58] Students also start reading classical texts at the first opportunity since it is only by 'praxis' that they will 'bring the whole language quickly into their power'.[59] And it is only when they have finished a truly heroic course of reading, including 'all the famous Politicall orations' which they should if possible commit to memory, that the task of 'forming them to be able writers and composers' can even begin. The result of this extended preparation is sure to be that 'honour and attention' will be 'waiting on their lips' whenever they speak in Parliament or from the pulpit.[60] Unlike Hobbes, Milton saw in such classically educated statesmen and

---

[52] Cicero, *On Duties*, p. 31; *De Officiis*, 1.23.79, p. 80: 'qui togati rei publicae praesunt'.
[53] Cicero, *On Duties*, p. 31; *De Officiis*, 1.22.77, p. 78; 'Cedant arma togae, concedat laurea laudi.'
[54] *CPW*, ii, 398.   [55] *Ibid.*, 385.   [56] *Ibid.*, 408.   [57] *Ibid.*, 409, 412.   [58] *Ibid.*, 398.
[59] *Ibid.*, 373–4.   [60] *Ibid.*, 401, 406.

orators not the destruction but the salvation of the commonwealth.

Often dismissed as inconsequential if charming, *Of Education* in fact represents something very close to a 'republican moment' for Milton. In it he brings together, for the first time in a political context, many of the themes which dominate his writings of the later 1640s and 1650s. He of course advocates the ancients as a touchstone of political wisdom, but turns to Cicero and *De Officiis* in particular for specific remedies. He also sees the solution to a political crisis as residing in the cultivation of virtue, the point of which in turn is to ensure that individuals will serve the commonwealth more effectively. Finally, he displays a deep contempt for wealth and private ambition.

The other sense in which the work can be characterized as republican is that it clearly expresses a wish to see the war against the king prosecuted more effectively.[61] However, what lay behind this new militancy (underscored by the abundance of martial imagery animating his prose) as much as anything was a shift in his religious allegiances. A break with the Presbyterians appears for Milton also to have meant a break with the political doctrines which they had made peculiarly their own. As Michael Mendle has shown, it was the Scots and Presbyterians who were at that time the leading exponents of the theory of the mixed constitution.[62] Thus in the early 1640s the Presbyterians – including Milton himself in *Of Reformation* – deployed the theory against the bishops as a way of ousting them from the Lords.[63] The theory also underpinned what they saw as the constitutional aim of the war: a limited monarchy (it is no accident that the parliamentary apologists who explored the implications of the theory most fully were all Presbyterians).[64] In 1643, for example, they insisted on a pledge entrenching the idea of a limited or mixed monarchy in Article III of the Solemn League and Covenant. And when the king was placed on trial in 1649, they sprang to his defence with the argument that those who had taken the Covenant were bound 'to preserve the King's Majesty's person and authority'.[65] By this time Milton was fiercely and openly anti-Presbyterian, and in

[61] For another aspect of Milton's militancy in 1643–4 – his possible involvement with Edmond Fenton's project for a parliamentary 'engine of war' – see Timothy Raylor, 'New Light on Milton and Hartlib', *Milton Quarterly*, 27, 1 (1993), 19–31.

[62] See Michael Mendle, *Dangerous Positions: Mixed Government, the Estates of the Realm, and the Making of the 'Answer to the xix propositions'* (University, Alabama, 1985), pp. 38–122.

[63] See Mendle, *Dangerous Positions*, pp. 122–8, 141–51; *CPW*, I, 599–601.

[64] See Richard Tuck, *Philosophy and Government 1572–1651* (Cambridge, 1993), pp. 233–5.

[65] S. R. Gardiner (ed.), *The Constitutional Documents of the Puritan Revolution 1625–1660*, 3rd edn (Oxford, 1906), p. 269.

The Tenure of Kings and Magistrates (February 1649) he denounced the Scots, the Presbyterians and the Covenant – and made a bonfire of constitutionalism. But the first step in this direction was arguably taken in *Of Education*.

IV

The High Court of Justice which tried Charles I was set up by an act passed on 6 January 1649.[66] But his execution on 30 January 1649 did not of itself do away with the monarchy. That had to wait until 17 March when the Act Abolishing the Office of King was passed, dismissing the office as 'unnecessary, burdensome, and dangerous'. But although the Act did refer to 'the Government now settled in the way of a Commonwealth' it did not of itself establish a republic.[67] That had to wait until an act was passed on 19 May declaring 'a Commonwealth and Free State'.[68] The drawn-out nature of this legislative process, in which no step necessarily implied the next one, testifies to the caution and even reluctance with which the revolutionaries approached the task of transforming England into a republic. But it also serves to highlight a number of distinctions which can be made (and evidently were) between the person of a king and his office, between monarchy as such and a commonwealth, between a commonwealth and the Commonwealth and even between both of these and a free state.

The most protean of these concepts is that of a commonwealth. Its elusiveness is illustrated by the variety of ways in which Milton himself used the term in *Observations upon the Articles of Peace* (May 1649), the first of his works to be commissioned by the Council of State whose Latin Secretary he had been appointed barely a month earlier. When Milton attacks the Irish rebels for seeking to alienate the 'Province of *Ireland* from all true fealty and obedience to the Common-wealth of *England*',[69] what he primarily has in mind is a legal entity, the 'way' of government assumed in the Act of 17 March and declared to exist on 19 May. When, however, he warns the Belfast Presbyterians that 'as Members of the Common Wealth they ought to mix with other Commoners, and in that temporall Body to assume nothing above other Private persons',[70] he means something quite different: that their clerical status does not exempt them from the

---

[66] *Ibid.*, pp. 357–8.   [67] *Ibid.*, pp. 385, 387.   [68] *Ibid.*, p. 388.   [69] *CPW*, III, 305.
[70] *Ibid.*, 320.

obligations which arise from belonging to the general body of citizens or community. And when he praises the 'remarkable Deeds' performed over the years by Cromwell, 'of whose service the Common-wealth receaves so ample satisfaction',[71] he means something else again. He is referring neither to the legally constituted government nor to the community which it governed but to something rather more abstract: that kind of body politic for the sake and on the behalf of which such services are usually performed.

It is this last notion of a commonwealth which is central to Milton's republicanism. Already a working assumption in his thought by the time he wrote *Of Education*, as we have seen, it predated the formal inception of the Commonwealth and survived the mutation of Commonwealth into Protectorate. What is most striking about the rare occasions when Milton attempts a formal definition, however, is the extent to which he relies on Aristotle. Despite his hatred of scholasticism, he was in fact always prepared to accept Aristotle as 'one of the best interpreters of nature and morality'.[72] In *Of Reformation*, for example, he resorts to the metaphor of the body politic, making clear its Aristotelian provenance: 'for looke what the grounds, and causes are of single happines to one man, the same yee shall find them to a whole state, as *Aristotle* both in his ethicks, and politiks, from the principles of reason layes down'.[73] The definition in *Eikonoklastes* (October 1649) also derives from Aristotle:

> For every Common-wealth is in general defin'd, a societie sufficient of it self, in all things conducible to well being and commodious life. Any of which requisit things if it cannot have without the gift and favour of a single person, or without leave of his privat reason, or his conscience, it cannot be thought sufficient of it self, and by consequence no Common-wealth, nor free.[74]

Here his notion of the 'well being and commodious life' to which society is 'conducible' clearly corresponds to Aristotle's *eudaimonia* (that is, the condition of flourishing which it is the purpose of the state to secure), while his notion of society as being 'sufficient of it self' relates no less closely to Aristotle's *autonomia* (that is, independence). A society or commonwealth is, in short, a body politic which is both flourishing and independent.

Of these attributes, Milton regards the latter as the more important, for a commonwealth which is not independent is *ipso facto* neither free nor a commonwealth. For Milton, to be independent and free is,

---

[71] *Ibid.*, 312.   [72] *Ibid.*, 204.   [73] *CPW*, I, 572.   [74] *CPW*, III, 458.

literally speaking, not to be dependent in the slightest degree. It is the same point as was being emphasized by Livy when he said that *libertas* 'does not depend on another's will'.[75] For a particularly clear example of how this idea of freedom as a state of non-dependency applies in practice, we need only turn to Milton's *Areopagitica*. Milton is of course primarily exercised by the fate of books which are censored or prohibited; in these cases, the freedom to publish what one likes has been denied *tout court*. But he is almost as indignant about those books which are licensed and published exactly as their author intended since, by virtue of the fact that they appear under 'tuition' and 'superintendence', they have been rendered intellectually worthless; and since no discerning reader will take such approved material seriously, the author might as well 'be silent'.[76] To enjoy a benefit under sufferance – or only by 'gift and favour' as Milton phrases it in *Eikonoklastes* – is in effect not to enjoy it at all. To put it another way, no actual threat to remove benefits but merely the threat of a threat to do so is sufficient to compromise autonomy. All this seems to have been crystallized for Milton by a passage in Cicero's eighth Philippic: 'What juster reason is there for the waging of a war than to repel slavery? A condition in which, though your master may not be oppressive, yet it is a wretched thing he should have the power to be so if he will.'[77] That is to say, even where there is no actual oppression, the potential threat of it is a sufficient spur to action. Milton quotes this passage verbatim in the *Defensio*,[78] but he had already paraphrased it in *The Tenure*: those without the 'natural and essential power' to 'dispose' of their own affairs as they wish, he says there, must be considered the 'slaves and vassals' of a 'Lord' whose 'goverment, though not illegal, or intolerable, hangs over them as a Lordly scourge, not as a free goverment; and therfore to be abrogated'.[79]

The key question therefore is how a society or commonwealth is so to arrange matters that the benefits which it enjoys and which are necessary to its being never come to be within the gift of any single person or group. Milton in fact gave two types of answer to this

[75] Livy, *Ab Urbe Condita*, trans. and ed. Evan T. Sage (London, 1958), x, p. 95 (XXXV.32.11): 'non ex alieno arbitrio pendet'. See C. Wirszubski, *Libertas as a Political Idea at Rome during the Late Republic and Early Principate* (Cambridge, 1960), pp. 9, 169.   [76] *CPW*, II, 533–4.

[77] Cicero, *Philippics*, trans. and ed. Walter C. A. Ker (London, 1969), p. 375 (VIII.4.12): 'Quae causa iustior est belli gerendi quam servitutis depulsio? in qua etiamsi non sit molestus dominus, tamen est miserrimum posse, si velit.'   [78] See *CPW*, IVi, 352.

[79] *CPW*, III, 237.

question, though which was predominant in any given work largely depended on when and why he was writing.

One response was to treat it narrowly as a question about constitutional arrangements, in which case Milton's answer was simply to say that those who govern the commonwealth are, and must at all times remain, its servants and not its masters. This is because the authority by which rulers govern is never transferred but merely delegated to them. As he puts it in *The Tenure*, the 'power of Kings and Magistrates' is 'committed to them in trust from the People, to the Common Good of them all, in whom the power yet remaines fundamentally'.[80] Far from becoming the people's 'Lords and Maisters' by virtue of their election, they are merely the people's 'Deputies and Commissioners' who administer matters of common interest on their behalf.[81] This view is reiterated throughout *The Tenure* and *Eikonoklastes*, but receives its most memorable expression in *The Readie and Easie Way* where Milton describes those who govern a 'free Commonwealth' as 'perpetual drudges and servants'.[82] However, it is rehearsed most exhaustively in the *Defensio* where Milton quotes at length from Cicero's *Pro Flacco*, *De Oratore* and *Pro Plancio* (as well as Suetonius and Tacitus) to establish the point that magistrates are not merely the servants but even the slaves (*servi*) of the people.[83]

Furthermore, since such authority is vested not in these servants themselves but in the offices they hold, on no account should they regard it as a personal possession. In *Eikonoklastes*, Milton therefore deplores the 'strange' tendency of 'entrusted Servants of the Common-wealth' (in this case, the king) to

esteem themselves Maisters, both of that great trust which they serve, and of the People that betrusted them: counting what they ought to doe both in discharge of thir public duty, and for the great reward of honour and revennue which they receave, as don all of meer grace and favour; as if thir power over us were by nature, and from themselves, or that God had sould us into thir hands.[84]

In Milton's view, such behaviour was quite as much a moral as a legal transgression, and the result of giving way to 'Injustice, Partiality, and Corruption'.[85] This was also the view of Cicero, who considers these topics in *De Officiis* as part of his analysis of the role of fortitude in public life. There he adjures magistrates to follow two pieces of advice

---

[80] *Ibid.*, 202.   [81] *Ibid.*, 199.   [82] *CPW*, vii, 425.   [83] *CPW*, ivi, 388.
[84] *CPW*, iii, 485–6.   [85] *Ibid.*, 487.

given by Plato; to forget their own interests and concentrate solely on the good of the citizens, and to care for the whole of the *res publica* rather than any part of it. They should remember that the 'management of the republic is like a guardianship, and must be conducted in the light of what is beneficial not to the guardians, but to those who are put in their charge'.[86] To do otherwise would lead to discord and even civil war.

It would be true to say, however, that there is nothing distinctively republican about this set of propositions. Republicans would naturally have subscribed to all of them, but so too would most sixteenth-century exponents of the constitutional theory of resistance (with whom Milton was certainly in close dialogue when writing *The Tenure*). What allows one to differentiate between the republican and neoscholastic traditions, as Quentin Skinner has pointed out, is that the neoscholastics 'are not generally republican in the strict sense of believing that the common good of a community can never be satisfactorily assured under a monarchical form of government'.[87] At first sight this means that there should be no difficulty in pronouncing Milton a republican. He defended the regicide in *The Tenure* while *Eikonoklastes* is devoted to smashing the posthumous image of the king purveyed in *Eikon Basilike*. Indeed the Aristotelian definition of the commonwealth is invoked in *Eikonoklastes* precisely in order to justify 'the taking away of King-ship it self, when it grows too Maisterfull and Burd'nsome'.[88] The allusion to the Act of 17 March underlines the point: the office of king was incompatible with the very being of a republic.

And yet, as has often been pointed out, Milton (like several other seventeenth-century republicans) managed to remain equivocal on the subject of monarchy as such; it was 'only after the protectorate had fallen' in 1659 that he 'briefly' voiced 'an unambiguous hostility to kingship'.[89] It is also true that Milton displayed a high degree of indifference with regard to constitutional forms; in *Eikonoklastes* and the *Defensio* he repeatedly spurns the opportunity to discuss which

---

[86] Cicero, *On Duties*, pp. 33–4; *De Officiis*, p. 86 (1.25.85): 'Ut enim tutela sic procuratio rei publicae ad eorum utilitatem, qui commissi sunt, non ad eorum, quibus commissa est, gerenda est.'

[87] Quentin Skinner, 'The State', in Terence Ball, James Farr and Russell L. Hanson (eds.), *Political Innovation and Conceptual Change* (Cambridge, 1989), p. 114.   [88] *CPW*, III, 458.

[89] Blair Worden, 'Milton's Republicanism and the Tyranny of Heaven', in Gisela Bock, Quentin Skinner and Maurizio Viroli (eds.), *Machiavelli and Republicanism* (Cambridge, 1990), p. 228.

form of government may be the best.[90] However, this was not, as Fink would have it, a consequence of adhering to the theory of the mixed state. Rather it appears to be a paradoxical outcome of the fact that the political theory which Milton developed in 1649 (and from which he never retreated in its essentials) went much *further* than was required merely to justify the regicide or the abolition of kingship (just as he drew the line not at the actual prohibition of books but at their appearing under tutelage). What he published in February 1649 after all was not *The Tenure of Kings* but *The Tenure of Kings and Magistrates*. The argument applied just as much to the Long Parliament as it did to Charles I. Not kings alone but all who governed could be removed if they abused their trust. More than this, they could be removed even if they did not abuse it. Thus Milton insists that the people may 'depose' or 'retaine' a ruler 'though no Tyrant, meerly by the liberty and right of free born Men, to be govern'd as seems to them best'.[91] The people may 'reassume' the power they have delegated 'if by Kings or Magistrates it be abus'd', but, crucially, they may also 'dispose of it by any alteration, as they shall judge most conducing to the public good'.[92] These assertions of the right of self-determination are about as categorical as can be imagined. They also go a long way to explaining Milton's lack of interest in precise constitutional forms. Since the threshold for political change was set so low (it could in principle be triggered simply by a new collective vision of what would be 'most conducing to the public good'), the powers of any ruler(s) of whatever description were severely limited. There is no doubt, however, that one of the decisive advantages of a republic for Milton was that political changes were easier to effect. As he explained in *The Readie and Easie Way*, whereas in a monarchy the king could not be removed 'without the danger of a common ruin', 'in a free Commonwealth' magistrates 'may be remov'd and punishd without the least commotion'.[93]

Much therefore rested on what might be called the moral economy of the commonwealth. This topic tended not to be discussed in any depth by writers in the neoscholastic or contractarian tradition, irrespective of whether they were proponents or opponents of absolutism. For example, John Locke, it has been argued, regarded 'political participation' as 'a burden, not a pleasure or a privilege: something to be abandoned gratefully when one's community is

---

[90] See *CPW*, III, 455, 516; IVI, 427.   [91] *CPW*, III, 206.   [92] *Ibid.*, 212.
[93] *CPW*, VII, 426–7.

fortunate to be governed well'.[94] But for republicans on the other hand it was a topic which it was vital to address since, in their view, it was only by *not* laying aside such burdens that one would be at all likely to be well governed. This is effectively the substance of the other answer which Milton gave to the question of how matters are to be arranged such that the commonwealth will continue to enjoy the benefits necessary to its being. If the commonwealth is to flourish and keep its autonomy, Milton insists, then both rulers and ruled must cultivate the virtues. There was nothing novel about this argument, either as far as Milton himself was concerned (it is the thesis of his own *Of Education* writ large) or in the tradition of republican thought.[95] Unless individuals were willing and able to place their capacities at the disposal of the commonwealth, so the argument went, then the commonwealth would collapse. But the commonwealth in turn could be relied on to safeguard and promote the virtues. This aspect of mutual support is summarized by Milton in *The Readie and Easie Way* where he maintains that 'freedom consists in the civil rights and advancements of every person according to his merit: the enjoyment of these never more certain, and the access to these never more open, then in a free Commonwealth'.[96] What he envisaged therefore was a virtuous circle in the literal sense: virtue as that which sustained, and was sustained by, the commonwealth.

For Milton, the Puritan virtue of godliness was of course foremost among those to be cultivated. But he places hardly any less emphasis on the four cardinal virtues to the study of which Cicero had devoted Book 1 of *De Officiis*: justice, prudence, temperance and fortitude. *Eikonoklastes*, for example, is shot through with praises of 'the old English fortitude', the 'prudence' and 'all the vertue of an elected Parlament', and 'the strength and supremacie of Justice'.[97] His conclusion is that:

The happiness of a Nation consists in true Religion, Piety, Justice, Prudence, Temperance, Fortitude, and the contempt of Avarice and Ambition. They in whomsoever these vertues dwell eminently, need not Kings to make them happy, but are the architects of thir own happiness.[98]

[94] John Dunn, 'The Concept of "Trust" in the Politics of John Locke', in Richard Rorty, J. B. Schneewind and Quentin Skinner (eds.), *Philosophy in History* (Cambridge, 1984), p. 297. For a contrasting view, see Mary G. Dietz, 'Hobbes's Subject as Citizen', in *Hobbes and Political Theory*, pp. 91–119.

[95] For the best account of this aspect of the republican tradition, see Quentin Skinner, 'The Republican Ideal of Political Liberty', in *Machiavelli and Republicanism*, pp. 293–309.

[96] *CPW*, VII, 458.   [97] *CPW*, III, 344, 409, 585.   [98] *Ibid.*, 542.

However, the prominence given to avarice and ambition suggests that Milton was not simply reiterating Ciceronian commonplaces. To some extent, a contempt for these vices was no more than the corollary of possessing the other virtues. Thus Cicero's discussion of these failings was subsumed under his treatment of fortitude and temperance. The evidence suggests, however, that Milton was relying at this point not so much on Cicero as on Sallust, the Roman historian whose works supply the Latin epigraphs for the title page of *Eikonoklastes*.[99]

Sallust's *Bellum Catilinae* provided the most compelling classical analysis of avarice and ambition. In his view, avarice and ambition were responsible for the decline of the Roman republic just as the virtues of justice and industry had been responsible for its rise. The key step had been the abolition of kingship. Since kings always see the virtuous as a threat (Sallust's statement of this claim was one of those chosen by Milton as an epigraph),[100] it was only when they had been expelled that men of virtue began to flourish, with the result that, as Sallust puts it later, the republic was 'raised from obscurity to greatness'.[101] But this held true only in adversity; with prosperity came decline. Men 'who had found it easy to bear hardship and dangers, anxiety and adversity, found leisure and wealth, desirable under other circumstances, a burden and a curse'.[102] The old virtues gave way to avarice and ambition, and the general collapse of morality which followed eventually ushered in the dictatorship of Sulla.

There can be little doubt that Milton was deeply impressed with and influenced by this account of the rise and fall of the Roman republic. In his capacity as an historian, he always aspired to match the standards set by Sallust (he admired Tacitus as well, but largely because Tacitus had succeeded to the extent that he had in emulating Sallust).[103] The lessons taught by Sallust were also of immediate political relevance for Milton, forming a key part of his attack on

---

[99] See *ibid.*, 337 for a reproduction of the title page bearing the epigraphs from Sallust's *Bellum Catilinae* (IV.7 and VI.7) and *Bellum Iugurthinum* (XXXI.26).

[100] *Sallust*, ed. Rolfe p. 12 (VI.7): 'Nam regibus boni quam mali suspectiores sunt semperque eis aliena virtus formidulosa est.'

[101] Ibid., p. 105 (LII.19): 'rem publicam ex parva magnam fecisse'.

[102] *Ibid.*, p. 19 (X.2): 'Qui labores, pericula, dubias atque asperas resfacile toleraverunt, eis otium, divitiae, optanda aliis, oneri miseriaeque fuere.'

[103] On Milton's view of Sallust as a model historian, see Nicholas von Maltzahn, *Milton's 'History of Britain': Republican Historiography in the English Revolution* (Oxford, 1991), pp. 75–7.

kingship in *The Tenure* and *Eikonoklastes*.[104] However, their pertinence
if anything increased as the dangers facing the republic in its early
years of adversity faded only to be replaced by the snares of
prosperity. Thus the peroration to *Defensio Secunda* (May 1654) is
delivered in the severely moralistic tones of Sallust. Milton warns his
countrymen that 'peace itself will be by far your hardest war, and
what you thought liberty will prove to be your servitude'.[105] And he
prophesies that unless they 'expel avarice, ambition, and luxury' from
their minds, then they will 'have passed through the fire only to perish
in the smoke'.[106]

An echo of all the themes I have been considering can be heard
issuing from a surprising quarter. During the course of the 'great
consult' in Pandemonium, Mammon almost succeeds in persuading
the fallen angels to accept an alternative to the choice of 'open war or
covert guile' which Satan has tabled as the motion for debate.[107]
What he advocates is, in almost every respect, unmistakably a version
of Milton's classical republic.

> Let us not then pursue
> By force impossible, by leave obtained
> Unacceptable, though in heaven, our state
> Of splendid vassalage, but rather seek
> Our own good from ourselves, and from our own
> Live to ourselves, though in this vast recess,
> Free, and to none accountable, preferring
> Hard liberty before the easy yoke
> Of servile pomp. Our greatness will appear
> Then most conspicuous, when great things of small,
> Useful of hurtful, prosperous of adverse
> We can create.[108]

Mustering a Ciceronian indignation, he scorns benefits which,
however 'splendid' they may be, are rendered worthless since enjoyed
only 'by leave'. His concepts of self-sufficiency ('Live to ourselves')
and autonomy ('to none accountable') are purely Aristotelian. He
envisages a future along Sallustian lines in which adversity gives way
to prosperity, and 'great things' come of 'small' (a direct translation of

---

[104] For example, see *CPW*, III, 190, where a paraphrase of Sallust, *Bellum Catilinae*, VI.7 features
prominently on the opening page of *The Tenure*: 'Hence it is that Tyrants are not oft
offended, nor stand much in doubt of bad men, as being all naturally servile; but in whom
vertue and true worth most is eminent, them they feare in earnest, as by right thir Maisters,
against them lies all thir hatred and suspicion.'   [105] *CPW*, IVi, 680.   [106] *Ibid.*, 681.
[107] *PL*, I, 798: II, 41.   [108] *PL*, II, 249–60.

Sallust's 'ex parva magnam'). Even the antithesis between 'Hard liberty' and 'the easy yoke' is appropriated from Sallust's rendition of a speech by Aemilius Lepidus attacking Sulla.[109]

The proposal is of course fatally flawed in principle by the fact that the fallen angels are accountable to God, and it is subverted in practice by the machinations of Beelzebub who reverses the 'popular vote' in favour of Mammon's republic and instead secures 'full assent' for Satan's 'bold design'.[110] But the proposal is doomed even in its own terms. Its spokesman is the very personification of wealth, the great enemy of republics. Moreover Mammon conspicuously fails to mention what alone could give it some hope of success: the virtues. For this reason, if no other, the fallen angels cannot be the architects of their own happiness. The outcome of this debate, in which a republican moment yields to the adventure of a single person, is obviously a re-enactment in miniature of the course of events in the 1650s. As such, it must be seen in part as offering Milton's verdict on the English experiment with classical republicanism. It would be doing him an injustice, however, to imply that these insights only became available with the experience of defeat. For not only was a critique of republicanism along these lines an integral part of the republican tradition, as we have seen, but, as I shall seek to show in chapter 10 below, Milton was bringing elements of it to bear on the politics of the later 1650s even as they unfolded.

[109] Sallust, 'Oratio Lepidi cos. ad populum Romanum', in *Sallust*, ed. Rolfe, pp. 394–5: 'potiorque visa est periculosa libertas quieto servitio' ('I looked upon freedom united with danger as preferable to peace with slavery'). See also Fowler's note, Milton, *Paradise Lost*, p. 101.
[110] *PL*, II, 313, 386, 388.

Milton and the characteristics of a free commonwealth

Thomas N. Corns

I

Milton's republicanism emerges after the event. Before the execution of the king, there is no evidence that he had added constitutional radicalism to the array of heterodox and oppositional opinions he had shown in his pamphlets of 1641–5. But the increasing radicalism of the positions he assumed within the debates of that period makes his later commitment to Revolutionary Independency unsurprising.

Certainly Milton's subscription to a militant and uncompromising version of antiprelatism, a root-and-branchism which excluded compromise with anti-Laudian episcopalians, had, as early as 1642, signalled an incipient alienation from the Presbyterian position. He had begun to part company with those among more moderate puritans who were prepared to entertain a new church settlement with an episcopacy purged of its Laudian innovations, as some of the Smectymnuans evidently sought. By the time he published *The Reason of Church-Government* early in 1642 a discerning reader could detect in his uncertainties about the right response to the sects the stirrings of the Independent tendency. In his tracts of 1643–5 he manifested a singularity of doctrine (on the issue of divorce) indicative of one who could not for long expect to find a place in even a newly reformed and Presbyterian Church of England. In a sense, one can often best place a political writer by the identity of his enemies. Milton's divorce tracts provoked the sustained and probably coordinated attack of Presbyterians and others of a militantly anti-Independent orientation. His response to these assaults was both to reiterate his thesis, in *The Judgement of Martin Bucer* (1644) and *Tetrachordon* (1645), and to develop in *Areopagitica* an argument for limited toleration of Protestant heterodoxy that finds analogy in Roger Williams's rather less carefully targeted and less subtly crafted *Bloudy Tenent of Persecution for cause of Conscience* (1644).

Milton's long silence, from mid-1645 and the publication of his first

collection of poems till his return to print with the publication in
February 1649 of *The Tenure of Kings and Magistrates*, has never been
satisfactorily elucidated, and no contemporary documents point to
an explanation. Surprising though that silence may have been for one
who had published so freely in the early 1640s, his re-emergence
among the civilian supporters of Revolutionary Independency poses
few mysteries; the anti-Presbyterian and unappeasing traits of his
early work and the radicalism of those with whom contemporaries
tended to bracket him, such as Roger Williams and the mortalist
'R.O.' (probably Richard Overton),[1] would have made such an
ideological trajectory predictable.

Milton emerges as a fully formed apologist of those who killed the
king; the stages in that particular development may nowhere be
discerned in his published writing. Yet he appears first as a regicide
rather than as a republican. While his earliest tract of 1649 is certainly
heavily theorized, it is legal theory and the case for the accountability
of monarchs, rather than the case for a republic, that chiefly exercise
him. Nor does he elsewhere in the tracts of 1649 address the
constitutional foundation of the new state. *Observations upon the Articles
of Peace* focuses on demonstrating the republic's superior record in
defending the national interest in its Irish colony. In *Eikonoklastes* he
expounds the culpability, not of kings in general, but of one king, and
the justification of the regicide state's conduct towards him.

In this theoretical reticence Milton follows the emphases and the
silences of other apologists of the new regime, and of those who
brought Charles I to trial and effected his prosecution. In a sense, the
most active and most militant of the senior army officers and their
civilian supporters blundered into the foundation of the republic,
without a constitutional theory, without a sustained critique of other
models (of course, specifically, monarchy), without a vision or an
image of the state they were founding, and even without an
appropriate political vocabulary.

This chapter argues that there is little in his vernacular writing of
1649 and almost nothing in his Latin defences to show that Milton
actively sought to argue for the English republic in terms derived
either from classical models or from Machiavellian political theory.
In his vernacular writing, he mirrors the emphases of the jurists,
politicians and soldiers who brought the king to trial. In his Latin, he

---

[1] See Daniel Featley, *The Dippers Dipt* (London, 1645), sig. B2ᵛ.

shows a guileful concern not to alienate continental regimes from the new state. Yet, especially in the vernacular works, there emerges an eloquent rehearsal, not of republican argument, but of republican values, inscribed both in his demystification of monarchy and in his assertion of the dignity of the English citizen, both of which find their fullest expression in 1660.

II

Blair Worden has perceptively documented the essentially conservative nature of the Rump Parliament in which constitutional power was invested in the period between Pride's Purge and its dismissal in 1653: 'The inauguration of the Commonwealth proved to be the end, not the beginning, of the Long's Parliament's revolutionary measures'; it made only 'occasional gestures' towards more radical opinion.[2] He has effectively situated Milton's early writings for the English republic in this paradoxically cautious political landscape. The trial and execution of the king, the pivotal events of the English revolution, emerge out of dark legalism, political muddle and a failure to secure an alternative settlement: 'The regicide was not the fruit of republican theory. Most of its organisers were concerned to remove a particular king, not kingship. They cut off King Charles' head and wondered what to do next. In that quandary they saw no practicable alternative to the abolition of monarchy.'[3] Given the strangulation of political theory in the native English context by the monarchy's long-standing assertion of its divine sanction and divine right to rule, it could scarcely have been otherwise.

The English language hardly had a vocabulary to describe the form into which the state was new moulded, nor did a vocabulary readily develop.[4] The term 'republic' is infrequently used in the

---

[2] Blair Worden, *The Rump Parliament 1648–1653* (Cambridge, 1974), p. 40.

[3] Blair Worden, 'Milton's Republicanism and the Tyranny of Heaven', in Gisela Bock, Quentin Skinner and Maurizio Viroli (eds.), *Machiavelli and Republicanism* (Cambridge, 1990), pp. 225–45 (p. 226).

[4] I have searched the electronic version of the *Oxford English Dictionary* for examples of the terms 'republic', 'republican' and 'republicanism', scanning all the material cited in quotations dating from the period 1630–80. The first occurs infrequently; the adjective and the abstract noun are not recorded in this period though 'republical' occurs occasionally. The term 'republic' occurs usually in discussions of Geneva or Venice, rather than England. The collocation 'English republic' is not captured by the *OED*. The word most frequently used for the English state during the Interregnum is 'Commonwealth', a very common word in political discourse in the mid-century. It occurs 193 times in quotations from the period 1630–80, and is in very frequent usage in the period 1649–60 (124 examples). But it is a

mid-century to describe the constitutional experiments of 1649–60. The more commonly used word for government in that period is 'commonwealth', though that remains throughout a deeply ambiguous term. Indeed, when the Rump declares itself a republic it does so in terms which reflect a certain anxiety about whether it will be understood. It terms itself 'Constituted, Made, Established, and Confirmed to be a Commonwealth *and Free State*' (my italics),[5] as if recognizing the importance of adding something to distinguish this English commonwealth from previous monarchical ones. The title of Milton's last substantial republican pamphlet, stressing the establishment of a *free* commonwealth, both echoes the idiom of the early days of the English republic and discloses the same terminological anxiety.

Many of the early acts of the Rump define the regime in terms of what it is not. The definitive measure, 'An Act for the Abolishing of Kingly Office in England and Ireland, and the Dominions thereunto belonging', establishes the new order in negative terms; that is, it is not kingly. The emphasis within that act is on the liberty of the people to live under 'the laws'. Kingship threatens legality and with that it threatens the rights of property. It impoverishes as well as enslaves the subject.[6] Indeed, the first constitutional legislation of the new republic shows a decided uncertainty about the future of monarchy in England. While it indicates a distinct unwillingness to see the en-thronement of any of the late king's children, it seemingly recognizes that a monarch from another quarter may at some point be considered. It commands:

> That no person or persons whatsoever do presume to Proclaim, Declare, Publish, or any way promote Charls Stuart, Son of the said Charls, commonly called, The Prince of Wales, *or any other person* to be King, or Chief Magistrate of England, or of Ireland, or of any the Dominions belonging to them, or either of them, by colour of Inheritance, Succession, Election, or any other Claim whatsoever, *without the free consent of the People in Parliament first had, and signified by a particular Act or ordinance for that purpose* . . . [my italics] [7]

complex term, applied to both the state, the constitution and the nation. Thus a commonwealth could assume the form of a democracy (or monarchy or oligarchy, etc.); each is but a 'forme of Commonwealth' (Thomas Hobbes, *Leviathan* (1651), II, 22). Again, 'The state of a Commonwealth is either Monarchical or Polyarchical' (R. Sherringham, *The King's Supremacy Asserted* (1660), cited *OED*).
5   19 May 1649; C. H. Firth and R. S. Rait (eds.), *Acts and Ordinances of the Interregnum, 1642–1660*, 2 vols. (London, 1911), II, 122.   6   Firth and Rait (eds.), *Acts and Ordinances*, II, 19.
7   'An Act prohibiting the proclaiming any person to be King of England or Ireland, or the Dominions thereof', 30 January 1649, in Firth and Rait (eds.), *Acts and Ordinances*, I, 1263.

The Rump Parliament indicated at the inception of the republic, on the very day of the king's execution, a palpable uncertainty about where the constitutional changes would come to rest. Indeed, it seems for a while uncertain even about how to refer to itself, before settling on the grand but vague term, 'The Keepers of the Liberty of England'.[8]

That sobriquet eloquently confirms Worden's thesis about the inherent conservatism of the outlook of those who dominated the purged parliament. It also points to the central thesis of governmental apologists of the early years of the republic; this is a regime not of innovators but of guardians of ancient rights, which are a legal inheritance protecting the property and lives of the subjects. That concept is felt very powerfully in the rhetoric associated with the trial of the king, which is always presented not as regicide but as tyrannicide, not the killing of a king but the killing of a particular king who has transgressed the laws which govern even kings. Thus, in the speech he had intended to deliver at Charles's trial, John Cook, the government solicitor, pins his whole case on the charge of tyranny, 'That if a King become a Tyrant, he shall dye for it'.[9]

Other arguments of a more theoretical kind or of a kind directed towards the establishment of the positive values of government without a king are rarely to be found among those writing to defend the actions of the purged parliament. A little later, John Cook returns to the issue in a less forensic frame of reference. Defining monarchy as 'the Government of one man over many, to give lawes and commands alone; to have thousands accomptable to him, and he alone and he to be accomptable to God', he unsurprisingly contends that even a good king, with such untrammelled powers, may allow the people to be 'less miserable for a season but it cannot hold long'.[10] However, the argument remains essentially a condemnation of kingship's potential for evil and illegality, rather than a celebration of the republican alternative.

The supple-minded Marchamont Nedham, writing in *Mercurius Politicus*, the principal pro-government newspaper of the Interregnum, seems to recognize earlier than his political masters the need for a theoretical argument in favour of the republic. His initial attempts,

---

[8] See, for example, 'An Act Declaring what offences shall be adjudged Treason', 14 May 1649, in Firth and Rait (eds.), *Acts and Ordinances*, II, 120.

[9] John Cook, *King Charls His Case: or, an Appeale to all Rational Men, Concerning His Tryal* (London, 1649), p. 23; see also Merritt Y. Hughes's sensible account of the charge of tyranny, *CPW*, III, 88–100.

[10] John Cook, *Monarchy No Creature of Gods Making & c.* (Waterford, 1651), pp. 1, 129.

however, flounder unpersuasively as he argues that political institutions should reflect the distribution of power, including military power, within a state in the condition of civil war 'where you may observe, *Force & Power* is put in equall Ballance with *popular Consent*, in relation to Change of Government':

> as in warr all other things fall to the Conquerors, by way of Acquisition. So likewise a Right to govern the People, & even that Right also which the People themselves have to Government: So that what Government soever it pleases the *prevailing Party* to erect, must be as valid *de jure*, as if it had the Peoples positive Consent.[11]

Or in Marvell's bluntly realistic phrase, the ancient rights, presumably of kings, 'do hold or break / As Men are strong or weak'.[12]

III

In such a context, it would have been inappropriate to expect to find in Milton an explicit rehearsal of the advantages of a republic. His political masters had largely blundered into it, claiming the power of the ancient law over the king but reluctant, for obvious reasons, to test their own mandate in an election and incapable of justifying in constitutional terms the purging from parliament of those who opposed them. In the cleverest of republican writers of the early years, Nedham and Marvell, he would find only a celebration of power and expediency. Nedham's earliest gestures towards a classical republicanism come in his satire, sustained through the early months of *Mercurius Politicus*, that the future Charles II is 'young Tarquin', directing his ravishing strides from his Scottish fastness towards the womenfolk of the English republic; the notion appears facetious throughout.

Milton's republican prose obeys the polemical exigencies of the time. *The Tenure of Kings and Magistrates* indicates in its title its engagement with the issues of legality, of the relationship of kingship to the law, that continued to exercise the government after the execution (George Thomason dated his copy a fortnight after the event). The issue, emphatically, is the response appropriate not to monarchs but to tyrants: 'turning to Tyranny they may bee ... lawfully depos'd and punished' (*CPW*, III, 198). Though the logic of

[11] *Mercurius Politicus*, 21 (24–31 October 1650), p. 342.
[12] Andrew Marvell, 'An *Horatian* Ode upon *Cromwel's* Return from *Ireland*', lines 39–40, in *Complete Poems*, ed. George deF. Lord (London, 1968), p. 56.

the contractual argument he espouses pushes him to a larger speculation, the perspective is ultimately conservative; tyrannicide does not initiate a new order but returns an aberrant state to its pristine legitimacy: 'to say Kings are accountable to none but God, is the overturning of all Law and government' (*CPW*, III, 204). Indeed, much as the 'Act for the Abolishing of Kingly Office' left the door ajar for a restored monarchy on a more acceptable footing, so *The Tenure* praises good kingship and distinguishes it from the regime of Charles I: 'look how great a good and happiness a just King is, so great a mischiefe is a Tyrant; and hee the public father of his Countrie, so this the common enemie' (*CPW*, III, 212). Charles would seem to be the first Protestant king to have merited such treatment (*CPW*, III, 237), a point Milton added as part of the tract for its second edition in 1650.

Worden has demonstrated how assiduously the purged parliament sought to effect a reconciliation with the supporters of the Presbyterians while attacking their leaders.[13] Milton makes a show of following that line: 'As for that party called Presbyterian, of whom I believe very many to be good and faithfull Christians, though misledd by som of turbulent spirit, I wish them earnestly and calmly not to fall off from thir first principles' (*CPW*, III, 238). But his own deeper animosities, manifested in the unpublished political poems of the mid-1640s, Sonnets XI and XII and 'On the New Forcers of Conscience under the Long Parliament', frequently break through into an uncontrolled malevolence, mapping the frenzy of his antiprelatical pamphlets onto an attack on Presbyterian divines 'rambling from Benefice to Benefice, like rav'nous Wolves seeking where they may devour the biggest' (*CPW*, III, 241). Indeed, Milton's strongest hostility seems not for the dead king but for the republicans' erstwhile allies, the now 'kingified' Presbyterian royalists.[14]

Whatever the inherent dissonances between its avowed overtures to Presbyterians and its ferocity towards them, *The Tenure of Kings and Magistrates* remains too guardedly and too consciously an endorsement of the official governmental line to function as a manifesto for republicanism. His controlled reiteration of that strategy is even more consistently felt in his next pamphlet, his first as employee of the new regime, his 'Observations' added to the *Articles of Peace, Made and Concluded with the Irish Rebels, and Papists* (1649). Again, the argument

---

[13] Worden, *Rump Parliament*, pp. 81–3.
[14] Thomas N. Corns, *Uncloistered Virtue: English Political Literature 1640–1660* (Oxford, 1992), pp. 194–200.

is framed in reassuringly conservative terms. The purged parliament acts to defend England's rights of property and government over Ireland, while Presbyterians and other Irish royalists contrive to betray those interests to Catholic 'rebels'. For supporters of the new republic, the opportunity to term others 'rebels', as they themselves had so often been termed, had obvious attractions. The new regime emerges as a bulwark of English national interest.[15]

The whole structure and tenor of *Eikonoklastes* excludes sustained argument at any level of abstraction. It is, necessarily, a retrospective tract, answering in detail and point by point *Eikon Basilike*'s account of events from the first calling of the Long Parliament through to January 1649. The word 'republic' does not occur in *Eikonoklastes*; 'commonwealth' occurs frequently, but never in reference to a system of government, rather as a collective term for the whole body of people constituting the nation. As I have observed elsewhere, kingship as such is not the issue: this king and his punishment are. Even the name, 'Iconoclastes', as Milton acknowledges, is 'the famous Surname of many Greek Emperors', godly monarchs who 'in thir zeal to the command of God . . . broke all superstitious Images to peeces' (*CPW*, III, 343).[16]

The vernacular tracts of 1649 plainly address an English audience, and they seek out, as the purged parliament in other ways sought out, at least the compliance of those who had formerly supported parliament against the king but who could not support his execution. The Latin defences of the English republic are targeted rather differently, and match the various stages by which the new regime and its successor, the Protectorate, positioned itself in the European context. Numerous allusions make it clear that readers in the United Provinces, in Sweden and perhaps in France were those to whom Milton addressed his argument and those whom the English republic wished variously to influence positively or to render at least neutral in its dealing with the threat it still faced from the future Charles II and his supporters at home and abroad.

 Only intermittently and guardedly does *Eikonoklastes* attack the king himself, and rarely in a tone below that of high seriousness.[17] In the Latin defences, his general avoidance of satirical or vituperative

---

[15] For a fuller account, see Thomas N. Corns, 'Milton's *Observations upon the Articles of Peace*: Ireland under English Eyes', in David Loewenstein and James Grantham Turner (eds.), *Politics, Poetics, and Hermeneutics in Milton's Prose* (Cambridge, 1990), pp. 123–34.
[16] Corns, *Uncloistered Virtue*, p. 208.   [17] Corns, *Uncloistered Virtue*, pp. 204–5.

attack on the king appears even more sharply, in that those tracts are characterized by their sustained and sometimes obscene mauling of the royalist apologists Milton is engaging. A polemicist who lashes his rival as 'a half-pint peregrinatory professor' who has 'turned from his pigeonholes and carpetbags stuffed with a mass of nonsense ... a nasty busybody' (*CPW*, IVi, 316) might be expected to spill a little vitriol over the chief enemy of the regime he defends, and in fact Milton does risk the occasional sally at Charles I's enthusiasm for drama ('even in the theatre he kisses women wantonly, enfolds their waists and, to mention no more openly, plays with the breasts of maids and mothers' – *CPW*, IVi, 408). In general though, his strategy is to focus the attack on Charles at the same level of sustained *gravitas* as in the vernacular tracts, while treating Salmasius and More to persistent and highly personalized abuse.

The arguments in *A Defence of the People of England* (1651) in part cover the same ground as the vernacular tracts of 1649, retaining a concern with demonstrating the supremacy of the law over the claims of monarchy, though Milton is drawn by the case he must confute into a concern with classical analogues and biblical arguments for and against monarchy. Yet perhaps more explicitly than in the vernacular tracts, he argues that he is defending the rights of a particular people at a particular time to deal with a particular king, rather than with the merits of republicanism. Indeed, he once more explores the distinction between good kings and tyrants, and declines to follow the republican argument to the exclusion of the former:

Whether the government of one man or several is in fact the better cannot be discussed here. Monarchy has indeed been praised by many famous men, provided that the sole ruler is the best of men and fully deserving of the crown; otherwise monarchy sinks most rapidly into the worst tyranny. (*CPW*, IVi, 427)

Indeed, he stresses that the logic of his argument 'does not mean that all kings are tyrants' (*CPW*, IVi, 367). What he persistently attempts in *A Defence of the People of England* is to establish the notion of the plurality of alternative governmental structures available to contemporary European civilization. Monarchy or republicanism are two possibilities; their advantages and disadvantages may be evaluated differently in different countries, and preferences may change in time.

It is therefore a task for men of the utmost wisdom to discover what may be most suitable and advantageous for a people; certainly the same government is fitting neither for all peoples nor for one people at all times; now one form is better, now another, as the courage and industry of the citizens waxes or wanes. (*CPW*, ivi, 392)

Persistently (and in a way that honestly reflects the events leading to the foundation of the English republic) he represents the constitutional revolution in England as a practical and perhaps imperfect solution to immediate political exigencies, and he uses that notion to defend the palpable unconstitutionality of a parliamentary republic maintained through the exclusion of many of its duly elected members of parliament:

Our form of government is such as our circumstances and schisms permit; it is not the most desirable, but only as good as the stubborn struggles of the wicked citizens allow it to be. If, however, a country harassed by faction and protecting herself by arms regards only the sound and upright side, passing over or shutting out the others, whether commons or nobles, she maintains justice well enough . . . (*CPW*, ivi, 316–17)

Much of the first Latin defence seems to engage a Dutch readership. The book he is attacking was published in the United Provinces; its author was a professional academic at the University of Leiden; much of the Latin controversy about the English republic was published in Amsterdam; and the English republic was contemporaneously engaged in a major diplomatic offensive directed at securing Dutch support. Four months after its first publication, the republic sent its first major embassy abroad, to the United Provinces, a mission which began very grandly but which met with much hostility, fomented in part by supporters of the House of Orange.[18] Dutch constitutional practices were both complex and dynamic, changing with the shifts in the balance of power between the assemblies of the individual states and the House of Orange. Milton's clouded vision of the English state, for the present a republic but imperfectly formed, was one an anti-Orangist Dutch contemporary could be expected to understand and to feel some sympathy with.

In *A Second Defence of the People of England*, published in May 1654, an engagement with immediate diplomatic exigencies more overtly shapes the argument about forms of government. The English republic's relations with Sweden had been congenial from the outset, and a month earlier the states had signed the Treaty of Uppsala, a commercial agreement the details of which remained to be worked out.[19] Moreover, Milton had (or believed he had or represented

---

[18] Robert Thomas Fallon, *Milton and Government* (University Park, Pa., 1993), p. 75.
[19] *Ibid.*, p. 161.

himself as believing he had) evidence that Queen Christina had responded both sympathetically to his first Latin defence and in hostile fashion towards Salmasius, who had been invited to Sweden. In the second Latin defence, Milton stresses that the English republic has no quarrel with good monarchs (and distinguishes them sharply from tyrants) and explicitly praises Christina as an exemplar of the former.

Indeed, few defences of regicide can have expressed such fulsome praise of a living monarch. As if embarrassed that republican ideology may seem a slur on 'Her Most Serene Majesty, the Queen of the Swedes' (*CPW*, ivi, 556), he asseverates, 'If I attack tyrants, what is this to kings, whom I am very far from classing as tyrants?' (*CPW*, ivi, 561). Indeed, Christina's panegyric becomes incorporated into the strong narrative of his own status that informs much of the polemical strategy of the tract:

When I had fallen on such a time in my country's history as obliged me to become involved in a cause so difficult and so dangerous that I seemed to attack the whole right of kings, I found such a glorious, such a truly royal defender of my honesty to testify that I had uttered no word against kings, but only against tyrants – the pests and plagues of kings. How magnanimous you are, Augusta, how secure and well-fortified on all sides by a well-nigh divine virtue and wisdom. Not only could you read with so calm and serene a spirit, with such incredible objectivity and true composure of countenance a work that might seem to have been written against your own right and dignity, but you could adopt such a judgment against your own defender that you seem to most men even to award the palm to his opponent. With what honor, with what respect, O queen, ought I always to cherish you, whose exalted virtue and magnanimity are a source not alone of glory to you, but also of favor and benefit to me! They have freed me from all suspicion and ill-repute in the minds of other kings and by this glorious and immortal kindness have bound me to you for ever. (*CPW*, ivi, 604–5)

Besides local advantages in terms both of Milton's own status and of the diplomatic imperatives of the mid-1650s, his explicit endorsement of the godly monarch may relate, too, to an emergence among republican apologists loyal to Cromwell of a sense of his status as another kind of godly monarch. Warren Chernaik has noted the ideological proximity of the second Latin defence and Marvell's 'The First Anniversary of the Government under O.C.'.[20] The apostrophe

[20] Warren Chernaik, *The Poet's Time: Politics and Religion in the Work of Andrew Marvell* (Cambridge, 1983), pp. 51–2.

to Cromwell the 'great Prince', with which the poem concludes (lines 395–402), suggests an image of constitutional continuity to those who may still have doubts about government without a king.[21] In similar fashion, Milton's panegyric to Cromwell late in the second Latin defence offers the Lord Protector as a godly monarch who transcends the achievements of kings and the category of kingship: 'The *name* of king you spurned *from your far greater eminence*, and rightly so' (*CPW*, ivi, 672, my italics). Wolfe notes that the 'list of high titles' that Milton confers on Cromwell culminates with 'the father of your country', and *pater patriae*, though the Senate gave it to Cicero after he scotched the Catilinarian conspiracy, was an epithet later bestowed on Julius and Augustus Caesar.[22]

IV

Milton appears a doubtful, conservative and perhaps reluctant revolutionary; but we should hesitate before we dismiss his radical credentials. He was, as he remained throughout the 1650s, a professional and loyal supporter of the republican regime in its various constitutional manifestations, drawing a civil servant's salary until the third quarter of 1659. He clearly shared that regime's initial uncertainties about what form of government would emerge after the killing of the king; indeed, why should he be more prescient than those most closely involved in driving events? He also took his polemical orientation in each of his regicide tracts from his sense of the immediate requirements of the debate and from the larger policy his government was developing. In Fallon's recent work we have a much fuller sense of his work in the service of the republic's foreign policy, and we now know that he continued to busy himself in the foreign secretariat headed by John Thurloe.[23] As I have suggested, his Latin defences in particular reflect the diplomatic concerns of the regime. His vernacular ones serve, rather, to second the efforts of the purged parliament in building a new consensus with those former supporters of parliament who had been reluctant to accept the regicide. The tracts assert an image of the republic as guardian of law and property and the traditional rights of the political nation. The endless discussion of the legal accountability of kings and of the criminal culpability of one king in particular in a sense hides the silences about

[21] Corns, *Uncloistered Virtue*, pp. 240–3.   [22] *CPW*, ivi, 672, n. 508.
[23] Fallon, *Milton and Government*, pp. 124–30 and *passim*.

the merits of republican government and its revolutionary characteristics.

Nevertheless, alongside his careful attempts to represent the regime
in terms acceptable to foreign governments and former allies, Milton
speaks a language and articulates a value system that are profoundly
subversive of old political assumptions about the nature of kingship
and the English state. The characteristics of a free commonwealth, as
they are most explicitly discussed, seem those of continuities with the
best aspects of the old regime, the defence of the laws, the protection of
property. But the characteristics of a free commonwealth, as they find
more oblique expression in those tracts, represent an utter sea-change
in English political life and thought. While the purged parliament
and later the Cromwellian ascendancy sought to conciliate some
opponents at home and to effect a *modus vivendi* abroad wherever that
was consonant with their perception of the national interest, nevertheless
in Milton's prose there emerges an awareness and an expression of
epochal change.

In a spectacular afterthought added to *Eikonoklastes* in its second
edition, Milton wrote,

Indeed if the race of Kings were eminently the best of men, as the breed at
Tutburie is of Horses, it would in some reason then be their part onely to
command, ours always to obey. But Kings by generation no way excelling
others, and most commonly not being the wisest or the worthiest by far of
whom they claime to have the governing, that we should yeild them
subjection to our own ruin, or hold of them the right of our common safety,
and our natural freedom by meer gift, as when the Conduit pisses Wine at
Coronations, from the superfluity of their royal grace and beneficence, we
may be sure was never the intent of God, whose ways are just and equal;
never the intent of Nature, whose works are also regular; never of any People
not wholly barbarous, whom prudence, or no more but human sense would
have better guided when they first created Kings, then so to nullifie and
tread to durt the rest of mankind, by exalting one person and his Linage
without other merit lookt after, but the meer contingencie of a begetting,
into an absolute and unaccountable dominion over them and thir posterity.
(*CPW*, III, 486–7)

Milton largely defines the characteristics of the free commonwealth in
terms of what it is not; it is not barbarous, it is not magical, it does not
depend on the whim and the permissions of a single man, it is not
irrational, it does not frustrate the reasonable interests of its citizens,
and it is not at odds with the principles of the Christian faith.

The sentiments are revolutionary; the idiom is utterly subversive. Note the opening analogy between men and horses. The argument is an ancient one, traceable to Aristotle, that only excellence should elevate an individual above others into the role of monarch. But the image Milton uses is profoundly reductive. The king, a semi-divine figure in the rhetoric of royalist panegyrists and apologists, is compared to a Tutbury stallion (the Staffordshire town was renowned for the quality of its draught horses), and found wanting. Then comes the sustained argument that, experientially, kings may be judged alongside other men; they are not by their kind off the scale of human virtue, and indeed their wisdom may be compared with that of ordinary citizens, whereupon it is found most certainly no better than most and worse than some. Throughout Milton's republican prose he asserts the dignity of the common citizen. A commonwealth without a king is a commonwealth in which the citizen enjoys his rights without permission, and what is permissive is not really a right. Again, the image is reductive. Freedom is not to be equated with the dubious benevolence of the traditional coronation celebration in which wine was poured into London's system of drinking water; 'pisses' does not disguise Milton's evaluation. Two remaining points relate to the godliness of the republic and to the nature of English civilization. This English republic is a state which seemingly has God's endorsement, something claimed for monarchy, with its ceremony of anointment, but really to be seen only here (as the argument will extend elsewhere, both in God's providence and in the way it protects the right of the godly to worship after their conscience). Again, republicanism marks the political maturity of the nation; monarchical leadership belongs to a barbarous age, now transcended.

The same values and a constellation of related ones pervade the radical subtext of his republican writings. In his 'Observations' there is a similar sense that merit, not inheritance, should determine who holds governmental office. Thus he compares the achievements of Cromwell and the Marquis of Ormond, Charles II's plenipotentiary in Ireland and scion of an ancient aristocratic house that traced its Irish nobility back to the late twelfth century:[24]

But seing in that which followes he [Ormond] contains not himself, but contrary to what a Gentleman should know of Civility, proceeds to the contemptuous naming of a person, whose valour and high merit many

[24] *CPW*, III, 312, n. 32.

enemies more noble then himself have both honour'd and feard, to assert his good name and reputation, of whose service the Common-wealth receaves so ample satisfaction, tis answerd in his behalf, that *Cromwell* whom he couples with a name of scorne, hath done in few yeares more eminent and remarkable Deeds whereon to *found* Nobility in his house, though it were wanting, and perpetuall Renown to posterity, then *Ormond* and all his Auncestors put together can shew from any record of thir *Irish* exploits, the widest scene of thir glory. (*CPW*, III, 312)

Inevitably the issues are confused by conflicting polemical imperatives. He wishes at the same time to assert that Cromwell is no propertyless *enragé* but one whose lineage has some noble blood (the force of 'though it were wanting' – it isn't really wanting). Again, there is a nationalist point about the inferiority of all things Irish to achievements in England and on behalf of England. Nevertheless, the message, about the superiority of merit over hereditary status, is clear. Cromwell's service for the commonwealth far outranks the service of Ormond and the Butler family to the English interest in Ireland. The abolition of monarchy in England was seconded by the revolutionary abolition of the House of Lords.[25] A free commonwealth chooses its servants, not for their blood, but for their godliness and their merit. Besides engaging the simple realities of the relative achievements of Cromwell and the marquis, Milton's language unmistakably is the idiom of the new man.

The passage exemplifies in miniature what is to be the informing subversive posture of *Eikonoklastes.* In the early 1640s Milton had spoken to bishops (at least to Bishop Joseph Hall in *Animadversions* (1641)) with a measureless contempt; in the late 1640s his contempt for kings (or at least Charles I) appears again, not in vituperation and rarely in satire, but in the forms of address he develops in the pseudo-dialogic format of *Eikonoklastes.* The idiom of monarchism depends on distinction, on proclamation from a posture of ascendancy; Milton pulls Charles down from the lofty and pious vagueness adopted in *Eikon Basilike* into the at least temporary parity of the disputation:

for their sakes who through custom, simplicitie, or want of better teaching, have not more seriously considerd Kings, then in the gaudy name of Majesty, and admire them and thir doings, as if they breath'd not the same breath with other mortal men, I shall make no scruple to take up (for it seems

---

[25] 'An Act for the Abolishing of the House of Peers', 19 March 1649, in Firth and Rait (eds.), *Acts and Ordinances*, II, 24.

to be the challenge both of him and all his party) to take up this Gauntlet, though a Kings, in the behalf of Libertie, and Common-wealth. (*CPW*, III, 338)

The image of the gauntlet is politically potent; certainly Milton engages the king as the champion of the new regime, but he does so as if in single combat on level ground. The king must fight him in his own person, and on terms which admit no differences of rank and degree. Just as Ormond, fairly compared with Cromwell, appears the overprivileged and overpromoted scion of an overrated provincial stock, so Charles, fairly compared with Milton the new man, appears dull, mendacious, duplicitous and vulgar. *Eikon Basilike* had aspired to the transcendency of devotional meditation; Milton pulls it into the role of a protagonist in a disputation, and toils assiduously and successfully to ensure that it is a disputation that he, John Milton, most surely wins.

The 'gaudy name of Majesty' implies, too, a new aesthetic at the heart of republican consciousness. Certainly Milton works to juxtapose (a version of) the truth next to Charles's pious vacuities and tendentious assertions; but he often does so in terms that express a republican sensibility deeply critical of the deceit and the self-deceptions of the displaced court. Thus he quotes Charles's account of the attempt to arrest the five members, and interposes a shrewder assessment:

> *That I went*, saith he of his going to the House of Commons, *attended with some Gentlemen*; Gentlemen indeed; the ragged Infantrie of Stewes and Brothels; the spawn and shiprack of Taverns and Dicing Houses: and then he pleads *it was no unwonted thing for the Majesty and safety of a King to be so attended, especially in discontented times*. An illustrious Majestie no doubt, so attended: a becomming safety for the King of *England*, plac'd in the fidelity of such Guards and Champions: Happy times; when Braves and Hacksters, the onely contented Members of his Goverment, were thought the fittest and the faithfullest to defend his Person against the discontents of a Parlament and all good Men. (*CPW*, III, 380–1)

> *Eikon Basilike* attempted to present the event in almost chivalric terms, as threatened majesty surrounded by a loyal retinue of gentlemen; Milton demystifies the language of royalism, juxtaposing a different image of court culture, dependent on the subcultural life of the brothel and the gaming house, with an image of the parliament and 'all good Men'.

V

Only in his last major republican pamphlet, *The Readie and Easie Way to Establish a Free Commonwealth* (two editions, 1660), does Milton ever articulate a constitutional model for good government without kings. Its unsatisfactoriness, both as a practical option and as a theoretical ideal, have frequently been remarked upon. As Worden somewhat impatiently observes, 'behind that rhetoric we would search in vain for a systematic republican theory'.[26] Yet if Milton as a political thinker falls far short of Machiavelli or of Harrington, he has other massive strengths. He is a brilliant and assiduous polemicist, and his late republican tracts, though composed under the shadow of the scaffold, show a resilient attempt to find the right strategy despite the circumambient disintegration of the political position he served.[27] But his abilities are not merely trained on gaining local advantage. His are the voice and the vision of the towering literary genius of his age. With an eloquence others could not approach, *The Readie and Easie Way* offers an image, rendered retrospectively poignant, of an English free commonwealth founded on the service of the godly. Republicanism, in Milton's writing, is more an attitude of mind than any particular governmental configuration. It produces a rational and unmystical state: 'The happiness of a nation must needs be firmest and certainest in a full and free Councel of thir own electing, where no single person, but reason only swaies' (revised edition, *CPW*, VII, 427). Only such a system respects the rights of the ordinary citizen, and observes the fact that some men do not transcend others in their abilities in the manner of those Tutbury stallions. In contrast kingship requires the surrender of self-respect:

> how unmanly must it needs be, to count such a one [as a king] the breath of our nostrils, to hang all our felicity on him, all our safetie, our well-being, for which if we were aught els but sluggards or babies, we need depend on none but God and our own counsels, our own active vertue and industrie. (*Ibid.*)

Moreover, kingship brings the unacceptable and displaced aesthetic of the court, its assertion of the divine status of the king and his family, together with the gaudy corruptions of cavalier culture. Once more, the merits of the free commonwealth may best be defined in terms of what it is not. It is not a state where 'a king must be ador'd like a Demigod, with a dissolute and haughtie court about him, of vast

[26] Worden, 'Milton's Republicanism and the Tyranny of Heaven', p. 245.
[27] On the polemical strategy of the tracts of 1660, see Corns, *Uncloistered Virtue*, pp. 279–93.

expence and luxurie'; nor where those who should become the principal servants of the commonwealth aspire instead to posts as regal lavatory attendants, 'bred up then to the hopes ... of court offices; to be stewards, chamberlains, ushers, grooms, even of the close-stool' (*CPW*, VII, 425).

Milton concludes both editions of *The Readie and Easie Way* with the assertion, 'What I have spoken, is the language of that which is not call'd amiss *the good Old Cause*' (*CPW*, VII, 462). The phrase is appropriate for, in a sense, that cause, the cause of English republicanism, is a language. It is an idiom in which a value system and an aesthetic are inscribed, and it is an undeferential posture which utterly subverts the assumptions of Stuart monarchism. In the various and increasingly careful polemical positioning and tactics of his republican writings from *The Tenure of Kings and Magistrates* through to the Latin defences, those who would deradicalize Milton may find some evidence, though only by ignoring that voice and vision. Not for nothing did Charles II's secretary of state, Sir Joseph Williamson, actively hound down and suppress the posthumous literary remains of 'that late Villain Milton'.[28] Republican forms of government could easily be changed – indeed, they showed little stability even with the Interregnum. But Milton's prose articulates something altogether harder to control, that republican consciousness, founded in a sense of political self-worth and a powerful suspicion of the mystery of kingship, that once found expression in England's free commonwealth.

[28] Sir Joseph Williamson, Public Record Office SP 104/66/120.

CHAPTER 3

Great senates and godly education: politics and cultural renewal in some pre- and post-revolutionary texts of Milton

Cedric C. Brown

In the early 1650s Milton had an amanuensis copy the following note into his Commonplace Book. It was in his own Latin but based on Machiavelli's *Discorsi*, one of seventeen notes from that work entered at about the same time:

Laudatissimos omnium inter mortales, eos esse qui vera Religione hominum mentes imbuunt, immo iis etiam laudationes qui humanis legibus Regna et Respub: quamvis egregie fundarunt. (*Discorsi*, 1.10)[1]
[He states] the most praiseworthy of all mortals to be those who imbue the minds of men with true religion, even more to be praised than those who have founded, with whatever distinction, kingdoms and republics according to human laws.

This was under the heading 'De Religione Quatenus Ad Rempub: Spectat' (Of religion, to what extent it has a bearing upon the commonwealth).[2]

The entry shows a characteristic partiality in appropriating the *Discorsi*. Machiavelli had actually written at the beginning of that chapter of his discourses on Livy:

Intra tutti gli uomini laudati sono i laudatissimi quelli che sono stati capi e ordinatori delle religioni. Appresso, dipoi, quelli che hanno fondato o republiche o regni.[3]

---

[1] *The Works of John Milton*, ed. F. A. Patterson *et al.*, 20 vols. (New York, 1931–40), XVIII, pp. 197–8; *CPW*, I, 475–6. All translations are my own.
[2] The various references to 'republic' below, in Latin, Italian and English, bear somewhat different meanings in different contexts. Here I have rendered the Latin 'res publica' as 'republic', because as will be seen the original Italian sets 'republiche' in opposition to 'regni'. In some other places I have put 'commonwealth'. In the citing of Machiavelli quoted below on p. 45, however, the reference is to 'status popularis' or democratic government.
[3] *Opere Politiche*, ed. Mario Puppo (Florence, 1969), p. 231.

Amongst all praiseworthy men those are most to be praised who are heads of
states and orderers of religions. Next after them are those who have founded
republics or kingdoms.

The burden of the chapter is that we should learn from the examples
of Roman history to support good leaders and not to serve tyrants,
like emperors, who do not have the interests of their cities at heart.
The main distinction is the separation of virtuous republics from bad
autocracies, and religion is not in focus after that first sentence. It is
Milton who has given religion priority, who has further coloured his
entry by using the phrase 'true religion', taking the Florentine into his
reforming vocabulary, and it is Milton the educator who is concerned
with imbuing minds. Here, as often in his work, matters of statecraft
are subordinated to the continuing educational cause of reformation.

This chapter draws together texts of Milton from pre- and
post-revolutionary periods in the context of examining in them the
ways in which formations of the polity are enmeshed with considerations
of religion, most especially of the progress or otherwise of reformation.
If in general scholars like to think that political thought was gradually
separating itself from the concerns of religion during this period, then
the case of Milton presents some complications. Although in his
reading, as far as we can trace it, and in the negotiations of his
writings with the changing political situations of the mid-seventeenth
century, he concerned himself with systems of government, and
although he had no wish to contaminate civil with ecclesiastical
powers, there remains a sense in which his ideas of the religious spirit
of the nation assumed a priority over matters of political organization.

More specifically, my concern is to link, in selected documents
chosen to span the Civil War and Interregnum, formulations which
support republican ideas or seem to refuse to endorse too much power
at an autocratic centre of government. They are texts written, on the
one hand, on the eve of Restoration, or published in the Restoration
years; and, on the other, in the pre-revolutionary period. That is, I
shall mainly use the Ludlow masque of 1634, the series of writings
leading into *The Readie and Easie Way*, and *Paradise Lost*.

These are very different kinds of text, and some attention will be
paid to the different ways in which political ideas are embodied in
them, especially in relation to *Paradise Lost*, a work about which
there has been some debate with regard to political expression. But,
questions of mode aside, there are some continuities to note between

the late texts, which come after the period of Milton's development of republican ideas, and the early ones, which may have more substantial political implications than are sometimes recognized. I shall find common ground in these various texts with regard to the relationship between regional or sectional interests and the centre of power, and by means of the inclusive idea of cultural renewal. By this I seek to identify Milton's educational drive to strengthen the spirit of his nation through the freedoms which he thought would result from the curbing or abolition of tyrannies in both court and church.

Underpinning my examples is also therefore an educational theme, concerned with readying the nation for the exercise of rational freedoms. This educational cause can also be seen to shape his other citations from Machiavelli in the Commonplace Book. A general argument in support of republics over monarchies which he drew from *Dell'Arte della Guerra*, in his first round of citations from Machiavelli apparently made as early as the early 1640s, was that republics better nurture men of virtue. In this entry he quotes from the Italian text, adding a brief cue in Latin at the beginning:

Resp. regno potior. perche delle repub. escano piu huomini eccellenti, che de regni. perche in quelle il piu delle volte si honora la virtù, ne regne si teme. &c. (*Dell' Arte della Guerra*, ii.63)[4]
A republic is preferable to a monarchy. 'Why do more excellent men come from republics than from kingdoms? Because in the former virtue is honoured most of the time and is not feared as in monarchies.'

A reference to the *Discorsi* some ten years later again registers Machiavelli as a simple champion of republicanism – no flexibility about political systems comes through – and at the same time confirms that the issue is the production of better leaders. His heading this time is 'Varius Reipub: Status' (various forms of commonwealth), and his marginal note 'status popularis' (popular form):

Machiavellus longè praefert Monarchie statum popularem, adductis rationibus haud inscitis toto capite. 58. l. 1 discors. et l.3 c.34. ubi disserit minus errare rempub: quam principem in eligendis magistratibus suis aut ministris.[5]
Machiavelli greatly prefers a popular form to a monarchy, adducing reasons of no little shrewdness in the whole of Chapter 58 of the first book of the *Discourses* and in Book 3, Chapter 34, where he argues that a republic makes fewer mistakes than a prince in choosing its magistrates or ministers.

[4] *Works*, ed. Patterson *et al.*, xviii, p. 164; *CPW*, i, 421.
[5] *Works*, ed. Patterson *et al.*, xviii, p. 199; *CPW*, i, 477.

One sees here what is evident in many other places in Milton's writing, a concern to produce and encourage an educated and responsible elite, which will in turn ensure the freedom of the people. As we shall see, maturity of this kind has its beginnings in right religion, for in Milton's militantly Protestant analysis servitude takes it origins in the institutions of false religion, which feed the institutions of tyranny. That is a pattern established out of the Old Testament, which takes me to my first text and the shadowing of a polity in the educational pilgrimage of the Hebrew people.

My first major text is *Paradise Lost*, XII, 214ff. This describes a moment in which an indication of a system of government is given, as Michael's narrative follows the Israelites after the Red Sea crossing, whilst they delay in the wilderness, with uncertain resolve and readiness, before finally entering the Promised Land:

> ... the race elect
> Safe towards Canaan from the shore advance
> Through the wild desert, not the readiest way,
> Lest entering on the Canaanite alarmed
> War terrify them inexpert, and fear
> Return them back to Egypt, choosing rather
> Inglorious life with servitude; for life
> To noble and ignoble is more sweet
> Untrained in arms, where rashness leads not on.

So, on the threshold of realizing a momentous promise, the Israelites delay their possession of the land, and despite a mixed verdict on the people Milton justifies that delay. He gives a reason bearing on preparation or education:

> This also shall they gain by their delay
> In the wide wilderness, there they shall found
> Their government, and their great senate choose
> Through the twelve tribes, to rule by laws ordained:
> God from the Mount of Sinai, whose gray top
> Shall tremble, he descending, will himself
> In thunder, lightning, and loud trumpets' sound
> Ordain them laws; part such as appertain
> To civil justice, part religious rites
> Of sacrifice, informing them, by types
> And shadows, of that destined seed to bruise
> The serpent, by what means he shall achieve
> Mankind's deliverance...   (*PL*, XII, 223–35)

A few lines later, beginning with line 244, there is an indication of a time of rare accord between God and His people:

> Thus laws and rites
> Established, such delight hath God in men
> Obedient to his will, that he vouchsafes
> Among them to set up his tabernacle,
> The holy one with mortal men to dwell...
>
> (*PL*, XII, 244–8)

The system of government endorsed by the Lord is a mode of republicanism, in the form of the Sanhedrin, or council of seventy drawn from the twelve tribes. It is a federal kind of republicanism, the central council respecting tribal representation. Like most at this time Milton elides various references and takes it, here at least, that Moses' calling upon the help of the seventy in the eleventh chapter of Numbers resulted in the same organization as is recorded in other books of the Old Testament.

This would seem to be a significant moment announcing a political model. In itself the reference would not have been surprising to readers who had lived through the middle years of the seventeenth century, especially to those who were attuned to anti-monarchical discourses. The model of the Sanhedrin had often been used to authorize non-monarchical forms of government by different groups during the revolutionary period. In the many tracts of the republican James Harrington, for example, some of them interconnecting with Milton's writings of 1659/60, the Mosaic 'senate' forms a basis of definition. Indeed, those of different persuasion sought to appropriate the Jewish model, so that many of the debates entered into in Harrington's tracts are conducted on the basis of biblical interpretation concerning the various systems of government of the Jews.[6]

Yet to recognize this sort of alignment in the text of *Paradise Lost* is to prompt further questions. For example, it raises the issue of just how fully the political is figured in the text. In one sense, the reference to the Sanhedrin is short-handed, confined to a bare factuality in an unelaborated reference. On the other hand, it is deliberate – this phase of history is not going to be passed without mentioning a divinely approved model of government which will be in place for

---

[6] *The Political Works of James Harrington*, ed. J. G. A. Pocock (Cambridge, 1977), pp. 176, 376, 573, 615ff, and in many other places. The most important English scholarship in this area came from John Selden: see Anna Strumia, *L'Immaginazione Repubblicana: Sparta e Israele nel Dibattito Filosofico-Politico dell'Età di Cromwell* (Florence, 1991).

future generations. The word 'senate' itself may seem firm enough. To the issue of how the political is defined in the text of *Paradise Lost* I shall be returning.

Another matter of difficulty is to understand how far that form of government is meant to be applicable to other nations and ages. Milton was a considerable historian, one who tended to contextualize historical texts and who was likely to demythologize and reinterpret historical precedents. Even biblical history is to be interpreted afresh, for whatever lessons the freely interpretative spirit might find in it.[7] He does not say what less cautious spirits might have said, that *the* form of government was inaugurated in the wilderness. He says that it was 'their' government, an arrangement appropriate to that nation at that time, with that nation's special relationship with God. The last books of *Paradise Lost* present an unfolding history, not a static allegory, for the education of Adam and the reader. The coincidence of civil and religious law within the jurisdiction of one body is a feature which belongs specifically to that situation and which Milton, insistent on the need to separate church from state, could not allow to the era of Christ, when under Grace men could break free from the schoolmastery of the Law. It should be noted as well that he presents the Mosaic council within a religious category, typologically: the descent of God himself in the thunder on Mount Sinai prefigures the later coming of the Messiah. For all that, a major model has been rehearsed, and Milton elsewhere invokes the Sanhedrin as model for contemporary republican government, together with the other models from the ancient and modern worlds – the Athenian Areopagus, the Spartan Ancients, the Roman Senate, the Venetian government, and the constitution of the United Provinces. There is a general approval of rule by a select council.

We might put a contemporary term to that model. A word commonly used of the Sanhedrin was 'aristocratic'. So, to pick two simple examples, if we turn to the antimonarchical Diodati's brief comments on Numbers 11, we find that he explains the change from Moses' sole leadership to the joint leadership of Moses with the Seventy as a shift from 'monarchical' to 'aristocratic' rule.[8] Or we find Thomas Godwyn ('the schoolmaster', as Harrington pat-

---

[7] See for example Mary Ann Radzinowicz, '"In those days there was no king in Israel": Milton's Politics and Biblical Narrative', *Yearbook of English Studies*, 21 (1991), 242–52.
[8] Giovanni Diodati, *Pious Annotations Upon the Holy Bible . . .* (2nd edn, London, 1648), pp. 93–4: 'But now *Moses* desireth that this Monarchicall form might be changed into Aristocracy: to which God consented . . .'

ronizingly calls him)[9] explaining at the beginning of his elementary book, *Moses and Aaron* (1625, but with over a dozen seventeenth-century editions), that between the Judges the tribes were governed by the Sanhedrin whose rule 'might be thought aristocratical'.[10] 'Gather unto me seventy men of the elders of Israel, whom thou knowest to be the elders of the people, and officers over them; and bring them unto the tabernacle of the congregation.' Thus said the Lord to Moses (Numbers 11:16). But selection of fit men from amongst leaders and magistrates for Milton's purposes was no such easy matter. As we look at what he was suggesting for models of government in 1659/60 we shall have reason to try to identify an aristocracy of civic and, I think, religious virtue. This is not quite the traditional aristocracy envisioned in mid-seventeenth-century English systems of government, based on Polybius, which described a balance between monarchy, aristocracy and democracy (or King, Lords and Commons).[11] What Milton like some others sought in place of a senate of greatly landed men was a principled and educated leadership in a freely reforming state.

Nor had Milton's experience of a ruling council been reassuring, as he confessed candidly to the Oldenburg emissary, Hermann Mylius, in February 1652. He wished to present the government in the image of republican Rome. His attempts to head state documents to be sent abroad 'Senatus Populusque Anglicanus' amply illustrate the point. But the scholar-secretary, who had often stood and waited on the wishes of the council he served, confessed that most of those who had been chosen were inexperienced and small-minded, mechanics, soldiers, home-bred people, forceful but lacking depth of education or experience of other countries in all but a handful of cases. Amongst such men, confesses one urbane public servant to another, one sometimes keeps prudently silent.[12] No wonder Milton showed considerable caution in determining principles of selection in 1659.

[9] Harrington, *Political Works*, ed. Pocock, p. 376.
[10] Thomas Godwyn, *Moses and Aaron: Civil and Ecclesiastical Rites used by the Ancient Hebrews...* (10th edn, 1671), p. 2: 'In these vacancies or distances of time, between *Judge* and *Judge*, the greater and weightier matters were determined by that great Court of the *Seventy* called the *Sanhedrin*; in which respect the form of Government might be thought *Aristocratical*. *Kings* succeeded the *Judges*...'
[11] The document most often referred to in this connection for this period in *His Majesty's Answer to the Nine Propositions of Parliament* of June 1642. See the survey in J. G. A. Pocock, *The Ancient Constitution and the Feudal Law*, A Reissue with Retrospect (Cambridge, 1987), pp. 306–34.
[12] On the Latin phrase, see Leo Miller, 'Lexicographer Milton Leads Us to Recover His Unknown Works', *Milton Quarterly*, 24 (1990), 58–62; the rest is paraphrased from Mylius' German and Latin entry in his record of his negotiations in England: Leo Miller, *John Milton and the Oldenburg Safeguard* (New York, 1985), pp. 171–2.

The coercive rhetoric of *The Readie and Easie Way* (of which I shall be citing the second edition to begin with) soon shows us why this episode in the wilderness was so formative in the political education of the Israelites, and in that of Adam; and the readers of the tract are in effect placed at an analogous historical moment in the progress of England. To have emerged from Egypt and come to the point at which a senate has been adopted by God is to have taken the people to the threshold of liberty; to contemplate monarchy again would be to behave like the ignoble waverers in the wilderness, those who thinking of return to the relative ease of Egypt wish idolatry and alien rule upon the nation. The institution of monarchy receives equally firm placement in *The Readie and Easie Way*: having established its government, Israel had become, in Milton's words, 'a Commonwealth of God's own ordaining, he only thir king, they his peculiar people',[13] and Moses' asking for help in leading the people was clearly a good thing; whereas the desire of subsequent generations of Israelites to have a king is seen as a falling off from that standard of government by senate which God had manifestly approved.

In Milton's political writings on the eve of the Restoration a main concern is to guarantee the quality and ideological correctness of these senators. Even before his proposals had reached their fullest, and perhaps most desperate, form in the second edition of *The Readie and Easie Way*, it had become clear enough, for all that others had proposed, that he did not wish a revolving council responsive to democratic pressure – 'being well chosen', the senate 'should be perpetual' (*CPW*, vii, 433). The broad electorate should be the last consulted, and he dismisses as dangerous 'the noise and shouting of a rude multitude' (*ibid.*, 442). The better and more educated should be the choosers. These true elders of Milton's times can save the people from their own tendency to enslave themselves. This is a terrible argument, it is remarked, by scholars who have harsh political lessons of the present century in mind, and as Milton's contemporary critics also declared,[14] and thoughts of the ageing council of parliament men have seemed close to absurd.

Faced with the extreme caution of Milton's methods of guaranteeing senators, scholars have sometimes tried to explain some of the features of his proposals away, thus in some cases saving him from his own

---

[13] *CPW*, vii, 449.
[14] The remark is that of Austin Woolrych (*CPW*, vii, 212). For a hostile contemporary view, see *The Censure of the Rota ... upon The Readie and Easie Way* (London, 1660).

tendencies to illiberality, just as we have tended to institutionalize a liberal reading of *Areopagitica*. It has often been pointed out that Milton's various writings of 1659/60, trying to respond to bewilderingly rapid change, were some of them hurried and others ill timed. It can also be said that he was writing the second version of *The Readie and Easie Way* in a situation in which it was obvious that popular feeling was in favour of a return of the monarchy, so that he had either to meet the mood of the nation in propounding a relatively safe form of government, tempering his real radicalism, as it were; or simply had to cut off considerations of the popular voice for monarchy, because they were counter-productive to his argument. He may therefore not be proposing an ideal government, but attempting a pragmatic solution for that moment, an interim arrangement until the nation should be ready for something more liberal.[15]

Despite all these considerations, the various writings of 1659/60 about the government have in them some consistent characteristics of Milton's thought, not all to be construed as desperate, because they accord with writings at other points in his career. His ideas of guaranteeing the quality of senators are not divorced from priorities of religious reform, and will prove to be connected with his proposals for regional government. Milton is in fact clearest and most consistent when he enumerates those institutions most to be avoided. These writings are, after all, presented to a nation seen as in crisis. England seems set to abandon the causes which for Milton have given it its heroic identity. The 'two ... most prevailing usurpers over mankinde' to be avoided in the pursuit of those causes are 'superstition and tyrannie' (*CPW*, vii, 421). The biblical rhetoric of glorious opposition to idolatry (or Catholicism) and tyranny he had displayed in his 1645 volume of poems as having exercised his mind back in psalm paraphrases done in 1624 following celebrations in London at Charles's escape from Spain – 'When the blest seed of Terah's faithful son, / After long toil their liberty had won'; 'O let us his praises tell, / Who doth the wrathful tyrants quell'; 'And freed us from the slavery / Of the invading enemy'[16] – was the rhetoric of 1588. Subsequently, in the heroic early 1640s, temporal and spiritual lordship unworthy of Christian liberty had been removed, and must never be replaced. In 'Christian libertie' (*CPW*, vii, 445) is a freedom of rational determination which men must be educated to learn to exercise, and,

---

[15] Critical understanding is reviewed by Woolrych, *CPW*, vii, 212–18.
[16] Paraphrase of Psalm cxiv, lines 1–2; Psalm cxxxvi, lines 9–10, 81–2.

although the main issue concerns civic freedom and the avoidance of the tyranny which he thinks inevitably comes with monarchical rule, he will say that 'the best part of our libertie' is 'our religion' (*ibid.*, 420). Those who rule will be tested against the great cause of Reformation as it is understood in these terms.

With this broad commitment in mind one may begin to seek, within the shifts of position which Milton shows in details of suggested government, according to precise audience and situation, consistencies between the 'Letter to a Friend', 'The Proposals of Certain Expedients', the first edition of *Readie and Easie Way*, the 'Present Means and Free Delineation of a Commonwealth', and the second edition of *Readie and Easie Way*, to put them in their probable order.[17]

In the 'Letter to a Friend' (*CPW*, VII, 322–33) Milton prescribes two levels of government. The first is 'a senate or general council of state', which raises revenue, preserves the public peace and conducts foreign negotiations. Such a group could consist, he says unrealistically, of the Rump Parliament, or, if the Rump is found wanting in establishing liberty of conscience or in abjuring the rule of a single person, then the council could be chosen by the army officers. Senators and army officers are supposed to support each other in their places, unless either side prove false to the afore-mentioned principles. As Woolrych noted (*CPW*, VII, 122), there is an indecision here, since Milton first suggests that senators and army officers should hold place for life, and then says it is a matter of indifference for the moment whether 'the civill government be an annuall democracy or a perpetual Aristocracy' (*CPW*, VII, 331). Then, to balance this senate, there would be a second tier of government at local level, what he calls 'well ordered committies of their faithfullest adherents in every county'. The 'Letter to a Friend' was not prepared for publication, is rough at the edges, but reveals a lot about the priorities in Milton's thought.

'The Proposals of Certain Expedients', a sketch of a pamphlet belonging to the autumn of 1659, suggests how the situation might be recovered from the dangers of confrontation between the rival armies of Lambert and Monck to something like the system of the early days of the Commonwealth. Milton recommends that the Committee of Safety should invite the Rump Parliament to resume, then this body

---

[17] A recent brief but closely contextualized appraisal of these writings can be found in Thomas N. Corns, *Uncloistered Virtue: English Political Literature, 1640–1660* (Oxford, 1992), pp. 269–93. Some materials here overlap with my *John Milton: A Literary Life* (London, 1995).

of well-principled men should be made into a permanent Grand Council, from which a Council of State should be chosen. The tests for those in authority should concern religious toleration and opposition to any form of monarchic rule.

The first edition of *The Readie and Easie Way*, says Corns, 'revives the notion of the sovereignty of the godly'.[18] After extended definition of religious and civil liberties, we have the same two tiers of government as in 'A Letter to a Friend', worked out with different detail. The Grand Council of ablest men has its duties defined much as in the 'Letter', but Milton now declares unequivocally that it should sit 'perpetual', because government is steadiest that way. It is here that he invokes support from the Sanhedrin, the Areopagus, the Ancients of Sparta and the Roman Senate, with conditional support from the constitutions of Venice and the United Provinces (*CPW*, VII, 370–1). There is also more detail on the county assemblies. Every county is 'made a little commonwealth, and thir chief town a city ... where the nobilitie and chief gentry may build ... befitting their qualitie, may bear part in the government, make their own judicial lawes, and execute them ... without appeal ...' (*CPW*, VII, 383). Woolrych (*CPW*, VII, 183) is surely right to suggest that the county governments were 'training grounds for future members of the Grand Council'. The idea is reinforced by the insistence on education at the local level, in schools and academies, for 'all learning and noble education, not in grammar only, but in all liberal arts and exercises' (*CPW*, VII, 384). As Woolrych remarks (*CPW*, VII, 184), 'the context suggests that he ... has in mind an education for public service intended primarily for the gentry'.

In 'Present Means', the unpublished letter of March 1660 to Monck (*CPW*, VII, 389–95), the two tiers are adapted to a new situation: Monck had readmitted the secluded members and hence ruined Milton's idea of using the Rump as the basis of fit men for his council. In this document, designed to secure a council another way, Milton suggests that the chief gentry in each county should be summoned to London to be instructed there about the dangers of monarchy, thence returning to their counties to conduct elections of standing councils, and from these standing councils the representatives for the central council would be chosen. The fitness of the central council is ensured by the *education* into anti-monarchic views

---

[18] Corns, *Uncloistered Virtue*, p. 281.

of the local gentry from which it would be chosen. Monck, following Milton's prompting, should teach the gentry what they need to
know.

Thus we come to the second edition of *The Readie and Easie Way*,
published when new elections were in process not on the principles
that Milton wished and it was clear that the ignorant would choose a
king again. New passages reinforce the sense of moral difference
between republicanism and kingly rule. The Rump, now gone, is
nevertheless defended. He is more circumspect in his definition of the
powers of the grand council, and, reacting to criticism and rival
schemes, he debates how far a perpetual assembly should be balanced
by a more popular assembly. But essentially he sticks to his perpetual
senate of aristocratic virtue, and it emerges that replacements will be
elected only by a process of refinement, keeping choice from the
popular voice. Selected spirits are to save the people from themselves
and compel them to liberty.

The modifications of the two-tier system through these texts
suggest first a pragmatic concern: a guarding of the Good Old Cause
by first trying to limit influence to those who had proved their loyalty
to the cause; and secondly an educational concern, the creating of
mechanisms by which the councillors coming forward from the
counties to the central council would be influenced in the right kind of
way, or at least would be likely to be most free from corruptive
influences at the centre. The elders of *his* Sanhedrin are, to begin with,
those who have shown their allegiance to reformation values in the
right for liberty of conscience. That is where he begins, in the 'Letter
to a Friend'. In *The Readie and Easie Way* he has also developed the
idea of renovating the centre from the provinces, something which he
had also put forward in *The Likeliest Means to Remove Hirelings* in
August 1659. Here, with the training of ministers chiefly in mind, he
proposes to set up schools and libraries in the provinces and hopes to
avoid the necessity of sending boys to the cities or the two universities
for their education. So the further guarantee of right-mindedness is in
the old Miltonic insistence on proper education, the *paideia* of a
leading class so as to ensure the liberty of the people. The letter to
Monck is also about education controlling choice, in this case in a
crash course taken in London. By the time of the second edition of *The
Readie and Easie Way*, in the face of virtually inevitable monarchy, he
hardens his views about the kind of aristocratic government of free,
educated spirits which would preserve the cause of reformation. In all
this, there is more than a constitutional concern to balance an

oligarchy with democracy in the provinces: there is also an attempt to identify or create ruling classes which can be trusted to do what he regarded as right.

At the end of his patient account of these texts, Woolrych attempted to make a distinction between Milton's secular prescriptions for government, and the rule of the saints optimistically envisaged by some radical parties. 'Nowhere', he remarks, 'does he stipulate godliness as an essential qualification for magistracy, either in the senate or the local councils' (*CPW*, vii, 217). He is in disagreement with Barker about whether Milton actually hoped that magistrates would support true religion, and also in disagreement with Fink concerning that remarkable passage (quoted below) in which the hope is expressed that, under such a senate and councils, peace and prosperity might last until the Second Coming. Fink had seen Milton like Harrington as visionary; Woolrych sees merely conventional expression and opportunistic persuasion. Idealism and pragmatism have been debated often in these texts.[19]

There is no denying that in relative terms Milton's language avoids open millenarian contaminations of the secular and religious, but I am not sure that priority of the religious is banished. It is there by implication, and not only in the matter of legislating for liberty of conscience. It is there in that search for a remnant of true leaders, for those whom Milton first wants to trust in the Rump and army are those who have already shown commitment to reformation in church and state. It is presumably there in the idea of educating gentry in the counties, for if Milton thinks here as he thought elsewhere, the freeing of minds would promote rationality in all spheres of activity, including religion. There would be something oddly inconsistent in these writings if, when he was bracketing the great enemies to true liberty – superstition in religion and tyranny in secular government, the 'great usurpers over mankind' – he did not associate freedom in secular and religious spheres.

And can one be sure that the highly rhetorical passage of hope for such a government until the Second Coming carries no belief? If the Grand Council is maintained, Milton says

ther can be no cause alleag'd why peace, justice, plentiful trade and all prosperitie should not thereupon ensue throughout the whole land ... shall

[19] *CPW*, vii, 214; Arthur E. Barker, *Milton and the Puritan Dilemma, 1641–1660* (Toronto, 1942), pp. 278–90, 308–26; Zera S. Fink, *The Classical Republicans* (Evanston, 1945), ch. 4. See also Barbara K. Lewalski, 'Milton: Political Beliefs and Polemical Methods, 1659–60', *Publications of the Modern Languages Association of America*, 74 (1959), 202; and Corns, *Uncloistered Virtue*.

so continue (if God favour us, and our wilfull sins provoke him not) even to the coming of our true and rightfull and only to be expected King . . . (*CPW*, VII, 374)

One appreciates the *mischief* – there is indeed a restoration of a monarch in view, but a greater monarch than some spirits imagine – but I do not see why the pious patterning need be discarded as merely a matter of rhetoric. As always the nation is on trial with God, and if it persists in good government, may God not approve it in a far greater way than He did in adopting the Sanhedrin in the wilderness, when the Promised Land was in sight?

I would like to create two perspectives on these writings by going back in time of composition to the pre-Civil War period, to some of the figurations in the Ludlow masque, and then forward to *Paradise Lost*, resuming the topic of how the political is figured within that poem. It may seem preposterous to compare prescriptions for government in 1659/60 with figurations in the masque of 1634, for the contexts are very different, and a Civil War had intervened. Milton had to write for a set situation at Ludlow in 1634 which on the face of it presents irreconcilable differences with the kind of government he was advocating in 1659: Bridgewater was a Privy Councillor, sent down from the centre, by the crown, to preside over a prerogative court in Wales and the Marches. The court's coming to Ludlow is a part of the conjunction of things to be celebrated in the masque. Yet, as many have said, Milton's celebrations for Ludlow do not glorify monarchical power, and the assumptions about the moral quality of courts in general, where Comus habitually reigns in his lax irreligion, are not optimistic. The masque offers a renovation stemming from a notable example given in the principality, in which well-schooled, pious aristocratic virtue meets a principle for virtue at the centre of the region, to create a pattern for governance which can rekindle a sense of national heroism. As in 1659, the regions play their part in building models for the training of a true-principled leadership.

Comus shows for a province what 'Arcades' shows for a demesne and family – prosperity built upon right culture, liberal education with godliness at its base. Woolrych's phrase 'aristocracy of virtue' fits both 1634 and 1659. If *The Likeliest Means to Remove Hirelings* and *The Readie and Easie Way* prescribe regional academies to guarantee well-principled, free-minded leaders, the masque gives us virtually an educational programme. Apart from her social graces, the Lady shows the application of virtuous principle in the face of habitual temptation in the courtly feast; the boys show precocious education; but the Attendant Spirit reminds us that the first preparation for meeting such influences as Comus represents is religious, as he cites the pastoral teaching of the shepherd lad as the best foundation against deceptive and blasphemous argument (lines 618–40). Good governance can only be guaranteed by true education and the example of the leading classes. Piety is not merely used politically to validate the powers of the magistracy, it is shown in the action to be the prior necessity for the kind of right discipline on which true prosperity should be based.[20]

Sabrina, still the least understood of entities in the action of the masque, carries the symbolism both of the potential of national heroism – through the Trojan/British myth rehearsed by the Attendant Spirit from his poet-pastor source, 'Meliboeus old' – and of chaste virtue as the renovative force in the principality. In pastoral figurations, past, present and future blessings are associated with her. She has always healed the herds along her banks and the local people are said to recognize in her a power which is providentially given, 'at their festivals / Carol her goodness loud in rustic lays, / And throw sweet garland wreaths into her stream...' (lines 847–9). After her sprinkling rites, the Attendant Spirit associates further prosperity in the region with her, in his thanks: 'May thy lofty head be crowned / With many a tower and terrace round' (lines 933–4). This potentiality in the region will be revealed, through the power of poetry, to the children coming from court as the resource they need to complete their fight against the residual powers of habitual laxness such as dwell in high palace halls. The principality plays its part in a pattern of renovation, as will the well-educated counties in 1659.

What is chiefly at stake, in all these thoughts about good governance, is cultural renewal leading to liberty; what is to be sought at all points is a leadership free from too much direction and habitual influence from the centre and liberated by religion and education to a free search for a renovated government. One may find analogies in other areas of Milton's thinking: in his insistence, for example, on the rational independence of ministers or writers, uncensored by central authorities. All is driven by an acceptance of ideas of reformation, which are based on ideas of the common enemies which depress and

---

[20] The interpretative arguments here are broadly similar to those in my *John Milton's Aristocratic Entertainments* (Cambridge, 1985).

enslave minds – superstition in the church and tyranny in the state – and also involve assumptions about educational discovery. The Israelites in the wilderness grow in understanding, so that they are ready for the Promised Land; those living in the era of grace must also grow and are freer in their responsibilities to use their reason, having been released from the bonds of the Law. Even in his younger days, in the 1630s, Milton seemed ready to admit that such cultural leadership was always likely to be in short supply. But at least a programme of cultural reformation validated Milton's own position, as teacher or prophet for the cause.

That Milton's ideas of government are always enmeshed with these large thoughts about cultural renewal, building on youthful assumptions about reformation, can be illustrated from many other places in the writings (and may indeed be regarded as self-evident), but I am tempted to end where I began, because the question of politics in *Paradise Lost* has been much discussed in recent years. Recent editors have said that the poem 'suppresses its politics'; this is rather like another thought, that the poem shows signs of being written under conditions of censorship, and that we should therefore be specially on the look out for ways in which its message is encoded.[21] This is as if to say, that Milton really wanted to be more political in this poem, that he really wanted to write a political poem, as twentieth-century discourse might require, instead of one about spiritual discipline, but was constrained. Religion may indeed mystify, but such thoughts make great assumptions about the kind of poem Milton wanted to write, and I think there are dangers in assuming either a simple suppression of politics or a method developed primarily because of censorship. Milton wrote a poem directed at the spiritual discipline of his countrymen, and with that function in mind one could conduct a counter-argument to say that he was as political as he needed to be. This is not to downplay the announced orientation of the poem as written in times of darkness and adversity, with danger compassed round. That is the context the author invites the reader to note. But it is to resist too simple conclusions about how the writing meets those conditions, and it is to question

---

[21] The remark is of the editors Stephen Orgel and Jonathan Goldberg in *John Milton* (Oxford, 1990), p. xx. My assumptions share some ground with those of Mary Ann Radzinowicz in 'The Politics of *Paradise Lost*', in Kevin Sharpe and Steven N. Zwicker (eds.), *Politics of Discourse: The Literature and History of Seventeenth-Century England* (Berkeley, 1987), pp. 204–29, especially where she dissociates herself from views that politics are either 'abandoned' or 'encrypted' in *Paradise Lost*.

tactical self-censorship with regard to the cause of Christian liberty.

There is nothing suppressed, for example, about the way that tyranny and idolatry are instituted in Books I and II, with such speed that we see those 'usurpers of mankind' in full operation by the time of the council in Pandemonium. Enslaving practices are easy to begin to list: the sacrifice of the good of the people to the interests of the tyrant; the use of a form of religion to awe the people into a submissive attitude to secular power; the diminishing of the size of the people, whilst the inner conclave sits in full size and splendour, lording it over them; the manipulation of a seemingly free council; and the acts of empire. Here the institutions of irreligious enslavement are in place, in the first great sweep of the action of the poem, ready to set the agenda of adversity for man, and the terms of earthly heroism. There is nothing suppressed, either, about a moment like that in Book IV, 179–93, in which Satan breaks into the enclosure of Paradise and simultaneously inaugurates the spoiling of the true church by those false pastors who enter it for gain – so since into his church false hirelings climb.

There is nothing unclear about the articulation of these great principles by which the endeavour for Christian heroism is defined, nor is there much that is indefinite either about the significance of those phases of history outlined by Michael in Books XI and XII. We are in no doubt as to how to understand, with Adam, prosperity based on piety and 'freedom and peace to men' (*PL*, XI, 580), or the collapse of godly discipline in the epoch leading into the Flood (*PL*, XI, 712ff); or the 'fair equality, fraternal rule' of the patriarchs (*PL*, XII, 26) to be supplanted by the time of Nimrod, the first lording of one man (*PL*, XII, 24ff); or, as we saw at the beginning, the instructive stage of Israel's experience in the wilderness, preparing for the Promised Land. Broad principles are elucidated, and these are what readers may apply to their own sense of things past and present, in free use of reason, prompted by the odd authorial hint. The method could be called censored; it could equally be called scholarly, with regard to history, and educational, with regard to the active participation of the reader.

It might also be said that political categories are clearly enveloped in a larger scheme which expresses godly discipline, and that the poem has as one of its main structures the marking of states of life as either being in the presence of God or being alienated from God. That is a chief meaning of the possession and loss of paradise, and of the learning about the paradise within thee happier far; and of the story of the temptations to alienation and the counter-working presence of Providence. The poem leaves the reader, as it leaves Adam and Eve, with a world of choice, solitary, self-responsible, yet with Providence their guide. The understanding of nations is much as with the understanding of individuals: free determination, subject to correction or to blessing, but within a providential frame.

All this bespeaks the function and perhaps the occasion of the poem: in times of adversity, when men have fallen and the fit are few, when the great efforts for renewal seem to have failed, there may be a turning to the basics of godly discipline, and a need to reaffirm the providential scheme. To that extent the details of a polity are subordinate to the need to speak in instructive healing to the spirit of the nation, or at least of its potential leadership. Yet, as I have said, the principles which motivate all Milton's reformist thought and writing are here, fully expressed, in domestic, public and religious fields; and as far as politics are concerned we find the same clear orientations of value as we do in the political tracts. Milton's political language was never free from the categories of religious and moral definition, and one scheme of reformation and recovery embraced it all.

I do not wish to make simple claims for unchanging characteristics in Milton's thought, as though he were immune from continuing history or never changed his mind, nor do I wish to deny that there is political theory in his works, or to refuse to see them as political interventions in themselves. This is an author whose Commonplace Book is full of references to his historical and political reading, who sought to play a full part in the political debates of the mid-century and who was certainly a good reader of political functions in other men's works. My brief has been more modestly to suggest some repeated priorities, and to suggest that ideas of cultural renewal, established within a reformation frame, control these and others works, even when their expressed agendas do not make it clear.

PART II

Milton and republican literary strategy

Biblical reference in the political pamphlets of the Levellers and Milton, 1638–1654

Elizabeth Tuttle

The margins of the religious and political pamphlets of the early 1640s were often crammed with abbreviated references to biblical texts; these are usually deleted from recent editions of the great Puritan writings. The original pamphlets of the Levellers, who were struggling for political change during the 1640s, often carry the same dense accumulation of references from the Old and New Testaments. This essay stems from the curiosity aroused by these italics in fine print. The question that arises is how did the Levellers use such a mass of biblical references and how did that use compare with the way Milton handled biblical tropes as he too attacked the established church and then worked to justify the revolutionary political strategy of the late 1640s?

During the first Civil War the imperatives of further religious reformation formed a driving force for political change. Later, in the years 1646 to 1649, they gradually gave way both to a more secular rhetoric and to more clearly political priorities. But at a crucial point in the virtually un-kinged community, religious images returned to the forefront within the 'Saints'' ideology as a remedy for disorder. These were cultural representations that men and women easily understood. Such images took hold and, among other factors, their seductive power became the cement of the fragile commonwealth of the 1650s, Britain's only experience of a republic.[1]

This paper addresses the question of the use of the material from the Bible – in the form of quotations and set, even stock images – in this political process. Given their common Puritan legacy, how was the

---

[1] Patricia Crawford, '"Charles Stuart, That Man of Blood"', *Journal of British Studies*, 16 (1977), 41–61; Blair Worden, 'Providence and Politics in Cromwellian England', *Past and Present*, 109 (1985), 55–99; Worden, 'Oliver Cromwell and the Sin of Achan', in Derek Beales and Geoffrey Best (eds.), *History, Society and the Churches* (Cambridge, 1985), pp. 25–45; see my *Religion et idéologie dans la révolution anglaise: salut du peuple et pouvoir des saints* (Paris, 1989), chs. 7–12.

Bible very literally used by men like John Lilburne, William Walwyn, Richard Overton and John Milton as they struggled first to disengage the individual's religious freedom from the hold of the state and then to develop a language expressing secular and natural rights? To what degree did the great poet's 'left hand' and the Levellers have a similar purpose? Did they use biblical quotations and images in the same way?[2] How did Scripture, the very source of 'Truth', contribute ideological support for a short-lived attempt to establish a republic? How did the Levellers' and John Milton's rhetorical strategies change as events transformed the political scene?

The Bible was central to the education of the vast majority of the English gentry and 'middling sort', and doubtless the totally illiterate had command of many biblical stories.[3] Biblical reference helped authors of every sort of treatise to communicate with their readers to an extent inconceivable to most modern readers. Among Puritans in particular, biblical images formed a common short-hand or code, a mythology in the Barthesian sense, whose referents were known to people who had read or been read to from the Bible since infancy.[4]

Beyond this common denominator, the cultural backgrounds of Milton and the Levellers were quite different. Highly educated and widely travelled, Milton had at his finger-tips instruments for creating unique combinations of traditional Ciceronian and Renaissance Ramist rhetoric and yet he did not scorn the exhortations of Puritan preachers and the techniques of dialogue close to those of the theatre in his time.[5] The Levellers, who were neither former students of the Inns of Court nor of the universities, wrote in narrower registers. The sources of their rhetoric were threefold: the Puritan sermon, the treatises on law and government such as those written by John Selden or Henry Parker and, finally, the satires on the princes and priests in the tradition of the Elizabethan Martin Marprelate tracts.

The Puritan ministers of the first forty years of the seventeenth century took liberties with the classical and academic model of

---

[2] A complete checklist of Milton's use of biblical references can be found in H. F. Fletcher, 'The Use of the Bible in Milton's Prose', *University of Illinois Studies in Language and Literature*, 14 (Urbana, 1929), pp. 14–103.

[3] Christopher Hill, *The English Bible and the Seventeenth Century Revolution* (London, 1993), ch. 8.

[4] Roland Barthes, *Mythologies* (Paris, 1957), pp. 193–4.

[5] ''Tis with a sermon as 'tis with a play, many come to see it, which do not understand it': John Selden, *Table Talk*, quoted in C. Richardson, *English Preachers and Preaching* (New York, 1928), p. 64; see also Michael Lieb, 'Milton's *Of Reformation* and the Dynamics of Controversy', in Michael Lieb and John Shawcross (eds.), *Achievements of the Left Hand: Essays on the Prose of John Milton* (Amherst, 1974), p. 69.

exposition and insisted on the 'plain style' in their preaching in order 'to shape and direct feeling and conduct'. The heart of the sermon often included possible objections and answers to those objections. The use of similitude or complex images relating to the lives of the audience became both a Puritan art of oratory and their particular art of memory. The preachers of the separatist congregations such as John Goodwin or, in a looser and more lyric style, John Saltmarsh, William Dell and Paul Hobson, broke away from the strict sequence of rhetoric of their predecessors.[6] One finds a mixture of classical oratory and the Puritan sermon both in Leveller writings and in Milton's pamphlets.

In fact, it is notable how much these polemicists did agree in the early 1640s about how and for whom to write. The main key to the renovation of language and therefore of communication was the Bible. The radical Puritan preachers had led the way whether they understood the biblical stories literally like the Baptists or used them figuratively as did the Antinomians.[7] If the cause of the radicals' struggle in the early 1640s was to give all men the opportunity to use their reason in searching for truth, John Milton and the Leveller spokesmen believed that the very means for this search lay in the Bible itself. In 1641 Milton writes *Animadversions upon the Remonstrants Defence, Against Smectymnuus* to defend his friends the Smectymnuan pamphleteers and there he stresses that the Bible is the perfect 'rule and instrument of knowledge'. Walwyn's *The Power of Love* and *The Compassionate Samaritane* plead the same cause. John Lilburne's *A Work of the Beast* or his more theological *Come Out of Her My People* demonstrate the impetus and rhythm that biblical quotations give to his early prose; in both pamphlets, the impassioned author supplies biblical references with each sentence to the point that he seems almost to out-do the very 'black-coats' (Presbyterian ministers) he scorned.[8]

Well-known biblical images were to assist Lilburne in his endeavour to assume the personification of the persecuted religious dissenter and

---

[6] Nigel Smith, *Perfection Proclaimed: Language and Literature in English Radical Religion, 1640–1660* (Oxford, 1989), pp. 16–19; William Haller, *Liberty and Reformation in the Puritan Revolution* (New York, 1955), pp. 200–3. For excerpts from such sermons, see A. S. P. Woodhouse (ed.), *Puritanism and Liberty* (London, 1938), pp. 180–5, 302–16, 390–6.

[7] William Haller, *The Rise of Puritanism* (New York, 1958), p. 135; Lieb, 'Milton's *Of Reformation and the Dynamics of Controversy*', p. 62; *CPW*, II, 490, n. 15; Smith, *Perfection Proclaimed*, pp. 14–15.

[8] *CPW*, I, 699–700; William Haller (ed.), *Tracts on Liberty in the Puritan Revolution 1638–1647*, (3 vols., New York, 1934), II, pp. 281–6; Lieb, 'Milton's *Of Reformation and the Dynamics of Controversy*', p. 59; Haller, *Tracts on Liberty*, III, p. 76; *Come out of Her, My People* (Amsterdam, 1639).

then of the Englishman demanding his rights. In the same way
Milton identified himself with his message and his public although he
never pushed it to such extremes as Lilburne: 'I conceav'd my selfe to
be now not as mine own person, but as a member *incorporate* into that
truth whereof I was perswaded.' Later, in *Areopagitica* Milton surely
has in mind the widening English public when he states that
censorship is a reproach 'to the common people'. The Bible was the
weapon both of attack and of pedagogy, 'a very sword and fire in both
house and City over the whole earth'.[9]

John Lilburne even stressed the very practical problem of the cost
of buying a Bible, a necessity in order the better to decode his prose. In
his full-flown political tract of October 1645, *England's Birthright
Justified*, 'free-born John' explains that he will quote fully from Job
instead of just providing the reference 'for the use of those that have no
Bibles, to read (they are become so dear and Monopolized like other
things)' and there follows a 36-line quotation to prove that the wicked
that oppress the poor shall perish. Biblical analogies were thereby
integrated into the discourse of political struggle.[10]

In turn, the author becomes the larger-than-life protagonist of a
plurisecular drama by explaining and defending biblical truth.
Milton saw himself as God's instrument, as 'mighty through God'.[11]
Lilburne of course uses his own and his readers' biblical knowledge of
Christ's passion to give emotional force to his arrest, whipping and
pillorying in 1638 which he describes both in *A Work of the Beast* and *A
Christian Man's Trial*. Richard Overton takes on different personae in
The Arraignment of Persecution, such as God's Vengeance or Christian
Martyr, both of which act as stand-ins for the author himself.

Milton and the Levellers use biblical invective to strengthen their
criticism of the clergy and to emphasize the need for further
reformation. Milton justifies the scorn he pours on his adversaries in
Of Reformation Touching Church-Discipline (1641): the church is a
'spiritual Babel'; 'prelates revell like Belshazzar' in Daniel and they
attempt to trample on civil power in the same way that King Ahaz
attempted to trample on priestly power (II Kings 16:1–3). He insists
that further reformation must come quickly as in the days of 'good'

---

[9] Haller (ed.), *Tracts on Liberty*, I, p. 102; *CPW*, I, 871; II, 536; I, 802; see also Joan Webber, *The
Eloquent 'I': Style and Self in Seventeenth-Century Prose* (Madison, 1968), pp. 60, 217.
[10] John Lilburne, *England's Birthright Justified* (1645), in Haller (ed.), *Tracts on Liberty*, III,
pp. 297–9; see also Richard Overton, *Vox Plebis* (London, 1646), pp. 1–3, 53, 65 E.362 (20).
[11] Quoted by J. A. Wittreich Jr, 'The Crown of Eloquence', in Lieb and Shawcross (eds.),
Achievements of the Left Hand, p. 8.

kings of Judah such as Asa, Hezekiah and Josiah.[12] In the heightening invective at the end of *Animadversions* Milton condenses the words of the prophet Ezekiel as he accuses Bishop Hall and his colleagues of being daubers: 'But hearken what God sayes by the prophet *Ezekiel*, Say unto them that daub this wall with untempered Morter, that it shall fall . . . and a stormy wind shall rend it.' Jeremiah is called upon a page later to remind the reader that these men are beyond the pale of Christian charity: 'Pray not thou for them, neither lift up cry or prayer for them'.[13] Milton turns visionary prophet as he brings together images from Ezekiel and Revelation to praise true religious zeal:

> then Zeale whose substance is ethereal, arming in compleat diamond ascends his fiery Chariot drawn with two blazing Meteors figur'd like beasts . . . ressembling two of those four which *Ezechiel* and S. *John* saw, the one visag'd like a Lion to expresse power, high autority and indignation, the other of count'nance like a man to cast derision and scorne upon perverse and fraudulent seducers.[14]

Lilburne often expresses heightened drama with references to the Old Testament. The conclusion to *A Work of the Beast* proclaims the prisoner's confidence in the Lord and in his own eventual triumph: he fears neither Daniel's Den nor the fiery furnace and like the prophet Elijah he will be nourished by God's providence. Then Lilburne appends a page-long poem in small italic print carefully inscribed with thirty-eight abbreviations as marginalia; of these, seventeen are from the Old Testament, mostly from Psalms and Isaiah. Overton in his playlet *The Araignment* attacks the persecutors and evokes at length the 'Iron fangs' of the beast in Daniel 7:19.[15] For these advocates of religious toleration and freedom of expression, the Old Testament provided means to orchestrate struggle and even to threaten established authority.

In the tracts of the early and mid-1640s, the references to the New Testament stand out as instruments of discussion and pedagogy. In Milton's anti-prelatical tracts, it is St Paul who shows the way as leader and preacher, and the references to his epistles are innumerable – more than a dozen in *Areopagitica* alone.[16] As the bishops and, after

---

[12] *CPW*, I, 590.
[13] *Ibid.*, 727, 729; the image of Samson in *The Reason of Church Government* is of course an even more famous example, *ibid.*, 858–61.   [14] *CPW*, I, 900.
[15] Haller (ed.), *Tracts on Liberty*, II, pp. 31; 33–4; III, pp. 253–4.
[16] Edward S. Lecomte, '*Areopagitica* as a Scenario for *Paradise Lost*', in Lieb and Shawcross (eds.), *Achievements of the Left Hand* p. 124; *CPW*, I, 625–6; II, 511–12.

1643, the Presbyterians held up the strictures of the Old Testament to justify the *jure divino* authority of ministers over the Christian conscience, the separatist ministers and the Levellers became wary of the Old Testament tropes. Walwyn warns in *The Power of Love*: 'nor are you under the Law, but under grace; the Law was given by *Moses* whose minister I am not'.[17] So Walwyn multiplies his references to St Paul and to the sayings of the Apostles in Matthew and Mark.

In the mid-1640s, as the struggle for political power increased in intensity in London and on the battlefield and as the Presbyterian ministers of the Westminster Assembly prepared to set up a strict Church discipline, Milton and the Levellers struggled to adapt their images and their communication to the need for massive protest and mobilization. References from the Old Testament and a growing use of references to Revelation took on the function of stirring up opinion to defend not just the Separatists but the whole people from a new tyranny. In *Areopagitica* Milton referred to God's words to the prophet Haggai, 'And I will shake all the Nations', as he wrote that 'God shakes a Kingdome with strong and healthfull commotions'. Walwyn defends Lilburne in his *England's Lamentable Slaverie* written in 1645 and assures him and all his allies that, quoting from Esther, 'God will deliver you as he did Mordicai and all his people'.[18] More and more the God of the Scriptures is directly associated with the success of the cause of religious and political reform.

The image of the Hebrews' Egyptian bondage is a favourite one to mobilize the people of Tower Hamlets and Southwark. In *England's Birthright Revisited*, Lilburne addresses ordinary working people: 'But as the Watermen of Queen-hive do usually cry Westward hough, hough, so according to the present ciment of the times most men have more than cause to cry in the Watermen's language Egypt hough, hough, the house of bondage, slavery, oppression'. In the same text where Lilburne brings Speaker Lenthall to task, he stops short to quote eight different Psalms, which speak of the oppression of the wicked, and he ends with Isaiah's promise, 'I will send him against an hypocritical nation and ... tread them down like mice in the streets.' The history of the chosen people, the stories and vehement exhortations

---

[17] William Walwyn, *The Power of Love* (1643), in Haller (ed.), *Tracts on Liberty*, II, p. 288; see also Richard Overton, *The Araignement of Mr. Persecution* (1645), *ibid.*, III, p. 225.

[18] *CPW*, II, 566; see John X. Evans, '*Imagery as Argument in Milton's Areopagitica*', *Texas Studies in Language and Literature*, 8 (1966), 204; William Walwyn, *England's Lamentable Slaverie* (1645), in Haller (ed.), *Tracts on Liberty*, III, p. 317.

of the Old Testament, were melded by the Levellers and at times by Milton in their comments on the state of England to represent the dangers, possibilities and necessities of a new settlement.[19]

As scholars have often stressed, for the radical pamphleteers Revelation was an essential source of dynamic images. Both the Levellers and Milton used them to castigate their enemies: Milton's famous 'queazy temper of luke-warmnesse' in *Of Reformation Touching Church-Discipline* (1641), 'the whore of Babylon' or Babylonian wickedness, 'the locusts and scorpions', and 'the bottomless pit' were all commonplace tropes which evoked the power and fatal destiny of the wicked. These images could act to stir up the anger of any public and fortify them in their resistance to new tyranny.[20] Here, in the uncertain times of the Civil War between 1641 and 1646, these images vied with the Old Testament in providing the pamphleteers with a powerful rhetorical stance; the Levellers used them to confirm the birth of a better world to men and women unaccustomed to even the possibility of political reform. If the Old Testament offered simple stories of struggle and victory along with imperatives for action, the apocalyptic vision of Revelation situated the continuing struggle in the saga of Christ's second coming; it set a mirror to the history of the future.[21]

For the period after the second Civil War and during the revolutionary crisis from 1647 to 1649 it is much more difficult to point to common aims and similar polemical style in Milton's pamphlets and in those of the Leveller leaders. From 1645 to February 1649, Milton remained silent.[22] Biblical references and marginalia disappeared almost completely from Leveller writings during this period as Richard Overton and John Lilburne drove home their conviction that natural law and natural rights are based on man's God-given 'sovereignty over himself'.[23]

Several explanations for the disappearance of most biblical references from the Levellers' writings come to mind. Their adversaries among the 'Grandees', the Independents and the Separatist preachers, such as Thomas Collier or John Owen, had practically monopolized the market for the biblical image. The pamphleteers who defended

[19] John Lilburne, *England's Birthright Justified*, in Haller (ed.), *Tracts on Liberty*, III, pp. 301, 303–5.
[20] *CPW*, I, 537, 524, 614; see also *Animadversions, ibid.*, 705–6.
[21] Overton, *The Araignement of Mr. Persecution*, in Haller (ed.), *Tracts on Liberty*, III, p. 256.
[22] Christopher Hill, *Milton and the English Revolution* (London, 1977), pp. 165–6.
[23] John Lilburne, *The Free-man's Freedom Vindicated* (1646), in Woodhouse, *Puritanism and Liberty*, p. 317.

Pride's Purge and preachers of the new regime constantly hammered away at identifying the members of the new regime's Council of State with 'the saints' of 'the New Creation'. By the end of 1648, to lean too heavily on biblical images was to join the chorus of these voices in favour of the Purge.[24]

William Walwyn was aware of this quite early: he wrote in 1647, 'the major voice ... is to these as the voice of God, and when they are zealous for vulgar opinions they think they are zealous for God'; after the king's execution Lilburne was even more adamant in *The Picture of the Councel of State*: 'they are all spiritual, all heavenly, the pure Camelions of the time ... the perfect figure of Angels of Light'.[25]

Perhaps more fundamentally, the disappearance of clear biblical references in Leveller writings and speeches, in the Putney or Whitehall Debates, for example, may be explained by their use of a different language or mode of communication: the discourse of natural rights. As early as 1646, Overton wrote: 'Every man by nature, being a King, Priest and Prophet in his own natural circuite and compasse...'. Lilburne, still quoting the Old Testament, but moving well beyond the religious sphere, similarly wrote: 'God ... gave man, his mere creature, the sovereignty (under himself) over all the rest of his creatures (Genesis 1: 26–9) and endued him with a rational soul or understanding.'[26]

It is not my intention to outline once again the contribution of the Levellers to political theory but it is essential to stress that the language of sovereignty and of the individual's 'property' over his or her choices and actions gave the Levellers' rhetoric a new independence in relation to their own cultural matrix where the Bible held such a central place. The Leveller spokesmen little by little replaced that frame of reference with a political one. Their political language had been developed by erudite lawyers, by men versed in political speculation such as John Selden or Henry Parker, but the Levellers transformed it into a rhetoric of communication; a logical exposition touched with irony was the natural form of discourse in Richard

---

[24] See my *Religion et idéologie dans la révolution anglaise*, chapters 11 and 12.

[25] William Walwyn, *A Still and Soft Voice from the Scriptures* (London, 1647), p. 4; [John Lilburne, et al.], *The Picture of the Councel of State* in *The Leveller Tracts 1647–1653*, ed. William Haller and Godfrey Davies (New York, 1944), p. 218; see also Richard Overton, *The Hunting of the Foxes* ... (March, 1649), p. 12, E548(7).

[26] Richard Overton, *An Arrow against All Tyrants* (October, 1646), in G. E. Aylmer (ed.), *The Levellers in the English Revolution* (London, 1975), p. 69; John Lilburne, *The Free-man's Freedom Vindicated*, in Woodhouse (ed.), *Puritanism and Liberty*, p. 317.

Overton's and John Wildman's treatises in 1646 and 1647. To defend the 'freeborn Englishman' in his addresses to Parliament, Overton and Lilburne gave up drawing direct similes between the Old Testament struggles; Lilburne relied on the works of Edward Coke and Henry Parker which contributed to his conception of natural law.[27] Marginalia still appear occasionally but they hold references to Coke's *Institutes* or to earlier Acts of Parliament. Overton refers to contemporary documents such as the *Declaration of the Army* of June 1647 in his attack on the new government in *The Hunting of the Foxes* published in March 1649.[28]

Nevertheless, in petitions and polemic passages directed to a wide audience of potential Leveller partisans, whether civilians or soldiers, the Leveller spokesmen indulged their taste for secular invective combined with pathos and explosive lamentations to move their audiences and readers. Here Overton, Lilburne and even Walwyn still evoke biblical images in order to mobilize their forces and drive home the villainy of their enemies. Lilburne in *The mournful Cryes of many thousand poor Tradesmen* written during the terrible winter of 1648 exclaims, 'is there no pity!' and refers to Jeremiah's Lamentations when he asks, 'are our Rulers become cruell like the Ostrich in the Wildernesse?' In August 1648, on the eve of Cromwell's victory at Preston, Walwyn warns his readers that the rulers in London may set up a greater tyranny than that of the king and attacks the Presbyterian conservative majority in Parliament: 'on your death-beds may you see yourselves the most horrid Murtherers that ever lived since the time that Cain killed his brother without a just cause'. Once again in prison in March 1649, this time on the order of the Council of State, Overton calls on one of the most well-known Old Testament stories to castigate his gaolers: 'Never were such Saints, such curious Angels of Light; Pharaohs Egyptian Sorcerers were short of these in their Art.'[29]

In the wave of petitions of the winter and spring of 1649, the Levellers' friends addressing the London crowds continued to evoke biblical history as the mirror of present struggles. In the women's

---

[27] William Haller and Geoffrey Davies, 'Introduction', in *Leveller Tracts*, 1, pp. 43–7; Christopher Hill, 'The Norman Yoke', in *Puritanism and Revolution* (London, 1958), pp. 81–7; in a different context see Quentin Skinner, 'History and Ideology in the English Revolution', *Historical Journal*, 8 (1965), 161–2.

[28] Overton, *The Hunting of the Foxes* ..., p. 3.

[29] John Lilburne, *A Declaration of Some Proceedings* (1648), in *Leveller Tracts*, p. 126; see also William Walwyn, *The Bloody Project* (August, 1648), in *Leveller Tracts*, p. 140; Richard Overton, *The Hunting of the Foxes* ... (London, 1649), p. 7.

petition of 24 April 1649, the authors recall that, 'By the counsel and presence of Deborah and the hand of Jaell, Israel was delivered from the King of Canaan, Sisera, and his mighty Host.'[30] Biblical references were no longer used as proof of the veracity of discourse; yet, to the Levellers' audience, biblical stories remained a powerful source of metaphor to stir up anger and resolution.

But basically the old reliance on Puritan tropes had been replaced by political concepts and Lilburne wrote proudly in his *England's New Chains* in the winter of 1649, 'we are ... the Common Idols of the World; our Cause and principles do *through their own natural truth and lustre* get ground in men's understandings'.[31] The defeat of the Leveller mutiny in May 1649 and the slow decline of the popular mobilization that they had been able to produce in the earlier years was to prove that Lilburne's confidence in 'the lustre' of these secular political principles was for the time being unfounded, but this secularization of political discourse may be seen in retrospect as a sign of things to come.

It is more difficult to compare John Milton's rhetoric of 1649 with that of the Levellers. Milton's political thought did become more and more anchored in the same fundamental radical concepts as the Levellers expressed: men's God-given right to political choice, the necessity of the consent of the governed, the bond of revocable trust established between authority and the people, and the God-given right of 'free born Men, to be govern'd as seems to them best'.[32] However, Milton continued to rely on biblical reference to maintain commitment to these principles.

Although, like the Levellers, Milton is very much aware of the possible misuse of biblical references and underlines this again and again, he continues to multiply them to sustain and enrich his own arguments. In his view, as in that of so many Reformation theologians and preachers, it was a legitimate rhetorical strategy to accommodate biblical texts to new circumstances. More particularly, Old Testament history provided concrete 'case histories' for his own careful interpretation of contemporary situations.[33] In the regicide pamphlets of 1649, *The Tenure of Kings and Magistrates* and *Eikonoklastes*, Milton

---

[30] *To The Supreme Authority ... the Humble Petition of Divers Wel-Affected Women ... of London* (25 April 1649) E551(14).

[31] John Lilburne, *England's New Chains Discovered ...* (1649), in *Leveller Tracts*, p. 166.

[32] *CPW*, III, 206 and *passim*; see also Christopher Hill, *Milton and the English Revolution*, chapter 12.

[33] H. R. MacCallum, 'Milton and the Figurative Interpretation of the Bible', *University of Toronto Quarterly*, 31 (1962), 404; Mary Ann Radzinowicz, '"In those days there was no king in Israel": Milton's Politics and Biblical Narrative', *Yearbook of English Studies*, 21 (1991), 242.

intensifies his use of biblical analogies. No longer in the political and religious opposition but standing beside the victors and anxious to defend the newly founded commonwealth, Milton aims at convincing the Presbyterian moderates who were not totally set against the new regime.[34] He marshals his biblical erudition first to defend the right of a people to destroy a tyrant and then to ridicule the so-called royal martyrdom described in Gauden's *Eikon Basilike*, the King's Book, that was fascinating the 'Image-doting rabble' (*CPW*, III, 601), to the dismay of all defenders of the commonwealth.

Milton often uses biblical comparisons to sharpen brief, sarcastic quips that exploded the sentimentality of *Eikon Basilike*. Using the same analogies that had filled the Presbyterian pamphlets of the 1640s, and clothing himself in the prophet Elijah's true righteousness, Milton mocks the inconsistency of Charles's Presbyterian mourners who had criticized the king in the early 1640s and now defended his royal image: the king 'was once their *Ahab*, now thir *Josiah*', first the wicked king ('and Ahab did evil in the sight of the Lord above all that *were* before him', 1 Kings 16:30) and then the pious king who rebuilt the temple in Jerusalem.[35]

In another rapid aside attacking Charles's tyranny over his kingdom, Milton uses Jacob's dying words to his sons in Genesis 49:14 to construct an original metaphor. The biblical text describes Jacob's son Issachar as an ass lying between his burdens, that is, as Merritt Hughes comments, the symbol of a 'hard-working lover of gain'; Milton picks up the image of the two burdens and transforms it to fit the radicals' view of Charles's reign: 'True; for he thought his Kingdom to be *Issachar a strong Ass that* would have *couch'd downe between two burd'ns*, the one of prelatical superstition, the other of civil tyrannie.'[36]

Milton multiplies his comparisons of Charles with the tyrants of Israel and assimilates the English commonwealthmen to their God-sent destroyers. In *The Tenure*, he passes in review the violent deaths of Old Testament tyrants such as Agag, Rehoboam, Eglon of Moab, Ahab and Jehoram and claims that their examples are more convincing than examples taken from Greek and Roman history. Yet Milton often uses the familiar biblical lessons to sustain his own arguments that do not necessarily follow traditional Protestant theology. Thus, as Martin Dzelzainis reminds us, Milton is convinced that Ehud was justified in killing Eglon of Moab *not* because he was a foreign prince

---

[34] *CPW*, III, 238; see Merritt Hughes's introduction, *ibid.*, pp. 54–6.
[35] *CPW*, III, 365; see nn. 51 and 52.   [36] *Ibid.*, 446, and n. 35.

as Protestant reformers had explained, but because, like that of Jehu who slew Jehoram, the act was 'a thing grounded in natural reason'.[37] In *Eikonoklastes*, Charles Stuart is described as more evil than Ahab, Jeroboam, Rehoboam or Saul. Milton draws the only possible conclusion from such analogies : the Scriptures and the history of the Reformation teach that the 'Kings of this World' are enemies of true piety. From Daniel's vision (Daniel 2:44), he is certain that their royal, arbitrary power shall be dissolved. Milton, iconoclast *and* republican, uses biblical images to contribute to this destruction.[38]

One of the elements of pathos used in the King's Book was Charles's complaint that he was not allowed his own chaplains when he was prisoner in his house at Holmeby, Northamptonshire. Milton devotes chapter xxiv of *Eikonoklastes* to blasting the self-righteousness out of the text. To do so, he takes up the example of Micah who made a graven image and a molten one and then hired a Levite as a priest, but the latter took off with the images to follow the people of Dan as their priest (Judges 17–18). Charles is represented as the lamenting 'superstitious Micah' who has lost his priest and his gods, and then Milton compares the king to the idolatrous Micah: 'And perhaps the whole Story of *Micah* might square not unfitly to this Argument ... *Micah* had as great a care that his Priest should be Mosaical as the King had that his should be *Apostolical*.' Then Milton lists the leaders of Israel, '*David, Salomon*, and *Jehosaphat*', who prayed even in public without the use of a priest. From there, using the story of Micah again and adding yet another reading to it, Milton leaps to an ironic exclamation that after all the king had set up his own prayer book so he almost thought himself as much a priest as Micah's son had been.[39] This single Old Testament tale is worked for all it is worth in a kind of gleeful *tour de force* of analogical reasoning.

The momentum of Milton's oration gathers power not only by his argument's use of Old Testament figures but also *through* an accumulation of biblical tropes. Answering the King's Book phrase by phrase in *Eikonoklastes*, Milton enlists a steady stream of biblical comparisons and contrasts to belittle Charles. Picking up biblical references used to defend Charles as head of the Church, Milton scoffs

---

[37] *Ibid.*, 212–16; Introduction, *John Milton: Political Writings*, ed. Martin Dzelzainis (Cambridge, 1991), p. xiii.

[38] *CPW*, iii, 509; David Loewenstein, *Milton and the Drama of History* (Cambridge, 1990), p. 64; Hill, *The English Bible and the Seventeenth Century Revolution*, p. 373.

[39] *CPW*, iii, 549–51.

at the king: 'with his glorious title of the *Churches Defender*, we leave him to make good, by *Pharaoh's Divinity*, if he please, for to *Josephs Pietie* it will be a task unsutable'. Then, commenting on the king's disdain for the ideals of equality and poverty prevalent among the Independent ministers who were chosen by the congregation and subjected to no hierarchy, Milton refers to Jesus' words, quoting Matthew, that the people should choose their minister and that he who gave away what he owned would inherit eternal life. Finally, Milton reminds his readers again that the English Church under Charles had been corrupt and the clergy 'be leper'd ... with a worse infection then *Gehezi*'s'. A page further on, Milton takes up the image of the fiery *'furnace of popular obloquie'* used in the King's Book to underline the conviction that Charles's enemies would soon roast there: 'I beleive not that a Romish guilded Portrature gives better Oracle then a Babylonish gold'n Image could doe, to tell us truely who heated that Furnace of obloquy, or who deserves to be thrown in, *Nebuchadnezzar* or the three kingdoms.'[40]

To today's reader the accumulation of such varied images culled from the whole breadth of the Bible may be confusing if not baffling. The modern, natural rights ideology, our political heritage, is expressed by Milton through often obscure biblical example. But confident of his readers' total familiarity with the whole biblical language of images and stories, Milton moves freely through examples from the history of Israel to Jesus' lessons and back again as a means of redefining the image of the king as arch-tyrant and evil-doer. Through Milton's countless references to the Bible, the refraction of the Word from past to present in multiple and accumulated images creates a wide-open space for enthusiasm and action.[41] As a political pamphleteer speaking within a fragile revolutionary moment, the outcome of this process could only be immediate human involvement: 'For Truth is properly no more then Contemplation; and her utmost efficiency is but teaching: but Justice in her very essence is all strength and activity; and hath a Sword put into her hand, to use against all violence and oppression on earth.'[42]

Milton increases the power of the biblical call for commitment by

---

[40] *CPW*, III, 496–8.
[41] See Terry Eagleton's remarks on Puritan discourse in *Walter Benjamin, or Towards a Revolutionary Criticism* (London, 1992), p. 14.
[42] *CPW*, III, 584; the biblical metaphor 'is a programme in shorthand': Hill, *The English Bible and the Seventeenth Century Revolution*, p. 125.

his own identification with prophetic or heroic figures. The scolding he addresses to the Presbyterians in *The Tenure* takes on the character of an Old Testament prophet's admonitions to a sinful people: '*Let them* not oppose thir best friends and associats ... *Let them*, feare therfore if they be wise.'[43] As Mary Ann Radzinowicz has underlined, 'The liberty of prophesying is Milton's paradigm for political liberty.'[44]

Milton's identification with the inspired leaders of Scripture is even more outspoken in chapter XXVIII of *Eikonoklastes* as he faces his most difficult task: the justification of the execution of Charles I. Milton positions himself as the Hebrew prince, Zerubabel, who proved to Darius that women are stronger than wine or kings, then claimed that truth will always prevail and eventually led the Hebrews out of Babylon to rebuild Jerusalem (1 Esdras, 3–4). Milton exclaims to his readers, 'I shall pronounce my sentence somewhat different from *Zorobabel*; and shall defend, that either Truth and Justice are all one, for Truth is but Justice in our knowledge, and Justice is but Truth in our practice', and two pages later: 'And if by sentence thus writt'n it were my happiness to set free the minds of English men from longing to returne poorly under that Captivity of Kings ... I shall have don a work not much inferior to that of *Zorobabel*.'[45]

It is from this stance that Milton summons up examples from the Bible, Roman Law and Greek tragedy along with ancient Greek and British history to maintain again that Charles could be tried like any private person. Not only does Milton accumulate vivid and time-honoured proofs for his argumentation, but biblical authority becomes Miltonic authority through his own rhetorical position. In *The Tenure*, Milton exemplifies the subject who is called to liberty by a performative God, 'our Supreme Magistracy'; in *Eikonoklastes*, the committed subject may be guaranteed success in a good cause, 'for God hath promis'd it to good men almost in every leafe of Scripture'.[46]

The context of the two *Defences*, published in 1651 and in 1654, was very different from that of the regicide tracts and Milton's manner of handling biblical images changed after 1649. As the officially designated champion of the republic, Milton was henceforth writing his prose pamphlets for a specific educated elite of Protestants

---

[43] My italics, *CPW*, III, 239.
[44] Radzinowicz, '"In those days there was no king ..."', pp. 243, 248; see also David Norbrook, 'The Politics of Milton's Early Poetry', in *Poetry and Politics in the English Renaissance* (London, 1984), pp. 280–4. [45] *CPW*, III, 583, 585. [46] *CPW*, III, 236, 599.

throughout Europe, *and* in Latin. Several fundamental changes had come about in the ideological stance of the Commonwealth since 1649. Most important, military victories had guaranteed the survival of the ever-contested governmental structure of the Commonwealth. Many of its domestic enemies of 1649 had been silenced. The hopes for the millennium that had stirred hearts in 1649 were now caught up in the rigid ideology of the Fifth Monarchists, who seemed to threaten the stability of the new regime. John Milton, who used apocalyptic lyricism to great metaphorical effect in his anti-prelatical tracts and in *Eikonoklastes*, never became involved in any such millenarian militancy.[47]

As Blair Worden has clearly demonstrated, the relative relaxation of censorship during the same years and the very existence of a republic in England brought about 'a shift of mood, of vocabulary' which gave a freer rein to the expression of a republicanism that had been developing in England in the first half of the century and which was based on the works of Greek and Roman authors, studied and revered by Italian humanists.[48] This transformation of the ideological landscape surrounding the government of which Milton was the servant doubtless modified Milton's own approach to the defence of the English republican experiment. His political stance is no longer that of an eloquent member of the radical opposition or the spokesman for a military coup as in 1649. Basing the concept of political authority on the consent of the people and positing the welfare of the people as the supreme law, Milton puts his faith firmly in the Cromwellian Protectorate, and sets about defending it.

As he spars with Salmasius and Pierre Du Moulin, biblical quotations continue to sustain Milton's arguments. As in *Eikonoklastes* the arguments of the two *Defences* are guided by the arguments of his adversaries. Despite its boisterous invective freedom, Milton's prose is carefully centred on rebuttal in the form of a monologue studded with direct questions and oratorical devices. Biblical references become

---

[47] Austin Woolrych, 'Political Theory and Political Practice', in C. A. Patrides and R. B. Waddington (eds.), *The Age of Milton: Backgrounds to Seventeenth Century Literature* (Manchester, 1980), pp. 55–6; for an example of such an apocalyptic outburst using Revelation, see the last pages of *Eikonoklastes*, *CPW*, III, 598–9.

[48] Blair Worden, 'Milton's Republicanism and the Tyranny of Heaven', in Gisela Bock, Quentin Skinner and Maurizio Viroli (eds.), *Machiavelli and Republicanism* (Cambridge, 1990), p. 226; see also his 'Classical Republicanism and the Puritan Revolution' in Hugh Lloyd-Jones, Valerie Pearl and Blair Worden (eds.), *History and Imagination* (London, 1981), pp. 190–3; Peter Lindenbaum, 'Milton and the Republican Mode of Literary Production', *Yearbook of English Studies*, 21 (1991), 126–30.

instruments of pedagogy in these tracts rather than metaphorical elements of a driving force stimulating active and even emotional response. Indirectly through his answers to the readers of Salmasius' and Du Moulin's tracts, Milton proffers advice from Scripture as to the best basis for government.

In chapter II of *Pro Populo Anglicano Defensio* (1651), Milton counters Salmasius' arguments that it is God's will that kings should rule over men and that they are only responsible to him. Systematically he uses to his own advantage the Old Testament examples: Samuel's teachings concerning kingship, Joash (II Kings 11), David, Moses, Abimelech, Solomon; in chapter IV, Milton counters Salmasius' Old and New Testament proofs of the necessary obedience of subjects to their kings, the Lord's anointed.

Contrary to his rhetoric in his earlier tracts, in the *Defensio* Milton refrains from exploring complex biblical images. Examples chosen from the Bible are soberly argued in relation to contemporary events (Charles's execution) and followed by adamant statements of personal conviction: 'In turn I assert that by God's testimony popular assemblies, elections, campaigns, votes and enactments are equally of God, and therefore on God's authority too it is equally forbidden for a king to resist the people.'[49] Milton is fundamentally concerned with defending the basis and instruments of the new government, hence his pragmatic approach.

The Bible had become only one of the sources that could be called upon to prove political validity. By the 1650s Milton had become convinced that the republican form of government was not only as valid as monarchy but intrinsically superior to it and, more frequently than before, he turned to the classical authors of Greece and Rome for support in his attacks against absolutist kingship as tyranny.[50] This was not a sudden change of direction; and many scholars have stressed the influence of classical form and content on Milton's prose works. Nigel Smith has recently reminded us of the importance of classical thought and oratorical structure in the much earlier tract, *Areopagitica*, where Milton expresses in republican vocabulary the dilemma of moral choice and virtue through self-control.[51] In *The Tenure*, addressing his Presbyterian adversaries, Milton used the

---

[49] *CPW*, IVi, 405–6.   [50] Zera S. Fink, *The Classical Republicans* (Evanston, 1945), p. 103.
[51] Nigel Smith, '*Areopagitica:* Voicing Contexts, 1643–5', in David Loewenstein and James Grantham Turner (eds.), *Politics, Poetics and Hermeneutics in Milton's Prose* (Cambridge, 1990), pp. 103, 110–12.

example of Seneca's Hercules 'the grand suppressor of Tyrants' and then hastily adds his own editorial comment: 'But of these I name no more, lest it bee objected they were Heathen; and come to produce another sort of men that had the knowledge of true Religion.' However he could not resist the forceful examples of the Roman texts well known to his educated countrymen, claiming that '[t]he *Greeks* and *Romans* ... held it not onely lawfull but a glorious and Heroic deed ... to kill an Infamous tyrant' and Milton calls on Cicero to defend the concept of a universal human law allowing people to defend themselves against tyranny.[52] In a similar manner Milton evokes Greek and Roman precedents – Solon, Lycurgus, the Roman Senate and Justinian – in *Eikonoklastes* to prove that human law permits the judgement of a king and compares Charles I to Sallust's villainous Catiline.[53]

But in the new republican context of the 1650s, Milton relies more on classical proofs than he did earlier. As he follows Salmasius' justification of kingship according to the law of nature in the *Defensio* he quotes Aristotle's *Politics* to prove that 'the king exists for the people ... the rights of the people remain supreme', and he does not hesitate to broadcast his belief in the superiority of ancient governments:

What is commanded by nature and good sense may best be seen in the case of the wisest nations rather than the greatest number of them. Greeks and Romans, Italians and Carthaginians and many besides have of their own accord preferred government by nobles or people to that of a king; and surely these nations were more important than all the rest.[54]

However arbitrary this profession of faith may seem today, it demonstrates Milton's confidence in the humanist heritage from the Mediterranean world. Consequently it is not surprising that Milton quotes Cicero's *Philippics* nine times in the *Defensio*. With the Roman orator's assistance Milton presents as 'an example to us all' the Romans struggling against such tyrants or potential tyrants as Tarquin or Caesar; when arguing that the army belongs to the people rather than the king, a parallel is drawn with the Roman legions which 'belong to the Roman people'.[55]

In the *Defensio* Milton does not hesitate to intertwine references to

[52] *CPW*, III, 213, 212, 214; Cicero, *De Officiis*, III. 6.
[53] *CPW*, III, 589–90, 441.   [54] *Ibid.*, lvi, 432.
[55] *Ibid.*, 469, 501; see Diane Parkin Speer, 'Milton's *Defensio Prima*: *Ethos* and Vituperation in a Polemic Engagement', *Quarterly Journal of Speech*, 56 (1970), 280.

classical authors with biblical ones as he contradicts Salmasius' use of these sources. In his discussion of the basis of kingly power, Milton moves with ease from Samuel's disapproval of kingship to Aristotle's description of monarchy, and then to Sallust's discussion of royal rights which degenerate into despotism.[56] In chapter III, where Milton concentrates on New Testament proofs and references from Plato, Aristotle and Cicero are mixed with quotations from St Paul to claim that law and right reason are above the power of kings. The Bible, English history and the works of classical authors all hold the keys to the understanding of the political process and to the meaning of justice.[57]

In *Second Defence*, Milton follows more closely the events of the years 1648–54 than in his earlier pamphlets and is particularly concerned with the defence of his government's leaders and of his own role as polemicist. Milton uses a wide variety of discursive modes but he begins by introducing himself as an orator, 'Now, on the very threshold of my speech', and describes the commonwealth as a purified state, returning to the values of the ancient Greek and Roman models.[58] Thus the religious radical of the 1640s who demanded the purification of the Church becomes the orator champion of a Christian state, itself purified from centuries of falsely established kingship and superstition. In the final sequence of *A Second Defence*, the orator gives advice to the leaders of the English commonwealth; liberty within his commonwealth will flourish only through Ciceronian stoic virtues: 'to be free is precisely the same as to be pious, wise, just, and temperate, careful of one's property, aloof from another's, and thus finally to be magnanimous and brave'.[59]

In the famous final lines of *Second Defence*, Milton no longer claims for himself the role of the Hebrew prince Zerubabel, but positions himself as his country's poet, an heir to Horace's lyricism. In doing so he expands the very breadth of the cause he defends:

I have borne witness, I might almost say I have erected a monument that will not soon pass away ... Yet there was not wanting one who could rightly counsel, encourage, and inspire, who could honor both the noble deeds and those who had done them, and make both deeds and doers illustrious with praises that will never die.[60]

Although Milton's frame of reference in *Second Defence* is deeply

---

[56] *CPW*, IVi, pp. 346–9.
[57] *Ibid.*, pp. 381–3; see Worden, 'Classical Republicanism and the Puritan Revolution', p. 195.
[58] *CPW*, IVi, pp. 548, 550; David Loewenstein, 'Milton and the Poetics of Defence', in Loewenstein and Turner (eds.), *Politics, Poetics and Hermeneutics*, p. 173.   [59] *CPW*, IVi, 684.
[60] *Ibid.*, 685–6.

anchored in classical texts, Milton continues to affirm his Arminian faith that God is very much at his side. In his defence of what he believes to be the established English republic, he repeatedly evokes His presence: 'God himself is truth! . . . For my part, I call upon Thee, my God, who knowest my inmost mind and all my thoughts'; what he writes he believes to be 'right and true and pleasing to God'.[61]

But biblical language as the unique means of expressing solutions to political questions had nearly run its course. The revival of classical concepts of the civic virtues were fused with those of radical Puritans – they too called for temperance, justice and piety – to form the modern language of natural rights and political liberty. The Levellers contributed much to this change during the struggles of the late 1640s; Milton and his republican friends continued to transform the referential framework of political thinking during the years of the English Commonwealth. However, notwithstanding the growing interest in classical political ideals, the energy and force of biblical images did not definitively fall into disuse with the demise of the English republican experiment. They remained a potential source not only of religious enthusiasm but also of political commitment.

[61] *Ibid.*, 585, 587.

CHAPTER 5

The metaphorical contract in Milton's Tenure of Kings and Magistrates

Victoria Kahn

> The Light of humane minds is Perspicuous Words, but by exact
> definitions first snuffed, and purged from ambiguity; *Reason* is
> the *pace*; Encrease of *Science*, the *way*; and the Benefit of man-kind,
> the *end*. And on the contrary, Metaphors, and senslesse and
> ambiguous words, are like *ignes fatui*; and reasoning upon them,
> is wandering amongst innumerable absurdities; and their end,
> contention, and sedition, or contempt.

When Hobbes expressed his fear in *Leviathan* that the 'equivocall
signification of words' would precipitate rebellion, he was articulating
a view widely shared by sixteenth- and seventeenth-century Englishmen.[1] Of particular concern was the ambiguity of Scripture, for
Renaissance Englishmen had experienced at first hand how the
metaphorical interpretation of Scripture could give rise to antinomianism, false prophecy and political anarchy. In *The Arte of English
Poesie*, George Puttenham had linked 'doubtfull speaches' with
'blind' prophecies designed to stir up 'insurrections', and had
recommended that the poet avoid such dangerously ambiguous
'propheticall rymes'. Thomas Wilson had similarly cautioned the
reader of *The Rule of Reason* not to construe the New Testament in an
illegitimately metaphorical sense: spiritual 'freedom' should not be
understood metaphorically to imply political 'freedom'.[2] Such views

---

[1] Thomas Hobbes, *Leviathan*, ed. C. B. Macpherson (Harmondsworth, 1975), ch. 5, pp. 116–17.
Hereafter references to *Leviathan* will be to chapter and then page. *The Tenure of Kings and
Magistrates*, ed. Maurice Kelley (*CPW*, III) will be abbreviated as *TKM*; *Christian Doctrine*, ed.
Maurice Kelley (*CPW*, VI) will be abbreviated as *CD*.

[2] On the association of metaphor and ambiguity with usurpation in classical and Renaissance
definitions of metaphor, see Patricia Parker, *Literary Fat Ladies: Rhetoric, Gender, Property*
(London, 1987), pp. 36–53, 97–103. Parker gives the examples from Puttenham and Wilson
on pp. 99–101. See also Steven Mullaney, 'Lying like Truth: Riddle, Representation, and
Treason in Renaissance England', *ELH*, 47 (1980), 32–47, on the link between the figure of
amphibology or ambiguous speech and treason.

were regularly articulated in sixteenth-century treatises on government and rhetoric; yet the Civil War, the regicide of Charles I and the outpouring of anti-monarchical pamphlets gave them a new urgency in the 1640s and 1650s. In these pamphlets, parliamentarians and radical sectarians marshalled the languages of biblical covenant and political contract to prove that political obligation was not absolute but open to interpretation. Among these pamphlets Milton's *The Tenure of Kings and Magistrates* would have been particularly distasteful to Hobbes, if he read it:[3] for, although Milton begins by arguing that monarchy involves a contractual relationship between the subject and the sovereign, he concludes that monarchy is itself a metaphor for which there is no literal, earthly referent. In the process, *The Tenure of Kings and Magistrates* dramatizes the belief that attention to the figurative or more precisely metaphorical nature of sovereignty dictates not only the regicide of Charles I but also republicanism.

The immediate occasion of *The Tenure* was the backsliding of the Presbyterians who, during the Civil War, had supported the parliamentary cause against the king.[4] Yet in 1648/9 they urged mercy for Charles on the eve of his execution. At the centre of Milton's quarrel with the Presbyterians was not only his view of the general covenant between the king and his people, but the particular Solemn League and Covenant which parliament had signed with the Scottish Presbyterians in September 1643 in order to win them over to the parliamentary cause. For one clause of this Covenant, that which bound parliament to respect the safety of the king, was a cornerstone of the Presbyterian plea for clemency in 1648/9. What the Presbyterians failed to understand, according to Milton, was that the Covenant was no longer binding not only because Charles had violated its conditions, but also because the Presbyterians themselves

---

[3] Hobbes certainly knew Milton's work for he mentions Milton's *Defence of the English People* in *Behemoth or the Long Parliament*, ed. Ferdinand Tönnies, intro. Stephen Holmes (Chicago, 1990), pp. 163–4: 'A' remarks: 'About this time came out two books, one written by Salmasius, a Presbyterian, against the murder of the King; another written by Milton, an Independent, in answer to it.' 'B' responds: 'I have seen them both. They are very good Latin both, and hardly to be judged which is better; and both very ill reasoning, hardly to be judged which is worse; like two declamations, *pro* and *contra*, made for exercise only in a rhetoric school by one and the same man. So like is a Presbyterian to an Independent.' As I suggest below, Hobbes here notices a rhetorical similarity which is deliberate on Milton's part in *TKM*.

[4] I follow Blair Worden who understands Presbyterian 'in its political sense . . . to denote that section of opinion which had supported the parliamentary cause in the civil war but which was alienated by, or which steered clear of politics after, Pride's Purge [December, 1648] and the execution of the king' (*The Rump Parliament, 1648–1653* (Cambridge, 1974), p. 10).

had acted on this assumption by subsequently taking up arms against the king.[5] Milton launched his attack on the Presbyterians by ridiculing their casuistical allegiance to the Solemn League and Covenant, and by attacking their interpretation of Scripture. In Milton's eyes, the Presbyterians were false prophets, who had 'gloss'd and fitted [Scripture] for thir turnes with a double contradictory sense, transforming the sacred verity of God, to an Idol with two Faces' (195).[6] In response to such backsliding, Milton proposed to discuss the nature of monarchy and tyranny by reference to 'autorities and reasons ... fetch't out of the midst of choicest and most authentic learning, and no prohibited Authors, nor many Heathen, but Mosaical, Christian, Orthodoxal, and, which must needs be more convincing to our Adversaries, Presbyterial' (198). In characteristic fashion, he then proceeded to turn the Presbyterian language of covenant and contract against the Presbyterians themselves. While Milton's understanding of covenant theology and of the revocability of political contract were commonplaces of both Puritan and constitutionalist thinking by 1649, the way in which Milton dramatized these insights in the rhetoric and dominant metaphors of his treatise was both biting and shrewd. In reasoning about the scriptural metaphor of covenant, as well as the secular metaphors of tenure and contract, Milton made metaphor itself the basis of a new contract with the reader, the aim of which was to further what Hobbes called 'contention, sedition, and contempt'.

Milton's metaphorical interpretation of the contract of sovereignty can only be fully understood in the context of seventeenth-century debates over the political meaning of covenant and contract. A brief review of this debate should help us see what is at stake in Hobbes's and Milton's contrasting accounts of the relation of political obligation to prophecy and the figurative interpretation of Scripture. We shall then be in a better position to understand the metaphorical logic of covenant and contract in *The Tenure of Kings and Magistrates*.

---

[5] *TKM*, 194, 229–33. Milton also discusses the king's and the Presbyterians' violation of the Solemn League and Covenant in *Eikonoklastes* (*CPW*, III, 593–7).

[6] This charge was particularly applicable to the Presbyterian Minister Stephen Marshall, who on 23 February 1641/2, had preached a sermon on the theme of 'Meroz cursed' (Judges 5:23), in which he urged parliament to take up arms against the king. Milton turned the example of Meroz against Marshall and other Presbyterians, implying that they were 'neuters' who, like Meroz, refused to fight in God's cause (*TKM*, 235, 242). The first edition of *The Tenure of Kings and Magistrates* ended with Milton's prayer that God visit upon the heads of the Presbyterians 'that curse ye Meroz, the very *Motto* of thir Pulpits, wherwith so frequently, not as *Meroz*, but more like Atheists they have blasphem'd the vengeance of God, and [traduc'd] the zeale of his people' (*TKM*, 242).

COVENANT AND CONTRACT

While the notion that the Old and New Testaments formed two covenants – one based on the law and the other on grace – is itself scripturally based, the doctrine of the covenant of grace was first fully articulated by seventeenth-century Protestant theologians who attempted to mitigate the rigours of Calvinism.[7] According to this view, God's covenant with the Hebrews was a covenant of works in the sense that their destiny as the chosen people was conditional upon their fulfilment of the moral and ceremonial law. This covenant was represented (and re-enacted) at various points in the Old Testament, particularly in Exodus and Deuteronomy. Christ cancelled the covenant of works and substituted a covenant of grace, according to which the individual believer's God-given faith was itself the enabling condition of works. Covenant theologians stressed that the covenant of grace was already available in the Old Testament: while the covenant between God and Adam was a covenant of works, after the fall the covenant between God and man became one of grace. This covenant was progressively realized in history: 'promised in the Garden to the fallen Adam, made more explicit in the dealings with Abraham, given added substance in the covenant of Sinai, and sealed and certified in the death of Christ, so that now men are incorporated under that New Covenant made most certain by him'.[8] In the revised account of predestination offered by covenant theologians such as William Perkins and William Ames, God binds himself by contractual

[7] Such theologians were sometimes referred to as 'covenant' or 'federal' theologians. On covenant theology, see Perry Miller, 'The Marrow of Puritan Divinity', in *Errand into the Wilderness* (Cambridge, Mass., 1964), pp. 48–98; and Miller, *The New England Mind: The Seventeenth Century* (Boston, 1961), esp. pp. 365–462, and the appendix listing seventeenth-century works on this subject; David Zaret, *The Heavenly Contract* (Chicago, 1985); Michael Walzer, *Revolution of the Saints* (Cambridge, Mass., 1965); Christopher Hill, 'Covenant Theology and the Concept of "A Public Person"', in Alkis Kontos (ed.), *Powers, Possessions and Freedom: Essays in Honour of C. B. Macpherson* (Toronto, 1979), pp. 3–21; William Haller, *Liberty and Reformation in the Puritan Revolution* (New York, 1955), esp. ch. 3; John F. Wilson, *Pulpit in Parliament: Puritanism during the English Civil Wars, 1640–1648* (Princeton, 1969); John von Rohr, 'Covenant and Assurance in Early English Puritanism', *Church History*, 54 (1961), 195–203.

Although the covenant of grace does not figure prominently in Calvin's theology, Calvin discusses the dispensations of the Old and New Testaments as two covenants in *Institutes of the Christian Religion*, esp. Book II, chs. 10 and 11. In *CD* Milton refers to Hebrews 8, where Paul distinguishes between the Mosaic covenant and the 'better covenant' established by Christ. He also cites Matthew 26:26–9, and Galatians 4:4.

[8] Von Rohr, 'Covenant and Assurance', p. 195. See also Miller, *The New England Mind*, ch. 13. Miller writes that 'the Covenant, its origin, its progressive unfolding, was thus the meaning of history and that which made intelligible the whole story of mankind' (p. 378). Milton shares this view of the covenant as available in the Old Testament but progressively revealed in time. See *CD*, 496, 514–20, 536.

obligation to save those who believe. One implication of this account was that the believer may contribute something to his salvation by virtue of his faith. Predestination is no longer simply a matter of divine fiat, but of the individual believer's response to a divine call. While covenant theologians insisted that the ability to respond was itself a gift of grace, the practical effect of covenant theology was to lessen the harshness of Calvinist predestination. Something like a doctrine of works crept back into Reformation theology. As Perry Miller has noted, covenant theologians at times drew 'perilously close' to the Arminianism they rejected.[9]

Historians of seventeenth-century political thought have long noted the intersection of the language of biblical covenant, with its emphasis on God's contractual relationship with man, and that of political contract. While it is uncertain in which direction the influence ran (or even whether it is possible to make such a discrimination), it is clear that references to God's covenants with Abraham and Moses – not to mention the simultaneous cancellation and fulfilment of that covenant by Christ – formed part of a symbolic language with a range of powerful political implications.[10] Of particular importance was whether one saw the law of grace as a spiritual covenant only, or one with civil and political consequences. In his *Commentary on Saint Paul's Epistle to the Galatians*, Luther had opposed spiritual matters to civil policy, insisting that 'in civil policy obedience to the Law must be severely required. There nothing must be known as concerning the Gospel, conscience, grace, remission of sins, heavenly righteousness, or Christ himself, but Moses only, with the Law and the works thereof.' In the *Institutes of the Christian Religion* Calvin had similarly distinguished between the spiritual and the political kingdoms: 'Through this distinction it comes about that we are not to misapply to the political order the gospel teaching on spiritual freedom, as if Christians were less subject, as concerns outward government, to human laws, because their consciences have been set free in God's sight.'[11] In contrast, some seventeenth-century

The
political
Connection

---

[9] Miller, 'The Marrow of Puritan Divinity', p. 78.

[10] J. W. Gough, *The Social Contract* (Oxford, 1957), ch. 7. Compare Peter Bulkeley, *The Gospel-Covenant* ... (London, 1646), pp. 345–6, on the analogy between spiritual and political Covenant; quoted in Hill, 'Covenant Theology', p. 7.

[11] Luther, *A Commentary on Saint Paul's Epistle to Galatians*, cited in *CD*, 538 n. 31; Calvin, *Institutes*, Book III, ch. 19, section 15. As Milton notes, however, in *TKM*, Luther and Calvin do at points justify resistance on the part of 'lesser magistrates', though not of individual subjects (243–6).

Englishmen drew on the scriptural language of covenant to undermine the distinction between the spiritual and political orders, specifically by arguing that the covenant with God may in some circumstances supersede the covenant with the king. Thus, for example, in the Fast Sermons before parliament during the early 1640s, Cornelius Burges and Stephen Marshall repeatedly return to the image of the covenant in their attempt to stir up opposition to Charles I.[12] In 1643, as we have seen, parliament signed the Solemn League and Covenant with the Scottish Presbyterians, an agreement intended to forge 'a close military and ecclesiastical alliance between the two kingdoms against the king'.[13] 'Charles' would condemn the Covenanters in the posthumously published *Eikon Basilike* for stirring up 'seditious Commotions' and for 'committing Sacriledge under the Zeale of abhorring Idols'.[14]

At the same time that the political implications of scriptural covenant were being developed, writers such as Henry Parker and Thomas Goodwin were articulating a notion of political contract, which rooted power in the people and made the sovereign their servant.[15] While such a contractual view of government was not incompatible with monarchy, it became so in the hands of the more radical exponents of the revolutionary cause. In *Jus Populi* (1644), Parker readily acknowledged that a people could contract to delegate authority to a king; he denied, however, that there was any 'sufficient rule, precedent, or authority for arbitrary [by which he meant absolute] power; neither Nature nor History from the Creation to the

---

[12] See in particular the first sermons by Burges and Marshall of 17 November 1640, reprinted in facsimile in *The English Revolution, I: Fast Sermons to Parliament, 1640–1653* (34 vols., London, 1970–2). Burges urged support of the parliamentary cause in scriptural terms which were to be resonant for Hobbes and Milton as well:

> what Good, in the issue, hath followed, or can be yet hoped for so long as men continue *Philistines*, enemies to God & his Church, *Anti-Covenanters* (even with *Hell*) rather than true *Covenanters* with God? Whether is our condition any what better [*sic*] now than heretofore, when those *Leviathans* were alive, in their height? I appeale to your selves. And the reason of all is this, that men mistake the meanes of Cure, or at least fall short of it. The cutting off of evill Doers (how necessary soever it be) is not all, nor the maine requisite to make a people happy; unlesse also there be a thorough joyning of themselves to God by *Covenant*. (1, 60)

[13] Haller, *Liberty and Reformation*, p. 103.
[14] *Eikon Basilike, or The King's Book*, ed. Edward Almack (London, 1907), ch. 14, pp. 122, 125.
[15] Parker and Goodwin were following a long tradition of English and continental reflection on the contract between subject and sovereign. Milton would have been familiar with similar arguments from the work of Fortescue, Ponet, Buchanan, and Huguenot writers such as Hotman, Beza and du Plessis Mornay. As I discuss below, Magna Carta was also invoked to support contractual and constitutional arguments for limited monarchy in the seventeenth century.

Redemption afford us any *vestigia* of it'. Even the Roman emperors, by this account, exemplified 'mixt' monarchy. He went on to argue that, although democracy is not always the best form of government, 'yet it is ever the most naturall, and primarily authenticall; and for some times, and places the most beneficiall'.[16] Men such as Parker and Goodwin came to espouse republicanism, by which they meant a form of representative government in which an elite few governed in the interests of the whole commonwealth. Inspired in some cases by Cicero, Tacitus and Machiavelli, in others by Arminianism and covenant theology, or by some combination of all these, they argued that the people reserved the right to resist tyranny, especially when it took the form of encroaching on religion.

HOBBES *v*. MILTON

Writing in the 1640s, in the midst of the Civil War, Hobbes was particularly sensitive to the unstable mixture of the languages of religious covenant and political contract; he saw clearly that the biblical notion of the covenant could be used to stir up political rebellion. As he tells us in *Leviathan*, his political theory was designed in part to answer those who 'have pretended for their disobedience to their Soveraign, a new Covenant, made, not with men, but with God'.[17] Hobbes conceived of his model of political contract as supplanting such spiritual covenants. Because he associated spiritual covenants with the false prophet's metaphorical interpretation of Scripture, he prosecuted his argument in large measure through an ostentatiously literal-minded interpretation of biblical texts.

Of particular concern to Hobbes was the interpretation of the biblical phrase 'the kingdom of God': construed as a spiritual or metaphorical kingdom, the phrase might seem to license antinomianism and thus rebellion against an earthly sovereign's literal or actual kingdom. Thus, it was important for Hobbes to declare that the covenant between God and Moses was a literal one – a covenant about actual rather than metaphorical government – precisely in order to counter the metaphorical interpretation of God's kingdom

---

[16] Henry Parker, *Jus populi, or A Discourse wherein clear satisfaction is given, as well concerning the Right of Subjects, as the Right of Princes* (London, 1644), pp. 54, 64, and 61.

[17] *Leviathan*, 18, 230. For further discussion of this point, see J. G. A. Pocock, 'Time, History, and Eschatology in the Thought of Thomas Hobbes', in *Politics, Language and Time* (New York, 1971), p. 181, and William Kerrigan, *Prophetic Milton* (Charlottesville, 1975), p. 105.

which would then act as a dangerous alternative source of authority to the human sovereign. In a witty refutation of the 'spiritual' understanding of 'the kingdom of God', Hobbes asserted that the controversy surrounding the interpretation of the phrase was itself evidence for his reading: 'If the Kingdome of God ... were not a Kingdome which God by his Lieutenants, or Vicars, who deliver his Commandements to the people, did exercise on Earth; there would not have been so much contention, and warre, about who it is, by whom God speaketh to us' (35, 448). No one, in Hobbes's view, would quarrel over a merely spiritual or metaphorical kingdom. He expanded upon this insight in the next chapter, remarking, 'he that pretends to teach men the way of so great felicity, pretends to govern them' (36, 466).

Hobbes's cynical account of what is at stake in the claim to speak prophetically is part of his argument for absolute sovereignty. Precisely because all men are naturally ambitious to govern, we should be suspicious of the claim to speak prophetically on the basis of a personal covenant with God.[18] Scripture itself warns us of this danger in the figure of Micaiah: 'that there were many more false then true Prophets, appears by this, that when Ahab [1 Kings 22] consulted four hundred prophets, they were all false Imposters, but onely one Michaiah' (36, 467). Contemporary politics illustrated even more powerfully for Hobbes the dangers of false prophecy:

For when Christian men, take not their Christian Soveraign, for Gods Prophet; they must either take their owne Dreams, for the Prophecy they mean to be governed by, and the tumour of their own hearts for the Spirit of God; or they must suffer themselves to bee lead by some strange Prince; or by some of their fellow subjects, that can betwitch them, by slander of the government, into rebellion, without other miracle to confirm their calling, then sometimes an extraordinary successe, and Impunity; and by this means destroying all laws, both divine, and humane, reduce all Order, Government, and Society, to the first Chaos of Violence, and Civill warre. (36, 469)[19]

This passage illustrates the sceptical logic which led Hobbes to conclude that the sovereign is the only legitimate interpreter of Scripture. Since there will always be false prophets and disagreements regarding the meaning of God's word, we must contract to assign this

---

[18] See Hobbes, *Leviathan*, 14, 197; 18, 230.

[19] As Hobbes knew very well, Cromwell in particular liked to use the 'extraordinary successe' of the New Model army to justify the parliamentary cause. I have discussed such appeals to success in *Machiavellian Rhetoric: From the Counter-Reformation to Milton* (Princeton, 1994), ch. 5.

power of interpretation to the Christian sovereign who, like the Calvinist God, rules absolutely and is not a party to the covenant. The alternative – individual interpretation (including the metaphorical understanding of the kingdom of God) – can only lead to the anarchy of civil war.[20]

As Hobbes's remarks illustrate, there was a close connection in seventeenth-century political thought between prophecy, covenant and political contract, not only because God's covenants with Abraham and Moses were important scriptural texts whose interpretation had political consequences, but also because prophecy and covenant could be construed as structurally analogous models of interpretation. Just as the covenants with Abraham and Moses established a literal kingdom of God on earth that will be realized again on earth in the future, so the 'sensus propheticus' for Hobbes is not a metaphorical sense, but a literal sense promised in the future. And just as Hobbes wants to construe the covenants of Abraham and Moses as covenants to which the Jewish people consented and which were absolutely binding, so he aims to define prophecy or the right to interpret Scripture as the absolute prerogative of the sovereign whom the subjects have consented to obey. Prophecy as the interpretation of sacred history serves to underwrite the logical (and in Hobbes's sense, ahistorical) authority of the sovereign.[21] The temporal deferral of the 'sensus propheticus' underwrites the metaphorical transfer of allegiance

---

[20] In Hobbes's view, the definition of words should, like the commonwealth, be a matter of irrevocable contract. His own definition of reason itself exemplifies this principle: 'For REASON ... is nothing but RECKONING ... of the Consequences of generall names agreed upon.' And, as in a commonwealth, part of the general agreement is to defer to the sovereign in cases of dispute: 'And therefore, as when there is a controversy in an account, the parties must by their own accord, set up for right Reason, the Reason of some Arbitrator, or Judge, to whose sentence they will both stand' (5, 111). On the link between government and language, see also *Leviathan*, 21, 267, where Hobbes compares the derivation of the principles of government from the books of Aristotle and Cicero to the grammarians' derivation of 'the rules of Language, out of the Practise of the time; or the Rules of Poetry, out of the Poems of *Homer* and *Virgil*'. In neither case, according to Hobbes, can practice or usage be the criterion of first principles. Rather, such principles must be generally agreed upon through a shared process of ratiocination, or imposed arbitrarily by the sovereign.

I have discussed Hobbes's attitude towards metaphor in *Rhetoric, Prudence, and Skepticism in the Renaissance* (Ithaca, 1985), ch. 6. See also Victoria Silver, 'The Fiction of Self-Evidence in Hobbes' *Leviathan*', *ELH*, 55 (1988), 351–79; and Quentin Skinner, 'Thomas Hobbes: Rhetoric and the Construction of Morality', *Proceedings of the British Academy*, 76 (1991), 1–61, on Hobbes's attempt to resolve the problem of paradiastole – the rhetorical name for the fact that evaluative terms such as virtue or vice are inherently slippery and may be used to redescribe a 'given action ... in such a way as to suggest that its moral character may be open to some measure of doubt' (3).

[21] On this point, see Pocock, 'Time, History, and Eschatology', esp. pp. 157–66.

to the sovereign and allows the potentially destabilizing effects of metaphor to be controlled in the present.

Beginning with the same equation of prophecy with scriptural interpretation, and allowing for the same possibility of false prophecy, Milton arrived at a number of opposed conclusions. Already in *Areopagitica*, he had argued that the uncertainty of interpretation dictated more rather than less freedom for the individual interpreter. The possibility of false prophecy implied, conversely, that truth might be misrecognized and therefore censored as falsehood; the only protection against the censorship of truth was to allow truth and falsehood to 'grapple . . . in a free and open encounter' (*CPW*, II, 561). This conviction took the form, in *Areopagitica*, of a striking proliferation of simile and metaphor, as though to dramatize in the rhetoric of the text the generative possibilities of free interpretation. Like Hobbes, Milton referred to the prophet Micaiah, who had tuned his voice 'according to the time' until, adjured to speak the truth, he warned that other prophets were inspired by 'a lying spirit' (1 Kings 22: 23; *CPW*, II, 563). Micaiah is thus simultaneously a figure of misrepresentation and of true prophecy. It was precisely the difficulty of telling the difference between the two that was the basis of Milton's argument against censorship.[22] He made the same point in *A Treatise of Civil Power in Ecclesiastical Causes* (1659) when he argued that Scripture could only be interpreted with the aid of 'divine illumination, which no man can know at all times to be in himself' and concluded that 'no man or body of men in these times can be the infallible judges or determiners in matters of religion to any other mens conscience but thir own' (*CPW*, VII, 242–3).

Like Hobbes, Milton believed that scriptural interpretation had political consequences, both in the sense that certain passages in Scripture could be construed to argue against coercion in spiritual matters or against absolute sovereignty,[23] and in the sense that our right (or obligation) to read and interpret Scripture for ourselves dictated a form of government that would support rather than undermine this free and open encounter with the Bible. Thus, in *Civil Power*, Milton allowed with Hobbes that the kingdom of God is not at the present moment a kingdom of this world (*CPW*, VII, 256–76); but

[22] I have discussed this passage at greater length in *Machiavellian Rhetoric*, ch. 6.

[23] Often such scriptural interpretation turned on an understanding of figurative language. In *A Treatise of Civil Power*, Milton argues that scriptural passages, such as Luke 14:6, where coercion is applied to spiritual matters, must be interpreted in figurative terms (*CPW*, VII, 260).

he drew the contrary conclusion that Scripture 'gives no judgment or coercive power to magistrates'. As a result, '*Erastus* and state-tyranie over the church' must be rejected (*CPW*, VII, 252). In *On Christian Doctrine*, Milton conceived of God's relationship to man as similarly involving persuasion rather than coercion: 'So we must conclude that God made no absolute decrees about anything which he left in the power of men, for men have freedom of action' (*CD*, 155). As supporting evidence, Milton cited the biblical account of Jonah's prophecy to the citizens of Nineveh that, unless they repented, the city would be destroyed (Jonah 3:4). The citizens repented and Jonah was angry with God that the prophecy did not come to pass. In Milton's reading, this outcome proves that the divinely inspired prophecy was not predictive, but persuasive and conditional upon the citizens' response: 'For if the decrees of God quoted above, and others of the same kind which frequently occur, were interpreted in an absolute sense without any implied conditions, God would seem to contradict himself and be changeable' (*CD*, 156).[24] Later in the treatise, Milton argued in similar terms for the doctrine of general rather than specific predestination:

the principle of predestination is founded upon a condition, – *whosoever hath sinned, him will I blot out*. This is announced more fully in the enforcement of the legal covenant, Deut. vii. 6–8. where God particularly declares his choice and love of his people to have been gratuitous; and in v.9. where he desires to be known as *a faithful God which keepeth his covenant and mercy*, he yet adds as a condition, *with them that love him and keep his commandments*.[25]

God's covenant is a conditional rather than an absolute covenant, dependent on the good will of the believer who strives 'to love him and keep his commandments'. And this is true not only of the covenant of works but also of grace, whose condition or 'work' is 'faith in Christ' (*CD*, 180). In a memorable phrase that also appears in *Paradise Lost*, Milton argues that the Gospel frees men 'from the works of the law' so that they may engage in 'works of faith' (*CD*, 536; *PL*, XII, 300–6).

One of the most important works of faith for Milton – one of the

[24] See also *CD*, 160. One could also use J. L. Austin's term 'performative' to describe Jonah's prophecy. A performative statement is one whose function is to perform or bring about a certain state of affairs, rather than to describe or designate an already existing one. I am indebted here to several conversations of many years ago with Ian Balfour.

[25] *CD*, 178. I quote here from the Sumner translation in John Milton, *Complete Poetry and Major Prose*, ed. Merritt Y. Hughes (Indianapolis, 1958), p. 920, because I prefer the translation of 'pactum' as covenant rather than compact.

most important manifestations of the 'new covenant' – was the work of reading, specifically reading and interpreting Scripture. As he writes in *Christian Doctrine*, 'all true believers either prophesy or have within them the Holy Spirit, which is as good as having the gift of prophecy and dreams and visions' (*CD*, 523–4). He who interprets under the new covenant interprets according to the spirit rather than the letter (*CD*, 536): 'on the evidence of scripture itself, all things are eventually to be referred to the Spirit and the unwritten word' (*CD*, 590).[26] Reading is a prophetic and ethical activity precisely because meaning is not simply or literally given but must be spiritually construed. The work of prophecy or interpretation is thus inseparable from attention to the figurative dimension of Scripture. Conversely, the figurative language of Scripture functions (like Jonah's prophecy) as a conditional covenant which demands the reader's interpretive and ethical response.

That Milton's view of the covenant has implications for the way we construe figurative language and ethical responsibility is apparent also in his discussion of the sacraments. Because the covenant of grace is conditional, it serves to demystify the sacraments. No sacrament is efficacious in itself; rather, the power of the sacraments is itself conditional upon the faith of the believer. In practice, this amounts to a recognition of the figurative dimension of Scripture, including such phrases as 'this is my body'. For, according to Milton, a sacrament is not itself a covenant but rather 'a sign of the covenant' (*CD*, 555). 'Failure to recognize this figure of speech in the sacraments, where the relationship between the symbol and the thing symbolized is very close, has been a widespread source of error, and still is today' (*CD*, 555).[27] Thinking tropologically serves to place the ethical burden where it belongs: not on the sacrament alone but on the individual agent and believer. As we will see in *The Tenure of Kings and Magistrates*, the logic of such reasoning could lead the defender of individual prophecy and conditional covenants to argue for republicanism.

---

[26] See also *CD*, 581–2: 'Each passage of scripture has only a single sense, though in the Old Testament this sense is often a combination of the historical and the typological . . . The right method of interpreting the scriptures [requires] . . . knowledge [of the] distinction between literal and figurative language.' Milton does not simply equate the spiritual sense with the figurative sense; he does, however, argue that an understanding of figurative language is an effect of a spiritual interpretation of Scripture.

[27] Maurice Kelley, the editor of *CD*, traces Milton's position on the sacraments to Wollebius and Ames (see the notes to Book I, ch. 27).

THE METAPHORICAL CONTRACT

In defending regicide in *The Tenure* Milton ran the risk of anti-nomianism: of arguing for an action 'above the form of Law or Custom' (194) – an action for which there appeared to be no sanction in positive or moral law.[28] Such arguments were familiar to Milton and his contemporaries from the antinomian preachers of the New Model Army, not to mention more radical sectarians. And Milton seems to echo them at various points in *The Tenure*, claiming that 'the Sword of God [is] superior to all mortal things, in whose hand soever by apparent signes his testified will is to put it' (193). Milton adopts a complicated rhetorical strategy to address the implicit charge of antinomianism and to defend his proto-republican arguments for what Henry Parker called *jus populi* (the right of the people): he appeals to arguments from reason and natural law, from Scripture, and from historical precedent. Although he provides historical examples of regicide, he also argues that the very lack of precedent should be a powerful incentive to kill the king.

What unites these diverse and in some cases contradictory arguments is Milton's metaphorical understanding of covenant and contract. Four points are important to note and will help us grasp the precise nature of Milton's republican thinking in this treatise. First, Milton construes biblical covenant and political contract in similar terms: both are structured as rational, open-ended and revocable agreements that depend for their realization on the performance of the contracting parties. Second, and consequently, biblical examples of God's covenant with the Jews are cited not so much as authoritative precedents for political contract as instances of the kind of God-given rational deliberation that should inform men's political covenants with each other.[29] Third, as in *Christian Doctrine*, covenant and contract are thus not only objects of

---

[28] See Michael Fixler, *Milton and the Kingdoms of God* (London, 1964), ch. 4, esp. p. 146; and William Haller, *Liberty and Reformation*, pp. 341–58.

[29] In 'The Politics of *Paradise Lost*', in Kevin Sharpe and Steven N. Zwicker (eds.), *Politics of Discourse: The Literature and History of Seventeenth-Century England* (Berkeley, 1987), Mary Ann Radzinowicz makes a related point about Milton's use of Scripture in *Paradise Lost*: 'He reads Scripture seeking its rational interpretation. Satisfied that he has rightly judged the significance of this or that occasion, his interpretation does not become the precedent to which current affairs are made conformable; rather, the free use of reason in an act of interpretation becomes the precedent, the mode by which current affairs are judged' (207). 'So it is with all Milton's political instances involving scriptural scenarios in *Paradise Lost*. In them Scripture is history and not authority; no interpretation is coercive; no public policy comes with God's fiat behind it to overrule freedom' (208).

interpretation for Milton, but also models of interpretation. Specifically, they are structurally analogous to Milton's understanding of scriptural prophecy and metaphor as conditional and performative rather than predictive. Covenants, contracts and metaphors all constitute ethical obligations which may be assumed or rejected. Finally, Milton's understanding of covenant and contract is rooted in the interest of the people and for that reason compatible with strategic considerations of reason of state. To the extent that it is possible to distinguish these strands in the intellectual history of the seventeenth century, Milton's republicanism in 1649 is Tacitean and Machiavellian as much or more than it is Ciceronian. But it is a Machiavellian republicanism that is (or claims to be) perfectly compatible with divine law and the covenant of grace.

Milton begins his account of the contractual 'origin' of kings with an Aristotelian narrative that differs from Hobbes's account in *Leviathan*: after the fall, men

agreed by common league to bind each other from mutual injury, and joyntly to defend themselves against any that gave disturbance or opposition to such agreement. Hence came Citties, Townes, and Common-wealths. And because no faith in all was found sufficiently binding, they saw it needfull to ordaine som authoritie that might restrain by force and punishment what was violated against peace and right. (199)

Unlike Hobbes, Milton imagines individuals initially contracting with each other for protection rather than conferring that power upon a sovereign. The subsequent establishment of a single – one might say, Hobbesian – 'authoritie' is attended, according to Milton, by the discovery of 'the danger and inconveniences of committing arbitrary power to any', and the consequent redefinition of the covenant as conditional rather than absolute and irrevocable: first, 'the law was set above the magistrate'.

When this would not serve, but that the Law was either not executed, or misapply'd, they were constrain'd from that time, the onely remedy left them, to put conditions and take Oaths from all Kings and Magistrates at thir first instalment to doe impartial justice by Law: who upon those termes and no other, receav'd Allegeance from the people, that is to say, bond or Covnant to obey them in execution of those Lawes which they the people had themselves made, or assented to. And this ofttimes with express warning, that if the King or Magistrate prov'd unfaithfull to his trust, the people would be disingag'd. (200)

In the remainder of the treatise Milton proceeds to demystify the logic
of Hobbes's account of the subject's transfer of allegiance to the
sovereign. Like the covenant of Moses, the contract between subject
and sovereign is a conditional contract which is continually subject to
renegotiation: 'It being thus manifest that the power of Kings and
Magistrates is nothing else but what is only derivative, transferr'd
and committed to them in trust from the People to the Common good
of them all, in whom the power yet remaines fundamentally and
cannot be tak'n from them without a violation of thir natural
birthright' (202). It thus stands to reason that when the common
good is not realized the power of the sovereign may be revoked and
reassumed by his subjects.[30]

Scripture is then adduced not, as in Hobbes, to underwrite the
argument for an absolute sovereign, but rather as evidence of the
historical revision of the original contract and of the impossibility of
any such permanently binding agreement. Milton cites Deuteronomy
17:14 and 1 Samuel 8 in support of 'the right of choosing, yea of
changing [one's] government' (207):[31]

It follows, lastly, that since the King or Magistrate holds his autoritie of the
people, both originaly and naturally for their good in the first place, and not
his own, then may the people, as oft as they shall judge it for the best, either
choose him or reject him, retaine him or depose him though no Tyrant,
meerly by the liberty and right of free born Men to be govern'd as seems to
them best. This, though it cannot but stand with plain reason, shall be made
good also by Scripture. *Deut.* 17.14. *When thou art come into the land which the
Lord thy God giveth thee, and shalt say, I will set a King over mee, like as all the Nations
about mee.* These words confirme us that the right of choosing, yea of changing
their own Goverment is by the grant of God himself in the People. (206–7)

Scripture teaches us that God's covenants with Abraham and Moses
were revised by David, Samuel, and others – both for good and for ill.
As Milton remarks of the Jews' request for a king in Samuel, 'God
himself joyn'd with them in the work; though in som sort it was at that
time displeasing to him' (208). The choice of a king is evidence of the
rational – though here faulty – exercise of free will that is the central
tenet of Milton's Arminianism. As Milton observes in *Christian
Doctrine*, 'God made his decrees conditional . . . for the very purpose of

---

[30] See Haller, *Liberty and Reformation*, 349, who fails to note that Milton argues that the covenant
is terminable only by the people, not by the king who is their servant.

[31] As Hughes notes, 'Deut. xvii, 14, had been interpreted adversely to popular rights by Grotius
in *De Jure Belli et Pacis* II, iv, 3' (206, n. 68). For Hobbes's interpretation of 1 Samuel 8, see
Leviathan, 35, 446; 40, 508–10; 42, 541. Hobbes reads 1 Samuel as evidence that God was the
Jews' literal king, before they abandoned him and chose another.

allowing free causes to put into effect the freedom which he himself gave them', including, as God sourly remarks in *Paradise Lost*, the freedom to err *(CD*, 160; *PL*, III, 99). Scripture and reason are not only compatible; Scripture is itself a record of the trials and errors of God-given reason.

To support this argument, Milton turns to 1 Peter 2:13 and Romans 13, which were regularly cited by royalists to justify monarchical power and absolute obedience to the crown:

> Therfore Kingdom and Magistracy, whether supreme or subordinat, is [without difference] call'd *a human ordinance,* 1 *Pet.* ii, 13, &c. which we are there taught is the will of God wee should [alike] submitt to, so farr as for the punishment of evil doers, and the encouragement of them that doe well. *Submitt,* saith he, *as free men.* [But to any civil power unaccountable, unquestionable, and not to be resisted, no, not in wickedness and violent actions, how can we submitt as free men?] *There is no power but of God,* saith *Paul, Rom.* 13. as much as to say, God put it into mans heart to find out that way at first for common peace and preservation, approving the exercise therof; els it contradicts *Peter* who calls the same autority an Ordinance of man. It must be also understood of lawfull and just power, els we read of great power in the affaires and Kingdoms of the World permitted to the Devil: for saith he to Christ, *Luke* 4.6. *All this power will I give thee and the glory of them, for it is deliver'd to me, & to whomsoever I will, I give it*: neither did he ly, or Christ gainsay what he affirm'd; for in the thirteenth of the *Revelation* wee read how the Dragon gave the beast *his power, his seate, and great autority*: which beast so autoriz'd most expound to be the tyrannical powers and Kingdoms of the earth. (209–10)

In this passage Milton employs his characteristic rhetorical strategy of enlarging the area of human discretion, even to the point of making the much cited, authoritative Romans 13 subject to debate. That is, Milton does not simply rebut his opponents' interpretation by proposing his own thematic paraphrase of Romans; rather, his interpretation of this passage is that it is open to interpretation. 'There is no power but of God' is not simply a statement of fact, but a test of human judgement, an exercise in deliberating about the best way to achieve 'common peace and preservation'. And such exercise is necessary because power is morally indifferent, and may be used well or badly. To illustrate this point, Milton refers to the passage in Luke where Satan offers Christ worldly power; and he insists that Satan's offer was genuine, because to deny Satan power would be to deny the power that tyrants have to oppress their subjects. At issue is not the possession of power but its right use. Only power that is correctly used may be correctly described as 'ordain'd of God' (210). And whether power is correctly used is a matter of rational deliberation: the people have the right to 'dispose of [sovereign power] by any alteration as they shall *judge* most conducing to the public good' (212, my emphasis).

In asserting the compatibility of Romans 13 and Peter – of divine and human ordinance – Milton makes the whole realm of politics coextensive with that of human judgement. In striking contrast, for example, to James VI, who in *Basilikon Doron* distinguished between the express commandments of God and the invention and the ordinance of man, Milton equates them: the power that is ordained by God is the same power that is ordered by man. He then develops the implications of this analysis by calling attention to the rhetorical dimension of sovereignty. Just as Romans 13 is open to interpretation, so the rule of a sovereign is open to interpretation by the people, who create legitimacy by their linguistic act of consent. Thus, if Romans 13 may be cited to support obedience to kings, it may also be cited to support resistance; similarly,

if the peoples act in election be pleaded by a King, as the act of God, and the most just title to enthrone him, why may not the peoples act of rejection, bee as well pleaded by the people as the act of God, and the most just reason to depose him? So that we see the title and just right of raigning or deposing, in reference to God, is found in Scripture to be all one; visible onely in the people, and depending meerly upon justice and demerit. (211)

As in Hobbes's *Leviathan*, authority is constituted by the metaphorical transfer of allegiance and power to the sovereign. But Milton's account differs in one significant respect: just as for Milton consent is not meaningful without the possibility of dissent, so the ability to transfer power to the sovereign is evidence of the power to revoke allegiance. Milton stresses what Hobbes labours to conceal: that political contract involves only a metaphorical transfer, since power remains fundamentally with the people. In this light, we might strengthen Hobbes's caution against allowing metaphors into political deliberation: metaphors are not less dangerous to absolute sovereignty 'when they openly profess their own inconstancy' – their own metaphoricity – but rather more (5, 110).[32]

THE LOGIC OF METAPHOR: TENURE *v.* CONTRACT

In characteristic fashion, Milton dramatizes his metaphorical understanding of covenant and contract in the metaphors of his

---

[32] See Hobbes, *Leviathan*, ch. 17. I have borrowed the preceding three paragraphs on Milton's interpretation of Romans 13 and Peter from *Machiavellian Rhetoric*, ch. 6.

treatise. That metaphor has ethical implications – and may dictate ethical obligation – is apparent from the very opening of *The Tenure of Kings and Magistrates*:

If men within themselves would be govern'd by reason, and not generally give up thir understanding to the double tyrannie, of Custom from without, and blind affections within, they would discerne better, what it is to favour and uphold a Tyrant of a Nation. But being slaves within doors, no wonder that they strive so much to have the public State conformably govern'd to the inward vitious rule, by which they govern themselves. For indeed none can love freedom heartilie, but good men. (190)

It is striking that the opening sentence of this treatise on the literal tyranny of Charles I should use tyranny and government as metaphors. But this is precisely Milton's point: it is metaphorical tyranny within that gives rise to literal tyranny without, to the demand for 'conformity' between inward and outward rule.[33]

Milton then harnesses the ethical logic of metaphor to argue for a different sort of conformity. In Milton's view, kingship is itself simply a metaphor – that is, the name of a contract or relation between two terms: 'We know that King and Subject are relatives, and relatives have no longer being then in the relation' (229–30). According to Milton's metaphorical logic, 'King is a name of dignity and office, not of person: Who therefore kills a King, must kill him while he is a King. Then they certainly who by deposing him have long since tak'n from him the life of a King, his office and his dignity, they in the truest sence may be said to have killed the King' (233). Although such a distinction between the king's 'two bodies' would seem to imply that there was no point in killing Charles once he had been deposed, Milton draws the opposite conclusion: he claims that since the Presbyterians have figuratively or metaphorically killed the king, they are logically and morally obliged to do so literally as well (190–2). It was precisely such an equivocal – or casuistical – understanding of 'king' that Hobbes feared, and with good reason. For, in a kind of parody of the scriptural distinction between the spirit and the letter, the figurative murder of the king is prior to and dictates his literal murder as its lethal consequence. Or, to put it another way,

[33] See *PL*, XII, 97–101:

> Yet sometimes nations will decline so low
> From virtue, which is reason, that no wrong,
> But justice, and some fatal curse annexed
> Deprives them of their outward liberty
> Their inward lost...

the king's official body proves to be fatally indistinguishable from his personal body. The contract of sovereignty and the metaphor of 'king' are thus prophetic in the sense of generating unforeseen meanings and actions, including the execution of the king himself.[34]

'Tenure' also figures prominently in the metaphorical logic of the treatise. The *OED* tells us that 'tenure' in this period could mean 'the action or fact of holding a tenement', 'the condition of service, etc., under which a tenement is held of a superior; the title by which the property is held; the relations, rights, and duties of the tenant to the landlord', and by extension, a 'title' or 'authority'. In Magna Carta, the freehold or free tenure of property was also a defining characteristic of the free subject as opposed to the king.[35] Significantly for our purposes, in his discussion of the definitions of tenure in the *Institutes*, Coke called attention to the connection between tenure and covenant: 'Also, *tenure* signifieth performance; as in the Writ of Covenant, Quod teneat conventionem, that is, That hee hold or performe his Covenant... And likewise it signifieth to be bound, as it is sayd in every common Obligation, teneri et firmiter obligari.' He argued further that all the meanings of tenant could be linked in the following formula: 'For (1) he hath the estate of the land, (2) he holdeth the land of some superiour Lord, (3) and is to performe the services due, and (4) thereunto he is bounden (5) by doome and iudgement of Law.'[36] From its first metaphorical reference in the title of Milton's tract to the authority or office of kings and magistrates, tenure gradually regains its literal meaning of feudal tenure. Milton plays on this meaning to suggest first that the people

---

[34] See William Kerrigan, *The Sacred Complex: On the Psychogenesis of 'Paradise Lost'* (Cambridge, Mass., 1983) on the similarity between prophecy and 'good metaphors': 'One cannot crack the meaning of a good metaphor by recourse to values already affixed to either of its terms... Tradition is decisive for the meaning of dead metaphors. By their very anomaly, good metaphors are prophetic – troublers of stability' (94).

[35] As Thomas Hedley said in a speech to parliament (28 June 1610): 'The sovereignty of the king hath his existence principally in matter of honor or government, the liberty of the subject in matter of profit or property... The words of Magna Carta, c.29, are these: *Nulla liber homo capiatur vel imprisonetur aut disseisietur de libero tenemento suo vel libertatibus consuetudinibus suis etc. nisi per legale judicium parium suorum vel per legem terrae*' (*Proceedings in Parliament*, 2 vols., ed. Elizabeth Read Forster (New Haven, 1966) vol. ii, p. 191). Edward Coke translated chapter 29 of the 1225 charter as 'No freeman shall be taken, or imprisoned, or be disseised of his freehold or liberties, or free customs [etc.] but by lawful judgment of his peers or by the law of the land' (quoted by Maurice Ashley, *Magna Carta in the Seventeenth Century* (Charlottesville, 1965), p. 12).

[36] Edward Coke, *Institutes*, Book i, ch. i, section i of the *First Institute*. I owe this reference to William Klein.

do not hold their land in a grant of tenure from the king so much as the king is a bondsman who holds his office or 'tenure' from the people on the condition that he fulfil his covenant with them (221); he then argues that the tenure of kingship – regardless of whether the king is a good ruler – reduces the people to the status of feudal subjects.

For the king to hold his subjects in feudal subjection is to arrogate to himself divine authority: 'to say that Kings are accountable to none but God, is the overturning of all Law and government ... for if the King feare not God, as how many of them do not? we hold then our lives and estates by the tenure of his meer grace and mercy, as from a God' (204). This, of course, was precisely the claim royalist defenders of divine right wished to make. But Milton draws the republican conclusion. A free nation, without 'the natural and essential power' of deposing its ruler, must

be thought no better then slaves and vassals born, in the tenure and occupation of another inheriting Lord. Whose goverment, though not illegal, or intolerable, hangs over them as a Lordly scourge, not as a free goverment; and therfore to be abrogated. (237)

In this slippage of meaning, tenure comes to stand not for the legitimate authority of the king but for the Presbyterians' and royalists' idolatrous interpretation of political contract.[37]

In literalizing the meaning of tenure here and elsewhere, Milton activates what J. G. A. Pocock, Christopher Hill and others have identified as the language of the 'Norman yoke' and the 'ancient constitution'.[38] In seventeenth-century political discourse, parliamentarians often referred to the so-called ancient constitution of immemorial custom, which rooted power in the people and subjected the king to the law. Royalists, in contrast, insisted that the king made the law and was thus above it; and they pointed for support not only to Scripture but also to the institution of hereditary feudal tenure

---

[37] This idolatrous interpretation of political contract is also one of the subjects of Milton's *Eikonoklastes*. Milton attacks the Presbyterian understanding of the Solemn League and Covenant in the introduction and in chapter 28, where he speaks of 'men so quell'd and fitted to be slaves by the fals conceit of a Religious Covnant' (*CPW*, III, 347, and 595; see 593–7).

[38] J. G. A. Pocock, *The Ancient Constitution and Feudal Law*, A Reissue with Retrospect (Cambridge, 1987); Christopher Hill, *Puritanism and Revolution* (London, 1958), pp. 58–125. In *TKM* Milton discusses the Norman Conquest (201); the 'ancient constitution' (220); the 'right of ancient laws and Ceremonies' (225). He also traces 'the most fundamental and ancient tenure that any king of England can produce or pretend to' not to William the Conqueror but to the year 446, when the British people elected a king after the Romans had relinquished their right of conquest (221).

introduced with the Norman conquest.[39] As Pocock and others have
shown, some Puritans and Presbyterians combined the idea of the
ancient constitution with that of England's divine mission as the Elect
Nation, arguing that the ancient constitution was a sign of England's
covenant with the Lord: godly rule reached its culmination with the
restoration of the ancient constitution. This was particularly true of
the Presbyterian William Prynne, who combined the language of
godly covenant and ancient constitution in defence of what Pocock
calls 'apocalyptic erastianism'. For those who (unlike Prynne) took
this position on the ancient constitution to its antinomian conclusion,
the Norman yoke with 'its feudal tenures, landed clergy, [and]
appropriation of the common lands' became a type of 'the Old Adam
not yet burned away in the fires of "the great spirit Reason"'.[40] In
passages such as the one quoted immediately above, we can see
Milton turning Prynne's language against him, while trying to avoid
the charge of antinomianism by appealing both to history and to
natural law. In Milton's view, a rational and revocable contract *is* the
form of God's covenant with the English people.

At this point in the treatise Milton is no longer simply justifying
tyrannicide; he is arguing for the abrogation of monarchical government
even when it is 'not illegal or intolerable'. And lest we think this
argument applies only to absolute monarchs, he turns sovereignty
itself into a metaphor without any literal referent except God: the
purpose of the trial of Charles I is 'to teach lawless Kings, and all who
so much adore them, that not mortal man, or his imperious will, but
Justice, is the onely true sovran and supreme Majesty upon earth'
(237). And, in the conclusion of the treatise, Milton makes the
exclusive identification of monarchy and God explicit:

Therfore he who is our only King, the Root of *David*, and whose Kingdom is
eternal righteousness, with all those that Warr under him, whose happiness
and final hopes are laid up in that only just & rightful kingdom (which we
pray uncessantly may com soon, and in so praying wish hasty ruin and
destruction to all Tyrants) eev'n he our immortal King, and all that love
him, must of necessity have in abomination these blind and lame Defenders

---

[39] See Pocock, *Ancient Constitution*, pp. 119–20. At the same time, because the royalists did not
want to base the monarchy's claim to legitimacy simply upon the right of (the Norman)
conquest, they also argued for the irrevocable consent of the people (as James VI does in *The
Trew Law of Free Monarchies*) and they even borrowed the language of the ancient constitution
and 'the immemorial custom of England' (*ibid.*, 151) to defend absolute monarchy.

[40] Pocock, *Ancient Constitution*, pp. 318, 317, 320. Pocock argues that the ancient constitution
argument was used by conservative Presbyterians from 1647 on.

of *Jerusalem* [the Jebusites, who are biblical precursors of the Presbyterians].
(256)

Like covenants, metaphors can be used to oblige or disoblige, to
engage or disengage: the metaphor of tenure obliges us to abrogate
hereditary kingship; the metaphor of sovereignty engages us to take
up arms against Charles, whose literal pretensions to absolute
monarchy have proven to be blasphemous.

In such pronouncements we see the inextricability of the language
of justice and that of reason of state for Milton. In his account of the
origin of monarchy, as well as his justification of the regicide, Milton
appealed to the 'autoritie and power of self-defence and preservation'
which is 'originally and naturally' in all individuals (199). 'Present
necessitie' and 'the Law of nature justifies any man to defend himself,
eev'n against the King in Person' (253, 254). The same is true of the
state: 'justice done upon a Tyrant is no more but the necessary
self-defence of a whole Common wealth' (254), the preservation of
'the public good' (220). The language of necessity, self-preservation
and *salus populi* was the language of reason of state in seventeenth-
century England – a language that, as Milton acknowledged in *Paradise
Lost*, could certainly be used for the purposes of tyrannical self-aggrand-
izement.[41] Yet for Milton in *The Tenure*, and for other defenders of
Cromwell and the New Model Army, such appeals to the preservation
of the commonwealth were perfectly consonant with true justice.[42]
In fact, since no one denied the justice of the legal maxim that, in
cases of individual assault, *vim vi licet repellere*, the extension of the
argument of self-defence to the defence of the commonwealth proved
to be a brilliant constitutionalist move.[43]

[41] Milton acknowledged the possible abuse of the language of reason of state in *Paradise Lost*
when he referred to 'necessity / The tyrant's plea' (*PL*, IV, 393–4).

[42] Compare Henry Parker who, in *The Contra-Replicant* (London, 1642), defended reason of
state as the legitimate use of extralegal means to preserve the state in times when the ordinary
workings of the law are not enforced or will not suffice: 'Lawes ayme at *Justice*, Reason of state
aimes at *Safety* ... To deny to Parliament recourse to reason of State in these miserable times
of warre and danger [is] to deny them self-defence' (24–5).

On the language of reason of state in England, see George L. Mosse, *The Holy Pretence: A
Study in Christianity and Reason of State from William Perkins to John Winthrop* (Oxford, 1957);
David S. Berkowitz, 'Reason of State and the Petition of Right', in Roman Shnur (ed.),
Staatsräson (Berlin, 1975), pp. 165–212; and Richard Tuck, *Philosophy and Government,
1572–1651* (Cambridge, 1993). In 'Republicanism and Reason of State', in Istvan Hont
(ed.), *The Politics of Necessity: Reason of State in Modern European Political Discourse* (forthcoming,
Cambridge), Alan Craig Houston argues against Tuck that reason of state was compatible
with constitutional concerns in seventeenth-century England; Milton's argument for a more
representative form of government in *TKM* would seem to bear out this contention.

[43] I owe this point to Quentin Skinner, who commented on an earlier draft of this chapter.

Despite Milton's defence of parliament and the army, the question of who could claim to represent and thus defend the commonwealth remained subject to debate; the danger of a satanic abuse of reason of state remained constant. The Army chaplain William Sedgwick both drew on the constitutionalist language of reason of state and illustrated its ambiguity when he argued in *A Second View of the Army Remonstrance* (1649), 'What makes a public person above a private but that he hath the civil sword in his hand to administer justice?' 'This Army is truly the people of the kingdom, in which the common interest most lies' (6, 11).[44] In the seventeenth century, a 'public person' was generally defined as legitimate representative of the people, a legitimate administrator of justice. Yet the view that justice and the sword, or justice and the trial of Charles I, were perfectly compatible was certainly a minority position in 1649. As Florence Sandler has written,

> When Milton ... justifies the regicide court as acting with the authority of the people, he offends the good parliamentarian by refusing to recognize the distinction between a free House of Commons and a Rump sitting at the behest of the Army, and he aligns himself with the small group of extremists who are prepared to force the actual forms of the law to fit their own arbitrary version of the 'fundamental law'.[45]

Here we return to the problem of antinomianism, the justification of an act 'above the form of Law or Custom' (194). We have seen how Milton understands scriptural covenant and prophecy as conditional or performative rather than predictive; and how he dramatizes in his own metaphors a similarly open-ended covenant with the reader. This understanding of covenant and prophecy also governs Milton's attitude towards precedent and example. While at times Milton seems to appeal to scriptural or historical precedent, he also sees the regicide as a uniquely heroic act that will serve as a precedent to future nations:

> And if the Parliament and Military Councel doe what they doe without precedent, if it appear thir duty, it argues the more wisdom, vertue, and magnanimity, that they know themselves able to be a precedent to others. Who perhaps in the future ages, if they prove not too degenerat, will look

---

[44] Sedgwick is quoted by Hill, 'Covenant Theology', p. 16. Fixler also discusses Sedgwick in *Milton and the Kingdoms of God*, pp. 151–2.

[45] Sandler, 'Icon and Iconoclast', in Michael Lieb and John T. Shawcross (eds.), *Achievements of the Left Hand: Essays on the Prose of John Milton* (Amherst, 1974), p. 168.

up with honour, and aspire toward these exemplary, and matchless deeds of thir Ancestors, as to the highest top of thir civil glory and emulation. (237–8)

Like scriptural covenants and prophecies, the regicide will prove in William Kerrigan's words to be a good metaphor, a 'troubler of stability'.[46] As Hobbes feared, the regicide threatens to teach others 'a better fortitude, to dare execute highest Justice on them that shall by force of Armes endeavour the oppressing and bereaving of Religion and thir liberty at home' (238).[47]

While Hobbes and Milton differed in their politics, they agreed on the contribution of scriptural exegesis to the Civil War, and on the relevance of scriptural models of covenant to political contract. Both used scriptural covenant to underwrite their views of political contract and for both, as a result, prophecy or the interpretation of Scripture was a crucial political act. As Hobbes knew very well, Milton's republicanism was as much a product of his interpretation of the biblical covenants of Abraham and Moses as it was of his reading the ancients.[48] Thus he remarked in *Behemoth*, a history of the Civil War written in the 1660s, Christian sovereigns should exercise more control over preaching, since 'the interpretation of a verse in the Hebrew, Greek, or Latin Bible, is oftentimes the cause of civil war and the deposing and assassinating of God's annointed'.[49] *The Tenure of Kings and Magistrates* exemplifies this intersection of scriptural prophecy, sacred covenant and political contract in Milton's thought.

---

[46] See *TKM*, 194, against 'disputing presidents [precedents]' and Kerrigan, *Sacred Complex*, p. 94, quoted above, n. 34.

[47] As I have been suggesting all along, Milton's forceful interpretation of God's covenant as a political contract paradoxically provides a mirror image of the 'mingling of force and covenant' that royalists found so distasteful in Hobbes's *Leviathan*. Royalists critics of *Leviathan* were aware that the arguments Hobbes put forth to justify allegiance to the sovereign would work as well for Cromwell as for Charles I. Pocock makes this point about *Leviathan* in *Ancient Constitution*, p. 164.

[48] Classical republicanism of the seventeenth century has often been interpreted as a secular mode of political thought; for a more nuanced view see Blair Worden, 'Milton's Republicanism and the Tyranny of Heaven', in Gisela Bock, Quentin Skinner and Maurizio Viroli (eds.), *Machiavelli and Republicanism* (Cambridge, 1990), pp. 225–47; Worden, 'Classical Republicanism and the Puritan Revolution', in Hugh Lloyd-Jones, Valerie Pearl and Blair Worden (eds.), *History and Imagination* (London, 1981), pp. 182–200; and J. G. A. Pocock's revision of his own thesis in the introduction to his edition of *The Political Works of James Harrington* (Cambridge, 1977).

[49] Hobbes, *Behemoth, or the Long Parliament*, p. 144.

CHAPTER 6

Milton, Satan, Salmasius and Abdiel

Roger Lejosne

It makes as much sense to see Milton as an unconscious
monarchist as an unconscious diabolist, an adherent without
knowing it, not of the Devil's, but of the king's party. There are
certainly passages in *Paradise Lost* which invite a royalist
interpretation.

Thus William Myers in *Milton and Free Will*.[1] In the preceding pages,
Myers has been contrasting the allusiveness of Milton's expression of
republicanism in his later poems with the obvious royalism prevalent
in Heaven and the just as obvious 'likeness between Satan's and the
Good Old Cause',[2] in *Paradise Lost*.

There is nothing strikingly original in such observations, which
were first made ages ago, and have sometimes led readers to believe
that in *Paradise Lost* Milton reneged on his old principles and
consigned rebels and republicans, including Cromwell, the regicides
and perhaps his own former self, to Hell in company with Satan. Or
conversely that being himself an old unrepentant rebel he must have
had some sort of lurking sympathy for Satan's politics.

It will be my contention in this paper, not only that both
interpretations are misguided, but that Milton's treatment of God's
heavenly kingship and Satan's rebellion can be viewed as complementary elements in his republican strategy. In other words, I believe
that he made monarchy in Heaven justify republicanism on earth – so
that Myers's notion of Milton as an unconscious monarchist in fact
makes much less sense than Blake's remark about his being 'of the
Devil's party without knowing it', which at least did not invite a
directly political reading.[3]

---

[1] William Myers, *Milton and Free Will* (London, 1987), p. 233.
[2] *Ibid.*
[3] I have already submitted something similar – as hardly more than a suggestion – as long ago
as 1967 in a paper entitled 'Satan républicain', in J. Blondel (ed.), *Le Paradis perdu, 1667–1967*

It has always been obvious to everyone that Satan's speeches in the early stages of his rebellion, i.e. in Books v and vi of *Paradise Lost*, are full of arguments which Milton himself had used in various pamphlets. Even the first, the one Satan whispers into Beelzebub's ear – 'Sleep'st thou companion dear...'[4] – with its repetition of the phrases 'new laws' and 'new commands', echoes not only Milton's but all the English, and Scottish, Puritans' revulsion at the Laudian 'innovations' in the Church, and more generally the received idea that the hallmark of tyranny was the imposition of 'new laws' according to the whims of the tyrant, 'an arbitrary sway according to private will', as Milton had said in *An Apology against a Pamphlet* in 1642.[5] In the *Second Defence of the People of England*, he urged Cromwell to 'propose fewer new laws than you repeal old ones'.[6]

More characteristically Miltonic is Satan's speech to his troops, beginning magnificently with a rollcall of the angels' titles, 'Thrones, dominations, princedoms, virtues, powers', and ending with the proud assertion of their 'being ordained to govern, not to serve'.[7] This piece of oratory is entirely based on Milton's most cherished principles, those of human (here angelic) dignity and human (angelic) liberty. Those 'magnific titles', Satan says, and their bearers, are now 'eclipsed under the name / Of king anointed' (*PL*, v, 773, 776–7). Similarly, Milton had pointed out in *The Tenure of Kings and Magistrates* that divine right monarchy is incompatible with the dignity of the subject:

And [surely] no Christian Prince, not drunk with high mind ... would arrogate so unreasonably above human condition, or derogate so basely from a whole Nation of men his Brethren, as if for him only subsisting, and to serve his glory; valuing them in comparison of his owne brute will and pleasure, no more then so many beasts, or vermin under his Feet...[8]

Satan refuses to pay 'knee-tribute' or perform 'prostration vile' (*PL*, v, 782) to a new-fangled 'lord' – just as Milton had insisted, in *The Tenure of Kings and Magistrates* again, that 'Titles of Sov'ran Lord, natural Lord, and the like, are either arrogancies, or flatteries, not admitted by Emperours and Kings of best note',[9] and as he had, in *The Readie and Easie Way*, expressed his disgust at a monarch who 'will have little els to do, but ... to pageant himself up and down in progress among the perpetual bowings and cringings of an abject

(Paris, 1967), pp. 87–103 and again, more briefly, in my study of *La Raison dans l' Œuvre de John Milton* (Paris, 1981), pp. 339–41. Being partly dissatisfied with what I then wrote, I now want to have another, closer look at the matter.   [4] *PL*, v, 673–93.   [5] *CPW*, I, 946.   [6] *CPW*, ivi, 678.   [7] *PL*, v, 772–802.   [8] *CPW*, III, 204.   [9] *Ibid.*, 202.

people, on either side deifying and adoring him for nothing don that can deserve it'.[10] What Satan calls 'prostration vile' Milton had called 'court flatteries and prostrations'.[11] Incidentally, one of the Laudian 'innovations' most obnoxious to the Puritans, Milton included, was the obligation to bend the knee in front of an altar. In *Of Reformation*, Milton had denounced the corruption of the Roman Church in which the Eucharist, 'even that Feast of love and heavenly-admitted fellowship, the Seale of filiall grace became the Subject of horror, and glouting adoration, pageanted about, like a dreadfull Idol'.[12] Satan, then, is a good Puritan, both in politics and religion. But of course in Heaven politics and religion are one and the same thing.

When Satan suggests that 'better counsels might erect / Our minds and teach us to cast off this yoke' (*PL*, v, 785–6), one is tempted to think of the '*Norman* Yoke' so often execrated in revolutionary pamphlets, and when he asks 'Will you submit your necks, and choose to bend / The supple knee?' (*PL*, v, 787–8) one is reminded of Milton, in *The Readie and Easie Way*, deploring the readiness with which his countrymen were preparing 'basely and besottedly to run their necks again into the yoke which they have broken'.[13]

Of course, the angels whom Satan addresses are 'Natives and sons of heaven possessed before / By none' as the English were 'freeborn Englishmen'. 'And if not equal all', the angels are 'free, / Equally free; for orders and degrees / Jar not with liberty' (*PL*, v, 790–3) – which Milton would probably agree with, though he tended to think that *virtuous* men were more or less equal in dignity as well as free. Anyway, 'all men naturally were borne free', he wrote in *The Tenure of Kings and Magistrates*.[14] And in his first *Defence of the People of England* he had maintained that 'It is neither fitting nor proper for a man to be king unless he be far superior to the rest',[15] thus subscribing in advance to Satan's Aristotelian contention that no one 'can in reason ... or right assume / Monarchy over such as live by right / His equals' (*PL*, v, 794–7).

As for '*Christian* liberty', it implied for Milton that the good man did not need to obey any law but that of his own conscience: in *Christian Doctrine*, he quoted St Paul to the effect that 'there is no law for the righteous'.[16] So does Satan proclaim that the angels 'without law/ Err not' (*PL*, v, 798–9) – thus claiming for their reason, however, an infallibility which Milton would never attribute to human reason, even when assisted by divine grace.

[10] *CPW*, vii, 426.   [11] *Ibid.*, 428.   [12] *CPW*, i, 523.   [13] *CPW*, vii, 428.
[14] *CPW*, iii, 198.   [15] *CPW*, ivi, 366.   [16] *CPW*, vi, 529.

Lastly, Satan's ringing conclusion about 'those imperial titles which assert / Our being ordained to govern, not to serve' (*PL*, v, 801–2) closely parallels Milton's own assertion in *The Tenure of Kings and Magistrates* that man, as the image of God, was originally 'born to command and not to obey'.[17]

Now the faithful angel Abdiel stands up to rebut Satan's argument.[18] Satan, however, is such a flamboyant figure that the somewhat less arresting Abdiel usually receives less attention. He is generally assumed to be impeccably orthodox in his defence of heavenly monarchy, both political and theological, and that's that. And indeed orthodox he is – to the point of being positively Salmasian. If one reads Abdiel's speech just after studying Milton's political pamphlets in conjunction with Salmasius' *Defensio Regia*, Du Moulin's *Regii Sanguinis Clamor* and a few other royalist writings, one cannot but realize, with some amusement, that Milton deliberately made the steadfast angel repeat, not only the most common, standard royalist arguments, but some of Salmasius' own which had attracted his attention and could be made to fit into the context of *Paradise Lost*.

To begin with, and unsurprisingly enough, the Son of God is king by the grace of God, or rather, to quote Abdiel, by 'the just decree of God' (*PL*, v, 814), and to him all kingly honour is due. This is of course a royalist commonplace: Salmasius, among many others, had maintained that a denial of divine right amounted to opposition to God: 'kings are appointed by God', he wrote, 'and it is wrong to do violence to them, nor can this be done without opposing the will of God'.[19] This has already been confirmed in *Paradise Lost* by no less a person than God the Father himself:

> him [the Son] who disobeys
> Me disobeys, breaks union, and that day
> Cast out from God and blessed vision, falls
> Into utter darkness...[20]

No doubt thinking of the correspondences in the 'Great Chain of Being' between God, the sun in the sky and kings, Salmasius had said that 'kings are coeval with the sun's creation', a sentence quoted by Milton.[21] It is almost as if the poet had remembered it when he depicted the Son of God as the first anointed king – a theological commonplace – thus becoming guilty of a kind of submerged pun, in

---

[17] *CPW*, iii, 198–9. [18] *PL*, v, 809–48.
[19] *CPW*, ivii, 1007. For convenience's sake, I choose my quotations of Salmasius from the chapters translated by Kathryn A. McEuen for *CPW*, iv. [20] *PL*, v, 611–14.
[21] *CPW*, ivi, 326.

English although Salmasius' text was in Latin. However that may be, the phrase 'rightful king' (*PL*, v, 818) in Abdiel's speech may just possibly give a hint of the Son as 'lawful successor and heir', or 'rightful heir', as Salmasius would have said.[22]

Now 'Shalt thou give law to God?' (*PL*, v, 822) Abdiel asks, just as Salmasius had repeated again and again in his *Defensio Regia* that a king gives laws but does not receive them, that he judges but cannot be judged.[23] The parallel is all the more interesting as Salmasius' view of absolute monarchy was rather extreme – it made subjects little better than the king's slaves – while Abdiel's necessarily *is* extreme: what monarch can be more absolute than God Almighty?

The next item of royalist lore in Abdiel's speech might come from almost any seventeenth-century royalist pamphlet; it is a description of the Good King: 'by experience taught', Abdiel says,

> we know how good,
> And of our good, and of our dignity
> How provident he is, how far from thought
> To make us less, bent rather to exalt
> Our happy state... (*PL*, v, 826–30)

Milton himself had copied down a quotation from Sir Thomas Smith in his *Commonplace Book*, presumably around the year 1640, to the effect that a good king 'doth administer the com-welth by the laws of the same and by equity, and doth seeke the profit of the people as his owne'.[24] But this was the tritest of commonplaces.

Now back to Salmasius, in the seventh chapter of *Defensio Regia*, for a lesson in political mathematics:

Some adduce ... that the king is more powerful than individuals, but not more than all taken together. These things are ridiculous and untrue. If, strictly speaking, he has more power than individuals, does he not have more than two, three, ten, a hundred, a thousand, ten thousand? Why not more than one-half of the people? What if another part of the other half is added?[25]

Salmasius goes on like this for another page. Milton made fun of this arithmetic in the *Defensio*[26] and he had already, in *The Tenure of Kings and Magistrates*, expressed indignation at the idea that the people should be regarded as 'all in one body inferior to' the king 'single, which were a kinde of treason against the dignitie of mankind to affirm'.[27]

---

[22] *CPW*, ivi, 336 (quoted by Milton), ivii, 1006.   [23] *CPW*, ivii, 986, 1007, 1013.
[24] *CPW*, i, 443.   [25] *CPW*, ivii, 1020.   [26] *CPW*, ivi, 470.   [27] *CPW*, iii, 204.

And now listen to Abdiel:

> Thy self though great dost thou count,
> Or all angelic nature joined in one,
> Equal to him begotten Son...
>
> (*PL*, v, 833–5)

Nowhere is the brave angel so glaringly a disciple of Salmasius. Then Abdiel proceeds to add that by the Son,

> As by his Word the mighty Father made
> All things, even thee, and all the spirits of heaven
> By him created in their bright degrees... (*PL*, v,
>   836–8)

which introduces the heavenly counterpart of that favourite idea of Salmasius and most royalists, that a king is like a father, or indeed that he *is* a father, since kingship originated in fatherhood. In the *Eikon Basilike*, King Charles was called 'Father of [his] Countrie'.[28] So did Salmasius call a king 'the father of the country and the people' and theorize on the derivation of kingdoms from patriarchal families.[29] The full title of Du Moulin's *Clamor* was *Regii Sanguinis Clamor ad Coelum Adversus Parricidas Anglicanos*. Since he actually created the angels, the Son of God – the Word – is literally in the position of a father to them.

He also is their feudal lord, since he

> Crowned them with glory, and to their glory named
> Thrones, dominations, princedoms, virtues, powers,
> Essential powers...   (*PL*, v, 839–41)

From him they hold their titles and estates. Milton had long before, in *The Tenure of Kings and Magistrates*, said of an unaccountable king that 'we hold then our lives and estates, by the tenure of his meer grace and mercy, as from a God, not a mortal Magistrate, a position that none but Court Parasites or men besotted would maintain'.[30] The 'court parasite' Abdiel adds that the angels are somehow the Son's peers of the realm – 'since he the head / One of our number thus reduced becomes' (*PL*, v, 842–3) – and that the Son himself is 'the root and trunk of dignity' (as Du Moulin would have it),[31] or 'the fountain of honour': 'all honour to him done / Returns our own' (*PL*, v, 844–5). This last point is a neat reversal of Milton's rhetorical question in

---

[28] Quoted by Milton in *Eikonoklastes*, *CPW*, III, 543.   [29] *CPW*, IVii, 1019, 1027–8.
[30] *CPW*, III, 204.   [31] *CPW*, IVii, 1058. The translator is Paul W. Blackford.

Eikonoklastes: 'And what were [the king's] most rightful honours, but
the peoples gift, and the investment of that lustre, Majesty, and
honour, which for the public good & no otherwise, redounds from a
whole Nation into one person?'[32]

Satan's 'haughty' answer is rather like a miniature first Defence of
the angelic people.[33] He denies that the angels were ever created,
thus effectively, *like Milton*, denying that the king is father of his
subjects: 'We know no time when we were not as now;/ Know none
before us...' (*PL*, v, 859–60). The people then existed before the
king. As Milton would say, in the *Defensio*: 'Our fathers begot us, but
our kings did not.'[34] Understandably enough, Satan does not add
with Milton 'and it is we, rather, who created the king' – since, as
events are going to show, he intends to set himself up as king in God's
stead and does not wish to weaken his future position.

God, then, is not a father, but a king, whose power and legitimacy
are therefore purely *political*, not natural, and consequently can be
challenged:

> Our puissance is our own, our own right hand
> Shall teach us highest deeds, by proof to try
> Who is our equal: then thou shalt behold
> Whether by supplication we intend
> Address, and to begirt the almighty throne
> Beseeching or besieging.   (*PL*, v, 864–9)

Thus did Milton in *The Tenure of Kings and Magistrates* point out that
by disobeying Charles and making war on him the Presbyterians had
'in plain termes unking'd the King'.[35] Similarly, after Salmasius had
defined the phrase 'royal power' as 'that which is highest and unique
in the state, over which no other is recognized', Milton had answered
tartly: 'Names give precedence to facts, and it is not our business to
worry about names when we have done away with the reality.'[36]
Royal power had been put to the test, defeated and destroyed, which
made Salmasius' definition pointless. This is precisely what Satan
intends – to do away with the reality of divine power without caring
for words such as 'almighty', for instance, which in his speech must be
understood as ironical.

The dispute between Satan and Abdiel is carried over to Book vi,
when they meet again on the battlefield. But by now they both seem

---

[32] *CPW*, iii, 524.   [33] *PL*, v, 853–70.   [34] *CPW*, ivi, 327.
[35] *CPW*, iii, 230.   [36] *CPW*, ivi, 454–5. Cf. *Royal Defence, ibid.*, 986.

more or less to have run out of arguments. Abdiel's pondering on 'strength' and 'virtue' – 'wherefore should not strength and might / There fail where virtue fails'[37] – reminds me of Salmasius' punning opposition of VIS and IVS, might and right, in *Defensio Regia*.[38] Anyway the issue of force versus right was one of those which had most exercised political writers on both sides: witness John Goodwin's well-known 1648 pamphlet *Might and Right Well Met*, in which the author justified Pride's Purge.

More significantly, perhaps, Satan still has a splendidly Miltonic few lines to deliver:

> At first I thought that liberty and heaven
> To heavenly souls had been all one; but now
> I see that most through sloth had rather serve,
> Ministering spirits, trained up in feast and song...[39]

This could easily pass for Milton's last words on the English revolution, and many parallels can be found in his prose works: in *Of Reformation*, in the very first lines of *The Tenure of Kings and Magistrates*, *Eikonoklastes*, the first *Defence of the People of England*, the *Second Defence*, *The Readie and Easie Way* and even the *History of Britain*.[40] It was a recurrent idea in Milton that vice and effeminacy render a majority of the people unfit for liberty, and that tyrants not only will take advantage of it, but will actually encourage debauchery in the people.

In his answer, Abdiel manages to be both Salmasian and Miltonic at the same time, since the burden of his speech – it is no servitude 'to serve whom God ordains / Or nature; God and nature bid the same'[41] – could be approved by either controversialist, on condition of implying widely different versions of the law of Nature: one, Salmasius', which regarded human monarchies as conformable to a universal natural rule, as mirror images of God's supremacy, and the other, Milton's, which recognized among men no other natural superiority but that of wisdom. Then Abdiel adds:

> Reign thou in hell thy kingdom, let me serve
> In heaven God ever blest, and his divine
> Behests obey, worthiest to be obeyed,
> Yet chains in hell, not realms expect...[42]

---

[37] *PL*, VI, 116–17.   [38] See *CPW*, IVi, 518–19.   [39] *PL*, VI, 164–7. See also IVii, 941–5.
[40] *Seriatim*: *CPW*, I, 572, 588–9; III, 190, 581; IVi, 457, 683–4; VII, 455; V, 402–3.
[41] *PL*, VI, 175–6.   [42] *PL*, VI, 183–6.

Thus had Salmasius pointed out that the leaders of the army had appropriated the whole power and made themselves 'both judges and kings and anything else that is supreme in ruling, even to the appearance and effect of tyranny'.[43] Thus also had he everywhere insisted, like nearly all true royalists, that a king's subjects are his servants and not he the servant of the people as was the doctrine of the English 'fanatics', and of Milton. Thus, lastly, had all English royalists – Du Moulin, for instance – called for the 'vengeance of heaven' against those 'gallows-birds' Milton and the English 'parricides'.[44]

So much for the Satan–Abdiel encounter, which appears as a compendium, an epitome of the pamphlet wars of the revolution and in particular of the Salmasius–Milton controversy.

In order to make the picture more complete, I must call to mind those speeches in Book I of *Paradise Lost* in which Satan describes himself as the irreconcilable foe of a heavenly tyrant 'upheld by old repute,/ Consent or custom'.[45] Of course, 'consent' and 'custom' were both standard justifications of the monarchy – and 'custom' was an old enemy of Milton's, at least since his first anti-prelatical pamphlet, *Of Reformation*, in which he wrote: 'Custome without Truth is but agednesse of Error.'[46] I must also point out that anti-tyrannical, anti-monarchical if seldom overtly republican sentiment is not in *Paradise Lost* the exclusive property of Satan and his confederates. Near the end of Book IV, Gabriel accuses Satan:

> And thou sly hypocrite, who now wouldst seem
> Patron of liberty, who more than thou
> Once fawned, and cringed, and servilely adored
> Heaven's awful monarch? Wherefore but in hope
> To dispossess him, and thy self to reign?[47]

In the *Defensio*, Milton had charged St Ambrose of Milan with substantially the same sin: 'It was his wish that all other men be servants of the emperor, that he might make the emperor his servant',[48] which somehow makes Gabriel's taunt a covert reminder of the fact that for Milton ecclesiastical and political tyranny were inseparable: priests abet the tyrant in order to establish their own tyranny. In Milton's mind, Archbishop Laud and King Charles

---

[43] *CPW*, IVii, 991.   [44] *CPW*, IVii 1078–81.
[45] See especially *PL*, I, 92–124, 245–63, 637–49.   [46] *CPW*, I, 561.
[47] *PL*, IV, 957–61. *Pace* Myers, *Milton and Free Will*, p. 232, these are *not* 'royalist reproaches'.
[48] *CPW*, IVi, 393.

had been a case in point.

The character who in Books xi and xii of *Paradise Lost* occasionally expresses anti-monarchical sentiment is the angel Michael, who even goes out of his way to refute, not Salmasius, but that other well-known upholder of absolute monarchy, Sir Robert Filmer. In his *Patriarcha* – not printed until 1680 but widely circulated in manuscript long before – Filmer contended not only that kingship stemmed from fatherhood, but that kings were literally the heirs of Adam's original authority and power (even of life and death) over his children and descendants. Now, in *Paradise Lost*, Michael, speaking of the garden of Eden which Adam is soon to leave, says:

> this had been
> Perhaps thy capital seat, from whence had spread
> All generations, and had hither come
> From all the ends of the earth, to celebrate
> And reverence thee their great progenitor.[49]

We should notice that no mention is made of Adam's 'authority' or 'power': in an unfallen world, he might have been an object of reverence, no doubt, but not a king. But then perhaps in a *fallen* world, kingship might become necessary, and who better qualified than Adam? Michael speaks on:

> But this pre-eminence thou hast lost, brought down
> To dwell on even ground now with thy sons...[50]

Well, it seems that after all Adam held no peculiar 'pre-eminence' and was his sons' equal, so that Sir Robert's most distinctive tenet is demolished. Michael is going to explain in the next Book that the first man

> who not content
> With fair equality, fraternal state,
> Will arrogate dominion undeserved
> Over his brethren[51]

was Nimrod, with Adam indignantly claiming that 'man over men' God 'made not lord'.[52] Incidentally, Salmasius also explained that 'Nembrot was the first to extend his power by arms', with only a very faint hint of disapproval.[53]

---

[49] *PL*, xi, 342–6.
[50] *PL*, xi, 347–8. Myers, p. 199, calls this 'a strong republican point' but misses the allusion to Filmer.   [51] *PL*, xii, 25–8.   [52] *PL*, xii, 69–70.   [53] *CPW*, ivii, 1027.

In *Paradise Lost*, Nimrod's kingship is explicitly contrasted with both 'paternal rule' – which obviously is not inconsistent with 'fair equality' and 'fraternal state' – and God-given dominion 'over beast, fish, fowl'. It is also made clear that only God can be called 'lord'.[54] It seems, then, that republicanism is not quite so devilish as might have been surmised from Books v and vi.

One last point – but a vital one, though it hardly appears in *Paradise Lost*: it does not need to. In the doggerel sonnet he prefixed to the *Basilikon Doron* in 1599, James VI of Scotland had said:

> God gives not Kings the stile of Gods in vaine,
> For on his throne his Scepter doe they sway.

The idea that kings are to be regarded as veritable gods was not new. It was taken up again by many supporters of the monarchy, though Salmasius himself, however stoutly he supported divine right and maintained that the king was subject to no law, seems to have stopped just short of doing so. Anyway, the idea was particularly obnoxious to Milton. In his *Observations upon the Articles of Peace with the Irish Rebels*, he asked 'why any mortal man for the good and wellfare of his brethren beeing made a King, should . . . make himself a God, exalted above Law'.[55] And when it seemed to him that in the *Eikon Basilike* King Charles laid claim to 'as much obedience and subjection, as we may all pay to God', that is, in his eyes, desired 'not less then to be a God', he called it sacrilegious.[56] Even more significantly, in the *Defensio* he wrote:

Monarchy has indeed been praised by many famous men, provided that the sole ruler is the best of men and fully deserving of the crown; otherwise monarchy sinks most rapidly into the worst tyranny. As to your saying it was 'patterned on the example of the one God,' who, in fact, is worthy of holding on earth power like that of God but some person who far surpasses all others and even resembles God in goodness and wisdom? The only such person, as I believe, is the son of God whose coming we look for.[57]

'The son of God.' Perhaps now we can understand better what Milton was up to when he made Abdiel a kind of celestial Salmasius and Satan a hellish Milton.[58] I believe he thought he could rely on his

---

[54] *PL*, xii, 24, 67–8, 70–1.   [55] *CPW*, iii, 307–8.   [56] *Eikonoklastes*, *CPW*, iii, 532–3.
[57] *CPW*, ivi, 427–8.
[58] The few studies focused on Abdiel's role which have been written since Mason Tung's 'The Abdiel Episode: A Contextual Reading', *Studies in Philology*, 62 (1965), 595–609, invariably concentrate on the moral and theological issues. One of the latest examples is Charles W. Durham's article on 'Abdiel, Obedience, and Hierarchy in *Paradise Lost*', *Milton Quarterly*, 26

'fit readers' to remember the controversies of the revolution. There was even a good probability that at least some of them would have read Salmasius' *Defensio Regia* and his own *Defences of the People of England,* and that they would be struck by the similarity of the dispute in Heaven. If the sole truly legitimate king was 'the son of God', then whatever Salmasius and the other royalists said of earthly kings was true of him, but him only. He only was king 'by the just decree of God' and could require kingly honours; he only could give laws – even 'new laws' – to his creatures, who of course were his servants; he only was in the position of both father and legitimate feudal lord, and was the true fountain of honour. He only was in power and dignity truly and naturally superior to all his subjects taken in the aggregate. To crown all, the Crucifixion had been the only true regicide, and indeed a parricide. In other words, Salmasius was right and Milton wrong in Heaven, but only in Heaven. And *consequently* Milton and the republicans were right on earth, where no man could rightly claim divine honours. This was corroborated by the almost explicit republicanism of Michael and Adam in the last two Books of *Paradise Lost.* In this way, Milton managed to overturn the age-old analogy between God and king, and make the universal hierarchy irrelevant to human politics, while the inadvertent reader might see nothing in it but perfectly orthodox and harmless theology, or even a confirmation of his own royalist opinions.

(1992), 15–19, which points out the anti-hierarchical implications of Abdiel's courageous stand against his superior, Satan. This may well have been part of Milton's meaning, although Abdiel, a seraph, cannot rank far beneath his leader in the angelic hierarchies, contrary to Durham's assumption (borrowed from Stella Purce Revard, *The War in Heaven: Paradise Lost and the Tradition of Satan's Rebellion* (Ithaca, 1980), pp. 63, 241). I would rather lay stress on the *loneliness* of Abdiel's stand, which puts him in the same company with such isolated heroes, so dear to the poet's heart, as Samson, Jesus, and no doubt Milton himself (see my *La Raison dans l'Œuvre de John Milton,* pp. 172–4). In this respect, Abdiel is very *unlike* Salmasius.

CHAPTER 7

Paradise Lost *as a republican 'tractatus theologico-politicus'*

Armand Himy

My purpose is to examine how on a few points *Paradise Lost* absorbs and reflects Milton's political experience. Even though *Paradise Lost* is not necessarily a political poem, it was written fairly late by a man who had a tremendous political experience that was both practical and theoretical. In my opinion, when politics are discussed in the first books, it is not so much the question of republicanism that is dealt with as the questions of government and of the source and foundation of political authority. It is only fairly late in the poem, in Books XI and XII, when the postlapsarian world is evoked by Michael, that indications are given on republicanism. And Milton's conclusion, as I see it, is that Christian liberty and republicanism cannot be separated.

Paradise Lost, as a literary work then, has its proper code and language. To adapt Pocock's vocabulary,[1] I will say that only after we have understood what means Milton had of saying anything can we understand what he meant to say, or what he succeeded in saying. The languages in *Paradise Lost* are multiple: literary, theological, political, and even to some extent historical. Though my purpose is not to study the various languages of the work, I must nonetheless recall the limits within which Milton's conceptions were at least theoretically framed, and then focus on some of the main paradigms utilized so as to see what bearing they may have on the question of republicanism.

The means Milton had of saying anything, imposed upon him by the literary genre, are the language of accommodation 'likening spiritual to corporeal forms',[2] and the language of indirection as defined by Christopher Ricks: 'Milton writes at his very best when something prevents him from writing with total directness.'[3] If accommodation

---

[1] J. G. A. Pocock, *Politics, Language and Time* (New York, 1971), p. 25.
[2] *Paradise Lost*, v, 570–6. On the question of accommodation, cf. *Christian Doctrine*, *CPW*, VI, 133.
[3] Christopher Ricks, *Milton's Grand Style* (Oxford, 1967), pp. 149–50.

serves as a kind of link between heaven and earth, indirection makes flexibility the rule when theology and literature, poetic and political style, are all involved at once. Milton's language is involuted; I am not thinking of involved grammatical style – although this is sometimes the case – but of the process of building language into language so as to create levels of meaning, or even so as to make a running commentary with the somewhat haughty and sarcastic father-figure of Milton bending over your shoulder. And this brings me to Milton's sarcastic temper, mentioned by Aubrey, in his *Life* of Milton: sarcasm that often leads to ambivalence, amphibology, and irony[4] which usually consists in saying one thing and meaning another, and in drawing unexpected conclusions from traditional premises.

Now the models or paradigms utilized by Milton for his plot are more or less those of the Christian epic – the monarchy of God, the role of Christ, the war in Heaven and the vision of the future. A few remarks on them will be necessary as they are utilized as foraging tools that help him to explore the matter of government, be it heavenly or terrestrial.

Paradise Lost is of course based on the Bible, which means that the work is set in a biblical time-scheme from the Creation to eschatology: it is the time-scheme of revealed history, both divine and human, within which Christian thought is conducted. It is only within such a time-scheme that we may envisage Milton's political thought. Government is the means through which history is forged under heavenly control. In *Paradise Lost*, the form of government is monarchy. This gives Milton the occasion to analyse the nature of power and its foundation. His arguing with himself results from the criticism of monarchy and the defence of God as monarch.

Historians generally agree that, in his early prose works, Milton did not oppose monarchy as such but only absolute and hereditary monarchy.[5] In *Paradise Lost* the criticism of monarchy is systematized. It rests upon an identification of monarchy with tyranny developed as a diptych: Satan as emperor, God as King.

On Satan as emperor, the main themes are constituted by historical

---

[4] Cf. Douglas Bush, 'Ironic and Ambiguous Allusion in *Paradise Lost*', *Journal of English and Germanic Philology*, 60 (1961), 631–40.

[5] 'This is the sum of their royal service to Kings; yet these are the men that stil cry the King, the King, the Lords Anointed. We grant it, and wonder how they came to light upon any thing so true...', *CPW*, I, 859. On this question, cf. Arthur E. Barker, *Milton and the Puritan Dilemma, 1641–1660* (Toronto, 1942), ch. 8.

archetypes and recurrent emblems such as the oriental tyrant and barbarous savagery, the Roman emperor and despotism, feudalism and warriors, together with remarks on the Roman Republic felt as irreparable loss. One of the best symbols of tyranny is the building of the triumphal arch in *Paradise Lost* (x, 298–304) which reflects the corrupt aspect of the empire, a society of soldiers devoted to pagan deities.[6]

The portrait of God as king and as tyrant is the subject of considerable debate. According to Satan, the origin of God is not clearly established. His fame may result from custom or tradition ('upheld by old repute / Consent or custom' (*PL*, i, 639–40)), unless his supremacy was gained through violence or favoured by chance ('upheld by strength or chance or fate' (*PL*, i, 133)). After his conquest, the new tyrant, as a Roman emperor, aimed at nothing less than deification. The full implications of tyranny and the steps leading to it are carefully discussed. Marked as it is by an insatiable thirst for power, tyranny aims at subordinating new territories still unexplored, including the empire of Chaos, through actions or decrees that are arbitrary. If Satan's attitude is seen as uncontrolled hubris, God's omnipotence cannot fail to lapse into violence. Power is submitted to the passions of power, autocracy engenders cringing vassals or slaves, who paradoxically keep faith in the pseudo-liberty bestowed upon them. Sovereignty is thus turned into a personal prerogative of the tyrant.

Satan's views on the tyranny of God serve several purposes. The immediate one is to illustrate Satan's lies. Accommodation and indirection, accepted as methods of interpretation from the outset, can leave no doubt as to what Milton means: God is no tyrant. But the description of tyranny is necessary to show what should be avoided in politics. Human kingship cannot fail to lapse into tyranny. The ironical tone reserved for the origins of God ceases to be ironical when applied to human kings. On the other hand, the text denounces the cringing kind of believer who can hardly imagine what true love or free worship voluntarily accepted, not imposed, can be. The criticism of the court of Heaven, if not that of the monarch, can be literally accepted. It opens the way to the worship of Christ as service of true love, and as genuine theocracy as opposed to tyranny.

After the ironical presentation of God as tyrant, the refutation

---

[6] Cf. Stevie Davies, *Images of Kingship in 'Paradise Lost': Milton's Politics and Christian Liberty* (Columbia, Missouri, 1983), pp. 94–5.

characteristically turns things round and asserts that the main foundation of power resides in the virtue of the subjects. Reverence and worship transmute fear into love, submission into active participation, individualism into union. Worship is an art of positive transfiguration. He who cannot obey cannot be free and consequently cannot command. Worship must be the bond between the Creator and the creatures. ('Him to love is to obey' (*PL*, VIII, 634); 'Whom to obey is happiness entire' (*PL*, VI, 741).) Obedience is not subjection. It is the condition for redemption. Authority then is not a simple political concept; it is a metaphysical prerequisite on which ontology is founded. The Pauline conception constitutes the traditional background (Romans 13:1). After all, the etymological root of hierarchy is *hieros*, 'sacred'. Obedience to hierarchy is religious service. *Paradise Lost* obviously rests upon a universe with a transcendent and immanent God as the fountain of all blessings. And this remains valid whatever the form of government. The commonwealth cannot lapse into tyranny if it is a Chistian commonwealth; the virtue of the subjects remains the fundamental issue.

We may infer from this that a commonwealth must be preferred to a monarchy, a view based on Milton's interpretation of history. When they left Egypt, the Hebrews, following the counsel of Moses, decided to transfer his power to no mortal; hence the foundation of theocracy, with the consequence that divine law and positive law became one and the same thing. Milton thinks that the adoption of a monarchical system later on by the Hebrews constituted a regression, as the only genuine monarchy is the monarchy of Christ.[7] Milton, on this question, shares the opinion of most of his anti-royalist contemporaries, and more particularly the millenarians whose doctrine was founded upon Daniel 7 and Revelations 20–1.[8]

In *Paradise Lost*, then, the tyranny of God denounced by Satan certainly casts light upon the fact that a human monarchy, though not the monarchy of God, leads inevitably to tyranny. However, I must now examine the second aspect of the monarchy of Heaven, the monarchy of Christ.

---

[7] '... who, in fact, is worthy of holding on earth power like that of God but some person who far surpasses all others and even resembles God in goodness and wisdom? The only such person, as I believe, is the son of God whose coming we look for'. *A Defence of the People of England, CPW*, IVI, 427–8.

[8] Compare the words of John Archer in 1642 quoted in E. L. Tuveson, *Millennium and Utopia* (New York, 1964), p. 86: 'All Princes shall fall by degrees to tyrannie and oppression, and enslaving their subjects ... Christ having a purpose to swallow all kingly power...'

The reign of the Son must be examined on two grounds: first as a reign marked by features different from those of the reign of the Father, and second as a monarchy in which servile service is excluded. The conception of the monarchy of Heaven is best understood only after a full analysis of the role of the Son and of his exaltation. Milton's argument is complicated by this.

> Hear my decree, which unrevoked shall stand.
> This day I have begot whom I declare
> My only Son, and on this holy hill
> Him have anointed, whom ye now behold
> At my right hand; your head I him appoint;
>
> . . .
>
>   him who disobeys
> Me disobeys, breaks union, and that day
> Cast out from God and blessed vision, falls
> Into utter darkness . . .   (*PL*, v, 602–14)

This sort of presentation of the elevation of Christ is not quite traditional – rather is it 'a theological fiction' according to Maurice Kelley – even though some critics have tried to establish its implications.[9] Whatever the source may be, the presentation remains typically Miltonic in its utilization of the principle of analogy or proportion:[10] *Paradise Lost* from beginning to end is based on the opposition image/idol, image of God opposed to *eidolon* (false image).[11] The Son of God is 'image of thee in all things' (*PL*, vi, 7) Satan is *eidolon*, 'Idol of majesty divine' (*PL*, vi, 101); hence a conception of the universe founded on the Word:

> . . . Son who art alone
> My word, my wisdom, and effectual might.
>   (*PL*, iii, 169–70)
>
> . . . begotten Son, by whom
> As by his Word the mighty Father made
> All things . . .   (*PL*, v, 835–7)

[9] Maurice Kelley, *This Great Argument* (Gloucester, Mass., 1962), p. 105. Christopher Hill, *Milton and the English Revolution* (London, 1977), p. 367 notes that 'The exaltation of the Son is one of Milton's inventions, and it appears to be a late insertion in the epic.' On the sources of the episode, see Stella Purce Revard, *The War in Heaven: Paradise Lost and the Tradition of Satan's Rebellion* (Ithaca, 1980), pp. 57–8.

[10] On such questions, cf. Etienne Gilson, *Le Thomisme* (Paris, 1948), p. 154: 'L'être des créatures n'est qu'une imitation de l'Etre divin . . . Si les créatures sont, de par leur origine radicale, des similitudes, il faut s'attendre que l'analogie explique la structure de l'univers comme elle en explique la création.'

[11] On this, Armand Himy, *Pensée, mythe et structure dans 'Paradise Lost'* (Villeneuve d'Ascq, 1977), ch. 8.

> ... true liberty
> ... which always with right reason dwells
> Twinned, and from her hath no dividual being...
>
> *(PL*, xii, 83–5)

The Word (*logos*), Wisdom (sapience), true (or Christian) liberty and right Reason are thus united in the person of the Son. Adam is integrated into this hierarchy: 'in his own image he /Created thee, in the image of God' (*PL*, vii, 526–7).

However, two consequences result from this decree: the rebellion of Satan and the Fall of Man. These are theological issues, but they have a far-reaching political aftermath in the poem. Let us examine first the rebellion of Satan and the war in Heaven that follows it. Milton at this stage took a number of decisions, and adopted a more radical perspective. He himself admits that his song is 'adventurous... / That with no middle flight intends to soar' (*PL*, i, 13–14). It was traditionally held that Michael opposed and defeated Lucifer[12] but Milton displaced Michael in favour of the Son of God (*PL*, vi, 671–866).[13] The battle is at first conducted by Michael and lasts three days; as it is not decisive, God finally asks the Son to settle the matter. The Son declares:

> Therefore to me their doom he hath assigned;
> That they may have their wish, to try with me
> In battle which the stronger proves, they all,
> Or I alone against them, since by strength
> They measure all...   *(PL*, vi, 817–21)

As he is the Word, and Truth, his intervention can only mean – especially if we keep in mind that he is alone (an adaptation and a parody of traditional single combat) – that the intervention of the embodiment of Truth must be sufficient to rout the enemies of Truth and dispel Satan's foggy sophistry. Of course, we may wonder why the demonstration of such a triumph of truth is illustrated by a battle:

> ... to subdue
> By force, who reason for their law refuse,
> Right reason for thir law, and for their king
> Messiah, who by right of merit reigns.
>
> *(PL*, vi, 40–3)

---

[12] C. A. Patrides, *Milton and the Christian Tradition* (Oxford, 1966), pp. 260–1.
[13] *Christian Doctrine, CPW*, vi, 347.

Even if Milton's devastating irony is hovering over the battlefield ('since by strength/They measure all' (*PL*, VI, 820–1)), Milton is quite aware of the difficulty created by one of his codes (the language of accommodation). Satan declares:

> ... who overcomes
> By force, hath overcome but half his foe.
>   (*PL*, I, 648–9)

To this, Book XII echoing Book VI, Milton offers a commentary:

> Dream not of their fight,
> As of a duel...
>   ... nor so is overcome
> Satan, whose fall from heaven, a deadlier bruise,
> Disabled not to give thee thy death's wound:
> Which he, who comes thy saviour, shall recure,
> Not by destroying Satan, but his works
> In thee and in thy seed...   (*PL*, XII, 386–95)

a commentary which practically reduces the language of accommodation to a dream. If the duel between Christ and Satan is an illusion or 'dream', the reader is invited, as in the analysis of the tyranny of God, to seek elsewhere the meaning of this conflict. The clue will not be given by the factual details of the war; the heart of the matter lies in the debate, in the ideas bandied about, when Satan asserts he also is a son of God, and therefore may pretend to equality with Christ, or to equal promotion. The question of the tyranny of God, through indirection, brought our attention to focus on the tyranny of human kingdoms and on the duties of man (which suggests that a society which is free must be made up of individuals with obligations). In like manner, the analysis of the elevation of Christ leads us from a pseudo-conflict between Christ and Satan to the question of equality (are individuals equal?). The theological questions are not questions which concern Heaven only. Milton, like God, never forgets the world of men. Theological paradigms, likening things heavenly to things corporeal, are indirect descriptions of human situations and problems.

Let us then examine the question of equality. As we have seen, there is a foundation laid by Christ, but history must continue the process of the unification of truth. Satan, once he has rejected the principle of the foundation laid down by God, gives his own definition of liberty, and a new debate is started:

> ... ye know your selves
> Natives and sons of heaven possessed before
> By none, and if not equal all, yet free,
> Equally free; for orders and degrees
> Jar not with liberty, but well consist.
>
> (*PL*, v, 789–93)

All men are not equal, but there is equality in freedom. Satan apparently means that each individual has potentialities that can be actualized without reference to a model, which implies a rejection of the image model, and of the Christocentric conception. If absence of equality appears in such a perspective, this is due to the limits of the actualization of such potentialities. This should not entail submission to a hierarchy. We have then a classical topos.[14]

This must be examined in the light of Milton's prose works, so as to see what evolution can be discerned in works written before *Paradise Lost*. In his *Art of Logic* Milton wrote:

Singular things, or individuals, as they are commonly called, have their own singular and proper forms; certainly they differ in number among themselves, which no one denies. But what does it mean for things to differ among themselves, if not to differ by reason of their singular forms? For number, as Scaliger correctly says, is a property consequent upon essence. Therefore things which differ in number also differ in essence, and never do things differ in number without also differing in essence. *Here let the Theologians take notice.*[15]

Such a view, even if we hold that Milton is not seriously influenced by Ramist logic, shows at any rate that the single character of individuality always fascinated him. When Satan in the above passage of *Paradise Lost* (v, 789ff) emphasizes equality in liberty for individuals, the principle of the singularity of each one lies at the core of his conception.

The younger Milton, in his *Prolusions*, upheld the traditional interpretation of the nature of man: 'It is, I think, a belief familiar and generally accepted that the great Creator of the world, while constituting all else fleeting and perishable, infused into man, besides what was mortal, a certain divine spirit, a part of Himself.'[16] Such a divine spirit infused into man certainly acounts not only for his

---

[14] On the refusal to admit the election of the leader of the group, there is the classic text of Numbers 16:3: 'And they gathered themselves together against Moses and against Aaron, and said unto them, Ye take too much upon you, seeing all the congregation are holy, every one of them, and the Lord is among them: wherefore then lift ye up yourselves above the congregation of the Lord?'　　[15] *Art of Logic, CPW*, VIII, 233. Italics in the text.

[16] *CPW*, I, 291.

immortality, but also for the single specificity of each spirit. Otherwise, what would immortality devoid of singleness amount to? Later on, it seems (the entry in *Christian Doctrine* cannot be properly dated) Milton sounded more reticent: 'We may . . . be absolutely sure . . . that when God breathed that breath of life into man, he did not make him a sharer in any thing divine, any part of the divine essence, as it were. He imparted to him only something which was proportionate to divine virtue.'[17] Although the last sentence is not quite clear, proportion or analogy apparently remains the main hinge in Milton's thought.

In *Paradise Lost*, with the consequences of the fall of man now being examined, Milton is even more vocal:

> Why should not man,
> Retaining still divine similitude
> In part, from such deformities be free,
> And for his maker's image sake exempt?
>   Their maker's image, answered Michael, then
> Forsook them . . .
> Therefore so abject is their punishment,
> Disfiguring not God's likeness, but their own,
> Or if his likeness, by themselves defaced
> While they pervert pure nature's healthful rules . . .
>   (*PL*, xi, 511–23)

Apparently analogy is obscured, the Maker's image having deserted man. The rule of nature is perverted to sickness. How is this made compatible with the possibility of the exercise of government?

Milton makes it clear that the Gospel has abolished the whole Mosaic law, the ceremonial, the judicial, and even the moral law. 'But in reality the law, that is the substance of the law, is not broken by this abolition. On the contrary its purpose is attained in that love of God and of our neighbor which is born of faith, through the spirit.'[18] We are at the heart of Milton's conception of liberty, which rests upon the abolition of outward restraints only so that an inward control may take their place.

> The law of God exact he shall fulfil
> Both by obedience and by love, though love
> Alone shall fulfil the law . . . (*PL*, xii, 402–4)

Milton here reverts to the law of God.

---

[17] *CPW*, vi, 317.   [18] *Christian Doctrine, CPW*, vi, 531.

As we have seen before, the outcome of the fight against Satan is almost irrelevant since the worm is undying (*PL*, vi, 739). The duties of man come first, and his conversion is the main objective. It is as if at this stage Milton repeated his famous

> Solicit not thy thoughts with matters hid,
> Leave them to God above, him serve and fear.
> (*PL*, viii, 167–8)

The decree of God then gives the general orientation; it rests on Christ as King and Messiah and as embodying right reason, but it cannot be interpreted as barring the way to human reflection and action. Satan's objections to the elevation of the Son, followed by the War in Heaven, are thus played down and the debate on equality is substituted. The only possibility left, in the fallen world (i.e. the world of history and politics), of recapturing the true spirit of the decree of God, lies in continuing the work of the unification of truth, under the guidance of Christ, without, however, knowing exactly how truth may be unified. This is confirmed in *Areopagitica*, in which the myth of Osiris, coupled with the myth of Orpheus, relates how the dismembered body of Truth is reconstituted; the parallel with the role of Christ suggests the divine character of the edification of such a temple of the Lord: 'out of many moderat varieties and brotherly dissimilitudes that are not vastly disproportionall arises the goodly and the gracefull symmetry that commends the whole pile and structure'.[19]

The theological issues lead us to the following four conclusions. First, Milton's treatment of the tyranny of God is ironical. The sloth of men, and their readiness to serve rather than be free, is Milton's main theme when he deals with the question of the tyranny of God. Next, the elevation of Christ and the war in Heaven that follows help Milton establish the full implications of the image system. If men choose Christian liberty, and Christ as true king, the definition of 'Imitatio Christi' is made more precise. This could not be done in the first part dealing with God as King. Thirdly, Satan rejects the image system. But the problem posed then is the problem of equality. Who can be an image, or a true image? What happens if, through two falls, Satan loses his lustre, and man becomes a degraded image? Finally, the conditions in history are described with the use of a secularized concept, the concept of the law of nature.

[19] *CPW*, ii, 555.

Milton's shift in attitude – and his manipulation of the language of accommodation and of the War in Heaven – reflects a return to realism. Realism here does not mean that he considers theological issues as useless abstractions. Realism on the contrary builds up the bridge binding together theology and history. History becomes his new preoccupation: after the law of God he must pass on to the law of nature. The foundation of power must now be re-examined in the light of the law of nature in terms that are in many respects classic ones. The origin of government in human history directly results from the Fall, the main source of divisions between men, which must inevitably lead to violence and destruction. Men 'foreseeing that such courses must needs tend to the destruction of them all, they agreed by common league to bind each other from mutual injury and joyntly to defend themselves against any that gave disturbance and opposition to such agreement. Hence came Citties, Townes and Commonwealths.'[20] For Milton, the structure of government should be inspired by the directly ordained divine code God gave to Moses on Sinai – the Ten Commandments, and the Mosaic laws, some religious, but others 'such as appertain / To civil justice' (*PL*, xii, 230–1). In the seventy elders of the magistracy devised by Moses as a sort of senate (*PL*, xii, 226) established 'Through the twelve tribes, to rule by laws ordained', historians have seen a source for the Great Council proposed in the *Readie and Easie Way*. Milton describes this kind of ruling as follows:

They knew the people of *England* to be a free people; themselves the representers of that freedom ... therefor not bound by any statute of preceding Parlaments, but by the law of nature only, which is the only law of laws truly and properly to mankinde fundamental; the beginning and the end of all Government; to which no Parlament or people that will throughly reforme, but may and must have recourse.[21]

Such a passage establishes the articulation between the law of God and the law of nature. We must try to see how such an articulation is established in the text of the poem. Milton in Book xii describes the conditions in which the law was bestowed upon men. Although the text, based on Exodus, is fairly long, it must be quoted, as Milton's terrestrial politics are founded upon it:

[20] *The Tenure of Kings and Magistrates, CPW*, iii, 199.
[21] *The Readie and Easie Way to Establish a Free Commonwealth, CPW*, vii, 411–13.

> the race elect
> Safe towards Canaan from the shore advance
> Through the desert wild, not the readiest way,
>
> ...
>
> This also shall they gain by their delay
> In the wide wilderness, there they shall found
> Their government, and their great senate choose
> Through the twelve tribes, to rule by laws ordained:
> God from the mount of Sinai, whose grey top
> Shall tremble, he descending, will himself
> In thunder lightning and loud trumpets' sound
> Ordain them laws; part such as appertain
> To civil justice, part religious rites
> Of sacrifice, informing them, by types
> And shadows...
>   ... But the voice of God
> To mortal ear is dreadful; they beseech
> That Moses might report to them his will,
> And terror cease; he grants what they besought
> Instructed that to God is no access
> Without mediator, whose high office now
> Moses in figure bears...   (*PL*, xii, 214–41)

Even though the donation of the law on Sinai takes place in the presence of God, it is immediately transferred into the hands of Moses, and later into the hands of Christ. What appears is the necessity of a covenant between men immediately following the covenant with God, or the transition from prophecy to magistracy. It is at this stage that natural law appears, when it is submitted to the threat of ambition:

> one shall rise
> Of proud ambitious heart, who not content
> With fair equality, fraternal state,
> Will arrogate dominion undeserved
> Over his brethren, and quite dispossess
> Concord and law of nature from the earth...
>   (*PL*, xii, 24–9)

In the text of *Paradise Lost*, the concept is alluded to rather than clearly defined. The main aspects of such a natural law are more precisely dealt with in the *De Doctrina Christiana*. 'The law of God is either written or unwritten. The unwritten law is the law of nature given to the first man. A kind of gleam or glimmering of it still remains in the hearts of all mankind. In the regenerate this is daily brought nearer to a renewal of its original perfection by the operation of the Holy Spirit.'[22]

The articulation between divine law and natural law is made more perceptible in this passage.[23] Natural law is a fairly complex concept that can hardly be disentangled from other notions with which it has been compared or sometimes assimilated in Milton's time, such as the law of reason, or the law of nations. But, though at times confused, the concept is none the less central to Milton's thought. Milton establishes a distinction between a primary law of nature equated with the unwritten law of God and a secondary law of nature, derived from it, and equated with positive law. Such a definition of the primary law of nature is different from the commonly received one which concerns the revelation of the oral law by Christ to his apostles. As for the secondary law, the distinction is made in *Tetrachordon* in which Milton argued that 'prime Nature made us all equall, made us equall coheirs by common right and dominion over all creatures', but as a result of the Fall, 'suffer'd not divorce onely, but all that which by Civilians is term'd the *secondary law of nature and of nations*'.[24] Government thus results from the secondary law of nature, yet Milton maintains that God never gave anyone dominion over other men who remain free, which sets strict limitations to any prerogative. The people had not appointed kings[25] and magistrates to be their masters, but rather to be their commissioners and deputies:

> Authority usurped, from God not given:
> He gave us only over beast, fish, fowl
> Dominion absolute; that right we hold
> By his donation; but man over men
> He made no lord; such title to himself
> Reserving, human left from human free.
>
> (*PL*, XII, 66–71)

The doctrine of the law of nature as it is briefly delineated in *Paradise Lost* implies, when explicated by the prose works, a contractual theory

---

[22] *Christian Doctrine, CPW*, VI, 516.

[23] '... the law of God does most closely agree with the law of nature.' *A Defence of the People of England, CPW*, IVi, 422.

[24] *Tetrachordon, CPW*, II, 661. On this, see Barker, *Milton and the Puritan Dilemma*, p. 114, and D. M. Wolfe, *CPW*, IVi, 422, n. 2.

[25] 'The power of Kings and Magistrates is nothing else but what is derivative, transferr'd and committed to them in trust from the People, to the Common good of them all, in whom the power yet remaines fundamentally, and cannot be tak'n from them, without a violation of their natural birthright.' *The Tenure of Kings and Magistrates, CPW*, III, 202.

of government. When kings began to use their power as despots, the people established laws that limited their authority. Positive laws, however, being human, are as a consequence imperfect and shadowy truths:

> With purpose to resign them in full time
> Up to a better covenant, disciplined
> From shadowy types to truth...
>
> (*PL*, xii, 301–3)

Yet, through discipline, they may lead to the truth of the foundation, previously described. Covenant politics and covenant theology are thus linked in Milton's mind.[26] Under the Gospel, there is a secondary, 'glimmering' of the eternal law originally communicated to Adam. Positive laws, derived from it, are of human origin, and as such are liable to deviations and distortions – hence usurpation and tyranny that nevertheless pretend to be grounded on law. Positive laws, varying with nations, may be termed the laws of nations, all of them concurring to the necessary process of the unification of truth.

But the question remains the same: who then are the men that can be free? Is there a natural equality of men? If not, is there a natural and equal freedom of unequal men? We examined this question earlier when we dealt with the conflict between Satan and Christ in the course of the war in Heaven. The question must be re-examined in history. Our conclusion was that true liberty rests on the capacity to reflect Christian liberty born of faith through the spirit. This was proportionate to the potentialities of each individual. How does this apply to the question of government, and to republicanism? And how is republicanism related to such notions as democracy or equality? Historians, in order to clarify Milton's attitude, have suggested a number of parallels. Arthur Barker, and later Merritt Hughes, have compared Milton's views with those of Filmer and Hobbes. Filmer had suggested: 'If the "sounder, the better, and the uprighter" part have the power of the people, how shall we know or who shall judge who they be?'[27] Hobbes, on the other hand, wrote:

If Nature . . . have made men equall, that equalitie is to be acknowledged: or if Nature have made men unequall; yet because men that think themselves

---

[26] Cf. *PL*, xi, 867, 982, 898; xii, 252, 302, 346.
[27] Robert Filmer, *Observations concerning the Originall of Government* in *Filmer: Patriarcha and Other Writings*, ed. Johann P. Sommerville (Cambridge, 1991), p. 199.

equall will not enter into conditions of Peace but upon Equall terms, such equalitie must be admitted. And therefore for the ninth law of Nature, I put this, *That every man acknowledge other for his Equall by Nature.* The breach of this Precept is *Pride*.[28]

Parallels may be established between Satan's claims (*PL*, v, 789ff) and a few lines extracted from the works of Hobbes. What such parallels suggest is the obvious fact that the debates and commonplaces that agitated Milton and his contemporaries are echoed in their works. Equality defined and supported by Satan, especially if it does not contradict one of the laws of nature defined by Hobbes,[29] cannot correspond to Milton's personal conviction, even if Milton mentions it so as to be able to reject it. In Milton, the multitude is not presented in a favourable light. It is certainly true that, in a number of texts, Milton creates the impression that his views are those of a Whig, if not of a modern democrat. Satan's republicanism has been compared with the language of *The Readie and Easie Way*.[30] And D. M. Wolfe suggested that Machiavelli's *Discorsi* may have been an important source for this work.[31] The trilogy Satan/Machiavelli/*Readie and Easie Way* (with Old Nick as common denominator) may be interesting as far as sources are concerned. But in *The Readie and Easie Way*, we do find a text that can leave no doubt as to Milton's evolution:

the main reason urg'd why popular assemblies are to be trusted with the peoples libertie, rather then a Senat of principal men, because great men will be still endeavoring to inlarge thir power, but the common sort will be contented to maintain thir own libertie, is found by experience false; none being more immoderat and ambitious to amplifie thir power, then such popularities.

In the same passage, he mentions a 'licentious and unbridl'd democratie'.[32] Now, *Paradise Lost* speaks of the 'herd' (*PL*, xii, 481) that is unfaithful:

> ... many will presume:
> Whence heavy persecution shall arise
> On all who in the worship persevere

[28] Thomas Hobbes, *Leviathan*, ed. Richard Tuck (Cambridge, 1991), p. 107.
[29] On Hobbes and Milton, cf. D. M. Wolfe, 'Milton and Hobbes: A Contrast in Social Temper', *Studies in Philology*, 41 (1944), 410–26.
[30] Blair Worden, 'Milton's Republicanism and the Tyranny of Heaven', in Gisela Bock, Quentin Skinner and Maurizio Viroli (eds.), *Machiavelli and Republicanism* (Cambridge, 1990), p. 235.   [31] *Commonplace Book*, *CPW*, i, 504, n. 8.
[32] *The Readie and Easie Way*, *CPW*, vii, 438–9.

> Of spirit and truth; the rest, far greater part,
> Will deem in outward rites and specious form
> Religion satisfied... *(PL, xII, 530-5)*

This apparently contradicts Milton's conception of natural law written in the hearts of all men, and perhaps, even more, such lines as these:

> The Spirit of God, promised alike and given
> To all believers... *(PL, xII, 519-20)*

But I do not think there is any contradiction here. The spirit is promised democratically, as it were, to all men; but Milton adds 'to all believers': that is the keyword, 'believers', people whose belief is as firmly established as Milton may wish; which of course limits the application of the word to just a few. This is discussed by Michael and Adam. Michael declares that the disciples of Christ, 'men who in his life/Still followed him' *(PL, xII, 438-9)* are left in charge to teach the nations; and when Adam asks 'what will betide the few/His faithful' *(PL, xII, 481)* when he reascends to Heaven, Milton's solution is that a Comforter *(PL, xII, 486)*[33] will be sent to 'guide them in all truth' *(PL, xII, 490)*. With the help of the Comforter, a few greater men – who may be the biblical remnant – must be in charge of the government of men. In *The Readie and Easie Way*, Milton gives the example of the Sanhedrin, the supreme council of the seventy among the Hebrews.[34] Great men may serve because of their capacities, but also as models and examples. There is a kind of 'appel du héros', as Henri Bergson put it.

I think that, in *Paradise Lost*, Milton believed in the role of a few men who fought against idolatry and tyranny in a republic.[35] This had been repeatedly asserted very early, in the *Commonplace Book*, in remarks on Machiavelli.[36]

What comes first at this stage is Milton's preoccupation with tyranny. The best form of government is the one that preserves mankind from tyranny. Acceptance of a limited form of the democratic principle (when he talks of the Spirit of God) is balanced by his conception of the few. Where Demos is concerned, what he fears above all is demagogy when 'wolves shall succeed for teachers' *(PL,*

---

[33] In *Christian Doctrine* the Comforter is the Holy Spirit, *CPW*, vi, 292.
[34] *The Readie and Easie Way*, *CPW*, vii, 436. On this, *PL*, xII, 225.
[35] Zera S. Fink, *The Classical Republicans* (Evanston 1945), p. 105.
[36] On the commentaries of Milton especially on Machiavelli's *Discorsi*, see *CPW*, i, 421 and 477.

xii, 508), and when 'secular power is ... feigning still to act / By spiritual' (*PL*, xii, 517–18) – which shows that he is aware of the risks of theocratic power. The foundation then does not bar the way to innovation, but then innovation and action are the prerogatives of the few.

Thus, his main conclusions, as I see them, are the following. A divine foundation is given. Natural law, which is divine in essence, but now only a gleam, may help us to develop imperfect laws that can be no guarantee against tyranny. Great men, few in number, must govern the majority of men, in whom the gleam of natural law is somewhat obscured. But the fact remains that a commonwealth, or a republic, is superior to a monarchy. Liberty – the essence of the foundation by Christ, as Milton understands it – must be maintained. That instils a glimmer of democratic inspiration. Implementation and specific questions such as the franchise cannot be directly dealt with in *Paradise Lost*. But equality and liberty are central points. The reason is that liberty and equality are philosophical notions discussed within the context of the foundation, whereas the other notions are more practical. When *Paradise Lost* is concerned, we may only infer what Milton thinks of such practical questions by establishing parallels with the prose works, as is often the case with theological questions. But there is one clear warning when it comes to the reality of government: and that is a firm, unmistakable warning against tyranny (the tyranny of individuals and the tyranny of the multitude), the most cruel of political evils. It follows that Milton's interpretation of Christian liberty as the abrogation of outward law 'has a profound effect on his conception of the state (if only because the state's purpose is to serve the regenerate)'[37] for the benefit of all.

[37] A. S. P. Woodhouse (ed.), *Puritanism and Liberty* (London, 1938), p. 93.

PART III
Milton and the republican experience

CHAPTER 8

Popular republicanism in the 1650s: John Streater's 'heroick mechanicks'

Nigel Smith

In the spring of 1662, the publisher, soldier and politician John Streater collected the blind poet, playwright and recently retired civil servant John Milton from his residence near the Strand and took him to a performance of his play *Macbeth* at the recently constructed public theatre next to Somerset House. Both men had cause to be grateful for the triumph and survival of the republic in the crisis of 1659–60, and their friendship had been forged during the anxious spring and summer months of 1660, when feverish negotiations and the deft deployment of the army had kept a threatened invasion of royalists at bay. Streater's military prowess (and his skill with artillery) had won him acclaim, and he was set to prosper as a publisher (the government had offered him much work). He had also recently been elected to the assembly of the people, one of the two chambers adopted by the constitutional legislation of November 1660. Milton had not been at all happy with this constitution at first (he had favoured a single perpetual chamber), but he had come to realize that a two-chamber constitution was the most effective means of reconciling all parties and interests to the continuing kingless state, as the constitution's chief author, James Harrington, had predicted. He contented himself with the dictation of a long poem on the triumph of the Puritan revolution, and he was refreshing his knowledge of educational and scientific advances made since the proclamation of a republic because these were to be given a book all of their own.

The preceding paragraph is, of course, all fiction. But its brief vision of what might have been provides, in the spirit of Erasmian 'folly' and Morean utopianism (much admired by 1650s republicans), a point of departure for considering afresh the history of republicanism, popular movements and literary activity during the Interregnum. It is often maintained that the republican ideas and activity that

flourished after the execution of Charles I and the proclamation of a
'free state' were of an aristocratic, gentry or elite character.[1] Historians
disagree over the character of this republicanism, and the extent to
which the regime that preceded the Protectorate was a true republic
or not.[2] They are nonetheless agreed that the popular parties of the
1640s, and in particular the Levellers, with their call for a very broad
extension of the franchise and regular elections to a representative
body, had little or nothing to do with the republican theories of the
state that addressed the politics of the following decade. Leveller
demands (many of which were religious rather than political in
nature) fell short of the steps that would have led them to design a
non-monarchical state. The nineteenth-century view (which survived
down to the middle of this century) that the Levellers were the only
true republicans is a case of mistaken identity. Individual Levellers by
and large do not figure in the major republican arenas of the
Interregnum. Only on the eve of the Restoration was it possible for a
very small minority to see that there had been a continuity between
Leveller and republican aims.[3]

John Streater, however, is a thorn in the side of every aspect of
this argument. He was a soldier, publisher and printer who sometimes
turns up on the fringes of 1650s historiography, but the significance
of his rich writings has not been given the recognition it properly
deserves (see note 71 below). He joined the forces of Parliament in
1642, and was present at the battles of Edgehill and Newbury.
Although active as a publisher in the mid-1640s, he was in the New
Model Army (one centre of Leveller support) in the late 1640s, and
when he first emerged in print in late March 1653 he was still a
soldier serving in Ireland.[4] His sentiments are typical of the junior

---

[1] Jonathan Scott, 'The English Republican Imagination', in John Morrill (ed.), *Revolution and Restoration: England in the 1650s* (London, 1992), pp. 35–54.

[2] Richard Tuck, *Philosophy and Government 1572–1651* (Cambridge, 1993), p. 222; Blair Worden, 'Marchamont Nedham and the Beginnings of English Republicanism, 1649–1656', in David Wootton (ed.), *Republicanism, Liberty, and Commercial Society, 1649–1776* (Stanford, 1994), pp. 416–17, n. 24.

[3] See *The Leveller: Or, The Principles & Maxims Concerning Government and Religion* (London, 1659), 16 Feb., E968(93), especially p. 7 on bicameral legislature. Harrington was not amused by the attribution of his own ideas to the authors of the *Agreement of the People*, and attacked *The Leveller* in *The Art of Lawgiving* (London, 1659), in *The Political Works of James Harrington*, ed. J. G. A. Pocock (Cambridge, 1977), p. 658.

[4] For Streater's biography, see *DNB* and R. L. Greaves and R. Zaller (eds.), *A Biographical Dictionary of British Radicals in the Seventeenth Century*, 3 vols. (Brighton, 1982–4) (hereafter *BDBR*). The most substantial account in a tract is to be found in Streater's *Secret Reasons of State* (London, 1659), 23 May, E983(24), a record of his persecution by Cromwell for

officers who had formed the backbone of Leveller support, although
when he left Ireland he had risen to be Quartermaster-General to
the infantry there. At least one other publication from an officer in
Ireland has close similarities with Streater's views on electoral
rights, the dissolution of the Rump Parliament, and his use of
classical history.[5] Streater's *A Glympse of that Jewel, Judicial, Just,
Preserving Libertie* (1653) is the first of a series of treatises in which a
genuinely popular classical republicanism is offered; it is an even
more significant treatise than some have claimed it to be.[6] Its
sentiments are close to those of the Levellers, notably with regard to
the popular origins of sovereignty, the protection of the poor from
oppression, an aversion to titles, and its sense that the abolition of
monarchy had produced 'a perfect equalitie, in respect of thy Rights
and Priviledges'.[7] It is true that Streater supported Pride's Purge
(unlike most Levellers), and the Rump Parliament (which he
thought was a true representative of England's liberties), so he
cannot be classed as a typical Leveller. Yet when Streater was
resisting imprisonment for publishing seditious literature in November
1653, he not only looked and sounded like Lilburne, but appeared
in court on the same day as him, and reported parts of Lilburne's
own defence in print.[8] In Streater's ideal republic, freedom is
consonant with the apprenticeship system, thereby exploiting another
Leveller goal.[9] A franchise that appears to be at least as broad as the
less extreme version demanded by the Levellers returns representatives

challenging the dissolution of Parliament, first in a paper distributed among army officers,
and secondly in a work entitled *The Grand Politick Informer* which has not survived (*Secret
Reasons*, pp. 2–7). Streater was discharged in late November 1653, but found himself forced
into hiding on account of his anti-Protectorate journalism. He promised quietism to
Major-General Desborough in October 1654, but was arrested again upon Thurloe's
suspicion of further seditious activity (*Secret Reasons*, pp. 18–20). Before publishing again after
the recall of the Rump, he may have published *The Picture of a New Courtier* (London, 1656), 18
April, E875(6), an outright attack on Cromwell, and *Sullogologia* (London, 1656), a discourse
on the antiquity of Parliament.
[5] See R. G. (?Richard Goodgroom), *A Copy of a Letter from an Officer of the Army in Ireland*
(London, 1656), but the tract is dated from Waterford on 24 June 1654, during a period of
intense activity for Streater.
[6] J. G. A. Pocock, 'Historical Introduction', in Harrington, *Political Works*, ed. Pocock, p. 9.
[7] *A Glympse*, sig. A2ᵛ.
[8] *Clavis ad aperiendum Carceris Ostia* (London, 1653), esp. pp. 2–3. For further invocations of
Lilburne's name and principles in the classical (and popular) republican cause, see *Lilburns
Ghost, With a Whip in One Hand, to Scourge Tyrants out of Authority* (London, 1659), 22 June,
E988(9). Printed for Livewell Chapman.
[9] See *Observations, Historical, Political, and Philosophical, Upon Aristotles first Book of Political
Government*, 4 (25 April–2 May, 1654), 26–9. For Streater, to be a servant, or to be bound to a
master, was not slavery.

and officers annually to assemblies and positions in an English version of the ancient city state.[10]

Moreover, in Streater's world, the freedom of speech which Levellers (and sectarians) so readily associated with religious toleration is imagined through the sharing of political wisdom among the populace. Where the Levellers' vision of freedom was rooted in an uncertain (and wholly English) conception of the constitution, Streater's popular republicanism went confidently further by means of a deep understanding of ancient classical literature, constitutions and political behaviour. Political openness, claims Streater, was encouraged by ancient rulers like Lycurgus.[11] All free men were to be given a political and legal education.[12] Indeed, in what is probably Streater's most powerful populist statement, he imagines that there must be a complete sharing of knowledge between rulers and ruled, in order to apply a brake on corruption and tyranny. There is no statement of such educational and political openness and democracy in any other proponent of English republicanism of the period.

Streater is most famous for printing Harrington's *Oceana* in 1656.[13] The connection has led some to see Harringtonian influences even in this early writing (which would mean that Harrington's ideas were circulating in the early 1650s, before they were available in print).[14] The persistent use of natural analogy in Streater certainly invites further comparison with Harrington's language. Or was Harrington the recipient of the army and urban republicanism of the earlier 1650s? While these questions remain to be answered, it is clear that Streater produced a vision that was truly populist and classical republican at once, and also in line with Leveller ideals as they had been articulated in the late 1640s.

We tend also to think of republican thought as being distinguished by its ability to frame non-monarchical models of government, as opposed to a mere objection to kingly tyranny or an assertion that the origins of government were popular. Central to this view is the significance of Marchamont Nedham and Harrington's preference for a bicameral constitution, where a popular assembly has a control

---

[10] See David Wootton, 'Leveller Democracy and the Puritan Revolution', in J. H. Burns (ed.), *The Cambridge History of Political Thought 1450–1700* (Cambridge, 1991), pp. 412–42.
[11] *A Glympse*, sig. A3ʳ.   [12] *Ibid.*, p. 5.
[13] J. G. A. Pocock, 'Historical Introduction', pp. 6–7, 9–11.
[14] Blair Worden, 'Harrington's *Oceana*: Origins and Aftermath, 1651–1660', in Wootton (ed.), *Republicanism, Liberty and Commercial Society*, pp. 430–1, n. 37.

over the deliberations of a senate.[15] It may be that Streater was an avid reader of the republican proposals published by Nedham in *Mercurius Politicus*, although he makes no obvious allusions to that newsbook. However Streater's ideas developed in this respect (complicated evidence suggests that he preferred a series of chambers dedicated to different aspects of public life), what matters for the development of his republicanism is that it was a broadly conceived and all-embracing cultural vision.[16] Reading classical philosophy and history was a means for the (New Model Army) soldier to come to understand that he was also a citizen:

The great preservation and cause of the growth of the Common-wealth of *Rome*, after their shaking off that yoak, Monarchie, was the yearly election of all Officers in greatest trust, both Military and Civil; for by this means they were prevented of obtaining to those advantages of making themselves Masters of the common Liberty.

... By this means also every one of the Commonwealth that affected Government, had hope of having share of the Government; therefore they endeavoured to improve themselves so, as to become capable of such and such trusts in Government: So that almost every one was an able defendant of their Libertie and Countrie: Therefore the greatnesse of that empire is not to be admired; for it is hard to oppose such a composed Bodie, by such a Body or power as is acted or supported by the Counsels or Interests of few. *Romes* power began to decline, when the power and secret reasons of State were assumed by few, or one person.[17]

In Streater's republic, there is an urgent sense of being driven by the quest for fame and honourable reputation: with only a year in office, people will be driven to complete their business and achieve goals only in the public interest.

Constitutional reform, however, is only one aspect of Streater's writings, which are most remarkable for the sense of what it would be like to live in republican culture. There should be, and there will be, a complete freedom from censorship, as well as the right to free speech and public assembly. Heroism will be a nationally shared public expression of these freedoms: 'some may say that the begetting and increasing of heroickness in the brest of the people may administer cause of fear in those that govern', but Streater thinks that all soldiers can be Caesars with no danger to the stability of the

---

[15] Worden, 'Marchamont Nedham and the Beginnings of English Republicanism', pp. 67–8.
[16] *Government Described: Viz. What {Monarchie,/Aristocracie,/Oligarchie,/Democracie,} is Together with a Brief Model of the Government of the Common-Wealth, or Free State of Ragouse* (London, 1659), pp. 6–8, E985(6).   [17] *A Glympse*, p. 1.

republic.[18] Equally, every citizen can become like Hercules, who was deified for 'imploying his strength in delivering the oppressed out of the hands of the oppressors'.[19] Every citizen would thus have the potential to rise to a position of great public authority, so that the machinery of state encourages meritocracy. Thus, one important element in ancient republican thought, and which Streater praised in the contemporary example of the Neapolitan rebel Masaniello, is permanently facilitated in his ideal vision.[20] In this martial state, that seems to take the heroism of both commonwealthsman and Leveller apology to a new extreme, public and private are seamlessly fused – there is no private interest that is not finally public (and unproblematically so). Life for Streater's citizens would therefore be rigorously demanding, since everyone would have to study the laws and 'mysteries' of the commonwealth, and the public good would always have to come before private interests. Each citizen would have to be as self-sacrificing as the stoical ideal rulers of the classical histories. If all were to share the knowledge of statecraft, all would have to be as exemplary and magnanimous as Aristotle's ideal monarchs. Rome flourished, he says, because its men and women desired more than anything the 'goods of the mind', believed in a citizen army, and wanted to procure the common good. Better to be poor in a rich city than *vice-versa*.[21] Yet Streater's republic is also a wealthy state (through trade and aggressive mercantilism, money will be 'as plentifull as dust'), and one with public art: public theatres show anti-tyrannical heroic drama.[22] Moreover, even by 1654, Streater was capable of identifying 'priestcraft' (albeit not by this name) – the perpetration of magic or superstition by kings and the Roman church.[23] In the ancient city-states a true apprehension of God as a series of causes in the natural world prevailed.[24] Reformation should be a return to these religious principles. It may be, in the mid-1650s at least, that Streater was appealing to the

[18] *Observations*, 4 (25 April–2 May 1654), 30.   [19] *Ibid.*, sig. A3^V.
[20] *Ibid.*, 9; see also Dion Cassius, Book 52, translated by 'A.R.' as *An Oration of Agrippa to Octavius Caesar Against Monarchy* (London, 1659), p. 6, E972(3).
[21] *Observations*, 9 (13–20 June 1654), 67.   [22] *Observations*, 4 (25 April–2 May 1654), 30.
[23] Religion as a means of social control (under tyrannies) was discussed by Streater with some 'Parliament men' in November 1654, and was regarded by Thurloe as a matter 'of dangerous consequence', *Secret Reasons*, pp. 19–20. Who were the 'Parliament men'? There is no record of Streater's association with the republican officers investigated and imprisoned at this time (Alured, Okey, Sanders), although he did sign a petition with them in November 1659: British Library, Add. MS 4165, f. 42. *The Picture of a New Courtier* mentions them on p. 4.
[24] *Observations*, 6 (10–16 May 1654), 44–6.

godly (and perhaps also to the Fifth Monarchists) in an attempt to fuse radical Puritan and republican agendas. Whether his version of ancient religion was related to Harrington's attack on priestcraft, or was even influenced by it, is even more uncertain. It is nonetheless similar to the respect for ancient stoicism exhibited by a radical Christian like John Lilburne, as we shall see. Elsewhere, Streater describes a domestic economy in which heroism is enhanced by the suppression of prostitition and adultery, and by selective breeding, so that only strong children are produced.[25] There must also be colonial expansion, so that these fruitful offspring may ensure a perpetual increase of society.

The extent of Streater's classicism is most evident in his newsbooks, the most important of which was *Observations, Historical, Political, and Philosophical, Upon Aristotles first Book of Political Government*, which ran for eleven numbers between 4 April and 4 July 1654.[26] It is an extensive serialized commentary upon Aristotle's *Politics*, and had reached the third chapter of the first book by its last issue (it was probably suppressed). In this newsbook Streater's republican vision is most extensively displayed, and his originality, anterior to Harrington's influence, is also established. Streater was primarily an Aristotelian, then a Ciceronian, and finally a Machiavellian republican, and he hoped that his discoveries would lead to the remedy of state diseases by peaceful policy rather than by force. A complete system of central and local government is recommended by grafting books of English law (from Coke's *Institutes* to Dalton's *Country Justice*) onto republican writings.[27] Both traditions are then reinforced by means of analogy with the behaviour of the natural world, on the authority of the writings of Galen and Hermes Trismegistus. Just as Nedham hid his criticisms of Cromwell in *Mercurius Politicus*, so Streater printed very largely foreign and Scottish news, together

[25] *Observations*, 3 (19–26 April 1654), 18–20. Streater considers that Venice did not expand its territories because adultery was tolerated, thereby compromising (heroic) desire. The optimum age of marriage is twenty-five for men, and eighteen for women.

[26] An earlier work, called *The Grand Politick Informer*, possibly in newsbook form, was published by Streater although it does not survive (see above, n. 4). It is referred to as a cause of Streater's imprisonment by the author of its apparent continuation, *The Politique Informer*, 1 (23–30 Jan. 1654), 1, E223(28). This newsbook (which ran for only two issues) was probably an officially sponsored 'replacement' for Streater's first newsbook. It is slavishly loyal to the Protector, and advises private men not to meddle in affairs of state.

[27] See Michael Dalton, *The Country Justice, conteyning the Practise of the Justices of the Peace* (1st edn, London, 1618). There were a total of fifteen editions of this work in the seventeenth century. Streater published the eleventh edition of 1666, as well as the editions of the four parts of Coke's *Institutes* (London, 1670–1).

with details of Protectorate legislation, but this did not stop *Observations* 'grating' the Protector.[28]

At the same time he published in three stages, and disguised as a newsbook (called *Perfect and Impartial Intelligence*), Suetonius' life of Julius Caesar: a more obvious attack on Cromwell. In fact, what appears to be a life is also a political commentary.[29] Streater was functioning here in relation to Suetonius as Machiavelli had commented upon Livy. This work of political theory masquerading as a newsbook deals with Caesar's gradual assimilation of power, from his control of the Senate (and his attempts to destroy it) to his control of the legal system. The news sections give details of the forthcoming elections to the Protectorate parliament of September 1654, although the oblique discourse refers to earlier examples of what was claimed to be Cromwellian tyranny. Streater's commentary contains a veiled incitement to revolt: for a flatterer to compare any ruler to Caesar (as much Cromwellian panegyric did) is to suggest that they should also be killed by a Brutus. The assassination of Cromwell is obliquely on the agenda here.[30]

There is no doubt that Streater is the voice of a simple and genuinely popular classical republicanism. It is also clear that in offering such a vision, he had seemingly made a leap of which few of his army or urban compatriots were capable, although it is one which we find growing in strength towards the end of the 1650s, and on the eve of the Restoration. It would certainly seem to have been in the army, or in his army period, that Streater developed the bulk of his ideas.

But if some army radicals were able to turn themselves into classical republicans with ease, others found the task more problematic. Many Levellers and agitators were first and foremost radical Puritans: their interests in political reform were initially motivated by a desire for greater religious toleration. Classical republicanism, properly conceived, would in many ways be in conflict with the millenarian, chiliastic and perfectionist Protestantism of the sects. To be a classical republican meant, of necessity, a clear engagement with the literature of classical antiquity. Here, the encounter of 1640s religious and political radicals with the political ideologies of classical antiquity was traumatic and complicated.

---

[28] Streater, *Secret Reasons*, p. 18.
[29] This newsbook may have been referred to erroneously as *The Grand Politick Informer* when Streater was investigated: *Secret Reasons*, p. 5.
[30] *Perfect and Impartial Intelligence*, 1 (16–23 May 1654), 6, E735(17).

Writing in 1653 to Christopher Feake, John Lilburne commented on his reading of classical literature:

I should have doted on the *Roman Poet* of the *Civil Wars*, had I not found him blessing his Fates for bringing forth a *Nero* through those bitter Pangs and Throws: And yet I must confesse, if I knew where, or could be so happy, to presage another New Birth of Tyrannie, to follow such a long and sore Travel of our State, I should also desire and play for one *Nero*, rather then one Hundred, or one million.[31]

The Roman poet was Lucan, author of *De Bello Civili*, the epic poem that told of the defeat of Pompey by Julius Caesar and the end of the Roman republic. Since Parliament's victory in the First Civil War, if not before, Lucan had become, through widespread citation in pamphlets, the poet of the Parliamentarians, the republicans and, eventually, the supporters of the Protectorate.[32] That Lucan's translator, Thomas May, had been both apologist and historian for Parliament confirmed this perception as he worked Lucanic perspectives into his histories of the Long Parliament.[33] Lilburne characteristically misses Lucan's ironic and sarcastic reference to Nero; Lucan's poem was of course a republican lament against tyranny.

Lilburne had been forced into exile in the early 1650s and, while in Amsterdam and Flanders, had the time to read Polybius, Plutarch and Machiavelli, in order to try to understand why the Leveller movement had failed:

Having red so much of famous Plutarchs Lives lately, with so much delight and seriousnes as I have done (reading for many daies together fiftie of his large Folios in a Day, and also largely takeing notes as I reade (my common practise in reading any book that pleaseth me)[)] I hope shortly in a few lines, which I intend to present him with, to let him know I now fully understand his meaning.[34]

What emerged as a result of this study was a merging in Lilburne's mind of the Leveller concern with tyranny and popular politics with the classical image of tyranny. Precisely the same examples from Plutarch that are found in Streater (Lycurgus and the giving of laws

[31] John Lilburne, *The Afflicted Mans Out-Cry* (London, 1653, 19 Aug.), p. 5, E711(7)*.
[32] See David Norbrook, 'Lucan, Thomas May and the Creation of a Republican Literary Culture', in Kevin Sharpe and Peter Lake, (eds.), *Culture and Politics in Early Stuart England* (London, 1994), pp. 45–66; Nigel Smith, *Literature and Revolution in England 1640–1660* (New Haven and London, 1994), pp. 203–7.   [33] See Smith, *Literature and Revolution*, pp. 343–4.
[34] *L. Colonel John Lilburne revived* (?Amsterdam, 1653, 27 March), p. 23, E689(32). Perez Zagorin's *A History of Political Thought in the English Revolution* (London, 1954), pp. 18–19, is one of the few studies to take Lilburne's reading seriously.

to Sparta; the virtue of Timoleon in freeing the Syracusans) occur here.[35] The writing is a curious hybrid, resulting in a kind of Leveller stoicism (although it is not so divorced from the quality of some of George Wither's verse at this time).[36] The poetry attributed to the Roman people in Sir Thomas North's translation of Plutarch is reworked into a characteristically Leveller use of the ballad (North and his French original were supposedly representing a Roman song of popular victory):

> The cleare unspotted Faith
>   Of Romans, we adore:
> And vow to be their faithfull friends,
>   Both now and evermore.
>
> Sing out ye Muses nine,
>   To Ioves eternall fame:
> Sing out the Honour due to Rome,
>   And Titus worthy name.
>
> Sing out, I say, the praise
>   Of Titus, and his faith:
> By whom ye have preserved bin
>   From Ruine, Doole and Death.[37]

Lilburne is trying to invent a spirit of popular republicanism, and he did so in a published letter addressed to the republican MP Henry Marten. Lilburne's blunders with Roman history (he made several confused and bizarre judgements of Roman figures) made him a target for controverters, but it is quite clear that he was interested in reviving ancient virtue, and in condemning the forms of tyranny that his new reading was helping him to understand. Lilburne asks Marten to pass on his regards to his old friend Mr Moyle, who had once called the Leveller 'Noble Cato'.[38] Lilburne says that at the time he did not understand the reference; now he does, for he had indeed become a republican.[39] The correspondence with Marten was part of a programme intended both to spread the English Revolution abroad and to advance true republican aims at home against the regime of the Rump. Not only Plutarch but also Machiavelli helped Lilburne

[35] *L. Colonel John Lilburne revived*, pp. 12–18.
[36] See e.g., George Wither, *Vox Pacifica* (London, 1645).
[37] *L. Colonel John Lilburne revived*, p. 22. Lilburne used the 1612 edition of North's translation.
[38] Was this John Moyle, member of the Rump and grandfather of Harrington's republican disciple Walter? If so, this is an instance of republicanism being transmitted inside one family. I owe this point to Blair Worden.   [39] *L. Colonel John Lilburne revived*, p. 23.

to understand that violence breeds violence. His writings stumble their way into a classical republican framework, and they never happily sit there.

And yet these later writings of Lilburne's (which only just preceded Streater's) are by no means the first engagements in classical republicanism by a Leveller. In some ways, Lilburne's awkwardness was an exception. As early as 1645 classical historians had been invoked in a defence of Lilburne that had used Livy and Machiavelli to justify popular sovereignty.[40] This is a fairly mild accommodation of classical views to Leveller ideals, since it is those ideals of popular sovereignty and not a republican constitution that govern the framework of the pamphlet.[41] There is nothing distinctively classical republican about it in this sense. Just over one year later, however, *Vox Plebis, or the Peoples Out-cry Against Oppression* began to use classical concepts of the state in a more dominant way, over and against the notion of an ancient constitution.[42] Magna Carta is regarded in this tract as but a confirmation of the earlier inheritances of freedom. The interesting opening passage of this tract reconciles a call for religious toleration (which it sees as the proper right of a state) with good government by laws. Also included is the pointed lesson of Rome: after the expulsion of the Tarquins, the Roman people had to struggle for their liberty against the new tyranny of the nobility in the senate. It is not certain who is responsible for this passage, but the similarity between it and later sections of editorial in *Mercurius Politicus* has led Blair Worden to propose Marchamont Nedham as its author.[43] If this is the case, then we have two important conclusions to draw, in addition to the fact that the Leveller party was indeed assimilating classical republican thought into its armoury as early as the mid-1640s. First of all, Nedham the journalist may be seen as a serious republican thinker at a much earlier stage than has been previously thought. Second, his collaboration with the Levellers at this stage provides further evidence of a continuity of Leveller and republican ideas. Worden goes as far as to

---

[40] *England's Miserie and Remedie in a Judicious Letter from an Utter-Barrister to His Speciall Friends* (London, 1654).

[41] S. D. Glover, 'The Classical Plebeians: Radical Republicans and the Origins of Leveller Thought' (unpublished Ph.D. thesis, University of Cambridge, 1993) explores the presence of republican, neostoic and Machiavellian components in radical Puritan, Leveller and army publications. I am grateful to Dr Glover for permission to cite his thesis.

[42] 19 Nov. 1646, E362(20).

[43] Worden, 'Marchamont Nedham and the Beginnings of English Republicanism', p. 66.

argue that the populist side of Nedham's thought amounts to a hijacking of Leveller ideas.[44]

There are increasing instances of republican thought 'creeping in' to Leveller tracts as the 1640s drew to a cataclysmic close. In 1647, John Wildman could write in a typically Leveller way on corruption and tyranny, but a year later he was writing about the shape of a state in terms that anticipate Harrington, by means of allusions to Aristotle, Polybius, Diodorus Siculus, Xenophon and Cicero:

> Every Nation is but a rude indigested *Chaos* a deformed lump untill Lawes or rules of Government be established, Lawes are the *vis plastica* or formatrix that formes the principall vitalls, the heart, the braine, the Liver of the Commonwealth.[45]

It was this kind of thinking – not as advanced as Streater's confident classicism but more forward than Lilburne's tentative classical explorations – that led ex-Levellers like Wildman and Edward Sexby to their own form of anti-Protectorate republicanism, in the context of the assassination attempt on Cromwell of Miles Sindercombe.

As we have seen, a crucial, distinguishing element of republican thought in the 1650s was the preference for bi-cameral government, as recommended in Harrington's *Oceana*. An executive or legislative body controlled by a popular representative has usually been regarded as the distinguishing mark of a republic where popular liberty can be defended (such as in ancient Athens, and eventually Rome), unlike the single chambers favoured by the 'democratical gentlemen' (such as Marten and Sir Cheney Culpepper) of the 1640s, and the much detested Rump Parliament itself. While this is a view that can be contested (was Streater's defence of the recalled Rump in 1659 in line with Harrington's bicameral model or not?), there is also an entirely different dimension to republican and late Leveller thought.

Or perhaps we should say feeling. Milton presumably supported Pride's Purge in a way that Lilburne did not. And Milton supported (or wrote in support of) the Rump on matters that Lilburne would not entirely have approved. And yet Lilburne was happy to refer to Milton as a great 'patriot' and translate his Latin from the *Defensio*.[46] What made this possible for Lilburne was his sense of a prevailing

---

[44] *Ibid.*, pp. 66–7.
[45] John Wildman, *The Lawes Subversion* (London, 1648), p. 2, 6 March, E431(2).
[46] Lilburne, *As You Were* (?Amsterdam, 1652), pp. 15–16.

'spirit of liberty', or 'spirit of republic', that sense of a shared and righteous purpose so aptly summed up in the phrase the 'good old cause'. His intricately detailed tracing of Plutarch's account of Timoleon's emergence from private retirement in Corinth to win the Syracusans their freedom shows neither a simple interest in a good man nor an exclusive interest in constitutions so much as an eager fascination with a heroic spirit or *ethos* of liberty. This may be judged from the urgent narrative detail of Lilburne's prose, which is entirely devoid of analysis, just as Milton's rhetoric is designed to communicate the spirit of liberty above all else, as opposed to the fine details of its implementation. Hence Milton could be seen as an intellectual grandfather to the conspiratorial urging of Sexby's *Killing Noe Murder* (1657) by being cited in its second edition (1659).[47]

To have a belief in a 'good old cause' and worthy patriots is not necessarily to regard differences with the opinions of others as absolute. The toleration of fruitfully productive differences in a non-repressive society was the aim of so many commonwealthmen, among whom are to be numbered many ex-Levellers. The 1650s might have suffered from the tyranny of the Rump and the Protector, but it was on the whole better than the tyranny of the Stuarts. Or at least ex-Levellers and republicans had a common cause against the tyranny of the Protector. And the entertainment of Leveller and republican ideas in the tracts of the mid and late 1640s and the early 1650s is anticipated by Milton's call (despite all its inconsistencies and qualifications) for free exchange in *Areopagitica* (1644). Both Lilburne and Streater in the early 1650s might be said to be exemplars of Milton's recommendations, and Streater, as a publisher and printer since at least 1646, would have had a special interest in press freedom.[48] Lilburne and Streater are the uncloistered and war[way]faring readers prophesied in *Areopagitica*. In Streater's case, the product of his reading was a merging of the classical and the Puritan remarkably faithful to Milton's own blend of these categories, even if Streater's republic and its spirit was constructed in necessarily different terms from those of *Areopagitica*.[49] Streater's call for unrestricted rights to public meeting, in honour of the God-given gifts of speech and public assembly, reads like a truly democratic Milton, as if

[47] *BDBR* suggests that Streater was responsible for the publication of this edition.

[48] Henry R. Plomer, *A Dictionary of Booksellers and Printers who were at Work in England, Scotland and Ireland from 1641 to 1667* (Oxford, 1907; 1968), p. 173.

[49] For *Areopagitica*'s articulation of the 'language of republicanism', see Nigel Smith, '*Areopagitica*: Voicing Contexts 1643–5', in David Loewenstein and James Grantham Turner, (eds.), *Politics, Poetics and Hermeneutics in Milton's Prose* (Cambridge, 1990), pp. 103–22.

Streater was a Milton who had not caught the pessimistic and elitist turns of the 1650s (or the late 1640s).[50] Both Milton and Streater praise the vigorous manliness of ancient Greece and Rome, both associate it with freedom of speech and of the press, and both are well aware of the precarious situation in which ancient freedom of speech often found itself.[51] Both stress a strong and heroic educational culture. Several images in Streater's writings are in fact the same as some in *Areopagitica*, although exact verbal echoes are missing.[52] We cannot regard Streater as a reader of Milton.

To have such a faith in the 'spirit' of a free state is to avoid those ways of thought that stress the definition of constitutions. Only when the Rump was recalled do we have a genuine flood of different models for a permanent free state. Harrington's calculus of liberty (defining proportions of land ownership against proportions of political representation) was the most exacting model in this respect.[53] While there is an element of 'good old cause' in Harrington's writing, and in the newsbooks and pamphlets that adopted his ideas, it is noticeable how much more of this 'spirit' there is in Streater's writings of this time. A series of shorter pieces desperately argue for the maintenance of the parliament as the best means of preventing either a return of the Stuarts or the tyrannous intervention of the Major-Generals. These works read like a combination of Lilburne and Harrington. In the collectively lived ethos of the republic there is a true experience of republican liberty, a time when the virtue of the ancient heroes is lived out. Streater's 'spirit' of a free state is most memorably expressed in his image of popular chivalric heroism that follows a passage in praise of the horse: 'the horse should be the Theater on whose back heroick men should act the part of their valour, to defend their liberty and country'.[54] To imagine a chief aspect of martial chivalry as a piece of living art is to represent the heroic English republic in just the same terms as Milton was to do in his *Second Defence of the People of England*.[55]

Milton's more desperate argument (in *The Readie and Easie Way to Establish a Free Commonwealth* (February–April 1660)) for one election to a permanent council to govern the kingdom in a Puritan oligarchy is markedly less democratic than Streater's vision, but both men share

---

[50] *Observations*, 7 (30 May–6 June 1654), 52; 8 (6–13 June 1654), 57–8; 10 (21–7 June 1654), 74.
[51] See John Milton, *Areopagitica* (1644), *CPW*, II, 494–500.
[52] See, for instance, the sponge as an image of censorship: *Observations*, 7 (30 May–6 June 1654), 52.
[53] James Harrington, *Oceana*, in *Political Works*, ed. Pocock, pp. 231–2, 236–41.
[54] *Observations*, 5 (2–9 May 1654), 34.   [55] *CPW*, IVi, 458.

the experience of imagining a truly free state. In no place is this more evident than in Streater's justification of public theatres as a revival of an ancient celebration of anti-tyrannical values, over and against later corruptions (one senses that licentious – possibly courtly – drama is Streater's target):

The wisest of Princes and States have esteemed of Plays and Interludes to heighten the minds of people, wherein are notably presented the Genues [*sic*] of a State, they are as passions and as lovers pulses, which do shew the soul more quicker then do words or actions; actions move more heavily only as time and opportunity present occasion. The Grecians in their Plays delighted much to see the destruction of Tyrants acted.

The first instituting of them was to a noble end and purpose, but by time they grew corrupt, and as the world declined in vertue and heroickness, so were they silenced with obscene and ugly parts, that indeed it was better to expel them, then to let them continue, unlesse they could have been corrected, and if corrected they might have served to moralize and methodize the best Historians.

But hear [*sic*] some may say what benefit would it be unto mechanicks to have such sparks of heroickness infused into them or to the Commonwealth, I answer that they would be the fitter for great and bold undertakings.[56]

Streater is objecting to the kind of argument put forward by Davenant and Hobbes in the early 1650s that heroic literature was for princes only.[57] Streater's faithful classicism also puts him at odds with Davenant's 1653 call for a new kind of drama in which the masses would be brainwashed into an admiration for the heroic by means of pictures and music, but not words.[58] We can be fairly sure that Streater's virtuous activism involved as much dialogue as one finds in Milton's one tragedy: a premium is placed on the power of eloquence.[59] And Streater's constituency of playgoers is undoubtedly largely artisanal: a feature to which he devotes considerable space, and which is derived from his knowledge of classical texts as much as from his own world.[60] More so than in Lilburne, but distinctly continuing the vision of urban merchant and artisan society cultivated by the Levellers, Streater's citizens are the artisans of central London.

[56] *Observations*, 4 (25 April–2 May 1654), 30.
[57] Sir William Davenant, 'The Author's Preface to his much Honor'd Friend, M. Hobbes', in Davenant, *Gondibert* (London, 1651), ed. David F. Gladish (Oxford, 1971), p. 13.
[58] See James R. Jacob and Timothy Raylor, 'Opera and Obedience: Thomas Hobbes and *A Proposition for Advancement of Moralitie* by Sir William Davenant', *The Seventeenth Century*, 6 (1991), 205–50.
[59] *Observations*, 10 (21–7 June 1654), 74, referring to Cicero, *De Oratore*, Book I.
[60] See above, n. 9.

Also significant is the fact that nearly all of the reading by which
republican ideas were entertained in Streater and Lilburne (and
other Levellers such as Walwyn, Wildman, Sexby, William Bray, and
so on) was not in Civil War and Interregnum pamphlet literature,
with its special ways of directing the reader's attention to how the
reader should be persuaded of the truth of the tract. Streater claimed
that *Observations* was not intended to 'divide, distract, or disturb', as if
it were a polemic on behalf of a specific interest. True republican
literature would avoid all faction and interests for the sake of the
common good. Rather, it would seek out the perfections and
corruptions of government, as if it were a *discorso* text.[61] Streater does
not imagine a Miltonic 'trial' of contrary opinions in an uncensored
public forum, but he does believe that the uncensored and widespread
availability of the best political wisdom will result in a free and
content republic. All the literature referred to by Streater and the
Levellers – largely heavy-duty ancient and Renaissance political
theory and historical writing – was available in English translation
before 1640, a fact that seriously qualifies our assessment of the
often-claimed effects of press freedom in the 1640s.[62] It was clearly the
political context of the 1640s and 1650s that made all the difference as
to how these texts could be applied. Streater's range of reference is
particularly wide, extending beyond Aristotle, Tacitus and Machiavelli
to far less well-known sixteenth-century historians.[63] Would Streater
(and Milton) have regarded pamphlets and tracts as inferior and
deceitful documents, or at least inferior to longer books, as was so
frequently claimed in the period? Or was it for Streater merely a
matter of the appropriate form for the sake of expediency?

In 1653–4 Streater, like Milton, praised the power of fully fledged
classical oratory and noted that Julius Caesar in his earlier career did
not prevail in politics because he was a poor orator. But then he is
equally aware of the deceptive power of oratory, and that 'the best
judgements and quickest wits are none the best Orators'.[64] At the
same time he also exploits the use of aphoristic knowledge and

---

[61] *Observations*, 1 (4–11 April 1654), 1.

[62] The role of translations in the formation of early modern political consciousness awaits an
extensive study. See, however, Glover, 'The Classical Plebeians', pp. 85ff.

[63] Among others, *Observations* contains citations of and references to Liudprandius, bishop of
Cremona, Thomas Fazellus, Philippe Camerarius, and Paulo Giovio, bishop of Nocera. In
Observations, Streater uses 'I.D.'s' English translation of Loys Le Roy's French translation of
Aristotle's *Politics* with Le Roy's commentary. Streater writes his own commentary, but he is
dependent upon Le Roy for a large number of his authorities.

[64] *Perfect and Impartial Intelligence/A Politick Commentary*, 1 (16–23 May 1654), 4, E735(17).

maxims (a discourse especially suited to the newsbook), while Milton appears to have regarded such compromises of the power of extensive oratorical delivery with dismay and distaste. The compressed discursive forms of the pamphlet and the newsbook were, as Nedham and Streater had shown, a potent means for disseminating ancient political theory and *discorso* writing, but it was a lesson that Milton found hard to learn.[65]

What had apparently been lost from the Leveller programme in 1650s popular republicanism was the concern with poverty. Perhaps Christopher Hill's relative lack of interest in the 1650s pamphleteers, and his preference for 'good old cause' emotion, is an expression of a misgiving that republicanism could in the end be a very selfish thing. Streater's calls for the cultivation of industry and trade do not convince the reader that he had a very central concern for the poor. Unlike the Digger claim to remove the taint of original sin through the collective cultivation of common land and the abolition of private property, Streater acknowledges property and labour as indelible consequences of original sin. Political liberty is the only way of mollifying this bondage: slavery is avoided when everyone is a servant to everyone else, rulers included. His republic is a commonwealth of increase in which wealth is enhanced by successful and aggressive trade battles with neighbours, like the Dutch, although he does have notions for reducing poverty, such as involving all women in the labour of spinning wool and pastoral farming.[66]

Moreover, and more like Milton than Lilburne, Streater's exemplary democracies (such as that of Ragusa) often have assemblies formed of social elites (with popular assemblies for other less important aspects of public life).[67] The difference from Milton's writing at the end of the Interregnum is the frequency of elections, which, Streater claims, preserves the interests of the commonwealth, and therefore of the people as a whole. And, in direct contradiction to Milton, Streater maintains that the fact that an election in England in 1659 would have resulted in a return to monarchy (or at least no free state) is no argument against depriving people of their rights.[68] He hoped that the 'legislators' (that is, the recalled Rump) would realize that the perpetuity of a free state depended upon this body denying itself perpetual power through the adoption of frequent elections.

[65] See Martin Dzelzainis' essay in this volume, below, pp. 193–4.
[66] *Observations*, 5 (2–9 May 1654), 36.　　[67] See Streater, *Government Described*, pp. 5–8.
[68] *Ibid.*, p. 8.

The army is also an important element for Milton and Streater, since it embodies the heroic spirit, and, as far as Milton was concerned, the will of Providence. But where Milton justified the army's acting on its own authority, the popular republican view was that it was always responsible to the people's representatives, just as the army of the Roman republic was responsible to the Senate and the people.[69]

The Restoration was, of course, to unite many of those supporters of the commonwealth who found themselves disagreeing during the 1650s and in the hectic days of 1659 and early 1660. Despite his volte-face in 1660, which earned him the disgust of Ludlow, Streater would again be investigated for seditious publishing in Charles II's reign.[70] That Milton felt his own lot to be with the 'good old cause' is in no doubt, although the precise nature of his sympathies and allegiances is still an open question. What is clear is that John Streater, and the form of republicanism he stood for, was a fulfilment of Milton's most optimistic ideas of free speech and of public heroism, and that Streater expresses those ideas with a learning and an incisiveness that Milton would have admired. It is also the case that Streater was making his republicanism occupy the position filled in the 1640s by Leveller ideas. The older generation of Levellers struggled to reach his position by incorporating classical republicanism. Lilburne did not quite make it, and the evidence concerning Wildman and Sexby indicates that they did not attain the degree of perception and insight achieved by Streater.[71]

---

[69] Dion Cassius, trans. A.R., *An Oration*, 7.

[70] See *DNB*, and Edmund Ludlow, *A Voyce from the Watch Tower*, ed. A. B. Worden (London, 1978), Part 5: 1660–1662, pp. 88, 114. *Calendar of State Papers Domestic* (1670), p. 322, identifies Streater as the author of *The Character of a True and False Shepherd* (London, 1670), a work that employs techniques akin to those of the Leveller Richard Overton, as well as some of Streater's typical classicisms.

   The connection between the books Streater printed or published and his convictions warrants future consideration. Streater is known to have printed 129 works, published seven and printed and published one. A further seventy-eight works may have been printed by him: see Paul G. Morrison's *Index* to Wing's Short Title Catalogue (New Haven, 1955). Before 1660 he printed or published mystical and republican works, and was associated with the radical publishers Giles Calvert and Livewell Chapman. After 1660, he turned to law books, including Coke's *Institutes*. Some almanacs, books and popular natural philosophy and 'physic' remained in his business in both periods.

[71] After this essay went to press, Dr Adrian Johns, of the University of Kent at Canterbury, allowed me to see his forthcoming article on Streater. In it, he deals extensively with Streater's interests in natural philosophy, his connections with the Hartlib Circle, and his involvement in attacks on the Stationers' Company Charter in the Restoration. He also provides further information on Streater's origins, and his activities during 1659–60.

Algernon Sidney may, by dint of aristocratic status, have been a focus for opposition during the Restoration, just as Sir Henry Vane stood for elite republicanism before it. But we should not let the lustre of these figures obscure an equally refined classical but popular republicanism that flourished in the 1650s. That Milton never mentioned the Levellers by name is, it has been said, no evidence that he was not in sympathy with them. Equally, his continuing sympathy and respect for the army is a strong indication of his interest in a reborn heroic citizenry. In this citizenry was authored the kind of democratic idealism of edification that is in fact articulated in *Areopagitica* and in John Streater's writing.

CHAPTER 9

Milton and Marchamont Nedham

Blair Worden

I

Milton's friendships can be hard to imagine. He yearned for friendship and treasured it when he found it. True friendship, he believed, survived when tested. It extended beyond conventional courtesies to Platonic unions of souls.[1] His early biographers tell us of the 'greatness' or 'intimacy' or 'particularity' of his friendships with Charles Diodati, with the wits of the Florentine academies, with Cyriack Skinner or Andrew Marvell or Edward Lawrence in England.[2] Yet the Milton we meet in his writings can seem a proudly solitary figure. Elsewhere in this volume (p. 117, n. 58) Roger Lejosne fittingly emphasizes the 'loneliness' of the stand of Abdiel in *Paradise Lost*, 'which puts him in the same company with such isolated heroes, so dear to the poet's heart, as Samson, Jesus, and no doubt Milton himself'. Milton cannot bring his friendships to life on the page, where they remain imprisoned within the conventions he wishes them to transcend. They seem witnesses less to intimacy than to the poet's egocentricity. *Lycidas* is ostensibly a poem on the death of Milton's friend Edward King, but famously tells us less about King than about Milton. When, in 'Mansus', Milton sighs for a friendship akin to that which had bound his friend John Baptista Manso to the poet Torquato Tasso, it is in the hope that Milton, like Tasso, will become, in an old age ripe with poetic triumph, the centre of a friend's attention. In prose, Milton addresses *Of Reformation* 'to a friend' in 1641 and writes the political tract *A Letter to a Friend* in 1659.

[1] *CPW*, I, 295, 326 (cf. *ibid.* I, 870, 872–3), II, 762–5; 'Samson Agonistes', lines 187–93. (I have argued for the autobiographical significance of that poem in 'Milton, *Samson Agonistes*, and the Restoration', in Gerald MacLean (ed.), *Culture and Society in the Stuart Restoration: Literature, Drama, History* (Cambridge, 1995), pp. 111–36.)

[2] Helen Darbishire (ed.), *The Early Lives of Milton* (London, 1932), pp. 2, 20, 21, 56–7, 74, 88, 95–6, 97–8.

Whether the friends are real or fictional, they take on no personality.

One friendship of Milton may seem hardest of all to imagine. Marchamont Nedham, records Anthony Wood, was a 'great crony' of Milton.[3] We might question that statement were it not for the testimony of Milton's nephew Edward Phillips, who names Nedham, together with Marvell, Lawrence and Skinner, among the 'particular friends' who 'all the time of [Milton's] abode' in Petty France, from 1652 to 1660, 'frequently visited' the poet.[4] Like the others in Phillips's list, Nedham was considerably younger than Milton. Born in 1620, twelve years after the poet, he became, through his pamphlets and still more through his newsbooks, the most widely read journalist of Puritan England. With Milton he served, and was paid a stipend by, the successive regimes of the Interregnum. The two men supported the Rump, Barebone's and the Protectorate, and welcomed the coups that destroyed each of them. They wrote the principal apologias for the Rump (in 1650–1, which produced Nedham's *The Case of the Commonwealth of England, Stated* and Milton's *Defensio*) and for the Protectorate (in 1654, the year of Nedham's *A True State of the Case of the Commonwealth* and Milton's *Defensio Secunda*). Milton's apologias were written in Latin for a European audience, Nedham's in English for a narrower, British one. In 1660 the names of Milton and Nedham were repeatedly linked by their royalist enemies, who hoped to see them hang together.[5]

Yet if the two writers were on the same successive sides, they can seem to inhabit different worlds. It is hard to envisage Nedham achieving, or wanting, a Platonic union of souls. Nedham was not the mere hack he can seem to be. His writings contain some risky moments of provocation or defiance of his political masters. Yet much of his career consists of naked opportunism and naked pragmatism. Milton and he could keep political company in the 1650s, but not in the years that preceded and followed them. Nedham, having written for Parliament in the first Civil War, wrote for the king in the second. After the Restoration he wrote for the monarchy again. His royalist writings include violently and merrily anti-Puritan propaganda. Even in the Interregnum his endorsements of the Commonwealth and Protectorate are calculated acts of persuasion, written with an air of measured detachment. It was only when in peril of his life for his royalist productions, and in dire poverty, that in 1649–50 he bought

[3] *Ibid.*, p. 44.   [4] *Ibid.*, p. 74.   [5] *CPW*, VII, 198–9.

his freedom, and a handsome salary, by agreeing to write for the
Commonwealth. Sincerity, the last virtue we could deny in Milton, is
the last word we would think of using to describe Nedham.[6]

Nedham liked the company of poets and wrote poetry, sometimes
accomplished poetry, himself. But his jaunty satirical ballads are a
world away from the burdened gravity of Milton's verse. We cannot
imagine Nedham insisting, as Milton does, that the life of a true poet
should exhibit the virtue of a true poem.[7] Milton's early biographers
stress his temperance and frugality, virtues which, in his writings, are
central to his system of values. The surviving correspondence of and
about Nedham testifies to a convivial, epicurean, bibulous lifestyle
and to some epic nights on the town. In their earlier prose the two
writers strove to instruct the nation in the principles of liberty and to
disabuse it of the ideological deceptions of royalism, Milton through
his pamphlets, Nedham through his newsbook *Mercurius Britanicus*.
Yet there is an obvious contrast between the direct and earthy prose
which Nedham aimed at a popular market, the market opened by the
collapse of censorship and the controversies of the Civil War, and the
elaborate Ciceronian periods of Milton's pamphlets of the 1640s,
which found so few readers. The contrast persisted into the 1650s.
Then Nedham addressed and hailed 'the common people of this
kingdom', whom the truth he tells 'most concerns'. The people, he
urged, must be given courses in popularized political wisdom because
they 'cannot attend to read chronicles'. They must be provided with
translations of works 'long locked up' in the Latin tongue.[8] Milton
hoped that a Dutch edition of one of his divorce tracts would appear
in Latin rather than the vernacular, 'because I know by experience
with these books how the common herd is wont to receive uncommon
opinions'.[9]

Friendships can be attractions of opposites, and between Milton
and Nedham there were many opposites to attract. Yet the two men

---

[6] There is a useful biography of Nedham by Joseph Frank, *Cromwell's Press Agent* (Lanham,
Md., 1980), though I sometimes dissent from its findings. I have discussed Nedham's career
(especially in the 1640s) and his character in '"Wit in a Roundhead": Marchamont Nedham
and the Civil Wars', in Susan Amussen and Mark Kishlansky (eds.), *Political Culture and
Cultural Politics in Early Modern England* (Manchester, 1995), and his political thought in
'Marchamont Nedham and the Beginnings of English Republicanism, 1649–1656', in David
Wootton (ed.), *Republicanism, Liberty, and Commercial Society 1649–1776* (Stanford, 1994) (and at
various points in my other three chapters in that book). The reader is referred to those
writings for statements not given documentary support here.   [7] *CPW*, I, 890.
[8] [Nedham], *A Cat May Look upon a King* (London, 1652), pp. 32–3; John Selden, *Of the Dominion
of the Seas* (London, 1652), trans. and ed. Nedham, ep. ded.   [9] *CPW*, IVii, 871–2.

may not have been quite as opposite as they seem. Writers choose what to tell us about themselves. Milton's self-representation, though it selects an important part of him, the part most consonant with the ethical purposes of his writing, has its omissions. We know from a letter of the young Milton that he hoped to find companionship in one of the Inns of Court,[10] but he does not disclose what we learn from Edward Phillips, that in the early 1640s Milton's course of 'hard study, and spare diet' was interrupted 'once in three weeks or a month' when 'he would drop into the society of some young sparks of his acquaintance, the chief whereof were young Mr. Alphry and Mr. Miller, two gentlemen of Gray's Inn, the beaus of those times', with whom he liked 'now and then to keep a gaudy-day' (gaudy-days being the regular festivals of the Inns).[11] Anthony Wood tells us that Milton was of an 'affable' temper, John Aubrey that he was 'of a very cheerful humour', even amidst the afflictions of his old age, when he would cheerfully 'sing'. He was, adds Aubrey, 'extreme pleasant in his conversation, and at dinner, supper, etc.: but satirical'. Milton's 'wit' was described by his nephews as 'prompt' and 'sharp', and by Wood as 'very sharp, biting and satirical'.[12] Nedham for his part liked to proclaim, what his writings so often reveal, his love of 'satire' and of 'wit' (a word which carried the connotation not only of humour but of nimbleness and inventiveness of mind). Wood thought of Milton and Nedham alike as men of culture and civility whom only perverted principles kept from the natural place of cultivated men, on the side of the king.[13]

Milton and Nedham alike claimed a high moral purpose for the 'satire' and 'wit' of their prose. Both men were ready to use and defend laughter as a literary and political tool. Nedham commends himself as 'a merry fellow' who likes to 'jest a little' and 'laugh in my sleeve now and then'. He is 'pleasant' to a 'purpose', for since 'all the serious treatises would not draw the people off from their liking for the king's ways, I thought it best to jeer them out of it'.[14] Milton's anti-prelatical tracts insist on the 'force of teaching there is sometimes in laughter' and on the capacity of mirth for 'serious reproof'. The 'grim laughter' of those pamphlets, he assures us, 'cannot be taxed of

---

[10] *Ibid.*, I, 327.   [11] Darbishire, *Early Lives of Milton*, p. 62.
[12] *Ibid.*, pp. 5, 6, 29, 39, 50, 54.
[13] Anthony Wood, *Athenae Oxonienses*, 4 vols. (London, 1813–20), III, 1183; Darbishire, *Early Lives of Milton*, p. 39.
[14] *Mercurius Britanicus*, 5 August 1644, p. 361; 3 November 1645, p. 913.

levity or insolence: for even this vein of laughing (as I could produce out of grave authors) hath oft-times a strong and sinewy force in teaching and confuting'. Those 'grave authors' were Nedham's warrants too. 'Eliah mocked the false prophets', explained Milton, 'to teach and instruct the poor misled people.'[15] Nedham invoked the model of Eliah to justify his own forays into satire in *Mercurius Britanicus*.[16] Milton and Nedham alike appealed to the Lucianic tradition of *joco-serio*, which stands or moves 'between jest and earnest'.[17] Milton's principal authority for the earnestness of laughter was Horace, who, in the translations from his Satires which Milton made in order to justify the mirth of his own attacks on prelacy, had laughed 'to teach the truth', for 'Jesting decides great things / Stronglier, and better oft than earnest can.'[18] Nedham's *Mercurius Politicus* carried in its regular heading Horace's words in *Ars Poetica*: '*ita vertere seria ludo*' (thus to turn seriousness to play).

In the early 1640s, when Milton enjoyed the gaudy-days of Gray's Inn with the beaux of those times, Nedham was a clerk at Gray's Inn, which would become a principal focus of his social and literary life. We do not know whether Milton and Nedham knew each other in the 1640s. In 1647 they were named next to each other in a list, drawn up by Samuel Hartlib, of prospective commissioners for a 'council of schooling' that would initiate educational reform, a subject in which Nedham (a former schoolmaster) and Milton (a private tutor) shared a keen interest.[19] Yet that moment of proximity, suggestive as it is, proves nothing. As far as we know the two men may only have become acquainted early in 1651, when Milton became licenser to Nedham's newsbook *Mercurius Politicus*, a position he would hold for about a year. From the outset of that period *Politicus* carried a series of references, coarsely derisive in the spirit of the *Defensio*, to Milton's duel with Salmasius. First it prepared the public for the appearance of the *Defensio*. Then it rejoiced in the impact of that work on the Continent and in Salmasius' consequent discomfort.[20] In the same period, too, the newsbook publicized Milton's *Eikonoklastes*, which Nedham also publicized elsewhere.[21]

[15] *CPW*, I, 663, 903.   [16] *Merc. Brit.*, 5 August 1644, p. 361.

[17] Nedham, *Mercurius Pragmaticus*, 4 April 1648, pp. 1–2; cf. *CPW*, v, 250.

[18] *CPW*, I, 903–4.

[19] J. Milton French, *Life Records of John Milton*, 5 vols. (New Brunswick, NJ, 1949–58), II, pp. 168–9.

[20] *Merc. Pol.*, 23 Jan. 1651, pp. 127, 128; 20 Feb. 1651, p. 604; 3 Apr. 1651, p. 697; 17 Apr. 1651, p. 722; 10 July 1651, pp. 914–15; 22 Apr. 1652, p. 1539; 22 July 1652, pp. [1750–1].

[21] *Ibid.*, 7 May 1651, p. 776; Nedham, *Cat May Look upon a King*, pp. 81, 83–4. (That pamphlet, published in 1652, shows signs of having been written earlier, perhaps in 1650.) And compare *Merc. Pol.*, 10 July 1651, p. 915, with *CPW*, III, 446.

The early 1650s are the first, and for the purposes of this essay the most significant, of the three periods when the political careers of Milton and Nedham come together and illuminate each other. It is a period of common radicalism and republicanism, when both writers seek to guide the infant Commonwealth into new political territory. To the second and third periods we shall come briefly towards the end of the essay. The second finds the two men at once the servants and the critics of the Cromwellian Protectorate. The third finds them standing together in 1660 against the impending Restoration.

II

Friends to each other, Nedham and Milton had a friend in common. This was the lawyer John Bradshaw of Gray's Inn.[22] Bradshaw presided over the court which tried and condemned Charles I and then over the Rump's Council of State. In a codicil added to his will in 1655 he remembered the two writers together.[23] Bradshaw, who may have been related to Milton on Milton's mother's side, acted as the poet's attorney in 1647 during his troubles with the Powell family. Milton's *The Tenure of Kings and Magistrates* (a copy of which Milton is known to have given to Bradshaw's brother) has clear echoes of the speech in which Bradshaw condemned the king.[24] It was to Bradshaw that Milton wrote in February 1653 to recommend the appointment of Andrew Marvell as assistant to the blind poet. It was from Bradshaw that Milton borrowed a manuscript of the *Modus Tenendi Parliamentum*.[25] Milton's *Defensio Secunda* contains a famous eulogy to Bradshaw, that 'friend of my own, of all others the most deserving of my reverence', that 'most faithful of friends, and, in every change of fortune, the most to be relied upon'. The eulogy begins with the description of Bradshaw as 'a name which liberty herself, wherever she is respected, has commended for celebration to everlasting memory', and ends with the claim that Bradshaw will 'spread the renown of his country's deeds among all foreign nations, and with posterity to the end of time'.

Milton identifies virtues in Bradshaw which Nedham was well qualified to appreciate. 'At home', writes Milton, Bradshaw 'is, according to his means, hospitable and splendid'.[26] Nedham, the poet

[22] For Bradshaw and Gray's Inn see *Mercurius Pragmaticus For King Charles II*, 19 June 1649, p. [8].

[23] W. R. Parker, *Milton: A Biography*, 2 vols. (Oxford, 1968), I, p. 540, II, p. 1071.

[24] *CPW*, III, 103–4; Parker, *Milton*, II, p. 953.   [25] *CPW*, VII, 497.

[26] *The Works of John Milton* ed. F. A. Patterson *et al.*, 20 vols. (New York, 1931–40), VIII, pp. 157–61.

John Cleveland tells us in 1650, took meals at Bradshaw's table.[27] Nedham had larger cause to value another of the merits recorded by Milton's eulogy: 'among his political enemies, if any has happened to return to his right senses ... no man has been more ready to forgive'. In his royalist journalism of 1649 Nedham had portrayed Bradshaw as a bloodthirsty 'monster'.[28] But in November Nedham was relieved of his difficulties by Bradshaw, whose 'favour', Nedham told a friend, 'hath once more turned the wheel of my fortune; who upon my single letter hath been pleased to indulge me my liberty'.[29] Soon Nedham had a chance to repay the debt. Early issues of *Mercurius Politicus*, which began life in June 1650, commended Bradshaw as 'a name that shall live with honour in our English histories', 'to whose especial vigilance, indefatigable industry and care, we owe much of our present peace and safety'.[30] Bradshaw reportedly helped Nedham to prepare the edition and translation which he published in 1652 of *Mare Clausum*, the defence of England's sovereignty of the seas by John Selden.[31] In the autumn of 1659, when Bradshaw died, Nedham published an obituary which recalls the eulogy of *Defensio Secunda* and which, in its length and fulsomeness, is unique among Nedham's voluminous publications. Like Milton's eulogy it has a personal touch: 'I cannot but sprinkle a few tears upon the corpse of my noblest friend.'[32]

In early 1651, when Milton began to license *Mercurius Politicus*, Bradshaw was a focus of bitter infighting within the government. Cromwell's victory at Dunbar in September 1650, where he had seemed to confront certain and final defeat, had been welcomed as a miraculous deliverance by the regime. But it also opened cracks within it. Hitherto the government had been held together by the gravity of the external threats to its survival. The basic division was between those who saw Pride's Purge, the regicide, and the abolition

[27] *The Character of Mercurius Politicus* (London, 1650), pp. 7–8.

[28] Anthony Cotton, 'London Newsbooks in the Civil War', Oxford D.Phil. thesis, 1971, pp. 317–18.

[29] Dorothy Gardiner (ed.), *The Oxinden and Peyton Letters* (London, 1937), p. 161. 'Once more' is alas ambiguous. Is it (as may seem the likelier reading) Bradshaw's favour that has 'once more' turned the wheel, or is it merely that the wheel of Nedham's fortune has once more been turned? If the former, we wonder when and how often Bradshaw had helped Nedham before.

[30] *Mercurius Politicus*, 25 July 1650, p. 101; 26 Sept. 1650, p. 276. Milton's eulogy likewise commended Bradshaw's 'indefatigable' industry: *Works*, ed. Patterson *et al.*, VIII, 158–9.

[31] John Selden, *Of the Dominion of the Seas*, ed. James Howell (London, 1663), 'Advertisement'.

[32] *Merc. Pol.*, 3 Nov. 1659, pp. 842–3; [Nedham], *The Publick Intelligencer*, 7 Nov. 1659, pp. 833–4. For Nedham and Bradshaw see also British Library, Add. MS 28002 (Oxinden papers), fol. 331ᵛ.

of monarchy and the House of Lords as preludes to further radical change, and those who wished to heal the wounds inflicted by those events and to dim the memory of them. Alongside the MPs who had supported the revolution of 1648–9 were large numbers who had kept out of parliament between the purge and the regicide and had contrived to avoid expressions of support for them.[33]

The expansive praise of Bradshaw in *Mercurius Politicus* was not a mere repayment of a personal debt. Bradshaw was the hero and symbol of the regicide court. In the weeks before the annual elections for membership of the Council of State, held in February 1651, there were moves to dislodge him from the presidency. (They failed, but he would lose the office nine months later.) Cromwell, who was in Scotland, and who, though he had been a regicide himself, was anxious to conciliate moderates, was believed to favour the termination of Bradshaw's presidency in February, and relations between the two men were testy. Bradshaw had other critics too, among them the trimming Councillor Bulstrode Whitelocke, who thought him an inept, garrulous and self-important chairman. By contrast George Bishop, firmly in the radical camp, rallied to Bradshaw's defence: 'he hath a plain and upright heart, full of courage, and nobleness for justice and the commonwealth', and 'whoever succeeds him, the commonwealth will find a great miss of him'. At the same time Bishop was successfully pressing for the uncompromising treatment by the Rump of royalists whom he had caught conspiring in Norfolk, a move which countered the conciliatory initiatives of moderates. Bradshaw and *Politicus* both gave their backing to Bishop's stance.[34]

In November 1650 the Commons debated a proposal that MPs be required to swear retrospective approval of the trial and execution of the king. Although that move was seen off, the House did issue a vote of congratulation to the regicides. It also ordered a day of thanksgiving to mark the second anniversary of the execution and took measures to remove royal arms and statuary from public places.[35] *Politicus* enthusiastically endorsed that programme.[36] The regicide, it pro-

---

[33] I have described the political background in my *The Rump Parliament 1648–1653* (Cambridge, 1974).

[34] *Ibid.*, p. 249 (cf. *ibid.*, pp. 243–5, 262); J. Nickolls (ed.), *Original Letters and Papers of State, Addressed to Oliver Cromwell* (London, 1743), pp. 33–4, 39, 49–51, 54–7, 65; Bulstrode Whitelocke, *Memorials of the English Affairs*, 4 vols. (Oxford, 1853), II, pp. 552, 558; Ruth Spalding (ed.), *The Diary of Bulstrode Whitelocke 1605–1675* (London, 1990), p. 254; *Merc. Pol.*, 2 Jan. 1651, p. 491.   [35] Worden, *Rump Parliament*, pp. 237–8.

[36] *Merc. Pol.*, 22 Aug. 1650, p. 178; 19 Dec. 1650, p. 464.

claimed, had been 'one of the most heroic and exemplary acts of
justice that ever was done under the sun'. 'That heroic and most noble
act of justice' was 'the basis whereon the Commonwealth is founded.
And if it ever be completed, it must be by honouring and entrusting
those noble instruments and hands who laid the foundation, or now
help with open hearts to carry on the building.'[37] There were,
Nedham argued, two 'irreconcileable' interests, the Commonwealth
and the Stuarts, between which all Englishmen must choose. There
was 'as vast a contrariety' between 'the Republic and the late family'
as between 'God and Belial, light and darkness, liberty and slavery,
free-state and tyranny'. Men who would not declare themselves
friends to the Rump must be declared its enemies. The regime must
penalize both 'the wild geese and the tame, the malignant and the
neutral'. It must take note of the 'jealousies and sorrows in the hearts
of the parliament's best friends', who 'think that surely there are some
persons in authority that have an evil influence to hinder the much
desired reformation'. It must root out, from central and local
government, 'lukewarm Laodiceans', 'those phlegmatic souls of the
moderate or middle temper', who would bend with the wind if the
royalist cause revived. It must confine power to 'that party' which
remained 'firm to the interest of freedom'.[38]

In May 1651 Nedham announced his intention – never, it seems,
fulfilled – to justify the regicide 'in a set treatise, by a cloud of
instances, derived from the scope of holy writ, the very principles of
right reason, law and example'.[39] The treatise, we may suppose,
would have been the equivalent for a native audience to Milton's
Defensio, which was published in February 1651. The *Defensio*, like
Politicus, speaks ostensibly for a government, but in reality for a party:
for what Nedham calls the Commonwealth's 'party of its own
throughout the nation'.[40] In the earlier 1640s both Nedham and
Milton had entertained views on kingship and on the Stuarts much
more critical than those on which parliament took its public stands.
Milton's feelings can be seen in his unpublished commonplace book

[37] *Ibid.*, 15 May 1651, p. 374; 3 July 1651, p. 886. Cf. *ibid.*, 2 Oct. 1651, p. 1100; 4 March 1652,
p. 1442.
[38] *Ibid.*, 22 Aug. 1650, p. 173; 24 Oct. 1650, pp. 323–4; 6 Feb. 1651, pp. 567–8; 27 Feb. 1651,
p. 607; 24 July 1651, p. 923; 21 Aug. 1651, p. 997; 6 Nov. 1651, p. 174; 5 Feb. 1652, p. 1385;
27 May 1652, p. 1511.   [39] *Ibid.*, 15 May 1651, p. 784.
[40] Nedham, *The Case of the Commonwealth of England, Stated*, ed. Philip Knachel (Charlottesville,
Va., 1969), p. 114.

and between the lines of his pamphlets.[41] Nedham's attitude emerges in *Mercurius Britanicus*, which attacked the tyranny of Charles I and insisted on the fiduciary character of kingship. In their concern to win and fortify public opinion, Nedham's masters in the first Civil War normally allowed him to express opinions more radical than their own. Both sides in the Civil War needed to answer, to caricature, to vilify each other. There resulted a process of polarization in which Nedham played a leading part.[42] He engaged in a similar process under the Rump.

So did Milton. The Rump's enemies – Presbyterians, royalists, Salmasius – had to be answered. In answering them, Milton, like Nedham, made points which only the more radical of his political masters would have been glad to hear. Milton had long scorned what he too termed 'lukewarm', 'Laodicean', 'neutral' men. He had long despised the sloth and equivocation that cloak themselves 'under the affected name of moderation'.[43] In 1649–51 he wrote, as Nedham did in 1650–2, for the 'best-affected' party.[44] In his eyes as in Nedham's the crisis of 1648–9 had divided the nation into two parties, the friends of 'liberty' and the friends of 'slavery'.[45] Like Nedham, Milton repeatedly recalled the wickedness and folly of the Presbyterian politicians and clergy of the late 1640s, behaviour which the moderate MPs in the Rump, anxious to bring Presbyterians back into the fold, wanted to forget. Those moderates also wished to distance the regime from its military origins and to subordinate the army, which had carried out the revolution of 1648–9, to civilian rule. They would not have enjoyed Milton's reminder, in the *Defensio*, that in the winter of 1648–9 'our soldiers showed better judgement than our senators, and saved the commonwealth by their arms when the other by their votes had almost ruined it'.[46]

---

[41] I have briefly discussed that topic in 'Milton's Republicanism and the Tyranny of Heaven', in Gisela Bock, Quentin Skinner and Maurizio Viroli (eds.), *Machiavelli and Republicanism* (Cambridge, 1990), pp. 231–2; there is more to be said about it.

[42] The process is described by Peter W. Thomas, *Sir John Berkenhead 1617–1679* (Oxford, 1969).

[43] *CPW*, i, 683, 690, 868; ii, 551; iii, 349, 600.   [44] *CPW*, iii, 512.

[45] *Works*, ed. Patterson *et al.*, vii, p. 511; cf. *ibid.*, vii, pp. 55, 493; viii, p. 177.

[46] *Ibid.*, vii, p. 55. Within the common support of Milton and Nedham for the Commonwealth's 'party of its own' there is admittedly a characteristic difference. In Nedham's explanations the party rules primarily by right of conquest: in Milton's primarily by right of virtue. Yet Milton does make use of the argument from conquest (*Works*, ed. Patterson *et al.*, vii, p. 367; *CPW*, vii, 455, 481, 483; cf. *ibid.*, iv, 917), while the argument from conquest – a Hobbesian argument – which Nedham advances on the Rump's behalf represents only a temporary phase in his thought; the appeals to public virtue which accompanied them, though initially more muted, would prove more persistent.

Milton and Nedham are close to each other in their celebrations of
the regicide. With Nedham, Milton hails the 'heroic virtue' of that
'memorable act of judicature', that 'impartial and noble piece of
justice', that 'exemplary' and 'matchless' triumph, 'so worthy of
heroic ages', which was carried out with 'matchless valour' and with
'the magnanimity peculiar to heroes'.[47] The 'proceedings' of the
regicides, asserts Milton, 'appear equal to what hath been done in any
age or nation heretofore': the 'high achievements' for which the king's
execution paved the way, declares Nedham, 'may match any of the
ancients'.[48] Nedham and Milton wrap their heroes in togas. 'In the
monuments of the Grecian and Roman freedom', recalls Nedham,
'we find those nations were wont to heap all the honours they could
invent, by public rewards, consecration of statues, and crown of laurel
upon worthy patriots' who had dared bring tyrants to justice.[49] The
Greeks and Romans, agrees Milton in the *Defensio*, praised and even
deified the slayers of tyrants.[50]

III

Milton and Nedham are not only champions of regicide. They are in
at the birth of English republicanism. The description of either man
as a republican may give us pause. Both of them, after all, supported
the overthrow of the Commonwealth in 1653 and its replacement by
the semi-monarchical regime of Cromwell. In endorsing that regime
Milton drew a distinction, which he had repeatedly made in his
publications of the Rump period, between tyrants, who are evil, and
kings, who are virtuous.[51] Only in 1659–60 did he unambiguously
renounce monarchy of any kind. Yet, at least under the Rump, his
tolerance of kingship is more theoretical than practical. He accepts
the Aristotelian principle of distributive justice, which awards supreme
power to a supremely wise and virtuous leader. But he usually invokes
Aristotle's principle to make an opposite point: to illustrate the folly of
subordinating wise and virtuous men to the rule of kings, who are
normally far less wise and virtuous.[52] He holds up virtuous kingship as

---

[47] *CPW*, III, 191, 233, 237, 311, 344, 561, 577, 589, 596; *Works*, ed. Patterson *et al.*, VII, pp. 63–5.
[48] *CPW*, III, 194; *Merc. Pol.*, 22 Jan. 1652, p. 1352.   [49] *Merc. Pol.*, 4 Mar. 1652, pp. 1442–3.
[50] *Works*, ed. Patterson *et al.*, VII, pp. 305–7, 329. Cf. *ibid.*, VII, p. 451; *CPW*, VII, 356.
[51] *CPW*, III, 198, 212, 388, 397, 453, 458, 530 (cf. *ibid.*, I, 439, 443, 453, 457, 507, 732); *Works*, ed.
      Patterson *et al.*, VII, pp. 111, 147, 235, 245, 267, 305, 307, 433–5, 475–7, 551; VIII, pp. 25, 27, 93.
[52] *CPW*, I, 420; II, 589; III, 204–5, 460, 486, 542, 585; VII, 364, 383, 448–9, 481–2; *Works*, ed.
      Patterson *et al.*, VII, pp. 127, 269–71, 279, 305, 377–9; cf. Nedham, *Case of the Commonwealth*,
      pp. 115, 120, 122.

a model with which to reproach tyrants, not for imitation or adoption by the Commonwealth. In and after *Eikonoklastes*, Milton uses a practical argument against kingship which counters his distinction between kingship and tyranny. Kings, whether hereditary or elected, are so 'frequently' or 'commonly' evil, so 'rarely' good, that wise nations will steer clear of them.[53] Often indeed Milton uses the word 'kings' pejoratively and treats kings and tyrants as indistinguishable.[54] Nedham explicitly abandons the distinction between them.[55] He lists the endless successions of evil kings that have been endured by England and other nations[56] and claims that good kings provide at best 'very rare' respites from a general rule of depravity.[57] It is of course true that in the course of his life Nedham was willing to write not only for Cromwell but for the Stuarts. Yet it is in his republican writings that his arguments are at their most innovative and incisive. While his royalist prose brings out best his gift for wit and satire, it is his republican prose that is most creative and productive in the realm of ideas. His Cromwellian prose, in comparison with either, is flat.

The republicanism of Milton and Nedham under the Rump is a critical moment in English political thought. Before 1649 political argument had been mainly (even if, as we are now properly reminded, not wholly) conducted in the insular and backward-looking language of custom, precedent and the ancient constitution.[58] In 1649 the ancient constitution collapsed. Supporters of the new regime had to look elsewhere for their arguments. Four ideas were developed during the Rump period to meet that need. First there was the appeal to providence, to a God whose outstretched arm has shattered earthly and customary forms. Secondly there was conquest theory, which entitled the victors of the Civil Wars to rewrite the constitution in their own interest. Thirdly there was the claim that the people were the origins of all legitimate authority and that they, or at least the

---

[53] *CPW*, III, 337, 409, 484, 486, 581; VII, 377 (cf. *ibid.*, III, 243); *Works*, ed. Patterson *et al.*, VII, pp. 115, 123. This was also the position of the radicals in the Rump who pushed through the abolition of monarchy: S. R. Gardiner (ed.), *The Constitutional Documents of the Puritan Revolution* (Oxford, 3rd edn 1906), p. 385.

[54] *CPW*, III, 337, 357, 509, 539, 598 (cf. *ibid.*, I, 431–2, 440, 471; III, 239; *Works*, ed. Patterson *et al.*, VII, pp. 119, 411). [55] Nedham, *Case of the Commonwealth*, pp. 62, 127.

[56] *Ibid.*, pp. 25–7, 68; *Merc. Pol.*, 24 Oct. 1650, pp. 325–6; 5 June 1651, pp. 831–2; 28 Aug. 1651, pp. 213–16; 4 Sept. 1651, pp. 229–32; *A Cat May Look upon a King*.

[57] Nedham, *Case of the Commonwealth*, p. 117.

[58] For the insularity: J. G. A. Pocock, *The Ancient Constitution and the Feudal Law* (Cambridge, 1957); for recent qualifications of Pocock's thesis: J. P. Sommerville, *Politics and Ideology in England 1603–1640* (London, 1986); Glenn Burgess, *The Politics of the Ancient Constitution* (London, 1992).

virtuous or the victorious among them, were entitled to abolish existing forms and create new ones at their wish. Those three arguments can be found, to varying degrees and with varying emphases, in Milton and in Nedham. But none of them pointed towards the adoption of one particular form of government in preference to another. That was the task of republicanism. In the England of the 1650s a decisive stage in the emergence of modern republicanism was formed. Nedham and Milton are the writers who initiated its formation.[59]

In *The Case of the Commonwealth of England, Stated* in 1650, and in *Mercurius Politicus* in 1651–2, Nedham expounded the virtues of a free state or republic. He urged his country to turn its back on the ancient constitution and to look instead to the wisdom of classical antiquity and especially of republican Rome. His editorials are a series of history lessons which imitate, both in form and in content, Machiavelli's *Discourses*. It is through them that Machiavelli's republican teaching breaks into the foreground of English political thinking, and that there is created the mental framework within which the writings of Machiavelli's disciple James Harrington make their impact later in the decade. Milton's republicanism of the Rump period is less conspicuous than Nedham's. It is to be found principally – though not exclusively – in writings which he did not publish: in the Digression to his *History of Britain*, written soon after the execution of the king,[60] and in his commonplace book, which contains his reflections on Machiavelli in 1651–2.[61] Milton, like Nedham, was not new to Machiavelli's republicanism. Both men had explored it well before 1649. But before 1649 republicanism in England could seem only a hypothetical ideal. Now it was advanced to meet a crisis and an opportunity.

Milton, like Nedham, urged his country to set the ancient constitution aside and to turn instead to the wisdom of Mediterranean republicanism.[62] Both writers depart strikingly from the general run of their contemporaries in appealing to historical examples – biblical, classical, medieval, modern – which range widely over time and

---

[59] Worden, 'Marchamont Nedham and the Beginnings of English Republicanism'.
[60] That dating, by Nicholas von Maltzahn, is controversial: see the debate between him and Austin Woolrych in *Historical Journal*, 36 (1993), 929–56. I hope to explain elsewhere my reasons for preferring von Maltzahn's view.
[61] Worden, 'Milton's Republicanism and the Tyranny of Heaven', pp. 231–5.
[62] *CPW*, VII, 451. In neither writer did that position exclude expressions of admiration for the substance and spirit of medieval liberty.

place, and in lining up those examples beside each other. In both their minds the classical examples are prominent. Their technique strips away the national self-absorption of so much writing of the time and offers the nation a much wider range of wisdom and example on which to draw. It places English experience within a comparative framework that demonstrates the operation of universal causes and patterns. Both writers maintain, in the same or similar phrases, that alongside the examples they have chosen they have countless others which they lack the space, or else the need, to reproduce.[63] The republican lessons of history must have been an eager source of conversation between the two friends. Our understanding of Milton's republicanism can be enhanced by comparison – and sometimes by contrast – with Nedham's.

The republicanism of both writers placed them in an ambivalent position towards the Commonwealth, which employed both of them and which both of them vigorously defended against its royalist and Presbyterian enemies, but about which both of them had critical views. The Rump, which abolished monarchy and the House of Lords, was the remnant of the ancient constitution, not a replacement of it. In so far as it introduced a republican form of government it did so by default, not by design. There was no king in the Rump period, but no republican constitutional architecture either. English republicanism of the 1650s is consequently more often a criticism of the English republic than an endorsement of it. Classical and Renaissance republicanism favoured mixed government, a principle to which both Nedham and Milton had been drawn in the 1640s.[64] The unicameral rule of the Rump answered not to the principle of mixed government but to the claim which Hobbes contemptuously opposed to it, for undivided and unlimited sovereignty. Milton laments his country's innocence about constitutional architecture. Its new leaders, he fears, have the habitual English disease: victims of too insular a political education, they are better versed in courage and warfare than in political skill and prudence.[65] In the *Defensio* Milton admits, though he does not specify, the deficiencies of the form of government established in 1649.[66] In 1660 he asserts that the failure to frame 'the

---

[63] For Nedham see Worden, '"Wit in a Roundhead"'; for Milton, *CPW*, I, 588; II, 489, 638; III, 201, 240, 539, 589; *Works*, ed. Patterson *et al.*, VII, pp. 307, 333.

[64] *Merc. Brit.*, 6 Mar. 1644, p. 198; 12 Mar. 1644, p. 206; *CPW*, I, 599.

[65] *CPW*, V, 451 (cf. *ibid.*, I, 796–7; II, 398–9); Leo Miller, *John Milton and the Oldenburg Safeguard* (New York, 1985), pp. 171–2.   [66] *Works*, ed. Patterson *et al.*, VII, p. 29.

form of a commonwealth' in 1649 had caused the ensuing calamities of the Interregnum.[67] With Nedham, Milton sees 1649 as one of those rare opportunities in a nation's history – what Machiavelli had called *occasioni* – when liberty is either seized or lost for generations to come.[68] The opportunity was missed.

And yet Milton never tells us how it should have been taken. His interest in constitutional architecture proves to be distinctly limited. He quickly loses patience with disputes about the 'intricacies' of constitutional forms.[69] As so often in his philosophy, forms count for much less than spirit. His republicanism feeds on, but is also confined by, his commitment to 'internal liberty', his certainty that moral or religious reform, reform of the soul or the household or the church, is a necessary and perhaps even sufficient condition of political reform.

Nedham's attitude to the Rump, like Milton's, is ambivalent. His editorials contrive to champion the regime explicitly and to criticize it implicitly. He too is evidently uneasy about the new form of government, or the lack of one. Agreeing with Machiavelli that true republicanism is popular republicanism, which prefers the claims of the people to those of the nobility or of the senate (or, in the case of England after 1649, of the parliament), he intimates that the Rump needs to introduce equivalents to the tribunes and popular assemblies which had protected popular liberties in republican Rome.[70] Yet that enterprising hint is not developed. Its eccentricity to the political thinking of its time made its development in Nedham's hands impracticable. For though *Mercurius Politicus* offered encouragement to radicals outside parliament who wearied of the Rump's rule and longed for its replacement, those radicals were as committed as the Rump to the undivided and unicameral sovereignty of the House of Commons. The main criticisms of the Rump ventured by Nedham are of its policies, not of its form of government. He voices the grievance of those who look for speedy parliamentary elections and for radical social reform. Into that territory Milton rarely follows him.

Nedham is a more concrete thinker than Milton, a more acute observer of history and politics. Yet his republicanism, too, has more to do with spirit than with form. Here again the two writers come

---

[67] *CPW*, VII, 430.

[68] *Ibid.*, III, 208–9; V, 441–3; VII, 430; *Merc. Pol.*, 1 Aug. 1650, p. 122; 9 Jan. 1651, p. 512; 5 June 1651, p. 832; 25 Sept. 1651, p. 1077; 30 Oct. 1651, p. 1158.   [69] *CPW*, VII, 331, 445.

[70] *Merc. Pol.*, 9 Oct. 1651, pp. 1110–11, 25 Dec. 1651, p. 1289; 1 Apr. 1652, p. 1490; 20 May 1652, p. 1596; 27 May 1652, pp. 1610–11; 22 July 1652, p. 1738.

close together. Pervasive in the writings of both of them is a vocabulary, indebted to Cicero and medieval tradition and given a modern edge by Machiavelli, which explains that freedom thrives on 'active', 'generous', 'magnanimous', 'manly' virtue and succumbs to corruption, degeneracy, effeminacy. There is the common insistence – despite Nedham's own social habits – on frugality and temperance and discipline and on the dependence both of virtue and of liberty upon them. There is the contrast between liberty and licence, and there is the Machiavellian conviction that luxury is an enemy to liberty.[71] There is the identification by both men of royalism as the political equivalent and extension of idolatry and superstition in religion.[72] The English instinct for what Milton calls 'a civil kind of idolatry in idolizing their kings'[73] is traced by both writers to the tyranny of custom and to the evils of education, in schools and universities alike.

The republican spirits of the two writers are not identical. Nedham's is uninhibited in its Machiavellian commitment to the primacy of the public sphere. The claims of the private mind, of conscience and of religious beliefs (or 'opinions' as he calls them),[74] he treats with scepticism. Milton's language of inward liberty and inward virtue is largely foreign to Nedham. Again, the licence which Nedham contrasts with liberty, and the discipline he identifies with it, are more often social and political qualities than, as they are for Milton, virtues of the mind.[75] And where, for Milton, England's failings in political education belong to wider defects of ethical and religious instruction, Nedham's concern with educational reform under the Rump is essentially political.[76] Even so, the resemblances between Milton's and Nedham's languages are more significant in the development of English republicanism than the contrasts.

The resemblances we have so far seen derive from the promotion by the two men of values which they thought desirable in all ages. There are resemblances too in their approaches to the opportunities and

---

[71] Worden, 'Marchamont Nedham and the Beginnings of English Republicanism', pp. 70–1.
[72] Nedham, *Case of the Commonwealth*, pp. 15, 114; *Merc. Pol.* 20 June 1650, p. 24; 8 Aug. 1650, pp. 131, 141; 22 May 1651, p. 813; 10 July 1651, p. 914; 18 Sept. 1651, p. 1067; 4 Mar. 1652, p. 1443; *CPW*, I, 923–4; II, 487; III, 237, 340, 341, 343, 438, 446, 484, 549, 570, 601; VII, 421, 425–6.   [73] *CPW*, III, 343.
[74] Nedham, *Case of the Commonwealth*, p. 123; *Merc. Pol.*, 12 Aug. 1652, p. 1781.
[75] Nedham, *Case of the Commonwealth*, pp. 96, 99, 103; *Merc. Pol.*, 15 Jan. 1652, p. 1335; 27 May 1652, p. 1511; 10 June 1652, p. 1641.
[76] Nedham, *Case of the Commonwealth*, pp. 111–12, 114; *Merc. Pol.*, 2 Oct. 1651, pp. 1093–4; 3 June 1652, pp. 1625–9.

challenges confronting England after the king's execution. The civil wars and the regicide belonged to a wider European pattern of revolution to which all republicans of the 1650s were alert. Milton had long hoped that the reformation planned by God for England would 'put an end to all earthly tyrannies'.[77] In *Eikonoklastes* he declares it to be 'an honour belonging to [God's] saints ... to overcome those European kings' who derive their power from Antichrist.[78] 'Most nations', proclaims the *Defensio*, will be brought by the example of Charles I's execution to realize that they too live under slavery, and will strive to free themselves.[79] Such sentiments were widely held after the regicide. They are present in the Horatian Ode of Andrew Marvell in 1650, which prophesies the liberation of 'all states not free' by Cromwell's army, and they are conspicuous in Nedham's publications of the same year.[80] Later they are propounded in Harrington's *Oceana*. 'This', declares Nedham in 1650, 'is an age for kings to run the wildgoose-chase.'[81] 'Take my word for it', writes Milton in the *Defensio*, 'the right of kings seems to be tottering.'[82] Sometimes Milton's vision seems to be that of Nedham and of Marvell: of an army of liberation marching through Europe. At other times he expresses scruples, which belong to his humanist intellectual equipment, about the pursuit of glory through warfare, and urges the nation to put justice at home before conquest abroad.[83] In such moods it seems that the overthrow of European monarchy will be won not by the sword but by the pen: by the pen wielded by Milton against Salmasius.

The conflict between monarchy and liberty, in the minds of Milton and Nedham alike, is being fought across Europe. It is being fought conspicuously in France, where the task of liberation falls upon the rebels of Bordeaux, whom both writers take to be emulators or prospective emulators of the English regicides.[84] It is being fought still more conspicuously in the United Provinces, whose anti-monarchical record, and whose achievement of independence from Spanish tyranny and popery in 1648, feats warmly admired by both our writers, gave needed confidence to the first stages of English

---

[77] *CPW*, I, 616; cf. *ibid.*, II, 231.   [78] *CPW*, III, 598.
[79] *Works*, ed. Patterson *et al.*, VII, p. 213; cf. *ibid.*, VIII, p. 15.
[80] Worden, 'Marchamont Nedham and the Beginnings of English Republicanism', p. 72.
[81] *Merc. Pol.*, 4 July 1650, p. 54.   [82] *Works*, ed. Patterson *et al.*, VII, p. 93.
[83] *Ibid.*, VII, p. 401; VIII, p. 185; *CPW*, I, 422, 499, 597; III, 238.
[84] Worden, 'Marchamont Nedham and the Beginnings of English Republicanism', p. 72; *CPW*, VII, 355–6.

republicanism. The conflict between the House of Orange and the republicans of Holland at once paralleled and interacted with the British conflict, where the Stuart pretenders were the relations and allies of the Orange family. As we might expect, Milton is more conscious than Nedham of the religious bonds between the two countries, Nedham more conscious than Milton of the political resemblances between the two infant republics. But the difference is one only of emphasis.[85]

The scale of the conflict between monarchy and tyranny inspires an ambitious programme in Nedham, which he promotes in *Politicus* in 1651–2. He advocates bold proposals for a union of England and Holland that will break up the United Provinces and emancipate its richest and most powerful province from the Orange threat, and thus help to free England from the Stuart one.[86] He proposes other ambitious initiatives in foreign policy, again with the destruction of the Stuart cause in mind. Following Machiavelli's advice about colonization, and invoking classical examples, he recommends the 'incorporation' of Scotland, which Cromwell has conquered, into England and the award of parliamentary representation to the Scots – a policy carried out by the Rump in 1652, if in terms less bold than those for which Nedham may have hoped. Nedham wants England to become, in Machiavelli's language, a commonwealth for expansion. Like Machiavelli, he exhorts his countrymen to avoid the employment of mercenary troops and to raise and train a citizen militia that will win glory abroad and preserve freedom at home. With Machiavelli he urges them to risk, even to welcome, the domestic 'tumults' that witness to the vitality of popular liberty and are a necessary price for it.[87] Those arguments do not figure in Milton's public writings, but they do give weight to entries in his commonplace book in 1651–2, where, among many telling references to Machiavelli, he registers his agreement with the Florentine about the desirability of leagues

---

[85] For Milton and the United Provinces see *CPW*, I, 586; III, 226–7, 240; VII, 179, 357, 374–5, 381–2; *Works*, ed. Patterson *et al.*, VII, pp. 19, 71–3, 203, 285; VIII, pp. 99, 141, 193; IX, pp. 101–3.

[86] For Nedham's representation of the common dangers to, and the shared opportunities open to, the English and Dutch republics in 1650–1 see *Merc. Pol.*, 8 Aug. 1650, pp. 136–9; 10 Oct. 1650, p. 307; 9 Jan. 1651, p. 512; 16 Jan. 1651, p. 529; 23 Jan. 1651, p. 542; 20 Feb. 1651, p. 600; 3 April 1651, pp. 696–7; 29 May 1651, p. 816; 5 June 1651, p. 834; 12 June 1651, p. 857; 10 July 1651, pp. 908–9, 913; 2 Oct. 1651, p. 1103; 9 Oct. 1651, p. 1110; 20 Nov. 1651, p. 1211; 13 May 1652, pp. 1586–7; 20 May 1652, p. 1595.

[87] Worden, 'Marchamont Nedham and the Beginnings of English Republicanism', pp. 71, 73–4; Worden, 'James Harrington and the Commonwealth of Oceana', in Wootton, (ed.), *Republicanism, Liberty, and Commercial Society*, p. 93.

between republics, about the acquisition of new conquests, and about the political benefits of tumults.[88] Milton also shares Machiavelli's and Nedham's dislike of mercenary troops.[89]

Yet on that last point, as in their discussions of forms of government, Milton and Nedham confronted a problem. What Milton calls the 'deliverance' of 1649 was not wrought by the militia forces of the counties, which republicans of a later generation would hail as England's equivalent to the citizen militias of ancient Rome and Renaissance Italy, but which the Rump dared not trust.[90] It was wrought by what had become a standing army, albeit an army characterized, as Milton and Nedham emphasized, by discipline and public spirit.[91] There is thus an ambivalence or unease running through the pronouncements of both writers on standing armies and militias.[92] There is a deeper ambivalence still about the leader of England's standing army, Oliver Cromwell, who became Lord Protector in December 1653 after his forces had broken up two parliaments within a year.

IV

Elsewhere in this volume Martin Dzelzainis persuasively represents Milton's publication in 1658 of *The Cabinet-Council* and of a new edition of the *Defensio* as veiled attacks on Cromwell and his regime (ch. 10 below). In the Protectorate, as so often in the early modern period, the most telling literary expressions of political opposition are to be found between the lines. Interlinear criticism presents scholars with obvious difficulties and obvious temptations. It may be too hard to prove and too easy to imagine. But sometimes it is unmistakable.

It is unmistakable in Nedham's writings about Cromwell. In the later 1640s, when advocating the restoration of the king, Nedham had played as large a part as anyone in forming the popular image of Cromwell as a man of ruthless ambition and bottomless dissimulation and hypocrisy. In *Mercurius Politicus* in 1651–2, when it was widely suspected that Cromwell would make himself king and betray both

---

[88] *CPW*, I, 499, 504, 505.   [89] *CPW*, I, 471, 497 (cf. *ibid.*, I, 414–15, 498).
[90] Cf. David Underdown, *Pride's Purge* (London, 1971), p. 307.
[91] *Works*, ed. Patterson *et al.*, VII, pp. 55, 493; VIII, pp. 177–9; Nedham, *The Lawyer of Lincolnes-Inne Reformed* (London, 1647), p. 1; Nedham, *Case of the Commonwealth*, pp. 59, 114–15; Nedham, *Interest will not Lie* (London, 1659), pp. 24–6.
[92] *CPW*, III, 448; VII, 435, 454; Nedham, *Case of the Commonwealth*, p. 77; *Merc. Pol.*, 27 May 1652, pp. 1609–10; Nedham, *Interest will not Lie*, p. 9.

the political and the social radicalism of the revolution, Nedham daringly recycled that earlier criticism. Though he did not now name Cromwell, Cromwell remains the intended target of Nedham's allusions to ambitious generals who had destroyed public liberty in classical antiquity. In 1656 the criticisms were cycled again, when Nedham reprinted editorials from *Politicus*, with amendments, in his treatise *The Excellencie of a Free State*. Ostensibly a defence of the Protectorate, *The Excellencie* is a risky and clever attack on it. The criticisms which had been aimed at Cromwell in *Politicus* are delicately rephrased so as to incorporate the evidence of Cromwell's character and intentions which had emerged in and since his usurpation of power in 1653.[93]

The Excellencie was one of three major anti-Cromwellian publications of 1656. The second was *A Healing Question Propounded* by Sir Henry Vane, the hero of Milton's sonnet of 1652. *A Healing Question* asks, with *The Excellencie*, how the supremacy of the 'good' or 'honest' or 'well-affected' party is to be restored. Like *The Excellencie* it hits subtly at Cromwell's ambition and hypocrisy, to which it alludes in dark and bitter biblical parallels. The third work was the *Oceana* of James Harrington. There Harrington represents Cromwell in fictional form, as the Lord Archon, who does what Vane and Nedham alike urge Cromwell to do. He surrenders the authority which he has seized by the sword. By deft quotation and adaptation of Cromwell's speeches, Harrington creates, in the supremely virtuous Lord Archon, a reverse image of Cromwell. The Archon is Cromwell as Cromwell represents himself, but the opposite of what Cromwell is.[94] The interlinear tactics of Nedham, Vane and Harrington show that Milton was not alone, under the Protectorate, in giving veiled expression to the hatred and mistrust which Cromwell inspired so widely, and which Milton, like Harrington, would express more plainly once the Protectorate had been toppled in 1659. But where Vane and Harrington wrote from outside the Protectoral regime, Milton and Nedham wrote from within it. Both escaped without punishment. In their hands, opposition from within became an art form.

Their tactics invite us to think again about the representation of

---

[93] Worden, 'Marchamont Nedham and the Beginnings of English Republicanism', pp. 66–7, 77–9.
[94] For Vane see my 'Oliver Cromwell and the Sin of Achan', in Derek Beales and Geoffrey Best (eds.), *History, Society and the Churches* (Cambridge, 1985), pp. 138–9; and for Harrington my 'Harrington's *Oceana*: Origins and Aftermath', in Wootton (ed.), *Republicanism, Liberty, and Commercial Society*, pp. 119–26.

Cromwell in *Defensio Secunda* in 1654. We need not doubt that one side of Milton's mind revered the achievements of Cromwell which are lauded in that work, or that he hoped (as he would evidently have ceased to do by 1658) that still greater ones would follow. But the celebration of Cromwell, like the many celebrations of England's current rulers elsewhere in Milton's prose, belongs to Renaissance conventions of praise, where praise serves not only to edify and encourage but to advise, even to warn, even to admonish. Milton was as alive as anyone to those conventions and to the responsibilities they carried.[95] In *Defensio Secunda* his admonition perhaps went beyond those conventions. That treatise takes up the question which had been left unanswered in Milton's sonnet to Cromwell in 1652, where the representation of Cromwell has an ambiguity not to be found in Milton's wholehearted tribute to Sir Henry Vane in the same year. In 1654 as in 1652 Milton asks whether Cromwell, who has met the challenge of war, can meet the challenge of peace. Peace will 'show what is the predominant disposition of your nature ... whether there is indeed in you that living piety, that faith, justice, and moderation of mind, for which we have thought that you above all others deserved, by the will of God, to be elevated to this sovereign dignity'.[96] In 1654 as in 1652 the question is left unanswered. Cromwell remains on probation.

Is he hero or villain? Nedham, like Milton, openly praises his heroism but covertly points to the man's darker side. In 1651–2 and again in 1656 Nedham represented Cromwell as a Machiavellian prince. He glanced at the false professions of integrity, humility and piety of which Cromwell's enemies so often complained.[97] Cromwell had become expert in giving outward encouragement to the radical programmes of his followers while obstructing those programmes behind the scenes.[98] Men who felt betrayed by that dexterity would have warmed to Nedham's repeated intimations that Cromwell had risen to power 'upon specious and popular pretences', by 'clothing himself with a pretence of the people's liberty', by 'pretending' himself a 'great patron of liberty'.[99] The same point is made in Milton's *The Readie and Easie Way* in 1660, which refrains, as does Nedham's anti-Cromwellian literature of the 1650s, from naming

[95] *CPW*, II, 487–8; cf. (e.g.) Ben Jonson's 'An Epistle to Master John Selden', lines 19, 28.
[96] *Works*, ed. Patterson *et al.*, VIII, pp. 227–9.
[97] *Merc. Pol.*, 13 June 1650, p. 13; 5 Aug. 1652, pp. 1769–73; Nedham, *The Excellencie of a Free State* (London, 1656), pp. 165–71.   [98] Worden, *Rump Parliament*, pp. 274–80, 291.
[99] *Merc. Pol.*, 1 Apr. 1652, pp. 1490, 1491; 5 Aug. 1652, p. 1773; Nedham, *Case of the Commonwealth*, p. 102.

Cromwell, but leaves Milton's readers as clear as Nedham's about its target: 'ambitious leaders of armies', remarks Milton, adopt 'hypocritical pretences' in order to destroy parliaments and to 'make way to their own tyrannical designs'.[100] Milton would not have levelled such a charge against Cromwell in 1654. Yet there is a sharp edge to the passage of *Defensio Secunda* which fears lest Cromwell, 'the patron himself of liberty' ('*patronus ipse libertatis*'), 'than whom none is esteemed a more just, a holier, or a better man', should 'offer violence to', and 'forcibly seize upon', 'the liberty of others'.[101] The passage recalls the anti-Cromwellian irony of Nedham's *The Excellencie* and Harrington's *Oceana*.

Cromwell's violence in April 1653 had expelled the Rump. When, on the same day, Cromwell broke up the Rump's Council of State, Milton's and Nedham's friend John Bradshaw declared defiantly that 'no power under heaven' could justly remove the MPs from power 'but themselves'.[102] Bradshaw would remain implacably opposed to the Protectorate. Milton and Nedham worked within it, but did not forget those principles of the 'good old cause' for which Bradshaw remained firm. The emphasis on the heroism and rectitude of the regicide in *Defensio Secunda*, as in the *Defensio*, vindicated the existing government from the charges of its enemies but at the same time revived a memory on which that government, or at least its more moderate members, had no wish to dwell. (The re-publication of the *Defensio* in 1658 – an event prominently advertised by *Mercurius Politicus*[103] – would revive that memory too.) *Defensio Secunda* contrives to remind its readers that the Long Parliament had been what, thanks to Cromwell's seizure of power, parliament no longer was, 'the supreme council of the nation'.[104] Nedham would play the same card in *The Excellencie*, which repeatedly insists that 'the supreme authority' of the nation properly belongs 'in the hands of the people's representatives'.[105] Under the Protectorate as under the Rump, Milton writes ostensibly for a government, in reality for a party. The attacks on Presbyterianism in *Defensio Secunda*, and the pleas for radical religious reform, ran counter to the Protector's policy of 'healing and settling', which aimed to reassure the gentry and orthodox clergy and to restore presbyterians to influence in church and state.

---

[100] *CPW*, vii, 380.   [101] *Works*, ed. Patterson *et al.*, vii, p. 227.
[102] C. H. Firth (ed.), *Memoirs of Edmund Ludlow*, 2 vols. (Oxford, 1894), i, p. 357.
[103] *Merc. Pol.*, 25 November 1658, p. 29.   [104] *Works*, ed. Patterson *et al.*, viii, p. 151.
[105] *The Excellencie*, p. v and *passim*.

Yet the most striking boldness of *Defensio Secunda* lies elsewhere. It lies in the praise – a warmer and more personal praise than that bestowed on Cromwell[106] – first of Bradshaw and then of Milton's friend Colonel Robert Overton, with whom the poet has been 'connected ... for these many years in a more than brotherly union, by similitude of studies, and by the sweetness of your manners'.[107] When *Defensio Secunda* appeared, Overton was about to be interviewed by Cromwell about his opposition to the Protector's elevation to power, an episode about which Andrew Marvell knew Milton to be concerned.[108] Overton would soon be arrested and would remain in prison for the remainder of the Protectorate. Among his papers the government found verses in his hand which derided the Protector as 'the ape of a king'. Writing to Cromwell in 1654, Overton compared his own predicament to that of 'Cremutius in Tacitus'.[109] Cremutius Cordus was the historian who under the Emperor Tiberius had resorted, as Milton and Nedham did under the Protectorate, to coded criticism of the regime under which he lived. Tacitus' account of the prosecution of Cordus had become, in early modern England, a reference point of protest, protest itself wrapped in code, against tyranny and censorship.[110]

v

In the winter of 1659–60, as the Puritan cause crumbled, Nedham's newsbooks, *Mercurius Politicus* and *The Publick Intelligencer*, endorsed Overton's mistrust of and opposition to George Monck, the eventual architect of the Restoration, and advertised Overton's firmness to his 'country's rights against any arbitrary or kingly innovation'.[111] Nedham's news reports in the same period risked and earned the wrath of the authorities by their defiant slants in favour of the good

---

[106] Austin Woolrych, 'Milton and Cromwell: "A Short but Scandalous Night of Interruption"', in Michael Lieb and John T. Shawcross (eds.), *Achievements of the Left Hand: Essays on the Prose of John Milton* (Amherst, 1974), p. 192. Woolrych's article is essential to an understanding of Milton's doubts about the Protectorate.   [107] *Works*, ed. Patterson *et al.*, VIII, p. 233.

[108] Parker, *Milton*, I, p. 452.

[109] Thomas Birch (ed.), *Thurloe State Papers*, 7 vols. (London, 1742), III, pp. 67, 75–6.

[110] Blair Worden, 'Ben Jonson among the Historians', in Kevin Sharpe and Peter Lake (eds.), *Culture and Politics in Early Stuart England* (London, 1994), pp. 78–9.

[111] *Merc. Pol.* 3 Nov. 1659, p. 844; 26 Jan. 1660, pp. 1049–50; 15 Mar. 1660, pp. 1163–5; *Publick Intelligencer*, 7 Nov. 1659, p. 835; 30 Jan. 1660, pp. 1037–9, 1041; 12 Mar. 1660, pp. 1156–8. In 1650 Nedham had acquired and published a letter from Overton to an (unnamed) 'dear friend': *Merc. Pol.* 26 Sept. 1650, pp. 266–7.

old cause.[112] When the crisis came in the spring of 1660 Milton and Nedham were almost alone in pleading against the royalist reaction and warning of the evils of a restored monarchy.[113] It was Nedham who, with his printer (also Milton's printer) Thomas Newcomb, advertised the first edition of *The Readie and Easie Way* and provided corrections to the misprints which troubled Milton.[114] Admittedly the plea in *The Readie and Easie Way* for a 'standing senate', and the attack in the pamphlet on 'the conceit of successive parliaments', are diametrically opposed to arguments for frequent parliamentary elections which Nedham had used in *Mercurius Politicus* in the Rump period.[115] But Milton, too, had favoured the principle of frequent elections at that time.[116] In the year before the Restoration Nedham, witnessing the electorate's state of mind, retreated into a view close to that of Milton in *The Readie and Easie Way*.[117]

Nedham and Milton alike had to buy their pardons in 1660, and were lucky to be allowed to do so. Both were said to have been approached by the restored regime to write on its behalf.[118] It was

---

[112] *Merc. Pol.*, 10 Nov. 1659–29 Mar. 1660, pp. 850–1, 867, 907, 967–8, 996–7, 1049–50, 1079–80, 1095–8, 1108–9, 1163–5, 1195; *Publick Intelligencer*, 10 Oct. 1659–5 Mar. 1660, pp. 778–80, 835, 842–4, 860, 898, 946–7, 956, 1037–9, 1041, 1051, 1079–80, 1127–8.

[113] David Masson, *The Life of John Milton*, 7 vols. (Cambridge, 1875–94), v, pp. 671–2. I believe there is a fair chance that Nedham wrote *Plain English*, a pamphlet discussed by Masson (*ibid.*, v, pp. 664–6).

[114] *Merc. Pol.*, 8 March 1660, p. 1151; *CPW*, vii, 409. Cf. Nedham's advertisements for Milton's *Considerations touching the Likeliest Means to Remove Hirelings out of the Church* in *Merc. Pol.* 1 Sept. 1659, p. 713; 20 Oct. 1659, p. 809. It was unusual for Nedham to carry advertisements for pamphlets arguing (as *Considerations* does) for radical religious policies. Though Nedham shares with Milton a profound anti-clericalism and a profound dislike of Presbyterianism, his stance in religion is normally Erastian, whereas Milton wished to separate church from state. But Nedham temporarily shifted his ground in 1652, at the time of Milton's alarm at the Erastian proposals advanced by Cromwell's chaplain John Owen, and favoured by Cromwell himself, for a religious settlement. Nedham then attacked the principle of a national church as Antichristian and, in terms familiar to Milton's readers, reproached the Erastianism of the Emperor Constantine, in whose conduct 'Satan had a new game now to play'. *Merc. Pol.*, 29 April 1652, pp. 1553–6; cf. *ibid.*, 6 May 1652, pp. 396–8; 12 Aug. 1652, pp. 213–17. I suspect that the prominent publicity given by Nedham, without editorial comment, to passages from anti-clerical and Socinian tracts condemned by the Rump in February 1651 (*Merc. Pol.*, 27 Feb. 1651, pp. 206–8) was intended to advertise rather than discredit the opinions expressed in the tracts, which accord with the Socinianism for which Milton was to run such a risk early in 1652.

[115] *CPW*, vii, 369, 374; *Merc. Pol.*, (e.g.) 23 Oct. 1651, p. 1142; 30 Oct. 1651, p. 1157; 18 Dec. 1651, p. 1271; 5 Feb. 1652, p. 1385.   [116] *CPW*, iii, 398–9.

[117] Nedham, *Interest will not Lie*, pp. 26–7. Nedham's earlier attitude had contained the seeds of his later one and offered foretastes of Milton's stand in *The Readie and Easie Way*: Nedham, *Case of the Commonwealth*, p. 105; *Merc. Pol.*, 9 Oct. 1651, pp. 1110–11; 5 Mar. 1652, pp. 1473–6; cf. *Works*, ed. Patterson *et al.*, vii, pp. 183, 371–3.

[118] Nedham: Public Record Office, sp29/114, fol. 155; Milton: Darbishire, *Early Lives of Milton*, pp. 32–3, 280.

well worth the government's while to sound Nedham: it cannot have been worth its while to ask Milton. There is no evidence of any contact between the two men after Charles II's return. In 1661 Nedham recycled his royalist ballads of the late 1640s. In the 1670s he would write pamphlets for the ministry of the Earl of Danby. From Milton the Restoration produced his greatest poems, all of them informed by the tragedy of the Revolution's failure. Yet if, in their later years, Milton and Nedham were divided, that separation need not obscure their earlier unity of purpose. Amidst marked differences we have found telling resemblances between the temperaments, the interests and the ideas of the two friends. Those conversations in Petty France may be lost to us, but they prove not to be beyond imagination after all.

CHAPTER 10

Milton and the Protectorate in 1658

Martin Dzelzainis

I

Towards the end of Hobbes's *Behemoth, or The Long Parliament*, speaker B in the dialogue, the pupil, obligingly poses a question: 'Seeing that there had been so many shiftings of the supreme authority, I pray you, for memory's sake, repeat them briefly in times and order.' This is the cue for a brisk resumé by speaker A, the master: the Long Parliament, he says, gave way to the Rump, followed in turn by Cromwell's Council of State and the so-called Barebone's Parliament. 'Fifthly', A continues, from

December the 12th 1653 to September the 3rd 1658, it was in the hands of Oliver Cromwell, with the title of Protector. Sixthly, from September the 3rd 1658 to April the 25th 1659, Richard Cromwell had it as successor to his father. Seventhly, from April the 25th 1659 to May the 7th of the same year, it was nowhere. Eighthly, from May the 7th 1659, the Rump, which was turned out of doors in 1653, recovered it again; and shall lose it again to a committee of safety, and again recover it, and again lose it to the right owner.[1]

The manner in which the story is told suffices to make Hobbes's feelings plain. A note of disdain is audible in the studied precision with which the succession of regimes is recorded, changing to one of derision as numbers and dates are abandoned for the final, headlong descent into anarchy. Of course Hobbes, an avowed enemy of

Earlier versions of this chapter were given at the Colloquium on 'Milton and Republicanism', Université de Paris x-Nanterre, April 1992; at the Conference on 'Politics in English Culture, 1525–1660', University of Reading, July 1992; and to a University of Oxford Renaissance Literature Seminar, New College, Oxford, February 1994. I am grateful to members of these audiences for their many helpful suggestions. Particular thanks are due to John Creaser and Jeremy Maule for their bibliographical assistance, to Barbara Everett and Emrys Jones for inviting me to present a near-final version at New College, and to the volume's editors for their meticulous scrutiny of the outcome.
[1] Thomas Hobbes, *Behemoth, or the Long Parliament*, ed. Ferdinand Tönnies, intro. Stephen Holmes (Chicago, 1990), pp. 195–6.

republicanism, could afford to be ironic about a sequence of events which he saw as a vindication of his political philosophy. For him, the moral of the story (as his choice of title for the work suggests) was the one taught by the Book of Job: after behemoth comes leviathan.

For a committed republican like Milton, the moral of the story was quite different: the republic collapsed not because republicanism was intrinsically inferior to other forms of government, but because its proponents had failed to keep faith with its guiding principles. Moreover, the vices it fell prey to – ambition and avarice – were precisely the ones which republican writers had always maintained would inevitably prove fatal to any free state which allowed them to take hold.[2] It was therefore possible to provide a coherent account of the failure of the republic in republican terms, and it follows from this that Milton too would have been entitled to regard these events as a confirmation – and not, as Hobbes would have it, a refutation – of his fundamental convictions.

But Milton would not have acquitted himself like Milton if he had merely stayed on the sidelines, deriving cold comfort from the fact that, if things were going wrong, then at least they were doing so in accordance with republican dogma. Time and again in his writings of 1659–60 he sought to arrest the descent at the latest point which had been reached, only to find that – as the strikingly high ratio of unpublished to published items indicates – some further turn of events had rendered his proposals obsolete. The full scale of the difficulties he faced can be gauged from the fact that the eight works which he published or composed in the final months of the Interregnum mark off no fewer than seven such 'shiftings of the supreme authority'. Thus *A Treatise of Civil Power in Ecclesiastical Causes* (published in February 1659) is addressed to Richard's Parliament, whereas its companion-piece, *Considerations Touching The Likeliest Means to Remove Hirelings out of the Church* (published in August 1659), is addressed to the restored Rump.[3] *A Letter to a Friend, Concerning the Ruptures of the Commonwealth* was drafted on 20 October 1659 in the aftermath of Lambert's coup

---

[2] See above, pp. 22–3. For the vices considered endemic to republicanism, and the solutions that were offered, see the following works by Quentin Skinner: *The Foundations of Modern Political Thought*, 2 vols. (Cambridge, 1978), I, pp. 56–64, 177–80; 'Machiavelli on the Maintenance of Liberty', *Politics*, 18 (1983), 3–15; 'The Idea of Negative Liberty: Philosophical and Historical Perspectives', in Richard Rorty, J. B. Schneewind and Quentin Skinner (eds.), *Philosophy in History* (Cambridge, 1984), pp. 193–221, esp. pp. 208–12; 'Machiavelli's *Discorsi* and the Pre-humanist Origins of Republican Ideas', in Gisela Bock, Quentin Skinner and Maurizio Viroli (eds.), *Machiavelli and Republicanism* (Cambridge, 1990), pp. 121–41.

[3] For these dates see *CPW*, VII, 236.

expelling the Rump, while *Proposalls of Certaine Expedients for the Preventing of a Civill War Now Feard, & the Settling of a Firme Government* (composed in November 1659) concerned itself with the prospects facing the Committee of Safety which had been set up in the interim.[4] The first edition of *The Readie & Easie Way to Establish a Free Commonwealth* (published in February 1660) was begun under the again-restored Rump, but completed under the Long Parliament (that is, after 21 February when Monck readmitted the members secluded in December 1648).[5] Finally, *The Present Means, and Brief Delineation of a Free Commonwealth, Easy to be Put in Practice, and Without Delay. In a Letter to General Monk* was composed in February–March 1660, before the Long Parliament dissolved itself, while the second edition of *The Readie and Easie Way* and *Brief Notes upon a Late Sermon* were both published in April 1660, after its dissolution but before the Convention Parliament assembled.[6]

These writings pose a formidable challenge to commentators, even if they do not always agree on the precise nature of the task facing them. To some, particularly those who are concerned with assessing how Milton, as a pragmatic pamphleteer, brought his convictions to bear on the immediate situation, the problem is one of establishing the relation between (to borrow from the title of an article by Barbara Lewalski) 'political beliefs and polemical methods'.[7] For others, particularly those concerned with upholding the image of Milton as a man of unbending integrity and commitment, it is above all (to borrow from the title of an article by Robert T. Fallon) 'a question of consistency'.[8] There is, however, one question raised by these writings of such importance that any commentator who seeks to evade it, or even to equivocate, can only do so to the detriment of whatever larger story he or she is trying to tell; namely, the question of whether Milton at some point came to repudiate Cromwell and the Cromwellian Protectorate.

The list of those who think that Milton did renounce, if not necessarily Cromwell himself, then at least his works, includes J. S. Smart, Don M. Wolfe, Barbara Lewalski, Michael Fixler and, most

[4] For these dates see *CPW*, VII, 139, 322, 335.   [5] For this dating see *CPW*, VII, 343–5.
[6] For these dates see *CPW*, VII, 389–90, 398–400, 465.
[7] Barbara Lewalski, 'Milton: Political Beliefs and Polemical Methods, 1659–60', *Publications of the Modern Languages Association of America*, 74 (1959), 191–202.
[8] Robert Thomas Fallon, 'Milton in the Anarchy, 1659–60: A Question of Consistency', *Studies in English Literature*, 21 (1981), 123–46.

recently and persuasively, Austin Woolrych.[9] At the heart of their case lies the belief that Milton cannot but have found objectionable the increasingly conservative religious, political and social trends which characterized the later Protectorate. Taking the Humble Petition and Advice of 25 May 1657 (supplemented by the Additional Petition and Advice of 26 June) as a benchmark, we can isolate a number of these trends.[10] Under this constitution, Cromwell was allowed to nominate his successor, thus placing the Protectorate on a semi-hereditary footing. He was also allowed to nominate the members of a newly constituted 'other House', and the controversy over whether this was tantamount to reinstating the House of Lords (abolished in 1649) was to be at the centre of political debate for the duration of the Protectorate. In a further deliberate echoing of monarchical forms, the Petition also substituted a 'Privy Council' for what had merely been a 'Council', the members of which would moreover be required to swear a personal oath of loyalty to the Protector. The Petition also envisaged a 'Confession of Faith' to 'be asserted, held forth, and recommended to the people of these nations' with a clause on heresy specifically designed to exclude antitrinitarians from enjoying liberty of conscience.[11] What Milton was later to call 'the superficial actings of State'[12] also became much more prominent. The regalia for the 1657 reinstallation of Cromwell as Protector included a sword, sceptre and purple robe.[13] It was now proper to speak of him as having a court. And, quite apart from baronetcies and knighthoods, he created two hereditary peerages in 1658, the patent for one of which listed the conferment of honours as being among the chief prerogatives of 'the imperial crown of these nations'.[14] The

---

[9] See J. S. Smart, *The Sonnets of Milton* (Glasgow, 1921), p. 92; Don M. Wolfe, *Milton in the Puritan Revolution* (New York, 1941), pp. 289–90; Barbara Lewalski, 'Milton: Political Beliefs', pp. 192–3; Michael Fixler, *Milton and the Kingdoms of God* (London, 1964), pp. 198–9; Austin Woolrych, 'Milton and Cromwell: "A Short But Scandalous Night of Interruption"?', in Michael Lieb and John T. Shawcross (eds.), *Achievements of the Left Hand: Essays on the Prose of John Milton* (Amherst, 1974), pp. 185–218; Austin Woolrych, 'Historical Introduction' to *CPW*, VII, 85–7.

[10] See S. R. Gardiner (ed.), *The Constitutional Documents of the Puritan Revolution 1625–1660*, 3rd edn (Oxford, 1906), pp. 447–59 (Humble Petition and Advice), 459–64 (Additional Petition and Advice).

[11] Gardiner, *Constitutional Documents*, p. 454. On attempts to arrive at a religious settlement see Blair Worden, 'Toleration and the Cromwellian Protectorate', in W. J. Sheils (ed.), *Persecution and Toleration, Studies in Church History*, 21 (Oxford, 1984), pp. 199–233.

[12] *CPW*, VII, 360.

[13] See Roy Sherwood, *The Court of Oliver Cromwell* (London, 1977), pp. 158–67 (Appendix A: Oliver Cromwell and Regality).

[14] Derek Hirst, 'The Lord Protector, 1653–58', in John Morrill (ed.), *Oliver Cromwell and the English Revolution* (London, 1990), p. 122.

assumption that Milton would have disapproved of any or all of these developments seems entirely reasonable.

The list of those who oppose this view includes David Masson, William B. Hunter and Robert T. Fallon.[15] Even though they would concede some (in Masson's case, a good deal) of what has been said about Milton's disenchantment with the Protectorate, they still find it inconceivable that he could have turned against it completely. The ensuing debate has largely turned upon the meaning of a single phrase in *The Likeliest Means* where Milton congratulates the Rump on having resumed its authority in May 1659 'after a short but scandalous night of interruption'.[16] Masson, followed closely by Fallon, finds it 'utterly impossible' that '"short"' could refer to anything other than the two weeks between the dissolution of 22 April forced on Richard by the army grandees, and the recall of the Rump, forced on the grandees by their junior officers.[17] Hunter takes it to refer to the whole nine months of Richard's Protectorate, arguing that his succession was, and was known to have been, irregular.[18] Woolrych's case for rejecting Hunter's claim is compelling, and he is almost as convincing in removing Masson's objections.[19] Woolrych's own argument, which currently holds the field, is that when Milton welcomed the recall of the Rump – as he did explicitly in the *Letter to a Friend*[20] – this was precisely because the clock had been turned back to before 20 April 1653. If this means that he disowned the whole of the Protectorate, then so be it.[21]

---

[15] See David Masson, *The Life of Milton: Narrated in Connexion with the Literary, Historical, and Political Events of his Time*, 7 vols. (London, 1859–94), v, pp. 577–80, 598–607; William B. Hunter, 'Milton and Richard Cromwell', *English Language Notes*, 3 (1966), 252–9; Fallon, 'Milton in the Anarchy', *passim.*   [16] *CPW*, vii, 274.

[17] Masson, *Life of Milton*, v, pp. 606–7; Fallon, 'Milton in the Anarchy', pp. 131–2.

[18] Hunter, 'Milton and Richard Cromwell', p. 257.

[19] Woolrych, 'Milton and Cromwell', pp. 201–9.

[20] Recalling the events of April and May, Milton remarks that 'I was overjoyed, when I heard that the Army under the working of Gods holy spiritt, as I thought & still hope well, had bin so far wrought to Christian humility & self-denyall, as to confesse in publick their backsliding from the good old cause, & to shew the fruits of their repentance in the righteousnesse of their restoring the old famous parlament, which they had without just autority dissolved': *CPW*, vii, 324. Fallon, 'Milton in the Anarchy', p. 326, insists that this too refers to the fortnight leading to the restoration of the Rump. However, the pamphlet to which Milton was alluding, *A Declaration of the Officers of the Army, Inviting the Members of the Long Parliament, Who Continued Sitting Till the 20th of April, 1653. to Return to the Exercise and Dis-charge of Their Trust* (London, 6 May 1659), E980(20), invokes the key date, 20 April 1653, no fewer than four times, sigs. A2, A3$^{r\ v}$.

[21] Woolrych now appears to think that Milton's repudiation of the Protectorate must have been more sudden; whatever the 'phases' were that 'worried' Milton before 1659, 'he either took them in his stride or ignored them', 'Dating Milton's *History of Britain*', *Historical Journal*, 36 (1993), 929–43, at p. 942. I am grateful to Professor Woolrych for sending me a copy of his article.

But rather than rehearse the various claims and counter-claims in detail, I propose instead to take a ready and easy way in an attempt to gain a wholly different perspective on the issue. My aim is to do so by challenging an assumption shared by all parties to the dispute, both those who maintain that Milton repudiated the Protectorate and those who disagree. For what many of them positively assert – and what none of them disputes – is that for several years prior to the publication of *A Treatise of Civil Power* Milton was completely silent on political matters. In the words of David Masson, 'nothing of a political kind [came] from Milton's pen during the last three or four years of Oliver's Protectorate, – nothing even indirectly bearing on the internal politics of the Commonwealth since his *Pro Se Defensio* against Morus in 1655, and nothing directly bearing thereon since his *Defensio Secunda* of 1654'.[22] Or, as Austin Woolrych puts it, in only marginally less emphatic terms: 'From *A Second Defence* until after Cromwell's death on September 3, 1658, Milton gave scarcely any indications of what he thought of the Protector and his government.'[23] In keeping with this, Arthur Barker speaks of a 'five-year silence between 1654 and 1659',[24] while Fallon refers to the 'sudden wealth of new material coming after four years of virtual silence'.[25] But perhaps the most telling manifestation of this orthodoxy is the breakdown in the sequence of historical introductions to the Yale edition of the *Complete Prose Works* when it comes to the mid-1650s. The editors of volume VII frankly admit that the series has left a 'gap in the story of national events between Don M. Wolfe's introduction to volume IV, which ends in 1654, and [Austin Woolrych's] to this volume, which begins logically with Cromwell's death in 1658'. The 'gap' to which they refer comprises the rule of the major-generals, the second Protectorate Parliament and the Humble Petition and Advice. They see no call, however, to make up for the deficiency with a 'comprehensive survey': all that is needed is a 'few retrospects' necessary 'to explain that crux in Milton's political attitudes which we find in the stark contrast between his eulogy of Cromwell's Protectorate in *A Second Defence* and his revulsion against it in the tracts of 1659–60'.[26]

My quarrel with this orthodoxy arises from its failure to take due account of two works published by Milton in 1658; first, perhaps in

---

[22] Masson, *Life of Milton*, v, p. 580.   [23] Woolrych, 'Milton and Cromwell', p. 197.
[24] Arthur E. Barker, *Milton and the Puritan Dilemma 1641–1660* (Toronto, 1942), p. 196.
[25] Fallon, 'Milton in the Anarchy', p. 124.   [26] From the editors' Preface, *CPW*, VII, ix–x.

May,[27] his edition of *The Cabinet-Council*, which he took to be by Sir Walter Ralegh, and secondly, probably in October,[28] a revised and augmented edition of his own *Pro Populo Anglicano Defensio*, which had first appeared in the very different circumstances of 1651. While the fact of their publication is often noted in the standard literature (though the Yale edition, supposedly 'complete', inexplicably neglects to print even Milton's prefatory note to *The Cabinet-Council*), the tendency has been to regard the works themselves as somewhat of a curiosity, to be added to the list of things with which Milton kept himself busy in these years, but otherwise of little interest.[29] As far as one can tell, the rationale behind this is that Milton was saying nothing new – in the case of *The Cabinet-Council* because the text was by someone else, and in the case of the *Defensio* because Milton himself had said it all (or almost all) before. At the very least, however, the juxtaposition of two such strikingly dissimilar texts is worthy of comment. Moreover, even if it is true that Milton was *saying* nothing new, then he was still *doing* something new in issuing these texts such that we ought to ask about his intentions, first, in offering (as he thought) the fruits of Ralegh's political wisdom to the public, and then in reiterating views of his own which had once commanded the attention of a European audience. For once we grasp these intentions, and so recover what I take to be the political significance of these two works, it will no longer be possible to say that between 1655 and 1659 Milton published nothing 'bearing on the internal politics of the Commonwealth'.

II

It is certainly true that Milton was very busy during these years with his own projects. He took up and substantially completed his longest English prose work, *The History of Britain*.[30] By 1658, he may have completed his longest Latin work, the theological treatise *De Doctrina Christiana*, and taken up his longest poem, *Paradise Lost*.[31] He also continued with what would have been the longest work of all, his

---

[27] See J. M. French, *The Life Records of John Milton*, 5 vols. (New Brunswick, 1949–58), IV, pp. 220–2.   [28] See French, *Life Records*, IV, pp. 238, 246.

[29] See Masson, *Life of Milton*, V, pp. 404–5, 573–4; W. R. Parker, *Milton: A Biography*, 2 vols. (Oxford, 1968), I, pp. 516–18; John T. Shawcross, 'A Survey of Milton's Prose Works', in Lieb and Shawcross (eds.), *Achievements of the Left Hand*, pp. 291–391, at pp. 322, 331.

[30] See *CPW*, VI, ed. French Fogle (1971), pp. xli–xlii.

[31] See *CPW*, VI, 23. For recent doubts about Milton's authorship of *De Doctrina Christiana*, see William B. Hunter, 'The Provenance of the *Christian Doctrine*', with comments by Barbara Lewalski and John T. Shawcross, *Studies in English Literature*, 32 (1992), 129–66.

Latin Thesaurus, which at his death reportedly consisted of 'a Manuscript Collection in three *Large Folio's* digested into an Alphabetical order ... out of all the best and purest *Roman* Authors'.[32]

Despite all this activity, he still made time to prepare a 200-page work for publication. Printed by Thomas Newcomb for Thomas Johnson, this was, to give it its full title, *The Cabinet-Council: Containing the Cheif Arts of Empire, and Mysteries of State; Discabineted in Political and Polemical Aphorisms, grounded on Authority, and Experience; and illustrated with the choicest Examples and Historical Observations. By the Ever-renowned Knight, Sir Walter Raleigh, Published by John Milton Esq.* Since Milton's manuscript is not known to have survived, there is no telling whether this was his title or not. As for the text, Milton explains in a one-sentence note '*To the READER*' that

Having had the *Manuscript* of this *Treatise*, Written by Sir *Walter Raleigh*, many years in my hands, and finding it lately by chance among other Books and Papers, upon reading thereof, I thought it a kinde of injury to withhold longer the work of so eminent an Author from the Publick; it being both answerable in Stile to other Works of his already Extant, as far as the subject would permit, and given me for a true Copy by a Learned Man at his Death, who had collected several such peices.[33]

Blandly understating his role and the effort involved, he claims that, reading a manuscript which he came across after several years of neglect, he suddenly felt impelled to publish it. The tone is so casual and matter-of-fact that one might easily forget that he had been blind for six years. It should also be noted that, uniquely, he signs himself 'Esquire' – a sudden and surprising show of concern for the social niceties. Usually signing himself without the least trace of servility as 'J.M.' or 'John Milton' or 'Mr John Milton' or 'John Milton Englishman', he here voluntarily subordinates himself to 'Sir Walter'. The impression is one of self-effacement and deference; Milton, it would appear, was anxious not to interpose himself between Ralegh and the reader.

Milton's willingness to promote Ralegh at his own expense would

---

[32] From the Preface to *Linguae Romanae Dictionarium Luculentum Novum* (Cambridge, 1693), sig. A2ᵛ. See also Helen Darbishire (ed.), *The Early Lives of Milton* (London, 1932), pp. 4, 29, 45–6, 47, 72, 166, 192, 339–40.
[33] John Milton (ed.), *The Cabinet-Council* (London, 1658), sig. A2ʳ ᵛ. Milton's note is reprinted in *The Works of John Milton*, gen. ed. Frank A. Patterson *et al.*, 20 vols. (New York, 1931–40), xviii, ed. Thomas Ollive Mabbott and J. M. French (1938), p. 273 (the title page is reproduced opposite). For the text see *The Works of Sir Walter Ralegh, Kt.*, ed. W. Oldys and T. Birch, 8 vols. (Oxford, 1829), viii, pp. 37–150.

have been underlined by the frontispiece, a rectangular half-length portrait of Ralegh, engraved by Robert Vaughan, with the motto 'Tam Marti, Quam Mercurio' above, and a three-line inscription below: 'The true and lively Portraiture / of the Ho.^{ble} and learned Knight / Sr Walter Ralegh'. Like other Ralegh portraits at the time, it derived from Simon van de Passe's 1617 engraving for the title page of *The History of the World*.[34]

Although the standard reference works by T. N. Brushfield, J. M. French, W. R. Parker and John T. Shawcross do not mention a frontispiece in their accounts of *The Cabinet-Council*,[35] the nineteenth-century bibliographers who came across copies of *The Cabinet-Council* bearing one were almost certainly correct in reporting this as a regular feature of the work.[36] What has not been noticed hitherto is that *The Cabinet-Council* was actually issued in four states. As the book went through the press, two separate errors were made in numbering the pages. Both errors were corrected but, when the volume was bound, both corrected and uncorrected sheets were used, with the result that some copies exhibit one error,[37] some the other,[38] some both[39] and some neither.[40] Most surviving copies of *The Cabinet-Council* do not bear a frontispiece but, given that there are copies in three of the states which do,[41] it can be assumed that

---

[34] For details and facsimiles of engraved portraits of Ralegh (though not this one) see T. N. Brushfield, *A Bibliography of Sir Walter Ralegh Knt.*, 2d edn (Exeter, 1908), pp. 77, 79, 88–90.

[35] See Brushfield, *A Bibliography*, pp. 129–31; French, *Life Records*, IV, pp. 220–2; Parker, *Milton*, II, p. 1066; Shawcross, 'A Survey', pp. 330–1.

[36] See William Thomas Lowndes, *The Bibliographer's Manual of English Literature*, 4 vols. (London, 1864), III, p. 2040; W. Carew Hazlitt, *Second Series of Bibliographical Collections and Notes on Early English Literature 1474–1700* (London, 1882), p. 510.

[37] Copies with sigs. D5–8ᵛ numbered irregularly (41, 40, 41, 44, 45, 45, 44, 48) include Durning-Lawrence Library, University of London, [D.–L.L.] (XVI.)Bc[Raleigh], and Bodleian Library, 232.g.105. Details of the Bodleian copy were kindly supplied by Professor John Creaser.

[38] Copies with sig. 16 misnumbered (213; should be 123) include British Library, 521.b.27; Cambridge University Library, Peterborough F.3.56 and Syn.8.65.49; and the copy described in *The Carl H. Pforzheimer Library: English Literature 1475–1700*, ed. E. Unger and W. A. Jackson, 3 vols. (New York, 1940), III, pp. 842–3 (item 817).

[39] Copies with irregularities in sigs. D5–8ᵛ and 16 include Christ's College Library, Cambridge, FF.5.8; Cambridge University Library, U*.8.107(G); John Carter Brown Library, D658 R163c; and the Yale University Library copy (University Microfilms, Ann Arbor, Michigan, Reel 224). Mr Jeremy Maule very generously supplied details of all the above-mentioned Cambridge copies of *The Cabinet-Council*; Professor David Armitage kindly reported on the John Carter Brown copy.

[40] On this point I am indebted to Professor Armitage, who confirmed the hypothesis that *The Cabinet-Council* was also issued in a fourth state made up exclusively from corrected sheets by locating the only known error-free copy: Butler Library, Columbia University, B823M64Z1658.

[41] For example, the Durning-Lawrence, Bodleian, Carl H. Pforzheimer, Christ's College and Yale copies.

the whole of the first edition was originally equipped in this fashion.

This finding tells us a good deal about how Milton, his printer, Newcomb, and his bookseller, Johnson, regarded the project. Their foremost concern was to associate *The Cabinet-Council* visually with the Ralegh canon, as this had taken shape in the 1650s.[42] Milton could vouch for the work's provenance and for its being 'answerable in Stile to other Works of his', but the familiar portrait of Ralegh would effectively serve as a logo conferring canonicity. Vaughan had in fact executed a second, inferior version of the Ralegh portrait which was used exclusively by the Shears family of booksellers.[43] It appeared, for example, in their editions of Ralegh's *Sceptick* in 1651, his *Observations, touching Trade & Commerce with the Hollander* in 1653,[44] and his *Remains* in 1657. Although this second plate was unavailable for commercial reasons, Newcomb and Johnson were able to secure the first plate which had been used only once before, for an edition of Ralegh's *Judicious and Select Essayes*, printed by T.W. for Humphrey Moseley, in 1650 (incidentally, a date which in principle makes it possible for Milton to have seen the Vaughan engraving).[45] Since Moseley had published Milton's *Poems* thirteen years earlier; since Newcomb had printed all of Milton's works from the second edition of *Eikonoklastes* onwards; since Newcomb and Moseley had collaborated on several volumes in the 1650s;[46] and since Johnson was advertising two Newcomb–Moseley volumes for sale in his shop in 1658,[47] there is no real difficulty in explaining how they managed to come by it.

---

[42] See Christopher Hill, *Intellectual Origins of the English Revolution*, corrected edn (Oxford, 1980), pp. 154–5, 204–5, 210–11.

[43] The Vaughan/Shears engraving is smaller and less fine; has only two rather than three books upright on the shelf in the top right-hand corner (the books are also untitled); and is styled differently beneath ('The Ho.^ble and Learned Knight / Sr Walter Raleigh').

[44] In Donald G. Wing (ed.), *Short-Title Catalogue*, 3 vols. (New York, 1972, 1982, 1988), *Observations* is assigned to John Keymor (Wing K391). For the other two items see Wing R180, R186A.

[45] See the description of *Judicious and Select Essayes* (Wing R170) in *Pforzheimer Library*, III, pp. 848–9 (item 822).

[46] For example, Robert Mossom, *Sion's Prospect*, By Thomas Newcomb (London, 1651), Wing M2867, By T.N. for Humphrey Moseley (London, 1653), Wing M2868; John Donne, *Paradoxes, Problemes, Essayes, Characters*, By T.N. for Humphrey Moseley (London, 1652), Wing D1866; Sir Ralph Maddison, *Great Britain's Remembrancer*, By Tho. Newcomb, to be sold by Humphrey Moseley (London, 1655), Wing M245.

[47] Johnsons' advertisement, appended to Theophilus Polwheile, Αὐθέντης *or a Treatise of Self-Deniall* (London, 1658), Wing P2782, sigs. Ee6, Ee8ᵛ, lists Jean Pierre Camus, *Elise, or Innocencie Guilty*, Printed by T. Newcomb for Humphrey Moseley (London, 1655), Wing C413, and Thomas Blount, *The Academie of Eloquence*, Printed by T.N. for Humphrey Moseley (London, 1654; another edn 1656), Wing B3321, B3322.

Given the concern shown by the Milton–Newcomb–Johnson consortium with the authenticity of *The Cabinet-Council*, it is ironic that, like many pieces appearing under Ralegh's name in the 1650s, it was not by Ralegh at all. As Strathmann has shown, it is actually an edited version of a treatise entitled *Observations Political and Civil* which survives in several manuscript copies. (The version published by Milton differs in that it is divided into twenty-six chapters and is shortened by about a tenth.) Written entirely in English, apart from a few Italian phrases and copious Latin tags (mostly from Tacitus), the treatise was put together by someone known only by his initials, 'T.B.', and dedicated between 1596 and 1600 to Lord North, Treasurer of Elizabeth I's household.[48] Far from being original in any meaningful sense, it is a synthetic compilation of material borrowed from other writers, often with little or no modification or commentary.[49] Thus (adopting the divisions of the 1658 text) chapters 1 and 2 are derived from Bodin's *Les six livres de la République*; 3 to 6 from Machiavelli's *Il Principe*; 7 to 12 from Bodin again; and 13 to 24 from Lipsius' *Politicorum sive Civilis Doctrinae libri sex*.

Chapter 25, which comprises almost a third of the text, differs in that 'T.B.' was drawing on a source – Francesco Sansovino's *Concetti politici* (or, possibly, a translation of it by Robert Hichcock[50]) – which itself consisted largely of material which had been recycled in whole or in part. The result is that there are several layers of indebtedness (for example, 'T.B.' borrowing from Sansovino borrowing from Machiavelli's *Discorsi*, a work which is of course cast in the form of a commentary upon Livy). Sansovino was born in Rome in 1521, and moved to Venice with his father in 1527. After studying at Padua, Florence and Bologna, and serving briefly at the court of Pope Julius II, Sansovino returned to Venice in 1553 and settled into a career as a prolific writer, editor and publisher.[51] It was at Venice, in 1578, that he published his *Concetti politici*, a collection of 805 aphorisms taken, sometimes verbatim, from Aristotle, Livy, Cicero, Polybius, Tacitus, Bembo, Guevara, Machiavelli and Guicciardini amongst others.

[48] See Ernest A. Strathmann, 'A Note on the Ralegh Canon', *Times Literary Supplement*, 13 April 1956, p. 228.
[49] See Nadja Kempner, *Raleghs staatstheoretische Schriften: die Einführung des Machiavellismus in England* (Leipzig, 1928), pp. 62–7, and Vincent Luciani, 'Ralegh's *Cabinet-Council* and Guicciardini's Aphorisms', *Studies in Philology*, 46 (1949), 20–30.
[50] See Luciani, 'Ralegh's *Cabinet-Council*', pp. 22, 29.
[51] See Paul F. Grendler, 'Francesco Sansovino and Italian Popular History 1500–1600', *Studies in the Renaissance*, 16 (1969), 139–80, at pp. 141–2.

Thanks to the work of Vincent Luciani, the full extent of Sansovino's borrowings from Machiavelli and Guicciardini has become clear (though, as John Donne's annotated copy of Sansovino shows, sharp-eyed contemporary readers soon spotted what was going on).[52] Indeed, when Sansovino republished the *Concetti* in 1583 (the year of his death), and appended texts of Guicciardini's *Avvertimenti* (or *Ricordi*) and Giovanni Francesco Lottini's *Avvedimenti civili*, he prudently deleted some of the *concetti* which he had previously appropriated from Guicciardini so as to make his dependence less obvious.[53] The markedly Italian flavour of this material was if anything intensified by 'T.B.' who, when choosing the *concetti* which make up the bulk of chapter 25 of *The Cabinet-Council*, opted exclusively for those which Sansovino had extracted from Machiavelli's principal works – the *Discorsi*, the *Istorie Fiorentine*, *Il Principe* and the *Arte della Guerra* – together with a liberal sprinkling of the aphorisms he had taken from Lottini and from Guicciardini's *Storia d'Italia* and *Avvertimenti*. Chapter 26, the second longest, which concludes the work, is more straightforwardly devoted to Machiavelli's *Discorsi* before concluding with a final flourish from the *Istorie Fiorentine* and Bodin.

What the provenance of *The Cabinet-Council* demonstrates – several times over – is that it belongs to the genre of the advice book. As we have seen, the original manuscript was dedicated to Lord North. At a further remove, Sansovino dedicated his *Concetti* to the Emperor Rudolf II, while Hichcock's English translation, *The Quintessence of Wit* (1590), was dedicated to Robert Cecil.[54] Taking another step back, to Sansovino's sources, we find Machiavelli's *Principe* dedicated first to Giuliano de' Medici and then to his nephew Lorenzo;[55] Lottini's *Avvedimenti*, published posthumously by his brother in 1574 and dedicated to Francesco de' Medici;[56] and Guicciardini's *Avvertimenti*, dedicated by its first editor, Jacopo Corbinelli, to Catherine de Medici in 1576.[57] It would scarcely be an exaggeration to say that *The*

---

[52] See Vincent Luciani, 'Sansovino's *Concetti Politici* and their Debt to Guicciardini', *Publications of the Modern Language Association*, 65 (1950), 1181–95, and 'Sansovino's *Concetti Politici* and their Debt to Machiavelli', *Publications of the Modern Language Association*, 67 (1952), 823–44; Grendler, 'Francesco Sansovino', p. 164.

[53] See Luciani, 'Debt to Guicciardini', pp. 1185–6.

[54] Francesco Sansovino, *Concetti politici* (Venice, 1578), sigs. *2–*3ᵛ; Robert Hichcock, *The Quintessence of Wit* (London, 1590), sigs. A2–3ᵛ.

[55] See Machiavelli, *The Prince*, ed. Quentin Skinner and Russell Price (Cambridge, 1988), pp. xii–xiii, 3, 94.

[56] See Maurizio Viroli, *From Politics to Reason of State* (Cambridge, 1992), p. 241; Giovanni Francesco Lottini, *Avvedimenti civili* (Venice, 1575), sig. A2ʳ ᵛ.

[57] Francesco Guicciardini, *Piu consigli et avvertimenti*, ed. Jacopo Corbinelli (Paris, 1576), sigs. Aii–iiiᵛ.

Cabinet-Council virtually recapitulates the sixteenth-century history of the advice book.[58] Machiavelli, many of whose most chilling precepts make their way into its pages, was of course a leading figure in that history. Guicciardini (also present) was possibly more influential still; Sansovino for one credited him with having been 'il primo inuentore di queste Propositioni, Regole, Massime, Assiomi, Oracoli, Precetti, Sentenze, Probabili'[59] – that is to say, with having forged the aphoristic form of prose to which exponents of the genre became increasingly addicted. But both these figures were outstripped by Tacitus, whose *Annals* and *Histories* were seen as a repertoire of the political techniques deemed indispensable for the efficient conduct of a Renaissance monarchy.[60] Guicciardini admired him, as did his editor, Corbinelli.[61] His sententious style was widely imitated, eclipsing Cicero as a model. Lipsius edited his works, while Lipsius' own *Politicorum libri sex*, it has recently been argued, was virtually a cento from Tacitus 'marshalled into a coherent argument and breathing the spirit of the contemporary Italian Tacitists' (it is no accident that most of the Latin quotations from Tacitus in *The Cabinet-Council* come in chapters 13 to 24 – the ones deriving from Lipsius).[62] Since Ralegh was among the most prominent English exponents of this Tacitean brand of humanism, it is easy to see why *The Cabinet-Council* was attributed to him and, in the case of one of the manuscripts, to Francis Bacon.[63]

But this was also the form of politics and – what amounted to much the same thing – the form of prose which Milton detested above all others. He was (to adopt the terms used on the title page of *The Cabinet-Council*) a sworn enemy of 'authority and experience'; he invariably elevated reason above 'examples'; for him, 'aphorism' was a term of abuse; and he had a profound distaste for 'Cabinet-Councils'. Thus, in *Of Reformation* (1641), he lamented that 'there is no art that

---

[58] See Quentin Skinner, *Foundations*, I, pp. 113–38 and 'Political Philosophy', in C. Schmitt, E. Kessler and Q. Skinner (eds.), *The Cambridge History of Renaissance Philosophy* (Cambridge, 1987), p. 441; Peter Burke, 'Tacitism, Scepticism, and Reason of State', in J. H. Burns with Mark Goldie (eds.), *The Cambridge History of Political Thought 1450–1700* (Cambridge, 1991), pp. 479–98; Richard Tuck, *Philosophy and Government 1572–1651* (Cambridge, 1993), pp. 31–6.

[59] Francesco Sansovino, *Propositioni, overo considerationi in materia di cose di stato* (Vinegia, 1583), p. 100b.

[60] For the English context, see now Malcolm Smuts, 'Court-Centred Politics and the Uses of Roman Historians, *c.* 1590–1630', in Kevin Sharpe and Peter Lake (eds.), *Culture and Politics in Early Stuart England* (London, 1994), pp. 21–43.

[61] See Tuck, *Philosophy and Government*, p. 42.

[62] *Ibid.*, p. 48.   [63] British Library, Harleian MS 1853, fol. 39.

hath bin more canker'd in her principles, more soyl'd, and slubber'd with aphorisming pedantry then the art of policie'. It was the 'masterpiece of a modern politician' to 'mould' the people with 'precepts' in order 'to break a nationall spirit'. He condemned Virgilio Malvezzi's *Discorsi sopra Cornelio Tacito* for cutting '*Tacitus* into slivers and steaks', had nothing but scorn for one 'super-politick Aphorisme', and finally wrote off 'all the Tribe of *Aphorismers*, and *Politicasters*'.[64] In *Of Education* (1644), he contrasted his Ciceronian ideal of education – 'that which fits a man to perform justly, skilfully and magnanimously all the offices both private and publike of peace and war' – with the actual outcome of the 'usuall method of teaching', where some 'betake them to State affairs, with souls so unprincipl'd in vertue, and true generous breeding, that flattery, and court shifts and tyrannous aphorismes appear to them the highest points of wisdom'.[65] In *Areopagitica* (1644), he juxtaposed the 'magnanimity of a trienniall Parliament' with the 'jealous hautinesse of Prelates and cabin Counsellours that usurpt of late'.[66] In *Eikonoklastes* (1649), he condemned the 'Politic Cabin at *Whitehall*' and claimed that the rights of Parliament had been '*invaded* by Cabin Councels'. And in the chapter dealing with the publication of Charles I's correspondence in an official pamphlet, *The Kings Cabinet Opened*, he dwelt contemptuously on the king's 'suttleties and mysterious arts' together with those of the '*Cabalists*'.[67]

It is true that at one point in *Eikonoklastes* Milton appears to reprove Charles for not being sufficiently schooled in Machiavelli. Chapter 18, 'Upon the Uxbridge Treaty', takes up Charles's claim that peace treaties represent 'a retiring from bestial force to human reason'. But, says Milton, 'his first Aphorism heer is in part deceav'd' since, given the way that 'Politicians' often 'handle the matter, there hath bin no where found more bestialitie then in treating'. All that the politicians do in resorting to negotiation is to shift 'from violence to craft, and when they can no longer doe as Lions, to doe as Foxes'. This of course alludes to the famous passage in the eighteenth chapter of *The Prince*, 'How rulers should keep their

---

[64] *CPW*, I, 571–2, 573, 582, 598. Interestingly, Milton must have read Malvezzi's *Discorsi* (Venice, 1635) in Italian since the English translation by Sir Richard Baker was not published until 1642. On the issue of whether the annotated copy of Baker's translation now in the Berg Collection was Milton's, see Edwin B. Benjamin, 'Milton and Tacitus', *Milton Studies*, 4 (1972), 120, 138–9.

[65] *CPW*, II, 375. The Ciceronian aspect of the tract is examined in greater detail above, pp. 12–13.

[66] *CPW*, II, 489. [67] *CPW*, III, 392, 465, 538–9.

promises'.[68] Milton's aim is in fact to expose Charles's pose of high-mindedness as a sham; in practice, he was only too willing to behave like a fox. The rest of the chapter is therefore given over to a demonstration of his constant willingness to break his word. According to Milton, in a deliberate play on words, his 'Principal Maxim' in any treaty was always to include a clause which would allow him to disavow it later.[69]

It follows therefore that in 1658 Milton published a work of a type of which he otherwise strongly disapproved. While this certainly demands an explanation, the answer does not lie in scrutinizing the text itself. There is very little to be gained by following the example of Parker, who sifted through the various maxims in an attempt to distinguish between those with which Milton might have agreed, and those with which he might have disagreed. It would be hard in any case to find fault with Parker's list, and even harder to disagree with his anodyne judgement that the book 'may or may not reflect in part [Milton's] own political views at the time'.[70] Shawcross reports a similar outcome to a similar piecemeal survey: 'the aphorisms frequently enough accord with Milton's views, but not always'. This too is unexceptionable. However, on the strength of this, Shawcross also ventures to conclude that 'such differences militate against this being offered for political reasons at this difficult time for the Protectorate': his verdict is that Milton must simply have 'thought it worthy of public perusal'.[71] But the leap from 'differences' within the text to the conclusion that the work as a whole was therefore not 'offered for political reasons' is unwarranted. This is because what matters about the contents is not whether they are internally consistent or not but the type of book to which they can properly be said to belong. The question we still have to answer is why Milton published an example of a genre, the advice book, of which he was normally so disapproving. And the only way in which we can do this is by recovering his intentions in publishing it.

Virtually the only evidence we have of these is the Latin epigraph under Milton's signature on the title page of *The Cabinet-Council*: 'Quis Martem tunicâ tectum adamantinâ dignè scripserit?' ('Who could

---

[68] *CPW*, III, 520–1. Professor Skinner points out that Machiavelli was in turn satirically inverting Cicero's advice in *De Officiis*, I.13.41; see Machiavelli, *The Prince*, ed. Skinner and Price, pp. xix–xx, 61. However, Milton's use of the adjective 'Principal' a few pages later suggests that he had Machiavelli in mind as much as Cicero.   [69] *CPW*, III, 527.
[70] Parker, *Milton*, I, p. 516.   [71] Shawcross, 'A Survey', p. 331.

fittingly tell of Mars clad in his adamantine tunic?')[72] This enigmatic question is taken from Horace, *Odes*, 1.6.13–14. To the best of my knowledge, it does not feature in any of the manuscripts of T.B.'s *Observations*.[73] Nor does it appear on any other Ralegh title page. And since Milton usually took great care over epigraphs, and obviously enjoyed complete familiarity with Horace's verse – what may be one of Milton's earliest poems is a translation of the immediately preceding ode[74] – the presumption must be that it represents his choice.

Horace's poem is a modest verse epistle addressed to Marcus Vipsanius Agrippa, politely declining to write about him and recommending Varius instead. The standard paraphrase of its argument is as follows: 'Varius will write of your military and naval exploits. I cannot handle such matters, Agrippa, any more than the conventional themes of epic and tragedy. Who would be the man to recount worthily the deeds of Diomede? I write συμποτικά and ερωτικά, and even there I am not serious.'[75] It is in fact an example of *recusatio* which, we are told, Roman poets found to be 'an elegant device to brush off importunate patrons, avid for commemoration in the grander genres. A diffident refusal to praise might prove the least exhausting form of flattery.'[76] As a literary device, *recusatio* is ironical through and through. For example, Horace here professes an incapacity for epic: he fears that he will only detract from the achievements of Agrippa and the emperor by writing bad epic poetry about them. To prove his point about incompetence, Horace deliberately botches his handling of the epic heroes: Achilles' divine wrath is reduced to a bad case of colic, and Odysseus' multiplex capacities are reduced to mere duplicity. At the same time, however, the expertise with which the professed ineptitude is demonstrated, and the fact that he has nonetheless briefly summarized the major themes of the *Iliad* and the *Odyssey*, go some way to achieving precisely what he has disclaimed all hope of being able to achieve.[77]

The difficulty is how much of this to allow into the equation when assessing Milton's epigraph. The Varius referred to by Horace was the leading epic poet of the day. He also wrote a tragedy, *Thyestes*,

---

[72] Horace, *The Odes and Epodes*, ed. and trans. C. E. Bennett (London, 1914), p. 21.

[73] I have checked the following British Library MSS: Add. 27,320 and 33,359; Hargrave 280; Harleian 1853 and 1889.

[74] Milton, *Complete Shorter Poems*, ed. John Carey (London, 1971), pp. 96–7.

[75] R. G. M. Nisbet and Margaret Hubbard, *A Commentary on Horace: Odes Book I* (Oxford, 1970), p. 80.   [76] *Ibid.*, p. 82.

[77] See *ibid.*, pp. 85–6; Steele Commager, *The Odes of Horace: A Critical Study* (New Haven, 1962), p. 71; Matthew S. Santirocco, *Unity and Design in Horace's Odes* (Chapel Hill, 1986), pp. 34–6.

which Quintilian compared favourably with the work of the Greeks, composed a panegyric on Augustus, and after Virgil's death helped to edit the *Aeneid* for publication (by order of Augustus). Agrippa (the same Agrippa who appears in Shakespeare's *Antony and Cleopatra*) was a lifelong friend and supporter of Augustus, and his greatest general and admiral: he defeated Pompey in two naval battles, and overcame Antony at Actium. Second only to Augustus, he was a key figure in the transition from republic to empire.[78] If we transpose one scenario into the terms of the other, then Milton stands in for Horace, and Ralegh for Varius. And when Milton poses the rhetorical question, 'Who could fittingly tell of Mars clad in his adamantine tunic?', the answer must be, 'Not I, but Ralegh.' Milton thus graciously recommends the work of an 'eminent' author more capable than he of handling such momentous themes. But who, then, is the Agrippa of whom Varius will write? Frankly, there seems to me to be only one plausible candidate: the commander-in-chief, Cromwell himself. And in this event we should understand Milton to be saying, 'I cannot, but Ralegh *will* write – indeed, already has written – of the exploits of Oliver Cromwell.'

Before drawing out the implications of this reading of the epigraph, and in particular the suggested identification of Cromwell with Agrippa, I wish to consider some possible objections to the way in which the epigraph has been handled. The first is that it goes too far in its extrapolation of intertextual features. In this case, the title page of the 1650 edition of Ralegh's *Select Essayes* – a volume which, as we have already seen, has connections with *The Cabinet-Council* – offers a close and instructive parallel since it too bears an epigraph from Horace (*Odes*, III.2.21–2): 'Virtus recludens immeritis mori/Caelum, negatâ tentat iter viâ' ('True worth, opening Heaven wide for those undeserving to die, essays its course by a forbidden path').[79] Whoever furnished this epigraph was (like Milton) trying to predispose the reader to take the desired view of the text it served, this being, after all, the *raison d'être* of the epigraph as a genre. By alluding to the salient facts of Ralegh's life – his fame as an explorer and a victim of Stuart tyranny, sacrificed on the altar of *rapprochement* with Spain – the reader is assured that the book will be typical of its author and reflect the master-themes of his life.[80] All of this is elegantly encapsulated in

---

[78] Nisbet and Hubbard, *Commentary*, pp. 80–1.
[79] Horace, *Odes and Epodes*, trans. Bennett, pp. 175, 177 (adapted).
[80] The contents comprise 'The First Invention of Shipping', 'The Misery of Invasive Warre', 'The Navy Royall and Sea-Service' and 'Apologie for his Voyage to Guiana'.

the quotation from Horace, with its references to forbidden paths, unmerited death and apotheosis. But there are other lines in the poem which can only strike one as grotesquely inapposite. As it happens, this is an ode which Ralegh himself knew well, and of which he translated part in *The History of the World*.[81] However, in view of his fate on the scaffold, line 13, 'dulce et decorum est pro patria mori', seems less than tactful, and lines 19–20, in which Horace defines *virtus* as residing in the unflinching discharge of duties, even less so: 'nec sumit aut ponit securis / arbitrio popularis aurae' ('nor takes up nor lays aside the axes at the fickle mob's behest').[82] It is clear in both cases that it is the epigraphs themselves which determine what is appropriate by way of interpretation. The one to the *Select Essayes* is transparent; there is no need to look to the rest of the poem, and to do so is to risk embarrassment. The one to *The Cabinet-Council*, by contrast, is opaque to a degree which forces one to look to the rest of the ode for enlightenment (it makes for a fitting irony that the epigraph to a volume devoted to the *arcana imperii* should itself require decoding).

It might be objected nevertheless that this is to overlook an altogether simpler possibility. The most obvious way of explaining the epigraph is that it takes its cue from the motto above the portrait: 'Tam Marti, Quam Mercurio'. It could be construed, for example, as issuing a plea for someone worthy to undertake a biography of Ralegh along the lines, say, of Greville's *Life of Sidney* published in 1652. However, the figure of Ralegh in the portrait is not 'clad in his adamantine tunic', or even a breastplate, but a doublet. And it would be odd to refer only to Ralegh's martial aspect when the aim of the motto was to highlight his conjunction of military and literary qualities. In any case, Milton was if anything more likely to have wanted to dissociate himself from such sentiments. All the evidence points to his having increasing doubts about the value of military prowess in the 1650s, so that he would be unlikely to refer to anyone as a Mars except in an ironic or disparaging sense.[83] It should also be remembered that Mercury was the god of traders and thieves as well as of eloquence. So that when Milton told Herman Mylius in February 1651 that too many members of the Council of State were

---

[81] See *The Poems of Sir Walter Ralegh*, ed. Agnes M. C. Latham (London, 1929), p. 62; Ralegh, *Works*, V, p. 145 (III.7.3).   [82] Horace, *Odes and Epodes*, trans. Bennett, p. 175.

[83] See Martin Dzelzainis, 'Juvenal, Charles X Gustavus and Milton's Letter to Richard Jones', *The Seventeenth Century*, 9 (1994), 25–34

'de Mercurii et Martis prole' ('sons of Mars and Mercury'), what he meant by this was that they were mere soldiers and tradesmen and hence, as von Maltzahn puts it, 'lacking that civic virtue appropriate to their political calling'.[84]

Finally, it might be objected that, however the epigraph is construed, it is surely unwise to rest any argument upon so slight a foundation. My reply to this is that I am only attending to details to which Milton himself devoted a good deal of care. For example, the elaborate title page of *Areopagitica*, with its epigraph from Euripides' *Supplices* (in Greek with an accompanying translation), is regarded by some as offering the key to interpretation of the work itself.[85] The Euripidean epigraph on the title page of *Tetrachordon* (1645), taken from the speech in which Medea disarms Creon's suspicions of her cleverness, both anticipates and discounts rejection of his views on divorce:

> For if thou bring strange wisdom unto dullards
> Useless thou shalt be counted and not wise
> And, if thy fame outshine those heretofore
> Held wise, thou shalt be odious in men's eyes.[86]

This dismisses the unlearned twice over (both in what is said and by virtue of its being said in Greek only) and invites the learned to rise above their envy. Mortified – though surely not surprised – when this tract fared no better than its predecessors, Milton composed a sonnet satirizing the incomprehension of the average browser: 'Cries the stall-reader, Bless us! what a word on / A title-page is this!'[87] When William Marshall produced his famously inept portrait of Milton for the frontispiece of the 1645 *Poems*, Milton's response was to compose a poem in Greek condemning the artist which the unwitting Marshall duly engraved beneath.[88] Years later, in his *Pro Se Defensio* (1655), Milton was still fretting publicly about Marshall and how he had been prevailed upon by Moseley to employ him.[89] Much more

---

[84] Nicholas von Maltzahn, *Milton's 'History of Britain': Republican Historiography in the English Revolution* (Oxford, 1991), p. 44.

[85] For a reproduction of the title page, see *CPW*, II, 485; for commentary, see David Davies and Paul Dowling, '"Shrewd books, with dangerous Frontispieces": *Areopagitica*'s Motto', *Milton Quarterly*, 20 (1986), 33–7, and Annabel Patterson, *Censorship and Interpretation: The Conditions of Writing and Reading in Early Modern England* (Madison, 1985), p. 115.

[86] For a reproduction of the title page and the translation of *Medea*, 298–301, see *CPW*, II, 577–8. I am grateful to Dr David Norbrook for drawing my attention to this.

[87] Sonnet XI, 5–6, *Shorter Poems*, ed. Carey, p. 303.   [88] See *Shorter Poems*, ed. Carey, p. 289.

[89] See *CPW*, IVii, 750–1.

significant, however, is the epigraph, adapted from Juvenal, on the title page of the second edition of *The Readie and Easie Way:* 'et nos / consilium dedimus *Syllae,* demus populo nunc' ('I too have given advice to Sulla, now let me give it to the people').[90] In this case, no convincing argument has ever been offered for identifying Sulla with anyone other than Cromwell.[91] As William Hayley remarked in 1796, 'the motto to this performance seems to display the just opinion that Milton entertained concerning the tyranny of Cromwell'[92] – a point which would have been taken even more readily in 1660.

There is one further piece of evidence to be considered. The phrase 'tunicâ tectum adamantinâ' seems to have had an enduring significance for Milton, being associated with both overbearing militarism and hypocrisy ('tectum' could just as well mean 'concealed' as 'clad', thus yielding the image of a dazzling exterior concealing what lies within).[93] In Book VI of *Paradise Lost,* just before hostilities commence in Heaven, Satan, the 'Idol of majesty divine', descends from his 'gorgeous throne':

> before the cloudy van,
> On the rough edge of battle ere it joined,
> Satan with vast and haughty strides advanced,
> Came towering, armed in adamant and gold.[94]

It is sometimes suggested that we should find a reflection of Cromwell in Satan: perhaps we should add to both the figure of Agrippa, the general who helped lay the foundations of imperial Rome on the ruins of the republic.

Taking a less defensive view of the matter, we can now begin to see *The Cabinet-Council* less as a literary curiosity which Milton disinterestedly made available to the public, and more as a tract for the times. For his

---

[90] For a reproduction of the title page, see *CPW*, VII, 405; trans. John Carey, *Shorter Poems,* p. 414.
[91] But see Austin Woolrych's remarks, *CPW*, VII, 205; Masson, *Life of Milton,* V, pp. 678–9. I am grateful to Dr Blair Worden and Professor Armitage for advice on this point.
[92] William Hayley, *The Life of Milton* (1796; reprint, New York, 1971), p. 144.
[93] One can only speculate as to the contents of Milton's MS Latin Thesaurus, but it is worth noting that Adam Littleton's *Linguae Latinae Liber Dictionarius Quadripartitus* (London, 1678), sig. CI^v (second pagination), has a very brief entry *s.v. Adamantinus,* citing only Pliny, whereas the expanded version (prepared with the assistance of Milton's MS), *Linguae Romanae Dictionarium Luculentum Novum* (1693), sig. D2, *s.v. Adamantinus,* adds 'Tunica adamantina, Hor. Armour impenetrable'. The prefatory note, 'TO THE READER', sig. A2^v, strongly implies that Milton's MS survived publication of the dictionary in 1693 and was available for consultation 'by the Curious or doubtful'. See also Leo Miller, *John Milton's Writings in the Anglo-Dutch Negotiations, 1651–1654* (Pittsburgh, 1992), pp. 82–5 (Appendix 3: Milton's *Thesaurus Linguae Latinae*).   [94] *PL*, VI, 101, 103, 107–10.

intention in publishing it was to offer something answerable to the state of affairs in 1658. The only assumption that we are required to make is that his intention in publishing it was entirely ironic: for if he was offering an advice book to Cromwell, then this was only because his regime had degenerated to the point at which such a debased form of advice had become appropriate. *The Cabinet-Council* was, in short, corrupt advice for a corrupt regime.

Once we assume an ironic intention on Milton's part, then the puzzles about the publication of *The Cabinet-Council* largely resolve themselves. In the first place, it means that Milton straightforwardly treated *The Cabinet-Council* as what it undeniably was – an advice book (though it could be said that, to the extent that Milton was offering the Protector an image of what he had become, the advice book was also functioning as a mirror for the prince). And, secondly, it means that Milton's publishing of it was perfectly compatible with his having maintained his long-standing hostility to the type of Renaissance statecraft it embodied. Indeed, the point of publishing it may in part have been to reassure doubters that he had indeed remained true to his earlier commitments.

III

David Masson suggested long ago that Milton's *Treatise of Civil Power* of February 1659 'can be construed no otherwise than as an effort on his part, Protectoratist and Court-official though he was, to renew his relations with the old Republican party'.[95] One who responded promptly and positively to this initiative was Moses Wall. In a letter to Milton, perhaps thanking him for a copy of the *Treatise*, Wall admitted that he had been 'uncerten whether your Relation to the Court, (though I think a Commonwealth was more friendly to you than a Court) had not clouded your former Light, but your last Book resolved that Doubt'.[96] What the letter signalled, according to Masson, was 'Milton's welcome back into the ranks of the old Republicans'.[97] This seems to me an entirely plausible reading of events, to which I would add only the suggestion that Milton began making overtures of this kind much earlier than Masson thought; not in the spring of 1659, but in the spring of 1658 with the publication of

[95] Masson, *Life of Milton*, v, p. 587.
[96] Moses Wall to Milton, 26 May 1659, *CPW*, vii, 510–11 (contractions expanded); for the suggestion of an earlier date, see *ibid.*, p. 83.   [97] Masson, *Life of Milton*, v, p. 603.

The Cabinet-Council. I shall therefore conclude by considering briefly the implications of this line of argument for the other work which Milton published in 1658: the revised and augmented *Defensio*.

In one sense, the contrast between the two works could not be greater. This is especially marked in chapter v of the *Defensio* where Milton takes up the challenge issued by his adversary, Salmasius, and agrees to examine the classical sources. Throughout, Milton is concerned to restore the reputation of the classical moralists and historians as upholders of political liberty rather than (as Milton thought Salmasius had presented them in his *Defensio Regia*) promoters of slavery. The most keenly contested figure is, as one might expect, Tacitus. When Salmasius quotes a remark from the *Annals* out of context, Milton replies that 'These are not the words of Tacitus, who was a noble writer most opposed to tyranny' but merely the utterances of one of the figures whose fate Tacitus is relating. If Salmasius had gone directly to the original text rather than, as Milton suspects, copying 'an excerpt' from somewhere – that is, from works like those of Lipsius or Malvezzi – this would have been immediately apparent. To prevent such unlicensed departures from the text, Milton insists on the orthodox humanist techniques of interpretation: 'we should consider not so much what the poet says, but who in the poem says it. Various figures appear, some good, some bad, some wise, some foolish, each speaking not the poet's opinions but what is appropriate for each person.'[98] But, as Milton himself seems to have realized, this concern with the rules of literary decorum and historical authenticity was, methodologically speaking, completely at odds with the priorities and practices of the writers of tracts on reason of state or the compilers of advice books, who ransacked their favourite ancient texts in search of aphorisms. The image of the classical moralists in the *Defensio* is one purified from any taint of Renaissance statecraft. In this respect at least, the *Defensio* stands at the furthest possible remove from *The Cabinet-Council*.

Even so, the 1658 edition of the *Defensio* raises almost as many questions as *The Cabinet-Council*. Given that Milton was, as is agreed on all sides, so busy, why did he make the time to prepare a fresh edition of a text which was still available? Copies of previous editions were advertised for sale in catalogues in 1657, 1658 and 1659, both in

---

[98] *CPW*, ivi, 439, 443.

London and Amsterdam.[99] If anything, the material from Homer, Virgil and Horace which is inserted into chapter v (the one most heavily revised in 1658) suggests how deeply he was engaged with *Paradise Lost* at the time.[100] Parker remarks lamely that it was done 'as if to remind the English people, at this critical moment in their history, that he had once served them well. It was a clear bid for remembrance, at a time when men might forget past deeds.'[101] In this he was echoing Masson who had also stressed Milton's personal motives, though he confessed that he found the spectacle of Milton yet again reliving his triumph over Salmasius rather trying: 'one begins to be a little tired of this high-strained exultation for ever and ever on the subject of his success'.[102] This may be so, but it begs the question; for we can accept that these were Milton's motives without trenching in the least upon the quite separate issue of his intentions in re-publishing the *Defensio*.

To judge from their silence on the point, Masson and Parker also assume that the fact that material has already been published before means that its re-publication cannot be a matter of any great significance or controversy. However, the perils of such an assumption are neatly illustrated by the actions of Milton's friend and colleague, Marchamont Nedham. In 1656, Nedham compiled some of the editorials he had originally written for *Mercurius Politicus* in the early 1650s and published them in book form as *The Excellencie of a Free State*. But four years later, as J. G. A. Pocock points out, these editorials 'calling for an armed popular republic, with frequent parliaments and rotation of officers, must have read like a radical manifesto'.[103] What had been published in support of one regime served equally well as a critique of its successor. There is no reason to suppose that Nedham did not know what he was doing – or that Milton in turn did not know what he was doing when, with the Protectorate well into its fifth year, he set about refurbishing the most famous of all defences of the Commonwealth. Moreover it should be borne in mind that the 'critical moment' to which Parker refers – the

---

[99] See John T. Shawcross, *Milton: A Bibliography for the Years 1624–1700*, Medieval and Renaissance Texts and Studies (Binghamton, 1984), pp. 187 (item 381), 188 (item 382), 190 (item 395), 194 (item 423).

[100] For variants in chapter v, see Robert W. Ayers, 'Appendix F: Variants in the London Editions of Milton's *Defensio*', in *CPW*, ivii, 1134, 1136 (misbound: should be 1135).

[101] Parker, *Milton*, I, p. 518.   [102] Masson, *Life of Milton*, v, p. 574.

[103] *The Political Works of James Harrington*, ed. J. G. A. Pocock (Cambridge, 1977), p. 13.

death of Oliver Cromwell and the succession of Richard – could not have been foreseen by Milton when he began revising the text of the *Defensio*. Although Cromwell showed signs of ill-health throughout 1658, his final collapse following the death of his daughter was relatively sudden. We should therefore proceed on the understanding that the regime under which Milton began revising the work was the one under which he expected it to be published.

As with *The Cabinet-Council*, Milton's intention in publishing the *Defensio* was to offer something answerable to the state of affairs in 1658, bearing in mind that the relevant context is that furnished by events in the first rather than the second half of the year. In fact 1658 began in turmoil for, as Underdown remarks, the 'Protectorate reached a point of acute crisis in February'.[104] The seeds of this crisis lay in the passage of the Humble Petition and Advice in May–June 1657 when, in refusing the offer of kingship, Cromwell fatally compromised the remainder of the constitution to which he did agree. In particular, the status and powers of the 'other House' were left unclear. Accordingly, this became the focus of the attack on the Humble Petition led by Sir Arthur Haselrig and Thomas Scot in the stormy Commons session of 20 January to 4 February 1658.[105] Their campaign was quickly supplemented by a petition provocatively addressed 'To the Parliament of the Common-wealth of England' which began to circulate in London on 25 January. It was prompted by 'affection to the good old Cause', which in this case amounted to a demand for government without a single person or a House of Lords, for liberty of conscience and for civilian control of the army.[106] Cromwell was so alarmed by the petition and the forces behind it – what was later to be dubbed by Prynne 'the confederated Triumuirate of Republicans, Sectaries and Soldiers'[107] – that he dissolved Parliament on 4 February before the petition could be presented. He then proceeded to cashier six Baptist officers from his own regiment of horse.[108] But while this dealt with the immediate situation, it did not resolve the underlying tensions which had produced it. Throughout the spring and early summer of 1658, rumours abounded that

---

[104] David Underdown, 'Cromwell and the Officers, February 1658', *English Historical Review*, 83 (1968), 101.

[105] For the debates see *The Diary of Thomas Burton*, ed. J. T. Rutt, 4 vols. (London, 1828), II, pp. 316–470.

[106] Barbara Taft, 'That Lusty Puss, the Good Old Cause', *History of Political Thought*, 5 (1984), 456.

[107] Austin Woolrych, 'The Good Old Cause and the Fall of the Protectorate', *Historical Journal*, 13 (1957), 134.   [108] Underdown, 'Cromwell and the Officers', pp. 101–7.

another Parliament would shortly be called, and that this time Cromwell would accept the offer of the crown.[109]

As we have seen, Milton's response to these developments was first expressed in the ironic performance of a common Renaissance ritual: the dedication of an advice book to a prince. However, given that his identifiable contribution – a note and the choice of an epigraph – was the work of a moment, and given that the gesture was sufficiently oblique to pass unnoticed,[110] there was clearly scope for a more positive and weighty intervention in the political debate. And since it must have been at around this time that Milton decided to embark on his revision of the *Defensio*, we need to ask exactly what kind of intervention it constituted.

Looked at in this light, the work takes on an immediacy and urgency which it would not have had at any other time in the years following its first publication. As rehearsed in the *Defensio*, Milton's position on the central issues agitating the nation in the early months of 1658 is perfectly clear. Although he did not absolutely oppose monarchy as such, non-elective or hereditary monarchy was a very different matter, and he flatly opposed it.[111] And while he was far from disapproving of aristocracy, suitably defined, he wholeheartedly approved of the abolition of the House of Lords.[112] It follows from this that for Milton to voice opposition to the retrograde tendencies of the Protectorate, and to warn against the drift back to monarchical forms, did not require a reformulation of his views: all that it required was a reiteration of views he had previously held. In many ways this was the essence of the Good Old Cause, and I would argue that Milton first declared his commitment to it not in 1659, but in 1658, and did so by publishing *The Cabinet-Council* and re-publishing the *Defensio*.

[109] See C. H. Firth, *The Last Years of the Protectorate, 1656–1658*, 2 vols. (London, 1909), II, pp. 270–4.
[110] See, for example, John Toland's bland comments in Darbishire, *Early Lives*, p. 188. Nevertheless it could be argued that such obliquity was entirely characteristic of the Cromwellian literature of counsel. I am grateful to Professor Armitage for this suggestion and for supplying me with a copy of his 'Parliaments and Eighteenth-Century British Political Thought' (unpublished conference paper, April 1993).
[111] *CPW*, IVi, 336, 472–3, 479–80.   [112] *CPW*, IVi, 457, 470–1, 484–6, 493–4, 509.

John Milton: poet against empire

David Armitage

I

In 1649 republicanism became available as a comprehensive political programme. With King Charles dead, the ancient constitution suspended, and 'a Commonwealth or Free State' declared, here was a moment to be seized for new-modelling the constitution at home and prosecuting grand designs abroad. Yet, as is well known, the Rump's political timidity restricted constitutional innovation even as it pursued a vigorous foreign policy with the conquest of Ireland and Scotland, and its proposals for Anglo-Dutch union. Republicanism was not responsible for internal renewal, but it did help to inspire external aggrandisement, with paradoxical effects: 'Nourished by constitutional failure at home, republicanism throve too on military and naval success abroad.'[1] England may not have become a new Rome by virtue of its constitution, but the infant commonwealth certainly looked set fair to imitate the martial achievements of the ancient republics.

The republican moment of 1649–53 – from the declaration of the Commonwealth to Cromwell's forcible dissolution of the Long Parliament – inspired a variety of Englishmen to apply the lessons learnt from the classical republics to their own political situation. John Lilburne, in exile, first read Machiavelli, Livy and Plutarch in

Earlier versions of this essay were presented in Princeton, Cambridge, Oxford, Nanterre and Reading. As well as to audiences on those occasions, I am particularly grateful to Martin Dzelzainis, David Kastan, David Quint, Quentin Skinner, Austin Woolrych and Blair Worden for their help and comments.

[1] Blair Worden, *The Rump Parliament, 1648–1653* (Cambridge, 1974), pp. 40, 173; Worden, 'Classical Republicanism and the Puritan Revolution', in Hugh Lloyd-Jones, Valerie Pearl and Blair Worden (eds.), *History and Imagination* (London, 1981), pp. 195–9; Worden, 'Milton's Republicanism and the Tyranny of Heaven', in Gisela Bock, Quentin Skinner and Maurizio Viroli (eds.), *Machiavelli and Republicanism* (Cambridge, 1990) p. 226.

these years.[2] In the same period, Marchamont Nedham's *The Case of the Commonwealth of England, Stated* (1650) and his editorials for the government organ *Mercurius Politicus* in 1651–2 applied ancient history to modern politics, and drew upon a wide range of classical and contemporary sources to celebrate the successes of the Rump and to point the way forward for republican regeneration. John Milton had his own republican moment during these years. He acted as licenser of *Mercurius Politicus* during the period when most of Nedham's republican editorials were published, and he seems to have begun reading Machiavelli's *Discorsi* seriously in November 1651, just as the first of them began to appear.[3] He was soon applying the Roman example to the analysis of the English constitution, as Herman Mylius reported in January 1652.[4]

Milton's reading of the *Discorsi* supplied him with positive arguments for a period of constitutional change and realignment in foreign affairs. The entries in his commonplace book show him ranging across the whole of Machiavelli's commentaries in search of timely lessons for the English commonwealth in these years – for example, that armed resistance to a tyrant is legitimate; money is not the sinews of war; it is necessary frequently to return to first principles; alliances with republics are more trustworthy than those with principalities; elective rulership is better than hereditary succession; and a republican form of government is to be preferred before all others.[5] Yet he also took a more salutary message from Machiavelli, which confirmed what the Roman historians and poets (particularly Sallust and Juvenal, as we shall see) had also told him: that in the case of a republic, it is both politically and morally artificial to distinguish internal from external affairs, and that each will compromise the other if not pursued prudently. A republic could only expand successfully on a foundation of a correctly balanced constitution: 'It is not the duty of every state to enlarge the boundaries of its power and to bring other nations under its rule. On the contrary, Machiavelli wisely shows that it is dangerous to do so unless that state is rightly ordered and unless the addition of that new

---

[2] Perez Zagorin, *A History of Political Thought in the English Revolution* (London, 1954), p. 18.

[3] William Riley Parker, *Milton: A Biography*, 2 vols. (Oxford, 1969), I, p. 394; II, pp. 993–4; James Holly Hanford, 'The Chronology of Milton's Private Studies', *Publications of the Modern Languages Association of America*, 36 (1921), 281–3; Maurice Kelley, 'Milton and Machiavelli's *Discorsi*', *Studies in Bibliography*, 4 (1951–2), 123–7.

[4] Leo Miller, *John Milton and the Oldenburg Safeguard* (New York, 1985), p. 128.

[5] John Milton, 'Commonplace Book', *CPW*, I, 456 (*Discorsi*, I. 58); 414–15, 498 (*Discorsi*, II. 10); 477 (*Discorsi*, III. 1); 504 (*Discorsi*, I. 59); 475 (*Discorsi*, I. 2, and I. 10); 477 (*Discorsi*, I. 58).

realm is justly administered.'[6] Milton drew this lesson from *Discorsi*,
II.19, in which Machiavelli contrasted the fate of the city-states of
contemporary Germany with that of other, less successful republics.
The German republics were defensive and eschewed expansion: for
that reason, they enjoyed freedom as they had done for some time.
Venice and Florence had been tempted to expand, and thereby
weakened themselves 'since conquests are harmful in a thousand ways
and for many reasons'. Though the Romans were exemplary in their
policies – expanding their population, making other states their allies
not their subjects, settling colonies in conquered territories – even
their republic was finally debilitated by the luxury it learned from its
conquests in the east, as Juvenal testified: 'Luxury, more deadly than
arms, laid its hand on us and avenges the conquered world.'[7]

If expansion harmed even the Romans, who had displayed conspicuous prudence and virtue, asked Machiavelli, what greater damage
could it do to states which did not have these moral resources? He had
warned that anyone who wished to set up a republic should first ask
whether it would expand, like Rome, or whether it was to remain
within strict physical limits, like Sparta and Venice. Yet even Sparta
and Venice were tempted to expand, with disastrous consequences for
their liberty and their stability, because their constitutions were not
suited to the strains of expansion. Under perfect conditions, Machiavelli
would advise any new republic to be defensive and non-expansionary,
for that way it might achieve political longevity; however, in the flux
of human affairs, he deemed such a recommendation idealistic, and
counselled that it should follow the Roman model instead, with the
risk of tumults as the price of greatness (*Discorsi*, 1.6).[8]

Machiavelli laid bare the collision at the heart of republican politics
between two overwhelmingly desirable but ultimately irreconcilable
goals: liberty, which distinguished the internal constitution of the
republic by allowing the human potential of its citizens to be realized
through active participation in political life, and *grandezza*, the aggressive
but potentially destructive pursuit of glory in external affairs. He used
the example of Rome throughout the *Discorsi* to show how an offensive
posture towards the outside world would be the only means to safeguard

---

[6] *CPW*, I, 499 (*Discorsi*, II. 19).

[7] '. . . saevior armis/luxuria incubuit victumque ulciscitur orbem' (Juvenal, *Satires*, VI. 292–3),
   cited in *Discorsi*. II, 19.

[8] For an excellent analysis of the problematic underlying Machiavelli's discussion see Patricia
   Springborg, *Western Republicanism and the Oriental Prince* (Cambridge, 1992), pp. 181–5, 212–21.

the liberty of a republic, yet he used the same historic example to show that the pursuit of greatness would inevitably lead to the loss of that liberty.[9] Rome's greatness could not have been achieved without prolonging military commands, but this led directly to servitude for the Roman people (*Discorsi*, III.24): the liberty which had been won with the expulsion of the kings ended in the dictatorships of Sulla and Marius, which in turn paved the way for the tyranny of Caesar (*Discorsi*, I.28, 37).

This moral analysis of the death of Roman liberty as the cost of Roman expansion derived ultimately from the early books of Sallust's *Bellum Catilinae*.[10] Sallust told how the people of Rome had created a republic after the rule of kings, 'which at first had tended to preserve freedom and advance the state, had degenerated into a lawless tyranny'. Under republican government, the people exerted themselves more forcefully, and put their talents forward more readily, because 'kings hold the good in greater suspicion than the wicked' and had therefore repressed the capabilites of the populace.[11] Sallust thought it remarkable how the state grew once it had become free (*civitas ... adepta libertate quantum brevi creverit*), so greatly were the people inspired by the desire for glory (*Bellum Catilinae*, VII.4). Martial valour was at its height, and good morals were cultivated at home. However, when the republic had grown through hard work and justice (*ubi labore atque iustitia res publica crevit*), fortune turned against Rome, and avarice, ambition and impiety slowly corrupted those who had formerly been so virtuous and hardy: 'finally, when the disease had spread like a deadly plague, the state was changed (*civitas immutata*) and a government second to none in equity and excellence became cruel and intolerable'. The dictatorship of Lucius Sulla set the seal on this declension, as everyone pursued his own advantage, the army became corrupted by eastern luxury, and 'virtue began to lose its lustre (*hebescere virtus*), poverty to be considered a disgrace, blamelessness to be termed malevolence' (*Bellum Catilinae*, IX.i; X; XI–XII).

The relevance of Sallust's analysis to the republican moment of 1649–50 was not lost on either Milton or Nedham. In the immediate aftermath of the regicide, they had high hopes of the potential for

---

[9] Maurizio Viroli, 'Machiavelli and the Republican Idea of Politics', in Bock, Skinner and Viroli (eds.), *Machiavelli and Republicanism*, pp. 158–9.

[10] Quentin Skinner, 'Machiavelli's *Discorsi* and the Pre-Humanist Origins of Republican Ideas', in Bock, Skinner and Viroli (eds.), *Machiavelli and Republicanism*, pp. 122–3.

[11] Sallust, *Bellum Catilinae*, VI. 7; VII. 2, in *Sallust*, trans. J. C. Rolfe (London, 1965), p. 13; compare Machiavelli, *Arte della Guerra*, II, cited in *CPW*, I, 421.

liberty to foster greatness, and both cited Sallust to affirm this belief. In 1649, on the title page of *Eikonoklastes*, Milton displayed Sallust's opinion that the monarchy had declined into tyranny, and hence that good men became suspect and their virtue a danger (*Bellum Catilinae*, VI. 7; VII. 1–2), a passage to which he had also alluded at the opening of *The Tenure of Kings and Magistrates* a few months earlier.[12] The following year, Nedham continued Sallust's narrative on the title page of *The Case of the Commonwealth of England Stated* (1650) with the epigraph, 'Incredibile est memoratu, quantum adeptâ libertate, in brevi *Romana* civitas creverit' (*Bellum Catilinae*, VII. 3), a verdict he was to repeat elsewhere in *The Case*.[13] Sallust's words clearly informed Nedham's most ringing endorsement of the Rump's foreign policy in 1652. Just as the loss of liberty debilitates a people morally, he told the readers of *Mercurius Politicus*, 'so on the other side, the People ever grow magnanimous & gallant upon a recovery [of it]; witness at present the valiant Swisses, the Hollanders, and also our own Nation; whose high atchievments may match any of the Ancients, since the extirpation of Tyranny, and a re-establishment of our Freedom in the hands of the People'.[14]

The republican confidence of the years under the Rump evaporated during the course of the Cromwellian Protectorate. Both Nedham and Milton came to feel that the story of moral decline, from freedom with greatness to servitude wrought by ambition, narrated by Sallust and warned against by Machiavelli, had – perhaps inevitably – run its course in England between 1649 and 1656. The evidence for Nedham's disillusionment comes from the version of his republican editorials published as *The Excellencie of a Free State* in 1656. When first published in *Mercurius Politicus* in 1651–2, these articles presented a set of warnings to the infant republic along with his celebrations of its fortitude. Liberty for the people, its most effective guardians, could only be secured once kingship had been thoroughly uprooted; it could only be maintained if the exercise of power could be limited by rotation of civil and military office-holders.[15] The reward for liberty

---

[12] *CPW*, III, 190. On Milton's reading of Sallust, his favourist historian, see especially Nicholas von Maltzahn, *Milton's 'History of Britain': Republican Historiography in the English Revolution* (Oxford, 1991), pp. 75–7; Martin Dzelzainis, 'Milton's Classical Republicanism', above, pp. 22–3.

[13] Marchamont Nedham, *The Case of the Commonwealth of England Stated* (London, 1650), p. 85.

[14] *Mercurius Politicus* 85 (22 January 1652), p. 1352.

[15] *Merc. Pol.* 77 (27 Nov. 1651), p. 1222; 72 (23 Oct. 1651), p. 1141; 78 (4 Dec. 1651), p. 1238, cf. 79 (11 Dec. 1651), p. 1256; 81 (25 Dec. 1651), p. 1289; 92 (11 March 1652), p. 1461; 100 (6 May 1652), p. 1572; 101 (13 May 1652), p. 1588.

and free assemblies would be power abroad and the extension of the empire. Yet, like Machiavelli and Sallust, Nedham warned that Rome's expansion had brought in luxury, a standing army and the extension of military commands. A succession of tyrants ensued. Liberty was lost, and with liberty, the empire itself.[16] When reprinted in 1656, these warnings looked like predictions, and they became a stick with which to beat the Protector.[17] Sallust's awed account of the achievements of Rome's new-won liberty had been celebratory when cited in *The Case of the Commonwealth* in 1650, but it became bitterly nostalgic when repeated in 1656; similarly, Nedham's praise of the Rump's foreign policy in 1652, when amended in *The Excellencie of a Free State*, became a lament for the republican opportunity which had been squandered by the Protector: 'the People ever grow magnanimous & gallant upon a recovery [of freedom]; witness at present the valiant Swisses, the Hollanders and *not long since* our own Nation when declared a Free-State, and a Re-establishment of our Freedom in the hands of the people procured, (*though not secured*) what noble Designs were undertaken and prosecuted with Success?'[18]

In 1660 Milton echoed Nedham's frustration with the failure to secure the free state in *The Readie and Easie Way*, as he put the achievement of republican *grandezza* firmly in the English past: 'Nor were our actions less both at home and abroad then might become the hopes of a glorious rising Commonwealth; nor were the expressions both of the Army and of the People ... other than such as testifi'd a spirit in this nation no less noble and well fitted to the liberty of a Comonwealth, then in the ancient Greeks or Romans.' Did Milton then believe that popular liberty had been extinguished by the rise of corrupting expansionism, personal ambition, and the entrenchment of over-mighty generals? He certainly believed that the moment for greatness to spring from liberty had passed, as he imagined the reproaches of the rest of Europe: 'where is this goodly tower of a Common-wealth which the *English* boasted they would build, to overshaddow kings and be another *Rome* in the west?' Like Nedham, he thought that the Dutch had not sacrificed their chance to be 'a

---

[16] *Ibid.*, 82 (1 Jan. 1652), pp. 1304, 1305–6; 85 (22 Jan. 1652), pp. 1349, 1351; 88 (12 Feb. 1652), pp. 1394–5; 90 (26 Feb. 1652), p. '1435' sc. 1427; 103 (27 May 1652), p. '1511' [sc. 1611]).

[17] *The Political Works of James Harrington*, ed. J. G. A. Pocock (Cambridge, 1977), p. 13; Blair Worden, 'Milton and Marchamont Nedham', above, pp. 174–5.

[18] Marchamont Nedham, *The Excellencie of a Free State* (London, 1656), pp. 19 (which reprints the passage from *The Case of the Commonwealth*, p. 85), 58 (my emphases).

potent and flourishing Republick': but who then was to be held responsible for squandering England's republican moment?[19]

Milton hinted at the answer when another republican *occasione* presented itself in 1660, with the recalling of the 'old Patriots' of the Long Parliament. The intervening period had seen some 'unhappie interruptions'.[20] Chief among them was what Milton called in *Considerations Touching the Likeliest Means to Remove Hirelings* 'a short but scandalous night of interruption', which had been ended by the recalling of the Rump in the spring of 1659.[21] Thanks to the researches of Austin Woolrych, we can be fairly certain that by this particular 'interruption' Milton meant the whole of the Protectorate, from the expulsion of the Rump in 1653 to the eve of its recall in 1659, as did the author of an anonymous pamphlet published shortly before Milton's which made *A Publick Plea, Opposed to a Private Proposal . . . in this Morning of Freedom, After a Short, but Sharp Night of Tyranny*.[22] This interpretation is strengthened by the fact that *A Publick Plea, Opposed to a Private Proposal*, the first edition of *The Readie and Easie Way* and *The Likeliest Means* were all published by Livewell Chapman, the fifth-monarchist house publisher to the good old cause.[23]

Malcolm Smuts has suggested that Tacitus and Juvenal 'provided languages capable of articulating the frustrations and cynicism' produced by the court in the 1590s.[24] For Milton, at least, Sallust and Juvenal performed a similar function in the 1650s, and both writers were much on his mind in the latter years of the Protectorate. Milton declared that 'I prefer Sallust to any other Latin historian whatsoever, which was also the nearly unanimous opinion of the ancients': as we now know, this was also the opinion of early modern Europe, where Sallust was the most popular ancient historian in the period 1450–1700.[25] Yet it is surely significant that Milton made this enthusiastic endorsement in July 1657, only weeks after the recon-

---

[19] *CPW*, VII, 357; in the second edition of *The Readie and Easie Way*, 'our actions' became 'thir actions' (*ibid.*, 420).   [20] *Ibid.*, 356.   [21] *Ibid.*, 274.

[22] Austin Woolrych, 'Milton and Cromwell: "A Short but Scandalous Night of Interruption"?', in Michael Lieb and John T. Shawcross (eds.), *Achievements of the Left Hand: Essays on the Prose of John Milton* (Amherst, 1974), pp. 200–9; *CPW*, VII, 85–7.

[23] On Chapman see Leona Rostenberg, 'Sectarianism and Revolt: Livewell Chapman, Publisher to the Fifth Monarchy', in *Literary, Scientific, Religious and Legal Publishing, Printing and Bookselling in England, 1551–1700*, 2 vols. (New York, 1965), I, pp. 203–36.

[24] Malcolm Smuts, 'Court-Centred Politics and the Uses of Roman Historians, c. 1590–1630', in Kevin Sharpe and Peter Lake (eds.), *Culture and Politics in Early Stuart England* (London, 1994), p. 30.

[25] Milton to Henry de Brass, 15 July 1657, *CPW*, VII, 500; Peter Burke, 'A Survey of the Popularity of Ancient Historians, 1450–1700', *History and Theory*, 5 (1966), 136–7.

stitution of the Protectorate on the footing of the Humble Petition and Advice and the reinstallation of the Protector.

The surest sign that Milton felt that the decline described by Sallust had afflicted England is the epigraph from Juvenal which he added to the second edition of *The Readie and Easie Way* in April 1660: 'et nos/consilium dedimus *Syllae*, demus populo nunc'.[26] This quotation recalls Milton's use of Juvenal in 1656 to criticize the victories of Charles X of Sweden and to discourage misplaced enthusiasm for militarism.[27] Though the Sulla to whom Milton claims to have given advice has been identified as General Monck (the presumed addressee of Milton's unpublished letter, *The Present Means and Brief Delineation of a Free Commonwealth* (February–March 1660)), the traditional reading of Sulla as Cromwell is more cogent, both literarily and politically.[28] He was not alone in applying Sallust to criticize the Protectorate, and in calling upon the figure of Sulla to accuse the Protector. As a satirical closet-drama of August 1660 put it,

> They that have read of *Catilines* deep plot,
> Have surely thought, such strange entrigues could not
> Be ever matcht; *Marius* and *Sylla* too
> Did much more harm than *Common-men* could do;
> Here's one out-does them all, *Cromwell* by name,
> A man of *mean extraction*, yet whose Fame
> Hath equall'd soaring *Caesars*.[29]

If Cromwell was the English Sulla – a military dictator extended beyond his term – then the Sallustian narrative had evidently run its course. It was remarkable how the republic had grown once it had recovered its freedom from kingly tyranny. But in due course, it had become corrupted. A semi-hereditary dictatorship had led to the rise of faction (as Machiavelli had warned in his analysis of the rule of Sulla and Marius); this could only lead to the return of kingship and

---

[26] *CPW*, vii, 405: 'I too have given advice to Sulla, now let me give it to the people' (Juvenal, *Satires*, i. 15–16, slightly adapted); compare *ibid.*, 440, on the dangers of popular government which led to 'the tyrannie of *Sylla*'.

[27] Milton to Richard Jones, 21 Sept. 1656, trans. in *CPW*, vii, 493–4, alluding to Juvenal, *Satires*, x. 47–50, on which see Martin Dzelzainis, 'Juvenal, Charles X Gustavus and Milton's Letter to Richard Jones', *The Seventeenth Century*, 9 (1994), 25–34.

[28] *CPW*, vii, 406; William Hayley, *The Life of Milton* (London, 1796), p. 144 (my thanks to Martin Dzelzainis for this reference); *The Sonnets of Milton*, ed. John S. Smart (Glasgow, 1921), p. 93.

[29] *Cromwell's Conspiracy. A Tragy-Comedy, Relating to our latter Times . . . Written by a Person of Quality* (London, [8 August] 1660), sig. [A2]ᵛ; see also Peter W. Thomas, *Sir John Berkenhead 1617–1679* (Oxford, 1969), p. 188, for Berkenhead's allusion to Sulla in 1655.

the final extinction of liberty.[30] Milton, who had once advised an
English Sulla, could now only turn to the English people to prevent
them from taking this path.

Milton had offered advice to Cromwell in the conclusion to the
Defensio Secunda in 1654. Though his panegyric is often taken as a
whole-hearted endorsement of the Protector, within the conventions
of rhetorical advice – as well as with hindsight – it was intended as an
admonition to Cromwell. After praising his achievements, Milton put
the Protector and his regime on probation as he warned that 'If the
republic should miscarry, so to speak, and as quickly vanish, surely no
greater shame and disgrace could befall this country'. In particular,
he counselled against mistaking the machinations of statecraft for the
true ends of the republic:

> For if the ability to devise the cleverest means of putting vast sums of money
> into the treasury, the power readily to equip land and sea forces, to deal
> shrewdly with ambassadors from abroad, and to contract judicious alliances
> and treaties has seemed to any of you greater, wiser, and more useful than to
> administer incorrupt justice to the people, to help those cruelly harassed and
> oppressed, and to render to every man promptly his own deserts, too late will
> you discover how mistaken you have been ... If you begin to slip into those
> same vices, to imitate those men, to seek the same goals, to clutch at the same
> vanities, you actually are royalists yourselves...[31]

When the *Defensio* was published at the end of May 1654, rumour was
already circulating that Cromwell was about to send an amphibious
expedition on his 'Western Design' to attack the Spanish possessions
in the New World,[32] to begin the Protectorate's first foreign military
engagement since the conclusion of the first Anglo-Dutch War. In
such a context, the warning not to confuse 'equip[ping] land and sea
forces' with 'help[ing] those harassed and oppressed' was peculiarly
timely. The Protector's failure to follow such advice ultimately
convinced Milton that Cromwell was the English Sulla who had
fatally compromised the republic's fragile liberty, and thereby
fulfilled the warnings of Sallust and Machiavelli, and gave new
topicality to the anti-court satire of Juvenal.

---

[30] *Discorsi*, I. 37; compare *CPW*, VII, 356–7, on 'the liberty ... successfully fought for' being
succeeded by 'a strange degenerate corruption', leading to the possibility that 'we return to
kingship'.

[31] *CPW*, IVi, 673, 681; compare *CPW*, III, 238 on 'the persuance of fame and forren dominion'
characteristic of the Stuarts, as opposed to 'a better fortitude, to dare execute highest Justice'
of the new commonwealth.

[32] See for example John Paige to William Clerke, 27 May 1654, in *The Letters of John Paige,
London Merchant 1648–1658*, ed. George F. Steckley, *London Record Society* 21 (London, 1984),
p. 107.

According to John Aubrey, Milton began work on *Paradise Lost* in 1658 – '2 yeares before the King came-in' – and finished it by 1663.[33] Though there was little falling off in Milton's activity as a Latin secretary in the latter years of the Protectorate,[34] his edition of Ralegh's *Cabinet-Council* and the reissue of the *Defensio* together suggest that by this stage he had already thrown in his lot with the republican opposition to Cromwell, and it has been suggested that his return to poetry is in itself evidence of his 'disenchantment' with the Protectorate.[35] Certainly, though Milton was not poetically silent in the 1650s, no poem of his saw print between Sonnet XIII in 1648 and the first printing of the Sonnet to Vane in 1662. He produced no panegyrics to Cromwell or his policies after the Sonnet of May 1652 ('Cromwell, our chief of men . . .'), no 'First Anniversary' or 'On the Victory Obtained by Blake', no 'Panegyric to My Lord Protector' or 'Of a War with Spain, and a Fight at Sea', to celebrate the Protectorate's martial achievements in the manner of Marvell or Waller. When he did return to poetry, he produced in *Paradise Lost* an epic narrative which with hindsight could be seen as critical of the kind of policies pursued by the Protectorate in the later 1650s and which was consistent with the Sallustian-Machiavellian analysis of the fatal temptations of empire for a newly liberated commonwealth. This was a conviction which later also informed *Paradise Regained* and hence can be seen as evidence of the continuity of his classical republicanism even beyond the Restoration.[36]

Paradise Lost is an epic of empire, though this was denied by Samuel Johnson, in his 'Life' of Milton: 'The subject of an epick poem is naturally an event of great importance. That of Milton is not the destruction of a city, the conduct of a colony, or the foundation of an empire. His subject is the fate of worlds, the revolutions of heaven and earth.'[37] The opening invocation of the poem places it as an imperial epic, even if not in the Homeric or Virgilian vein, as Milton calls upon the 'Heavenly Muse' for

[33] John Aubrey, *Brief Lives*, ed. Oliver Lawson Dick (London, 1960), p. 202.
[34] Robert Thomas Fallon, *Milton in Government* (University Park, Pa., 1993), p. 4.
[35] Martin Dzelzainis, 'Milton and the Protectorate in 1658', above; Worden, 'Milton's Republicanism and the Tyranny of Heaven', p. 241.
[36] For a rather different reading of Milton's attitude towards empire, and its relationship to his republicanism, see Andrew Barnaby, '"Another Rome in the West?": Milton and the Imperial Republic, 1654–1670', *Milton Studies*, 30 (1993), 67–84.
[37] Samuel Johnson, *The Lives of the English Poets*, ed. George Birkbeck Hill, 3 vols. (Oxford, 1905), I, pp. 171–2.

> aid to my adventurous song,
> That with no middle flight intends to soar,
> Above the Aonian Mount, while it pursues
> Things unattempted yet in prose or rhyme.
>
> (*PL*, I, 13–16)

The 'adventurous song' is a song about adventure, and which takes
risks, especially spiritual risks. This spirit of adventure has been seen
as characteristic of nonconformist writing after the Restoration, and
its presence at the very opening of *Paradise Lost* may confirm the epic's
place in the literary culture of nonconformity.[38] However, a more
precise allusion marks *Paradise Lost* as a poem about exploration and
colonial plantation. Milton takes his description from a context which
confirms an intent to reflect on colonial expansion, the invocation to
Josuah Sylvester's translation of du Bartas's 'Les Colonies' from *The
Divine Weeks and Works* in which he described his poem as 'mine
adventurous Rime'.[39] This allusion defined the subject-matter of an
'adventurous' poem as the migrations of peoples, the planting of
colonies and the growth of empires. With only two exceptions in
Paradise Lost – once to describe the true heroism of the heavenly
bands, and once to brand Eve's complicity in Satanic overreaching
(*PL*, VI, 66; IX, 921) – 'adventure' and its cognates are used exclusively
to denote the designs of Satan and his

> squadrons and gross bands
> On bold adventure to discover wide,
> That dismal world, if any clime perhaps
> Might yield them easier habitation,
>
> (*PL*, II, 570–3)[40]

designs which are the enterprises of a fallen pride, like Milton's
'adventurous' essayings of 'things unattempted yet in prose or rhyme'
itself.

    Paradise Lost is built around only two narratives – the biblical
narrative of the Fall, and the story of Satan's colonization of the New
World. Satan's voyaging drew its most immediate inspiration from
Camoens' *Lusiads*, the only ten-book epic before *Paradise Lost*, which
had first been Englished by the Royalist Sir Richard Fanshawe in

[38] N. H. Keeble, *The Literary Culture of Nonconformity in the Later Seventeenth Century* (Leicester, 1987), pp. 267–8.

[39] *The Divine Weeks and Works of Guillaume de Saluste Sieur du Bartas*, trans. Josuah Sylvester [1613], ed. Susan Snyder, 2 vols. (Oxford, 1979), I, p. 442, line 17.

[40] Compare *PL*, II, 204–5; II, 473–5; II, 615; X, 254–5; X, 440; X, 468.

1655.[41] The prose Arguments first added to the reissue of 1668 made clear the narrative of New World conquest and territorial expansion which is played out throughout the epic. The most immediate temptation Satan presents to his followers after the expulsion from Heaven is the promise of new territory: 'he comforts them with hope yet of regaining Heaven, but tells them lastly of a new World and new kind of creature to be created'. The assembled demons are in doubt 'who shall be sent on this difficult search: *Satan* thir chief undertakes alone the voyage ... He passes on his Journey to Hell Gates ... with ... difficulty he passes through, directed by *Chaos*, the Power of that place, to the sight of this new World which he sought.' Finally, his conquest complete, and man tempted to fall, Sin and Death 'by wondrous sympathie feeling the success of *Satan* in this new World, and the sin by Man there committed, resolve to sit no longer confin'd in Hell, but to follow Satan thir Sire up to the place of Man'.[42]

The wisdom of such expansion is debated in *Paradise Lost* in idiomatically Machiavellian terms when, in the first part of Book II, the fallen angels debate whether Pandemonium should be either a commonwealth for preservation or a commonwealth for expansion. The demons have secured their liberty from the monarchy of Heaven and have the potential to see their new-formed republic achieve greatness, perhaps like Rome after the expulsion of the Tarquins or the English republic after the regicide. Mammon proposes, in the language of classical republicanism, that Pandemonium should be a Sparta, 'preferring/ Hard liberty before the easy yoke/ Of servile pomp' and 'the settled state/ Of order' (*PL*, II, 255–7, 279–80), rather than 'Armed with hell flames and fury all at once/ O'er heaven's high towers to force resistless way' (*PL*, II, 61–2) as Moloch had earlier advised. In response, Beelzebub takes the cold-eyed Machiavellian line that even if it were possible 'to continue, and build up here/ A growing empire' in self-sufficient security, in the end Pandemonium would still be overwhelmed by the forces of heaven, and God would inevitably 'over hell extend/ His empire' (*PL*, II, 314–15, 326–7).

---

[41] On Milton's debt to Camoens in *Paradise Lost* see especially James H. Sims, 'Camoens' "Lusiads" and Milton's "Paradise Lost": Satan's Voyage to Eden', in Philip Mahone Griffiths and Lester F. Zimmerman (eds.), *Papers on Milton* (Tulsa, 1969), pp. 36–46; Louis Martz, *Poet of Exile* (New Haven, 1980), pp. 155–68; David Quint, *Epic and Empire: Politics and Generic Form from Virgil to Milton* (Princeton, 1993), pp. 253–7, 265.

[42] *CPW*, VIII, 16, 17, 26. For Milton's presumed authorship of the 'Arguments' see *ibid.*, 7–8. On the connection between 'adventure' and the new world in *Paradise Lost*, see also William C. Spengemann, *A New World of Words: Redefining Early American Literature* (New Haven, 1994), pp. 107, 111–12.

The Republican
cycle in Hell

Under such circumstances, to remain a commonwealth for preservation
would only invite disaster, so the moment should be seized to expand.

Since the invasion of Heaven is deemed to be too great a risk for the
fallen forces, Beelzebub proposes to take the conflict into 'another
world, the happy seat/ Of some new race called Man' (*PL*, II, 345–6).
He then asks, 'whom shall we send/ In search of this new world . . .?'
(*PL*, II, 402–3), but, in a parodic foreshadowing of Christ's self-sacrifice
in the councils of Heaven, only Satan himself is willing to 'undertake/
The perilous attempt' (*PL*, II, 419–20). Once arrived in the New
World, he makes a reproachful address to the sun as 'God/ Of this new
world' (*PL*, IV, 33–4),[43] then concludes with the resolve,

> Farewell remorse: all good to me is lost;
> Evil be thou my good; by thee at least
> Divided empire with heaven's king I hold
> By thee, and more perhaps will raign;
> As man ere long, and this new world shall know.
>
> (*PL*, IV, 109–13)

The poem's action is thus enacted as a territorial raid in a new world
by an invading force which comes upon inhabitants who, once
seduced into falling, are comparable to the 'American so girt/ With
feathered cincture, naked else and wild' encountered by Columbus in
the New World (*PL*, IX, 1116–17). Yet the newly discovered territory
has to be made accessible and exclusive for colonization and traffic.
Sin and Death see the potential of Satan's new dominion for the
extension of their own, and propose to build

>   a path
> Over this main from hell to that new world
> Where Satan now prevails, a monument
> Of merit high to all the infernal host,
> Easing their passage hence, for intercourse,
> Or transmigration, as their lot shall lead.
>
> (*PL*, X, 257–61)

The arch they spring across the gulf of Chaos, 'a ridge of pendent
rock/ Over the vexed abyss', confirms Hell's right to intercourse with
the new world 'by wondrous art/ Pontifical' (*PL*, X, 312–14). Sin tells
her father Satan that their work together has confirmed him as
monarch of the new world by right of conquest, despite his earlier
defeat in Heaven:

---

[43] According to Edward Phillips, Milton wrote the invocation to the sun (*PL*, IV, 32–41) in the
early 1640s: 'The Life of Mr John Milton', in Helen Darbishire (ed.), *The Early Lives of Milton*
(London, 1932), p. 72.

> here thou shalt monarch reign,
> There didst not; there let him still victor sway,
> As battle hath adjudged, from this new world
> Retiring, by his own doom alienated,
> And henceforth monarchy with thee divide.
>
> *(PL*, x, 375–9)

When Satan returns to Pandemonium, his conquest complete, he offers the demons 'a spacious world, to our native heaven/ Little inferior, by my adventure hard/ With peril great achieved' *(PL*, x, 467–9). However, instead of 'their universal shout and high applause' he hears 'from innumerable tongues/ A dismal universal hiss, the sound/ Of public scorn', before becoming 'A monstrous serpent on his belly prone' *(PL*, x, 507–9, 514) as the reward for his colonial ventures. Though Satan had achieved his aim in the new world, the fruits of victory are at least as bitter as those of defeat, as Satan and his fellow-demons are all transformed into serpents in the moment of their triumph, 'the dire form/ Catched by contagion, like in punishment,/ As in their crime' *(PL*, x, 543–5). As Milton had insisted in *Defensio Secunda*, 'A cause is neither proved good by success, nor shown to be evil': it should not be judged by its outcome, but rather the outcome should be judged by the cause.[44]

Martin Dzelzainis suggests elsewhere in this volume that the debate in Pandemonium can be seen to parallel the events of the 1650s in England 'in which a republican moment yields to the adventure of a single person', and that it therefore hints at Milton's judgement on the Protectorate's dereliction of the republican cause.[45] The parallel might be pressed further by recognizing the Machiavellian language in which the debate is conducted, and the significance of Satan, a single person 'with monarchal pride/ Conscious of highest worth' *(PL*, II, 428–9) embarking upon a risky enterprise in the new world. Cromwell, too, was a single person with quasi-monarchical powers, in the eyes of republicans, and it was also clear that under his rule Britain faced the Machiavellian dilemma of whether to become a Sparta or a Rome, a commonwealth for expansion or a commonwealth for preservation. James Harrington had attempted to cut this Gordian knot in his *Commonwealth of Oceana* (1656), which reimagined Britain as a commonwealth both for increase and for preservation,

---

[44] *CPW*, IVi, 652. This passage marks the lowest point of Milton's faith in victory as the basis of *de facto* power: compare the account of his views in 1649 in Victoria Kahn, *Machiavellian Rhetoric: From the Counter-Reformation to Milton* (Princeton, 1994), p. 154.
[45] Dzelzainis, 'Milton's Classical Republicanism', above, p. 24.

and thereby able to 'take the course of Rome' while also becoming a perpetual republic – a clearly utopian plan for Cromwellian Britain.[46] This was intended less as a blueprint for constitutional reform than as ironic – and thereby critical – counsel to the Protector. *Oceana*, like Nedham's *Excellencie of a Free State*, was published to coincide with the first Protectoral Parliament and offered advice to the Protector at the height of a major crisis for republican government in England. The choices lay between the revival of the ancient constitution, with Cromwell as king, or the re-establishment of parliamentary sovereignty.[47] These choices had been made the more pressing by the rising opposition to the regime of the major-generals, and by the failure of Cromwell's Western Design which had embroiled the nation in a costly war with Spain, deflated the Protector's own confidence in his providential role, and brought the justness of his cause into question among many of his former supporters.[48]

To turn a commonwealth for preservation into a commonwealth for expansion was, Machiavelli warned, to court destruction; similarly, the costs of expansion for a republic might be greatness in the short term, but ambition, luxury, debilitation and tyranny in the long run, as Sallust had shown. Both of these complementary narratives could easily be mapped onto the experience of England's passage from Commonwealth to Protectorate, first as a warning, then as a diagnosis of corruption and collapse. Perhaps the surest sign in *Paradise Lost* that Milton had Cromwell in mind when framing his account of the adventure in the new world is Satan's appeal to the language of reason of state when he approaches Adam and Eve, and stiffens his resolution to corrupt and conquer them:

> And should I at your harmless innocence
> Melt, as I do, yet public reason just,
> Honour and empire with revenge enlarged,
> By conquering this new world, compels me now

---

[46] Harrington, *Political Works*, ed. Pocock, pp. 273–4 (paraphrasing Machiavelli, *Discorsi*, I. 6), 330; Blair Worden, 'English Republicanism', in J. H. Burns and Mark Goldie (eds.), *The Cambridge History of Political Thought 1450–1700* (Cambridge, 1991), p. 467.

[47] On Harrington, Nedham and the first Protectoral Parliament see David Armitage, 'The Cromwellian Protectorate and the Languages of Empire', *Historical Journal*, 35 (1992), 548–9; Blair Worden, 'Marchamont Nedham and the Beginnings of English Republicanism, 1649–1656', in David Wootton (ed.), *Republicanism, Liberty, and Commercial Society, 1649–1776* (Stanford, 1994), p. 82.

[48] Blair Worden, 'Oliver Cromwell and the Sin of Achan', in Derek Beales and Geoffrey Best (eds.), *History, Society and the Churches* (Cambridge, 1985), pp. 25–45; Armitage, 'The Cromwellian Protectorate and the Languages of Empire', pp. 540–4.

> To do what else though damned I should abhor.
> So spake the fiend, and with necessity,
> The tyrant's plea, excused his devilish deeds.
>
> (*PL*, IV, 388–94)

The relationship between republicanism and reason of state was a fraught one, for it was far from clear that necessity – however defined – could be held to override the common good of the *res publica*.[49] Milton's attitude to statecraft elsewhere – and his identification of 'public reason' with tyranny in this passage – suggests that he felt that no such plea of necessity could ever legitimate the suspension of justice and the public good, least of all in the antithetical interests of 'honour and empire'. We can only imagine his reaction to Cromwell's declaration at the opening of the 1656 Protectoral Parliament justifying his unpopular war with Spain, which had been sparked by his adventure in the New World, that he was 'ready to *excuse* most of our actions, (and to justify them as well, too, as *excuse* them) upon the grounds of *necessity*; the grounds of *necessity* being, of justification, above all considerations of instituted law'.[50] So spake the Protector, and with necessity, the tyrant's plea, excused his devilish deeds.[51]

Satan and his minions were once angels; through ambition and self-interest, coveting 'honour and empire', and pleading reason of state, they fell. Such temptations could corrupt even a Cromwell – hailed as a hero by republicans like Milton and Nedham in their defences of the Protectorate – when England followed the course of Rome as plotted by Sallust and Machiavelli. Such degeneration is revealed by Michael to Adam in his vision of the world before the Flood in Book XI of *Paradise Lost*:

> Those whom thou last saw'st
> In triumph and luxurious wealth, are they

---

[49] For a more sanguine reading of the compatibility of republicanism and reason of state in the seventeenth century see Alan Craig Houston, 'Republicanism and Reason of State', in Istvan Hont (ed.), *The Politics of Necessity: Reason of State in Modern European Political Discourse* (forthcoming, Cambridge).

[50] Cromwell's speech to the first Protectoral Parliament, 17 Sept. 1656, in *The Writings and Speeches of Oliver Cromwell*, ed. Wilbur Cortez Abbott, 4 vols. (Cambridge, Mass., 1937–47), IV, p. 261.

[51] The Protectorate's public defence of the Spanish War – *Scriptum Dom. Protectoris . . . In quo hujus Reipublicae Causa contra Hispanos justa esse demonstratur* (London, [9 November] 1655) – has been attributed to Milton since the eighteenth century: see [Thomas Birch (ed.)], *A Complete Collection of the Historical, Political, and Miscellaneous Works of John Milton*, 2 vols. (London, 1738), I, p. xxxiv; John T. Shawcross, 'A Survey of Milton's Prose Works', in Lieb and Shawcross (eds.), *Achievements of the Left Hand*, pp. 360–3; for more recent denials of the attribution see *CPW*, V, 711–12; Fallon, *Milton in Government*, pp. 98–100.

First seen in acts of prowess eminent
And great exploits, but of true virtue void;
Who having split much blood, and done much waste
Subduing nations, and achieved thereby
Fame in the world, high titles and rich prey,
Shall change their course to pleasure, ease, and sloth,
Surfeit, and lust, till wantonness and pride
Raise out of friendship hostile deeds in peace.

(*PL*, xi, 787–96)

Yet there is a benign alternative: 'The paths of righteousness . . .,/ And full of peace' (*PL*, xi, 814–15) recommended by Noah instead of 'subduing nations'. This could be achieved in the vision of the world which Michael spreads before Adam, where Europe has yet to be conquered by Rome, and 'Rich Mexico, the seat of Motezume,/ And Cusco in Peru, the richer seat/ Of Atabalipa, and yet unspoiled/ Guiana' (*PL*, xi, 405–11) have not yet been overrun by the Spanish monarchy. Such visions had become a cliché in English colonial writing by the 1650s, in which the world before Babel, the tyranny of Nimrod and the attendant ills of monarchy and territorial empire was presented as *terra nullius*. All the world was America, in which human beings could migrate and plant without need for conquest, usurpation or violence. Sir Hamon L'Estrange in 1652 called this a time when 'I suppose that mankind having then (as wee use to say) the world before them, and room enough, spread, dilated and extended into that same moderate and temperate clymate', while Ferdinando Gorges expressed a similar sentiment in 1659 when he wrote of the world before the Flood, when people might travel without fear of enemies 'to hinder their passage having the wide world before them, to pick and choose where they please'.[52] This is the scene occupied by Adam and Eve themselves at the very end of *Paradise Lost*, in which 'The world was all before them, where to choose/ Their place of rest, and providence their guide' (*PL*, xii, 646–7), though they too are fallen and their descendants will not be able to escape the compulsions of ambition and empire, whether in the age of the biblical giants, under the rule of republican Rome, or as citizens of the commonwealth and free state of England.

---

[52] Sir Hamon L'Estrange, *Americans No Jewes* (London, 1652), p. 9; Ferdinando Gorges, *America Painted to the Life* (London, 1659), sig. A3ʳ.

III

When Milton began work on *Paradise Lost,* in the last months of the Protectorate, his treatment of the problem of empire would have been a timely reflection on the betrayal of the English republic by Cromwell, an English Sulla. When the poem was first published, in 1667, it retained its topicality as a retrospective republican reading of the failures of the 1650s. Though we know all too little about the continuity of republican thought immediately after 1660, it is clear that many of those who had nurtured their republicanism hopefully after 1649 still held to their beliefs after the Restoration, whether nostalgically, critically or admonitorily. In 1665, Algernon Sidney weighed the respective merits of governments for 'enlargement' and those intended to be 'free happy and safe'. Though he commended the successes of commonwealths, and preferred the 'victories obtain'd by the Romans before all that have been gain'd by Kings since the beginning of the world', he echoed Sallust's analysis and warned that 'the prodigious power [Rome] arriv'd to brought in Luxury and pride destroy'd discipline and Virtue soe then ruin necessarily followed'.[53] Sidney also compared Cromwell to Caesar, charged that 'he came to be a Monarch' and thought him a 'tyrant, and a violent one' whom he had always opposed.[54] In 1668 Sidney's fellow-exile, the republican Slingsby Bethel, similarly called Cromwell 'this late Tyrant, or Protector', lambasted his 'unjust Invasion of the Spanish Territories in the *West-Indies*' as an act of self-interested ambition, and counselled that it was 'our true Interest ... to neglect especially *Europian* acquisition, and colonies'.[55]

In the context of the later 1660s, Milton's critical treatment of territorial expansion and empire-building in *Paradise Lost* marks a stage in the gradual transformation of the strenuous classical republicanism of the 1650s into the Whig thought of the latter part of the century. One sign of this shift was a turn away from whole-hearted approval of the Machiavellian ideal of a commonwealth for increase

[53] Algernon Sidney, 'Court Maxims Discussed and Refelled' [*c.* 1665], MS Warwickshire County Record Office, fols. 13, 15 (my thanks to Blair Worden for a photocopy of this manuscript); compare Sidney, *Discourses Concerning Government* [*c.* 1681–3; first published 1698], II, 22, ed. Thomas G. West (Indianapolis, 1990), pp. 203–8.

[54] Sidney, 'Court Maxims', fol. 70; Jonathan Scott, *Algernon Sidney and the English Republic, 1623–1677* (Cambridge, 1988), p. 113; Alan Craig Houston, *Algernon Sidney and the Republican Heritage in England and America* (Princeton, 1991), p. 174.

[55] Slingsby Bethel, *The World's Mistake in Oliver Cromwell* (London, 1668), pp. 2, 8, 7; see also Bethel, *The Present Interest of England Stated* (London, 1671), pp. 1, 34.

to an espousal of the calmer policy of self-containment, avoidance of continental commitments, and rejection of conquest in favour of commerce.[56] The successes of the Rump which were celebrated by so many republicans had seemed to confirm Sallust's maxim that a newly liberated republic can achieve greatness in a short time; however, the transition to the Protectorate fulfilled the republicans' worst fears that greatness leads in due course through debility back to tyranny and the revival of kingship. Since conquest, and hence the transformation of a republic into an empire, had played so large a part in this disillusioning pattern, republicans were forced to reconsider the merits of *grandezza* when the cost was so rapid a loss of liberty.

Since Cromwell could be held personally responsible for this declension, republicanism itself was not at fault: this could encourage the belief that the republican experiment had never been given a fair trial in Britain. If *Paradise Lost* stands as a monument to that lost republican moment as much as to the recrimination and regret which followed its collapse, then the words of Jesus in *Paradise Regained* provide the epitaph to the republican dream that liberty and empire might be reconciled, and hence also to the hopes of 1649–53:

> They err who glorious count it to subdue
> By conquest far and wide, to overrun
> Large countries, and in field great battles win,
> Great cities by assault: what do these worthies,
> But rob and spoil, burn, slaughter, and enslave
> Peaceable nations, neighbouring, or remote,
> Made captive, yet deserving freedom more
> Than those their conquerors, who leave behind
> Nothing but ruin wheresoe'er they rove.
>
> (*Paradise Regained*, III, 71–9)

Dr Johnson was not wrong in his opinion that the treatment of empire in *Paradise Lost* placed the epic beyond the bounds of convention, though he missed the positive thrust of its anti-imperial strain and hence also of its republicanism. Milton's anti-imperialism has been variously attributed to his response to Fanshawe's translation of the *Lusiads*, to the influence of Lucan's republican epic of the vanquished,

---

[56] See for example [John Trenchard and Walter Moyle,] *An argument, Shewing, that a Standing Army Is inconsistent with a Free Government, and absolutely destructive to the Constitution of the English Monarchy* (London, 1697), p. 18; Charles Davenant, *Discourses on the Public Revenues, and on the Trade of England* [1698], in *The Political and Commercial Works of Charles Davenant LL.D.*, ed. Charles Whitworth, 5 vols. (London, 1771), II, p. 26; [Andrew Fletcher,] *A Discourse of Government with Relation to Militia's* (Edinburgh, 1698), p. 63.

and to his dissolution of the constraining closure of the epic in favour of the open-endedness of romance.[57] Such questions of genre and allusion still demand a further order of explanation. Though *Paradise Lost* has been held to embody a critically proleptic view of British imperialism,[58] this is clearly unhistorical, and the source of Milton's antipathy to empire must be sought in his own reading and his political experience. As I have suggested, his most formative sources were classical and republican, and they gave him a coherent reading of the moral narrative played out between 1649 and 1660. Milton remained true to his republicanism even in his anger and his regret. Throughout, he was guided by its historical typology, disillusioning as that was; he was aware of the incompatibility of liberty and *grandezza* at its very heart, chastening as that was. In the end, it was his reading of Sallust and Machiavelli, and his experience of the rule of an English Sulla, which confirmed him in these convictions, lent a critical and nostalgic edge to his republicanism, and caused him to become a poet against empire.

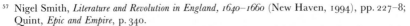

[57] Nigel Smith, *Literature and Revolution in England, 1640–1660* (New Haven, 1994), pp. 227–8; Quint, *Epic and Empire*, p. 340.
[58] Christopher Hill, *The Experience of Defeat: Milton and Some Contemporaries* (London, 1984), p. 328; Keith W. F. Stavely, 'The World All Before Them: Milton and the Rising Glory of America', *Studies in Eighteenth-Century Culture*, 20 (1990), 154–5.

PART IV

Milton and the republican tradition

CHAPTER 12

The Whig Milton, 1667–1700

Nicholas von Maltzahn

The Whig Milton is first of all the Milton of the prose works. In the last decades of the seventeenth century, Whigs found sustenance especially in his assaults on the sacerdotal view of kingship, and also in his pleas against the licensing of the press and in his anti-clerical arguments for a Protestant toleration. One great figure after another in the Whig tradition drew on Milton for inspiration and instruction. James Tyrrell, John Locke, Algernon Sidney, John Toland, John Dennis, Daniel Defoe, the Third Earl of Shaftesbury, Joseph Addison: these and many less-remembered Whigs read Milton's works with interest and often with approval. Their reading was selective, however, and would only slowly lead to a richer valuation of his achievement. The sacrilege of Milton's *Eikonoklastes* and *Defensio* – books proscribed and publicly burnt at the Restoration – made him so notorious that he often went unnamed by Whigs, even when his arguments and rhetoric were useful to them in late seventeenth-century controversy. They sometimes thrilled to his determined republicanism, but they were more often embarrassed by it. Tories were eager to discover his presence in their opponents' writings and to tar them with his notoriety. Not all Whigs were alike, moreover, nor was their response to Milton. The growth of party featured tensions and eventually schisms that add to the complexity and diminish the coherence of the Whig 'tradition', especially after the Revolution of 1688–9.[1] The name 'Whig' needed more and more stretching to cover divergent points of view. This led to a corresponding variety in appraisals of Milton's works and reputation.

Milton's republicanism had origins both humanist and religious. For later readers the attractions of the former were often outweighed

I am especially indebted to Blair Worden for his assistance with this chapter (and related work of mine), which owes much to his essays on republicanism and on Milton in particular.
[1] A less differentiating view of its subject limits the value of George F. Sensabaugh, *That Grand Whig Milton* (Stanford, 1952), especially where it touches on his readership after the Revolution.

by discomfort with the latter. Milton's soaring assertions of God's purpose might look like so much cant to readers wearied by their experience of the Interregnum or wary of its legacy. In the Restoration the distinction was often drawn between Milton's dubious opinions and his exemplary learning (especially the fund of fine Latin in his prose). Whigs came therefore to recommend Milton's politeness at the expense of his politics and prophecy. Religion was often an awkward subject for Whigs owing to their associations with Dissent; Tories loved to dub them 'fanatics', charged them with enthusiasm and fomenting rebellion, and identified them with their Puritan predecessors. From this bad reputation they were eager to defend themselves. Hence their difficulty with Milton, who looked like a zealot because of his regicide writings and his uncompromising self-presentation as a servant of God. Even *Paradise Lost* might at first seem too much the work of an enthusiast: Milton's ill fame fostered suspicions of the epic's devotional aims, and doubts about the work were compounded by its lack of rhyme and by its humble presentation in the modest formats of the early editions (1667, 1674, 1678).

For Whigs as well as for a wider readership, *Paradise Lost* at first played a secondary part in Milton's reputation. But over time its profound humanism came to recommend it as a monument of Whig culture, and as a devotional work in which the force of inner light was richly expressed. Thus an increasingly positive valuation of Milton's poetry coloured what had hitherto been a more purely political interest in his prose. As rationalism in religion became more prevalent, so *Paradise Lost* gained in popularity, and its success expressed a hunger for an 'originality, poetic sensibility, and prophetic insight' lacking in the Church.[2] The Whig Milton who emerges in the bitter controversies of the Exclusion Crisis and the Glorious Revolution is the ancestor of the very different Whig Milton, at once polished and sublime, whose poetry would find such elegant notice in the essays of Addison's *Spectator*.

I

Milton was famous first as a regicide writer, but it is not too anachronistic to style him also one of the first Whigs. At the Restoration he again dedicated himself to poetry, and yet he did not

---

[2] Gerald Cragg, *The Church and the Age of Reason 1648–1789* (Harmondsworth, 1960), p. 140.

acquiesce in the new regime as much as traditional biographies have claimed. Although he was chastened by his narrow escape in 1660, he never finally retired from the public sphere. In view of the dangers he faced, it is not surprising that his further contributions should have been discreetly made. But *Paradise Lost* provided timely advice in the Toleration Debate; it may be seen among the publications greeting the parliament of October 1667 with pleas for a Protestant toleration.[3] This puts Milton at the origin of English Whiggery. Moreover in some of his last publications he again addressed matters central to the Whig agenda. *Of True Religion* (1673) demands a Protestant toleration at the time of the first Test Act. Milton's bitterness about Presbyterian impositions in matters of faith had led him to articulate his earlier claims for toleration largely against them; in *Of True Religion* his approach is more irenical. A contemporary could say of this pamphlet that 'J. Milton has said more for [toleration] . . . in two elegant sheets . . . than all the pr[elates] can refute in 7 years.'[4] Milton also anticipates Whig concerns in *A Declaration, or Letters Patents* (1674), which contests the Catholic succession by proposing the merits of elective kingship. As Exclusion became an issue, publications favouring elective monarchy came under severe scrutiny: hence the value of this 'neutral' translation of a Polish advertisement for the value of such an election.[5] Martin Dzelzainis has shown, however, that Milton's bad reputation as a regicide writer denied him an effective role in present debate.[6]

Milton could only be a Whig of a peculiar kind. The extremes of his earlier republicanism were not easily translated into the compromises of Restoration constitutional thought. Already in the Interregnum he had had to soften his revolutionary claims for popular resistance – such compromise was needed when he came to serve the common-wealth[7] – and in the longer term the argument of *The Tenure of Kings and Magistrates* had much less influence than his spectacular expressions

---

[3] My fuller arguments about the publication date and first reception of *Paradise Lost* is forthcoming in *Review of English Studies*.   [4] *Calendar of State Papers Domestic, 1675–76*, p. 89.

[5] The licenser Roger L'Estrange, for example, could later take particular exception to a history that described the Saxons' 'Election of Kings . . . The Chiefest for worth, not by Descent', Public Record Office, London: PRO 29/421: III, fol. 43. The pertinence of Milton's translation of the *Declaration* to English politics is therefore quite clear, *pace* W. R. Parker, *Milton: A Biography*, 2 vols. (Oxford, 1968), I, p. 638; II, p. 1151; and also *CPW*, VIII, xiii, 442; Christopher Hill, *Milton and the English Revolution* (London, 1977), pp. 219–20 (cf. *CPW*, VIII, 596–604).

[6] Martin Dzelzainis, 'Milton's *Of True Religion* and the Earl of Castlemaine', *The Seventeenth Century*, 7 (1992), 55–6, 64.

[7] *John Milton: Political Writings*, ed. Martin Dzelzainis (Cambridge, 1991), pp. x–xxv.

of hostility to the sacerdotal view of kingship in *Eikonoklastes* and the *Defensio*. Although Sexby's *Killing Noe Murder* would restate Milton's argument for tyrannicide (in 1657 against Cromwell, and against James or William when republished in 1689), such extreme views found few exponents, and even Locke's theory of revolution in the *Second Treatise* was largely overlooked in the settlement after 1688/9.[8] The more lasting memories of Milton were of his swingeing attack on tyranny, especially that of Charles I: Milton's historiography in *Eikonoklastes* and the *Defensio* often proved more useful to Whigs than his political theory. His republicanism was not much use to Whig proponents of the ancient constitution. Whigs favoured limited monarchy, and only after the failure of the Exclusion parliaments did some of them contemplate still more revolutionary ways to keep the Catholic James from the throne, and explore more strongly republican claims, in which the role of the one was further attenuated in favour of the few and the many. Moreover, the strongly religious terms in which Milton at first expressed his resistance theory were foreign to later Whig writing, and when Whigs drew on his work they often passed over its religious dimension.

The first Whigs were not republicans, nor were many later Whigs. Even those who favoured resistance to the crown seldom entertained republican alternatives. The distinction may be illustrated with reference to the original Whigs, those Scottish Covenanters after whom the English party was named. They did adopt a radical resistance theory based on that of earlier Presbyterian reformers, and one which shares much with Milton's position in the *Tenure*, where he had worked from this tradition in part to rebuke latter-day Presbyterians for betraying their earlier opposition to Charles as well as their ancestral reformers' pronouncements on the subject. Citing Presbyterian writings of the 1640s, especially Rutherford's *Lex Rex* (1644), the authors of *Naphtali* (1667) sought to demonstrate the legitimacy of any 'Action and Call Extraordinary' against its betrayers, because of 'the lawfulnesse of private Persons defending their Lives, Libertyes and Religion'. The episcopal response was to scorn this 'pretext of Heroick motions, and rare excitations of the Spirit': the fear justified by recent rebellion was that 'private persons ... under colour of high pitches of zeal and fortitude' might 'by Gods Spirit ... execute justice

---

[8] Edward Sexby, *Killing Noe Murder* (London, 1657), p. 11; John Locke, *Political Writings*, ed. David Wootton (Harmondsworth, 1993), p. 88.

upon all the powers and people of the Land'.[9] This was just the kind of resistance that Milton had urged in the argument of the *Tenure*, and would consider again in *Samson Agonistes* (1671). In the Scottish Whigs' work, however, we find nothing like Milton's republicanism nor the humanism that informs it. Despite their bitterness in the 1660s about the betrayal of Presbyterianism since the Restoration, and especially the royal apostasy from the Covenant, the intransigent Scots did not propose commonwealth solutions in their revolt against the episcopal oppressors of their church, even as they cried up the strongest version of resistance theory. They viewed 1651–60 as a time of foreign usurpation, and hated the yoke of the Commonwealth as well as that of the Protectorate.

Milton has in common with the Covenanters an urgent religious imperative, but he had further connected resistance theory with classical republicanism. In the 1660s neither was very applicable in the milder south, and with other republicans Milton may have thought discretion the better part of valour. In England a different kind of opposition was emerging. Anti-episcopal polemic, for example, did not publicly reach anti-monarchical conclusions[10] since dissenters pressing for a Protestant toleration did so with high expectations of Charles II, who seemed a likely sponsor of toleration (although fears of royal leanings towards Catholicism complicated these hopes). Even if Milton did not address present issues very directly, what he brought to the press met with suspicion. The episcopal licenser only grudgingly accepted *Paradise Lost* in 1667. Roger L'Estrange helped to prune Milton's *History of Britain* in 1670. *Of True Religion* (1673) appeared with an anonymous imprint. After Milton's death, the government moved swiftly to obstruct the publication of his state letters and *De Doctrina*. Seeking to publish Milton's works on the Continent (with Elzevir in Amsterdam), Daniel Skinner found the enduring scandal of that author enough to draw Joseph Williamson's ire. The reaction to these *Literae* (which had already found another Dutch publisher, probably through Milton's nephew Edward Phillips) was aggravated by fears that plans were afoot to print Milton's

[9] James Stewart and James Stirling, *Naphtali* (n.p., 1667), pp. 21, 76; Andrew Honyman, *A Survey of . . . Naphtali* (Edinburgh, 1668), pp. 104–5, 107, 112–14; James Stewart, *Jus Populi Vindicatum* (n.p., 1669), t.-p., pp. 251–67, 409–26.

[10] Compare the extreme of the twin publication *Mene Tekel; or the Downfal of Tyranny* and *A Treatise of the Execution of Justice* (London, 1663) with Nicholas Lockyer, *Some Seasonable and Serious Queries* (London, 1670), pp. 13–15.

collected works. The Secretary of State 'could countenance nothing of that man's writings' and forced their retraction from the press, with the worried Skinner offering to put 'my copies and all my other papers [from Milton] to the fire'.[11] Through the years others too would find themselves tarnished with 'the ill name [of] Mr Milton's Friendship', both personally and through political association.[12]

Whigs had every reason to be silent about Milton or to deny his presence in their thinking. As fears grew about James's succession to the throne, they sought to alter the line of title and to diminish the prerogatives of the crown. Despite their dismay at the growth of popery and arbitrary government, however, their programme until 1681 depended ultimately on royal consent, and even a republican like Henry Neville would present his proposals in a more accommodating language than that of Milton in the Commonwealth. By contrast, their Tory opponents increasingly claimed that Whig ambitions in parliament revived the religious and political sedition of the earlier generation, whose authors might now be recalled to prove the point. Among these Milton featured prominently, and his writings were cited more by foe than by friend. In Tory hands, Milton's anti-tyrannical arguments appeared simply anti-monarchical, and thus might now appal a later generation. His anti-Presbyterian writings also served Tory purposes. Thus Hobbes, while admiring the Latinity of Milton's controversy with Salmasius – they wrote 'very good Latine both, and hardly to be judged which is better' – could deplore the 'very ill reasoning' of both, 'hardly to be judged which is worst'.[13] 'So like is a Presbyterian to an Independent' that they might both feature in those lists of 'Milton, Goodwin, Rutherford, and a hundred more' that Tories recited with bitter satisfaction against Whig pretensions. Tories knew, moreover, that both parties had learned sedition from earlier Jesuit authors such as Mariana and Suarez. In the Popish Plot, Titus Oates even testified that 'Milton was a known frequenter of a Popish Club', a claim that at once surprised and gratified Tory pamphleteers.[14] The ever-active Roger L'Estrange

---

[11] Nicholas von Maltzahn, *Milton's 'History of Britain': Republican Historiography in the English Revolution* (Oxford, 1991), pp. 14–17; Bodleian: MS Rawl. A.185, fols. 271^r–272^v; PRO, SP 84/203, fols. 24^r, 105; Parker, *Milton*, I, pp. 610–11, 656; II, pp. 1130–2, 1167.

[12] Bodleian: MS Rawl. A.352, fol. 295^r; E. S. de Beer (ed.), *The Diary of John Evelyn*, 6 vols. (Oxford, 1955), III, p. 365; *Historical Manuscripts Commission* 36 (1911), Ormonde, n.s. 6, p. 335.

[13] Hobbes, [*Behemoth or*] *The History of the Civil Wars of England* (London, 1679), pp. 229–30.

[14] Roger L'Estrange, *The Reformed Catholique* (London, 1679), p. 17; L'Estrange, *A Further Discovery of the Plot* (London, 1680), p. 3; Bodleian: MS Wood F. 49, fol. 189^r.

was only the most insistent of those who quoted scandalous passages from the *Tenure* and *Eikonoklastes*, the latter causing special outrage as the 'bitter invective' of 'a needy Pedagogue', that 'villanous leading Incendiarie *John Milton*' whose 'bloody Schoole of King-killing' Tories recalled with horror.[15] L'Estrange also warned of the Whig threat to the kingdom by advertising the historical parallels between present sedition in 1679 and past rebellion in 1641, not least in his publication of the Digression from Milton's *History of Britain* as *Mr John Miltons Character of the Long Parliament and Assembly of Divines* (1681). After the dissolution of the last Exclusion (Oxford) Parliament, Tory polemic charged the Commons with its failings, and L'Estrange and others were pleased to have Milton available as a critic of parliament and Presbyterianism.[16]

Whigs were therefore reluctant to name Milton, even when they found him serviceable. Suppressing his name might save Milton's arguments from his reputation. This shows clearly in a few tracts, and may be supposed in a number of others. Eager that the Licensing Act be allowed to lapse in 1679, for example, Charles Blount could tailor *Areopagitica* for present purposes, but even as he drew on Milton's text at length he only once conceded the least obligation to that work, and this only when he used the most memorable of phrases from his original ('as good kill a Man, as a good Book'), thus disguising the wider debt. A less Whig author was even more reluctant to cite such a source: William Denton failed to note Milton as the 'I.M.' of the admirable *Treatise of Civil Power*, and also drew much on *Areopagitica* without acknowledgement.[17] Two decades later, country Whigs could similarly revive *Areopagitica* in yet another licensing controversy, still without acknowledgement.[18] Even when Milton proved useful, therefore, his notoriety as an anti-monarchical writer made any positive reference to him impossible in the polemics of the day. Thus a

[15] Roger L'Estrange, *An Answer to the Appeal* (London, 1681), p. 34; L'Estrange, *The Dissenter's Sayings* (London, 1681), p. 31; L'Estrange, *Dissenters Sayings. The Second Part* (London, 1681), pp. 32, 47, 74–5; William Dugdale, *A Short View of the Late Troubles in England* (Oxford, 1681), p. 380; Bodleian: MS Wood F. 47, fols. 626ᵣ ᵥ.

[16] Von Maltzahn, *Milton's 'History'*, pp. 3–12. Milton's *Character* appeared at just the time that 'Charles II in his Declaration of 8 April had called on his subjects to consider "the rise and progress of the late troubles"': Locke, *Political Writings*, ed. Wootton, p. 56.

[17] *A Just Vindication of Learning* (London, 1679), p. 3; William Denton, *Jus Caesaris* (London, 1681), pp. 1–3, 67, 'An Apology for the Press', pp. 1–9; Sensabaugh, *That Grand Whig Milton*, pp. 56–65.

[18] Matthew Tindal, *A Letter to a Member of Parliament* (London, 1698); E. Sirluck, '*Areopagitica* and a Forgotten Licensing Controversy', *Review of English Studies*, 11 (1960), 260–74.

bad reputation helped narrow perceptions of Milton, and much contracted his legacy.

Owing to the pressure of political debate, the scope and variety of Milton's writings found few admirers in the 1670s and 80s. Milton the republican could not easily become Milton the Whig. It would be Tory writers who helped in this transformation, as their reaction against Milton came to evoke a Whig response in which he could play a more positive part. Until the failure of the Oxford parliament (March 1681), Whigs stopped short of any truer republicanism or more radical line of resistance, and 'that grand Whig, Milton' was more a Tory invention than any real presence in controversy. Despite the burst of print activity in 1679 and after, in which Whigs (re)published many earlier texts (including Marvell's *Miscellaneous Poems*, 1681), Whig presses did not bring out much under Milton's name: the second edition of *Paradise Regain'd/Samson Agonistes* (for John Starkey, 1680), the first translation of *Miltons Republican-Letters* (a badly printed Dutch product, 1682), and *A Brief History of Moscovia* (for Brabazon Aylmer, 1682). At the same time, however, Tories sought further to buttress their position with the (re)publication of more royalist works on church and state, and among these the posthumous publication of Filmer's works was of special importance. This included Filmer's attack on Milton's *Defensio* (in *Observations*, 1652), part of the influential *Free-holders Grand Inquest* (1679) from which Tories learned to deplore 'those grand Patriots of Rebellion and Confusion' among whom Milton featured prominently.[19] Filmer's claims became commonplace among Tories in the subsequent decade, but he also prompted some major restatements of the Whig position, in which Milton could play some part.

Reacting to Filmer's egregious assertion of royal power, Whigs renewed far-reaching questions of sovereignty and the role of the people, both in the state and in the church. The key issues here emerge in brief in Filmer's rebuttal of Milton. He focused on two problems in the republican position. The first is Milton's inconsistency in defining 'the people', which Filmer sees as evasive in a way characteristic of populist arguments. In such constitutional proposals, did the people equal a *populus universus*, *pars major* or *pars potior et sanior*? The question remained how these might be determined: 'If the sounder, the better,

[19] Andrew Allam – White Kennett, British Library: MS Lansdowne 960, fol. 34ᵛ; White Kennett, *A Letter from a Student at Oxford* (n.p., 1681), p. 14.

and the uprighter Part have the Power of the People, how shall we know, or who shall judge who they be?' The second difficulty lay in Milton's hostile view of the arbitrariness of power, and in his claims for liberty. Filmer thought power arbitrary by definition,[20] and his argument with Milton exemplifies the logic of his influential *Patriarcha, or the Natural Power of Kings* (1680). Tories seized on his patriarchal theory for passive obedience and made it a central tenet in their doctrines of sacerdotal kingship. The bitter denunciation with which Milton's regicide tracts had long met was now to be renewed, as Tories sought to style Whigs as sacrilegious republicans, the enemies of *jure divino* kingship and an unbroken succession. But Whigs benefited from Filmer's shortcomings as a political theorist: his old arguments invited refutation and then induced a more profound reconsideration of political obligation.

Of Whig writers who responded to Filmer the most significant was Locke, and questions about power and the people lie at the heart of his inquiries. In the evolution of Locke's position Milton had more of an influence than has been recognized, although it may have been only indirect and cannot be determined with much confidence. Locke knew a number of Milton's works and much admired his Latinity owing to a familiarity with the *Defensio*.[21] In the 1680s if not before, he must have found Milton congenial reading. The radicalism of Locke's *Two Treatises* (1690) is now agreed upon by scholars, even as they propose different dates for its composition (1679–83, revised 1689). Though there is no necessary connection, Locke's resistance theory shares much with that of Milton's *Tenure* (it is suggestive that he should later have known Milton to be the author of the anonymous *Pro Populo Adversus Tyrannos*, 1689, an adaptation of the *Tenure*[22]). What remains of Locke's *First Treatise* answers Filmer in detail, and shows a close knowledge of *Observations*, including the section on Milton, as well as of *Patriarcha*.[23]

The degree to which Locke's *Second Treatise* addresses his friend James Tyrrell's *Patriarcha Non Monarcha* (1681) has also become apparent, and here Milton has an interesting part. Tyrrell, writing in the context of the Exclusion Crisis, and seeking some moderate path

[20] Filmer, *The Free-holders Grand Inquest* (London, 1679), pp. 19–20, 23–4, 25, 26, 32; sig. s2ʳ.
[21] Bodleian: MS Locke fol. 14, pp. 5–7, 10, 40, cf. 115; in a booklist perhaps prepared for Shaftesbury around 1670, Locke cites Milton under 'Politici' and lists *Of Reformation, The Doctrine and Discipline of Divorce* and *Areopagitica* (PRO 30/24/47/30, fol. 43ʳ).
[22] Bodleian: MS Locke c. 44, fol. 63ᵛ ('Miltons sovereigne right of the people 4° Lond: 89').
[23] Locke, *Two Treatises of Government*, ed. P. Laslett (Cambridge, revised edn 1988), Preface; First Treatise, sect. 78.

by which the ancient constitution might be protected against more aggressive claims for royal power, could cite Milton as notorious for defending 'downright Murder and Rebellion'. He thus dismisses him in *Patriarcha Non Monarcha* as being as extreme in his claims for popular power as Filmer was for royal power.[24] This may have been in part a strategic disclaimer: it is consistent with the Whig reluctance to cite Milton that he be more valuable to Tyrrell as a radical voice to be dismissed than as an authority to be approved (although later evidence suggests that Tyrrell took a special interest in Milton). In the changing political climate of spring 1681, moreover, Tyrrell seems to have reworked his book even as it went through the press, and this at least in part in order to mute his response to Filmer's *Observations* on Milton. As the Whig cause suffered successive reverses after having seemed near victory, Tyrrell appears to have decided against publishing a discussion of tyrannicide prompted by Filmer's attack on Milton's *Defensio*.[25] Tyrrell's defence of the ancient constitution was always more conservative than Locke's theory of revolution. But any argument of Milton's that Tyrrell could remove from consideration, Locke could restore. After the Whig defeat Locke seems in reconfiguring Tyrrell to have revived the logic of those Miltonic claims that Tyrrell had suppressed. Thus, whether or not Locke drew directly on Milton, through Filmer and Tyrrell Milton's radical resistance theory lent itself to the more revolutionary considerations of the *Two Treatises*. Later divisions in Whig thinking can already be seen in the different responses of Tyrrell and Locke to Milton's extreme position on resistance, the former reluctant to accept Milton's conclusions, the latter ready to embrace them and extend them in a contractual theory justifying revolution.

For Whigs some form of revolution seemed more necessary as the 'Stuart revenge' gathered force in the early 1680s. Filmer's views on the *Defensio* seem to have prompted other readers to return to Milton's illegal work. In 1682–3 two Whigs were seen to use the *Defensio* as their guide in developing seditious arguments about church and state: Samuel Johnson sought to undermine 'the

---

[24] James Tyrrell, *Patriarcha Non Monarcha* (London, 1680), p. 97 = [137]. Tyrrell collaborated with Locke in 1681–3. Bodleian: MS Locke c. 34; J. W. Gough, 'James Tyrrell, Whig Historian and Friend of John Locke', *Historical Journal*, 19 (1976), 585–9; J. G. A. Pocock, *The Ancient Constitution and the Feudal Law* (Cambridge, 2nd edn, 1987), pp. 346–8, 354.

[25] Locke, *Political Writings*, ed. Wootton, pp. 58–60. Tyrrell was hampered 'not being in town dureing the impression, & so never seeing the work untill it came forth'. MS note in Bodleian: 8° c 101 Linc., *Patriarcha Non Monarcha*, p. 261 (presentation copy to Bishop Barlow).

foundation of the Church in her Ministry' and Thomas Hunt 'that of the State in the Royal Authority', each with undisclosed reference to Milton. Attacking the Tory position, Johnson elaborated contemporary arguments about the reign of the ancient emperor Julian, in whose strange career Tories saw an argument for passive obedience and Whigs for Christian rebellion. Here Johnson was directly indebted to Milton's arguments against royal prerogative, and his Tory opponent saw him as 'truly an Ecclesiastical Milton, the most impudent and ill-natured fellow, that an honest man can have to do with'. That Hunt drew on Milton is less evident, although the convergence of a number of his and Milton's positions made the accusation a telling one, and satisfactory enough for Roger L'Estrange to trumpet the discovery in his *Observator*. The debt to Milton had been spotted by Thomas Long, who lamented the swarming libels of 'the Late Unhappie Times', now revived, and singled out Milton and Goodwin for having 'publickly defended the Parricide committed on that incomparable King'. Again, 'Antimonarchical principles' were the stock in trade 'of the Sectaries and Phanaticks', whose 'Seditious and Rebellious Practices' had long plagued the nation.[26] The Tory response to *Julian* was soon amplified in successive editions of *Jovian*. It was reported that Johnson 'despises' *Jovian* and 'saith he will answer it with a wet finger', but the response never came. The failure of the Rye House Plot foiled the hopes of desperate Whigs: Johnson was chaplain to William Lord Russell, martyr to that disaster, and would endure persecution and imprisonment until the Revolution. With Russell, Johnson could favour resistance against tyranny, his sentiments perhaps Miltonic in part,[27] but it was left to another author, a more famous Whig martyr still, to articulate the radical position at this crisis in terms of enduring value to later republicanism.

In Algernon Sidney's *Discourses Concerning Government* we hear a voice closer to Milton's than any other in the Restoration, one sharing his republican vocabulary and priorities to a remarkable degree. Sidney too wrote in response to Filmer, and his work evolved in the

---

[26] Thomas Hunt, *Mr. Hunt's Postscript* (London, 1682); Samuel Johnson, *Julian the Apostate* (London, 1682); Thomas Long, *A Vindication of the Primitive Christians* (London, 1683), sig. a1ᵛ–a2ʳ, Aᴠɪɪɪʳ, B1ʳ; Long, *The Original of War* (London, 15 Jan. 1683/4), sig. A2ʳ, p. 22; Long, *A Compendious History* (London, 1684), pp. 20–1, 25, 93; Dean and Chapter Library, Durham: MS Raine 32, fols. 143–5 (George Hickes – Thomas Comber, 29 Aug. 1682); MS Raine 33, fols. 4–5 (Hickes–Comber, 14 Feb. 1683); Sensabaugh, *That Grand Whig Milton*, pp. 77–89.
[27] Sensabaugh, *That Grand Whig Milton*, pp. 91–9.

more extreme conflict after the failure of the Exclusion parliaments, when the failure of such compromise won from this republican a larger plea for resistance. That Sidney owed much to Milton cannot be established from his writings, where Milton's name never appears, and where no passage requires the earlier author's presence in the later's thoughts. But Sidney's services to government in the 1650s must have introduced him to Milton the Secretary for Foreign Tongues, and he could not but have known Milton's contemporary fame (one of Sidney's friends records him telling a story about Milton in the late 1670s). Recent students of Sidney have documented the convergence in their thinking, and especially in the insistent identification by these 'moral humanists' of liberty with virtue, to which may be added their willingness to combine such arguments for positive liberty with claims for natural rights.[28] Failing any more direct connection, Blair Worden's description of the shared circumstances of their evolving republicanism in the 1650s and after does much to explain their common political vision. Their more cosmopolitan sense of the requirements of liberty and virtue could not easily be joined, however, with Interregnum or Whig commonplaces about the ancient constitution. In the 1650s Milton attempted the marriage of republicanism with arguments from the ancient constitution at some cost to consistency, not least with his writings elsewhere.[29] In the early 1680s, Sidney sought a fuller political and historical explanation of the error of any such compromise, and instead articulated anew the demands of virtue, liberty and discipline, as well as their rewards. For this he did not need Milton, but the convergence of their views would again be apparent when in the late 1690s they both found a publisher in the Whig John Darby.

The failed revolution of 1683 was the nadir in Whig fortunes and in Milton's posthumous career. With the discovery of the Rye House Plot and the prosecution or flight of its perpetrators, real and imagined, Whig hopes seemed doomed. Wider reaction to the Plot included the Oxford Decree of 1683, with its proscription of Milton's regicide writings and the consignment of further copies of his works to the flames. L'Estrange's was only the loudest of the many voices

---

[28] Paris, Bibliothèque Nationale, Fr. MS 23254 ('Lantiniana'), fols. 99–101; Blair Worden, 'Republicanism and the Restoration 1660–1683', in David Wootton (ed.), *Republicanism, Liberty, and Commercial Society, 1649–1776* (Stanford, 1994), pp. 153, 155, 165, 172–4; Jonathan Scott, *Algernon Sidney and the English Republic, 1623–1677* (Cambridge, 1988), pp. 15, 23–7, 29–30, 100, 106–9, 193, 248; Alan Craig Houston, *Algernon Sidney and the Republican Heritage in England and America* (Princeton, 1991), pp. 114–78, 137n., 141, 212.

[29] Von Maltzahn, *Milton's 'History'*, pp. 198–221.

decrying such authors as Milton; it remained a Tory commonplace that 'those Wild and Barbarous Principles... Collected out of the Writings of Knox, Buchanan, Milton, and other Authors' were still current in Whig thinking.[30]

In the 1680s, therefore, Milton was loathed by Tories, and Whigs refrained from naming him despite his relevance as they evolved their positions. The exception was the slow recognition of the importance of *Paradise Lost*. Here Tory poets such as Dryden and Oldham were able to respond more freely to Milton's example than their Whig counterparts. More accessible than *Paradise Lost*, for example, was Dryden's *State of Innocence*, a fashionably dramatic reworking of the epic in rhyme, which very much outsold Milton's original in this period. Still more remarkable is that some Tories associated with Christ Church, Oxford, that bastion of reaction, played an instrumental role in illustrating and promoting Tonson's famous fourth edition of *Paradise Lost*, the subscription folio that finally appeared in 1688.[31] This publication marks a new synthesis, beyond the contest of earlier faction. In part it reflected the distinction that could be made between Milton's prose and his poetry. But this handsome edition, which did so much to secure Milton's growing fame as an epic poet, also may be seen as a product of the 'Anglican Revolution' in the late 1680s,[32] that profound change of political and religious alignments under James II, which soon would be further transformed into the Whig triumph of 1688–9. In the subscription list for the 1688 folio may be seen the common rallying of Whig and Tory behind a national Protestant poet, a cultural bulwark against the oppressive Catholicism of James. His succession to the throne had finally forced Tories to make common cause with their Whig coreligionists. The deep conflict this produced in Tory ranks would last for decades. But the Whigs' success would occasion conflicts in their ranks as well, with notable consequences for the Whig Milton.

III

Milton was 'the great Anti-monarchist'.[33] But the Revolution of 1688/9 overthrew a monarch, not monarchy itself. Recent historians

---

[30] John March, *The False Prophet Unmask't* (Newcastle, 1683), sig. A2ᵛ.
[31] This paragraph draws on my argument in 'Wood, Allam, and the Oxford Milton', *Milton Studies*, 31 (forthcoming 1995).
[32] Mark Goldie, 'The Political Thought of the Anglican Revolution', in R. Beddard (ed.), *The Revolutions of 1688* (Oxford, 1991), pp. 102–36.
[33] Anthony Wood's note in Bodleian: Wood 363, flyleaf 1ᵛ.

have described how the Revolution Settlement forced Whigs, moderates and Tories to decide whether the reign only of James II was to be repudiated, or whether older resentments of Charles II might also govern a new constitutional settlement. Generally, the former course prevailed. Only the more extreme Whigs attempted any wider polemic against the Stuarts or the crown itself, and only in this quarter did Milton's complaints against Charles I enjoy much favour. In the Revolution of 1688/9 Whig publishers prepared for a new edition of his complete prose. But it did not soon appear. The triumph of 1688/9 proved a more conservative one than that for which many Whigs of the 1680s had worked and suffered. Only the radical Whigs who found themselves disappointed in William's rule ever much articulated the extreme resistance theory of Milton or Locke. Their claims were for the most part muted until the rise of the country party later in the decade.

In the 1690s it was Milton's poetry that had a more receptive audience on the strength of the folio edition of *Paradise Lost* (1688). In the flowering of Whig literary culture in the 1690s (such as it was), Milton came to have a wider appeal not because of his politics but because his politics might now be more readily overlooked. The challenge was to transform Milton from a republican to a Whig moderate enough to applaud the Revolution Settlement. Nahum Tate, for example, could now imagine Milton posthumously abandoning his republicanism and instead praising William's royal government:

> Behold where MILTON Bow'rd in Lawrel Groves,
> A Task beyond his Warring Angels moves;
> Himself a Seraph now, with sacred flame
> Draws Scheme proportion'd to great WILLIAM's Fame;
> (For Common-wealths no more his Harp he strings,
> By NASSAU's Virtue Reconcil'd to Kings).[34]

Tate acknowledges the tension between Milton's commonwealth legacy from mid-century and the present state of affairs. He nonetheless enlists Milton as a proponent of the providential arguments for William's succession. The year before, Tate had dodged the issue in *A Pastoral Dialogue*, in which his ambitions for a national poetry take him to 'Elysian Bow'rs' where, like Ferdinand the Bull, a pacific Milton 'on Eternal Roses lies, / Deep wrapt in Dreams of his own

---

[34] Nahum Tate, *A Poem, Occasioned by His Majesty's Voyage to Holland* (London, 1691), p. 5.

Paradise'.[35] Such celebration of the Revolution, for which Tate soon found laureate reward, could not of course patch over the divide between Milton's determined republicanism and the Revolution Settlement. In both poems Tate shows himself happier with Cowley as his visionary guide than with Milton.

Milton's was not an easy poetic example to follow. *Paradise Lost* was emerging as an admired and influential poem: its success in the folio format appears from its re-publication (1688, 1691, 1695), from the further editions of Dryden's derivative *State of Innocence* (Herringman, 1690, 1692, 1695), from the re-publication also of *Paradise Regain'd/ Samson Agonistes* and Milton's *Poems* (1688, 1695), and from related translations. Success invited imitation. But as the original became familiar to a wider audience, and as Milton grew in stature, the imitators worked with less confidence than such earlier poets as Dryden or Oldham. The young John Dennis, a Whig acolyte of Dryden, could already cite Milton in 1692 as 'one of the most sublime of our English Poets', although he still wished that the language of *Paradise Lost* had been 'as pure as the Images are vast and daring'. But within the decade he came to profess Milton 'perhaps the greatest Genius that has appear'd in the world for these seventeen hundred years'.[36] The anxiety of influence was correspondingly more acute, and it became more difficult to escape the dangers of derivation in synthesizing Milton's example with a new poetry.

Milton's wider poetic influence is first conspicuous in the flood of elegies occasioned by the death of Queen Mary (1695), which prompted a laureate competition, especially among Whigs. The elegists include three notable Miltonists: Dennis, Patrick Hume and Samuel Wesley. Hume's contribution bears special mention because he is otherwise known only for his admiring commentary on *Paradise Lost*, published in over three hundred folio pages by Tonson (6th edn, 1695). His annotation does not show much political bias, although the complaint against tyranny in the Nimrod/Babel passage at the beginning of Book XII draws some Whig notice: if indeed 'all Primitive and Natural Power was Paternal', Noah had later denounced 'the Dominion of Brethren over one another, as a Curse on the Posterity of wicked Cham'. Hume's poetry too shows him learning from Milton's

---

[35] Nahum Tate, *A Pastoral Dialogue* (London, 1690, reissued 1691, also as *A Poem, occasioned by the late discontents*), sig. A1^r, A2$^{r\ v}$, pp. 13, 27.

[36] John Dennis, *The Passion of Byblis* (London, 1692), sig. C1; James Winn, *John Dryden and His World* (New Haven, 1987), pp. 461, 469, 472–4; Dennis, *Iphigenia* (London, 1700), sig. A3^v.

example, as when he transposes Milton's scales of heaven into the
golden scales of conscience, in which Queen Mary balances her filial
duties against her 'Duty to God, and to her Native Land', or where he
revolves questions about the cosmos, or evokes the terrors of death's
'fatal Dart'. Hume could not do without rhyme, but the fluent use of
polysyllabic words in his iambic pentameter is a tribute to Milton's
precedent.[37] Likewise Dennis's memorial *The Court of Death* (1695)
improves where it imitates Milton, especially in scenic passages such
as when 'the great Consult began' before the 'Chief of the pow'rs'.
Dennis himself attests that Milton's achievement governed 'these
Pindarick Verses': he 'was resolv'd to imitate him as far as it could be
done without receeding from Pindar's manner'. *Paradise Lost* finds a
more local application in Samuel Wesley's contribution: Wesley had
earlier seen *Paradise Lost* as a model for his own Christian epic, and
had long been familiar with Milton's prose and verse, but he was less
able than Dennis to synthesize Miltonic narrative with the urgent
movement of an ode, not even when his Charles I finally welcomes
Mary into heaven.[38]

The growth of Milton's influence appears more strikingly still in Sir
Richard Blackmore's *Prince Arthur. An Heroick Poem in Ten Books*
(1695), which draws heavily on Milton's example, especially in its
description of the historical origin of its action in Lucifer's ancient
rebellion and the fall of man, which lead to our redemption in Christ
but also to Lucifer's later attempt with the Saxons to quash British
Christianity. Readers in the 1690s were quick to observe the debt and
to prefer Milton's original: 'Instead of this', wrote one in mounting
exasperation, 'Read Miltons Paradise Lost.' Despite his debt, or
because of it, Blackmore conspicuously fails to mention Milton in his
Preface, where he reports on the challenge of epic 'that no one for near
seventeen hundred years past has succeeded in it'.[39] But in this and
later epics Blackmore's imitations show Milton beginning to emerge
as the major poet in the Whig tradition. Others responded to *Paradise
Lost* with more critical tributes and parody, especially in collegiate
verses where Tory suspicions of Milton combine with a lively interest
in his poetic example, which soon came to replace that of Cowley

---

[37] *Paradise Lost* (London, 1695), p. 310; *Poem Dedicated to the Immortal Memory of Her Late Majesty the Most Incomparable Q. Mary* (London, 1695), pp. 7, 9, 10, 11, 14, 15.

[38] John Dennis, *The Court of Death* (London, 1695), sig. a2ʳ, pp. 4–5; Samuel Wesley, *Elegies on the Queen and Archbishop* (London, 1695), p. 11; Wesley, *The Life of our Blessed Lord* (London, 1693), p. 345, *passim*.

[39] Bodleian: Shelfmark fol. △ 686, Richard Blackmore, *Prince Arthur* (London, 1695), sig. a2ʳ–b2ᵛ, pp. 35, 160.

whether for versification and or fuller narration and description. Here, in Johnson's phrase, the young poets might achieve 'a momentary triumph over that grandeur which hitherto held its captives in admiration'.[40]

Even as Milton's poetry grew in fame, his prose was less valuable *His prose* for the times than more radical Whigs might have wished. At the *reputation* Revolution the booksellers' response had been almost immediately to attempt the publication of Milton's complete prose, consistent with the re-publication of other Interregnum tracts at this date.[41] As early as 30 January 1689, Awnsham Churchill registered a collection of Milton's works as licensed for publication.[42] There are a few notable omissions in this list: the *Tenure* and *Eikonoklastes* are missing (both of which would find separate publication within the year, but without an imprimatur), as well as the *History* (less Whig than might have been wished, and of a separate copyright), and *The Judgement of Martin Bucer* (also in another bookseller's hands). There were to be two editions of Milton's complete prose but these only appeared late in the decade, when new political controversy contributed to interest in his work in 1697–8. Instead, the earlier publication history of the regicide tracts repeated itself: the revolutionary opinions of the *Tenure* (1649) now reappeared in *Pro Populo Adversus Tyrannos* (1689); then the lasting cult of the *Eikon* was again answered by *Eikonoklastes* (1690); and the subsequent French translation of Salmasius' *Defensio Regia* (1691) met with an English translation of Milton's *Defence of the People* (1692).

The publication of the anonymous *Pro Populo Adversus Tyrannos* in 1689, was sufficiently risky that its imprint ventured the name of neither printer nor bookseller, and only a few years later did the trade publisher Randal Taylor advertise it as 'The Right of the People over Tyrants, by John Milton'.[43] This version of the *Tenure* has been described as 'an effective instrument of Williamite propaganda', but the radicalism of Milton's theory of popular resistance finally leaves

---

[40] Samuel Johnson, *The Lives of the English Poets*, ed. George Birkbeck Hill, 3 vols (Oxford, 1905), I, p. 317.

[41] Mark Goldie, 'The Revolution of 1689 and the Structure of Political Argument', *Bulletin of Research in the Humanities*, 83 (1980), 522–3.

[42] G. E. Briscoe (ed.), *A Transcript of the Registers of the Worshipful Company of Stationers from 1640–1708 A.D.*, 3 vols. (London, 1913–14), III, p. 345 (30 Jan. 1688/9).

[43] Alicia D'Anvers, *Academia* (London, 1691), p. 68; Edward Arber (ed.), *Term Catalogues 1668–1709*, 3 vols. (London, 1903–6), II, p. 361; W. R. Parker, 'Milton on King James the Second', *Modern Language Quarterly*, 3 (1942), 41–4. A trade publisher like Taylor was often used for 'concealment and convenience' in selling topical tracts: Michael Treadwell, 'London Trade Publishers 1675–1750', *The Library*, n.s. 6, 4 (1982), 104–16, 120–1.

the work a monument instead to Whig positions that were betrayed as
the Convention Parliament gave way to the new realities of William's
regime. Sensabaugh's catch-all term 'Williamites' is an oversimplifi-
cation: such unity was not long capable of being foisted on the range
of Tories, Trimmers and Whigs who had helped in the succession.[44]
Pro Populo Adversus Tyrannos now directs at Revolution backsliders the
accusations that the *Tenure* had levelled at Presbyterians. Its comments
'on the late posture of Affairs' are notably anticlerical, if along
Milton's lines, but the editor characteristically omits other passages in
the original devoted to proof-texts from the Bible and the reformers.
It is the voice of a true Whig that here asserts that kings and
magistrates govern 'in trust from the People'. Government is by
contract, and the *Tenure* again provides an extreme version of the
popular right to resistance. Commenting on the work, a Tory noted
its claim that 'Any who can may kill' a tyrant, and questioned the
underlying assumption that men are 'born free', a phrase answered
by the Filmerian objection that 'Noe man ever borne free from
subjection to parents, wch they (jure naturae) were necessarily bound
to obey'.[45] Claims for contract were of course denied by Tories. But
they were also repudiated in the Revolution Settlement, despite the
wishes of the less compromising revolutionaries.

Radical Whigs were also responsible for the re-publication of
Eikonoklastes (1690). Milton's fame as a scourge of Charles I, and
thus of Stuart kingship, made him especially useful to those who
sought to impugn not only James II but also his brother, father and
grandfather before him. The reappearance of *Eikonoklastes* enraged
Jacobites and occasioned bitter quarrels over the memory of Charles
I. Of course the renewed animus lay in James's present case. The
authorship of the *Eikon Basilike* had long been subject to suspicion as
well as to heated defence, and had often occasioned hostile comments
about Milton.[46] In anniversary sermons each 30 January, churchmen
lamented the execution of Charles I and extolled the royal portrait;
conversely, 'in Derision of the Day, and Defiance of Monarchy' some
dissenters might even celebrate the execution of the king by drinking
off toasts from a 'calves-head'. Milton's regicide writings, anathema

---

[44] Sensabaugh, *That Grand Whig Milton*, pp. 134–42.
[45] *Pro Populo Adversus Tyrannos* (London, 1689), t.-p., pp. 5–6. 8; Bishop Barlow's annotated
copy is Bodleian: B 12.10 (4) Linc., pp. 6–7.
[46] F. F. Madan, *A New Bibliography of the* Eikon Basilike, *Oxford Bibliographical Society Publications*,
n.s. 3 (1949), 126–63.

to Tories, were '*in Deliciis*' with these 'Calves-head' Whigs.[47] Controversy rekindled because in a 'Memorandum' now published with *Eikonoklastes* the late Earl of Anglesey had testified that the *Eikon* was not Charles I's work, as many had long known or suspected. Much violent debate followed, in which Milton's name often surfaced, with reference either to his discovery that 'Charles' had stolen Pamela's prayer from the *Arcadia* or to his scathing evaluation of Charles as a possible author of the *Eikon*. The 'Calves-head' Whigs were delighted to explore the matter, notably in a series of pamphlets putatively written by General Ludlow, the old hero of dissent, two of which draw on *Eikonoklastes* (1690) and three of which share its spurious Amsterdam imprint. When Jacobites consulted *Eikon Basilike*, Whigs could consult *Eikonoklastes*.[48] Tories might deplore Milton, and note his fluency whenever his 'Argument, and his deprav'd temper met together', as for example with Satan in *Paradise Lost*.[49] But to recall Milton was to risk reviving him. Thus the eccentric Edmund Elys, ever spoiling for controversy, now hastened to write his 'Joannis Miltoni sententiae Potestati Regiae Adversantis Refutatio' in 1690, but failed to publish it until a decade later when the Whig publication of the 1698 *Complete Collection* renewed 'the villain Milton' as a polemical presence. In 1690 the question was whether Elys judged the 'publishing of [his response] at this time proper & seasonable'.[50] For the rest of the decade, the controversy allowed Jacobites to comment on the succession but also invited radical Whigs to pour scorn on the Stuarts and argue anew for limits on the powers of the crown.

Anti-Stuart feeling also motivated *A Defence of the People of England* (1692), a translation of the *Defensio* by Joseph Washington of the Middle Temple, a prominent Whig lawyer and 'favorite of sir Joh.

[47] Edward Ward, *The Secret History of the Calves-Head Club* (London, 1703), pp. 4, 6–7, 9–10. That these rites were not just a Tory invention appears from the pious Samuel Wesley, *A Letter from a Country Divine* (London, 1706 [3rd edn]), pp. 3–4, 8, and *A Defence of a Letter* (London, 1704), pp. 4–5.

[48] Richard Hollingworth, *A Defence of King Charles I* (London, 1692); *A Letter from General Ludlow to Dr. Hollingworth* (Amsterdam, 1692), pp. viii, 31–49; *Ludlow No Lyar* (Amsterdam, 1692), pp. xx; G. W. Whiting, 'A Late Seventeenth Century Milton Plagiarism', *Studies in Philology*, 31 (1934), 37–50; Edmund Ludlow, *A Voyce from the Watchtower*, ed. A. B. Worden (London, 1978), pp. 19–22, 34–42, 50–1.

[49] *Vindiciae Carolinae* (London, 1692), p. 3.

[50] Bodleian: MS Ballard 12, fol. 65^r (George Hickes – Arthur Charlett, 6 Sept. 1690); MS Ballard 25, fol. 24^r (John Willes – Arthur Charlett, 9 Sept. 1690); MS Smith 49, p. 203 (Elys – Smith, 1690); MS Smith 60, p. 130 (Smith – Elys, 23 Oct. 1690).

Somers'.[51] Washington's translation may have been in some part a commission for the 'Calves-head' edition of Milton's prose (1698), in which it appears under a 1694 half-title. As published in 1692 it provided a Whig response to Jacobite fulminations in the *Eikon* controversy. These included the publication in Paris of a French translation of Salmasius' *Defensio Regia*, the preface to which expressed hostility to Milton's sacrilegious handling of the king's memory.[52] The Erastian and deist emphases of Washington's translation emerge here and there: for example, a marginal hand (the only one in the whole text) points to the passage in chapter 4 where Milton comments on the episcopal danger to the crown, and elsewhere Washington translates Milton's *'optime'* as 'exactly' in order to claim that 'The Law of God does exactly agree with the Law of Nature'.[53] Tate, now the Whig laureate, would soon memorialize Washington's premature death and, noting his talents as a linguist, could more especially praise his 'Roman virtue at the needful Hour' when he had 'Oppos'd encroaching Tides of Lawless Pow'r'. Well might 'Great Milton's Shade with pleasure oft look ... down' on this servant of Liberty.[54]

Now in preparation were the two folio editions of Milton's prose, of which the more important is the great *Complete Collection* (1698). As with *Eikonoklastes* (1690) and the Ludlow pamphlets, the identity of the editors of this 'Calves-head' edition of Milton's prose remains obscure. His nephews Edward and John Phillips appear to have assisted, and John Toland is likely to have had a supporting role (he also has been associated with the Ludlow pamphlets, which he echoes in *Amyntor: or a Defence of Miltons Life*, 1699). Collectively, the political impulse behind these publications is unmistakable, not least a sharp dislike of the Stuarts and also growing misgivings about William III and the Revolution Settlement. The first volumes of the *Complete Collection* (1698) feature a series of separate title pages for Milton's English works all dated 1694, giving Amsterdam as their place of publication although they are printed in London

---

[51] John Toland, 'The Life of Milton', in *A Complete Collection of the ... Works of John Milton* (London, 1698), p. 31; Bodleian: presentation copy, Vet. A5 e. 2041; Mark Goldie, 'The Roots of True Whiggism 1688–94', *History of Political Thought*, 1 (1980), 203; Goldie, 'The Revolution of 1689', 495n.

[52] *Le Traité de l'autorité royale* (Paris, 1691); Erich Haase, *Einführung in die Literatur des Refuge* (Berlin, 1959), p. 82.

[53] *Defence* (London, 1692), pp. 106, 113; cf. *The Works of John Milton*, ed. F. A. Patterson *et al.*, 20 vols. (New York, 1931–40), VII, p. 267; *CPW*, IVi, 422; *Milton: Political Writings*, ed. Dzelzainis, p. 149.   [54] *In Memory of Joseph Washington* (London, 1694), p. 4.

(consistent with earlier 'Calves-head' productions). The latter ruse has been thought to reflect concerns about official reprisal, but it may also have been an attempt to evade some awkward question of copyright. The *Complete Collection* issued from the printer John Darby, Whig and dissenter, who was later to advertise the work and who cooperated closely in the 1690s with the Whigs likely to have been its editors, and especially with Toland who finally supplied the prefatory biography for this edition, dated 3 September 1698.[55] The copyright for many of Milton's works belonged instead to Joseph Watts, who in a contract with Elizabeth Milton in 1695 extended renewed claims to Milton's prose, perhaps owing to fears of losing his property, or to prevent the other imprint – it is suggestive that now too the owner of Milton's *History* should have re-published that work. That Watts had no part in *Complete Collection* appears from his failure in his 1695 contract to mention in his list of 'Mr. John Miltons Works' a number of the titles already printed in the 1694 volumes. Instead his incomplete list of Milton's titles corresponds exactly to the less complete English *Works* published in 1697 (which omits of Watts's properties only the Latin titles).[56] The separate publication of Phillips's version of the *Letters of State* (1694) may reflect frustration at a delay in publishing the 'Calves-head' prose with which it shares the 1694 imprint. The *Letters* allowed him in his prefatory 'Life of Mr. John Milton' to provide an admiring Whig portrait of his uncle, as if a corrective to that which had recently appeared from the Tory Anthony Wood (*Athenae Oxonienses*, 1691). Phillips's biography does not much refer to Milton's verse here, even though he had helped prepare the text of *Paradise Lost* and now published for the first time the 'republican' sonnets praising Cromwell, Fairfax and others, but if his 'life' was designed to preface this edition of Milton's prose it was to be displaced by the more sophisticated and politically more pointed biography by John Toland,

[margin note: Toland's ed. ↓]

---

[55] Among his sources, Toland drew on the papers and the assistance of the Phillips brothers as well as James Tyrrell. *Complete Collection* (London, 1698), pp. 5–6, 44; R. E. Sullivan, *John Toland* (Cambridge, Mass., 1982), p. 6. In 1694 Edward Phillips implies some editorial activity in connection with the *History*: Helen Darbishire (ed.), *The Early Lives of Milton* (London, 1932), p. 75. Toland seems likely to have intruded the further 'Calves-head' material hostile to Charles I that disrupts the original pagination of the *Complete Collection* (pp. 527–8, 525–6, 527–8).

[56] Bedfordshire County Record Office, Bedford: MS P11/28/2, fols. 309, 313–15. I am grateful to Peter Lindenbaum for sharing with me before publication his article on Watts's contracts for Milton's prose, although I differ from him in arguing that they lead to the 1697 *Works of Mr. John Milton* (rather than the 1698 *Complete Collection*).

which puts its stamp on the *Complete Collection* as published finally in 1698.

Already in the early 1690s Toland seems to have been among the 'Calves-head' republicans, and he emerged as a writer of unusual flair as the decade progressed. With the printer and bookseller Darby he had a standing contract to write and translate works supportive of their common cause.[57] The 'Life of John Milton' shares with other of his works a combination of lively synthesis and some unreliability, much shaped by his republican and deist aims. He wrote the 'Life' as a contribution to controversy, and it was as such that it was read by many of his contemporaries. Toland's critics observed how far he had foisted upon Milton a portrait of himself: he either shared Milton's opinions or imposed still worse ones on 'so great a Man'.[58] Toland could here address the causes of the hour: for example, several references in the 'Life' reflect the country Whigs' interest in reducing or eliminating the standing army after the Treaty of Ryswick (1697), and even as Toland prepared his biography Milton's style already influenced another tract from his hand against standing armies, *The Militia Reform'd* (1698). Toland's 'Life' does not much emphasize Milton's resistance theory or republicanism. As if reluctant to provoke unnecessary outrage, Toland professed a Whig acceptance that 'our Constitution is a limited mix'd Monarchy', although the degree of limitation remained very much in question. He disliked Milton's emphasis on men and not laws.[59] He may also have resented the oligarchic character of Milton's republican proposals at the Restoration; in reaction to the Junto Whigs Toland instead advertised Harrington's plans for rotation and produced his great edition of that better republican's works.

But Toland's admiring 'Life' of Milton was influential because he was able to animate his subject, and provide a more rounded portrait of the poet and controversialist. The *Complete Collection* thus offered all of Milton's prose but also an enriching sense of the exemplary life in which these works had their origin. If Toland's now seems a narrow view of Milton, and especially of Milton's religion, he nonetheless began the work of restoration in which the scope and vitality of

[57] A co-signer of this contract is the Whig Thomas Raulins to whom Toland dedicates the 'Life of Milton', British Library: Add. MS 4295, fol. 6.
[58] *Remarks on the Life of Mr. Milton* (London, 1699), pp. 1–2, 12–14.
[59] John Trenchard, *Argument* (London, 1697), pp. 2–3; Toland, *Militia Reform'd* (London, 1698), p. 11.

Milton's achievement would find wider recognition. Here too began Toland's transformation of the 'Calves-head' Milton into Milton the apostle of toleration, a more attractive figure to eighteenth-century readers. Toland was always glad to offend the cult of King and Martyr, and the 'Life' continued the controversy over the authorship of the *Eikon Basilike*, and again provided the Anglesey memorandum and related materials supporting Gauden's authorship of the King's Book, as well as long quotations from the *Tenure*, *Eikonoklastes* and the *Defensio*. One of Toland's opponents, at least, almost knew enough not to encourage him further. Others were less wary, reacting to his assertions and insinuations without anticipating his larger agenda.[60] They now occasioned Toland's *Amyntor: or a Defence of Miltons Life* (1699), in which he set Milton aside in order to turn to the authority of the biblical canon. Even as he denied any heterodoxy on this score, the freedom of his speculations on the authorship of the New Testament strongly implied some sceptical conclusions, and not just about the Apocrypha. It was so difficult to prove the authenticity of the Gospel! Even in modern times, for example, a text that some almost took for Holy Writ might have been foisted on its putative author by interested parties, first in collusion and then, perhaps, in good earnest. The example Toland cited was of course the *Eikon Basilike*.

Toland was eager to doubt the reliability of 'authoritative' texts, since this permitted him to insist instead on the authority of reason, not tradition. Rationalism in religion might follow from a wider toleration, and a second purpose in his writing about Milton was to impugn priestcraft by means of Milton's anti-clericalism. Here he again followed the logic of his *Christianity Not Mysterious* (1696) in decrying the abuses of church and state, as he anatomized how the powerful advance their interest by fostering unreason in the population at large and then by manipulating its fears; thus it was useful in the 'Life' to dwell on Milton's Aristotelian observation 'that the deepest Policy of a Tyrant has bin ever to counterfeit Religion'.[61] Toland's object was finally to debunk sacralism, and to this end he quoted from *Of True Religion* especially in favour of toleration. His views would soon find a wider audience through the second edition of the Huguenot Pierre Bayle's compendious *Dictionnaire historique et critique* (1720 [1697]), where Bayle added much from Toland to his entry for

---

[60] Offspring Blackall, *A Sermon Preached . . . January 30th. 1698/9*, p. 16; *Mr. Blackall's Reasons for Not Replying to a Book Lately Published* (London, 1699), p. 2; *A Letter to the Author of Milton's Life* (London, 1699).   [61] *Complete Collection* (London, 1698), p. 27.

The 18th-c transformation of John Milton

Milton. In successive editions of this influential work, Milton first appeared as a regicide, but then also as a supreme defender of 'la Tolérance'. Milton might now be seen as a deist *avant la lettre*, and as a professor of reason against royalist impostures such as the King's Book. This Whig Milton now had an established reputation as a poet, with *Paradise Lost* to the fore as 'un des plus beaux Ouvrages de Poësie que l'on ait vu en Anglois'.[62] As a tolerant Protestant and writer of the national epic, Milton was increasingly redeemed from the darker associations of mid-seventeenth-century fanaticism and partisanship.

IV

A synthesis was emerging in which Milton the famous republican, at first silenced among English Whigs, came to be rehabilitated first as a religious poet, and then again as a writer on political and religious matters. But owing to his changing posthumous reputation, some of Milton's distinction as a poet and controversialist would be lost in a limited understanding of his legacy. The alteration can be traced in the response to Milton of three Whigs with influential views on literature. The first is John Dennis, who thought that his 'Country's welfare' and the 'defence of our Liberties' followed from 'those happy Enthusiasms, those violent Emotions, those supernatural transports which exalt a mortal above mortality ... [which] shake and ravish a Poet's Soul with insupportable pleasure'.[63] Dennis knew Milton best of all to have answered the national need for a religious poet, and he fervently admired *Paradise Lost*. He valued the very excesses of that epic, which he saw as exhibiting its sublimity: he saw that Milton's capacity for enthusiasm combined with an aesthetic that strove after 'Things unattempted yet in prose or rhyme'. Questioning enthusiasm and excess alike, Anthony Cooper, the Third Earl of Shaftesbury, was much less taken with Milton's epic, and could not brook the unmannerliness of Interregnum republicanism. His own prescription for politeness on a model of gentlemanly conversation did not readily admit the example of the poet-prophet or the pamphleteer fighting in the wars of truth. His ideal of civic religion led him only hesitantly to praise Milton as a religious poet, since the expression of private revelation suggested to Shaftesbury that self-aggrandizing spirituality

---

[62] Pierre Bayle, *Dictionnaire historique et critique* (Rotterdam, 1720), pp. 1987, 1991.
[63] Dennis, *Miscellanies in Verse and Prose* (London, 1693), sigs. A5ʳ, A7ʳ, A8ᵛ.

that he resented in both priestcraft and enthusiasm.[64] The last and much the most influential of these Whig voices was that of Joseph Addison. Like Shaftesbury, Addison disliked enthusiasm; like Dennis, he deeply admired *Paradise Lost*. In his historic series of essays on *Paradise Lost*, which lastingly established it as the national epic, Addison trimmed the poem of its excesses, so that it no longer seemed the work of a regicide writer or poet-prophet. Bringing its classical dimension to the fore, and sharing with his readers his own bland theology, Addison also emphasized the visual imagination governing the poem. He demoted questions of doctrine, shunned controversy, and defined even the epic poem as primarily a literary undertaking, the truth claims of which were subordinated to his narrower vision of poetic excellence. Thus the Whig Milton, in the reign of Queen Anne and after, could become a more professional man of letters, a commercial property of special value to Addison's associate the publisher Jacob Tonson. Milton's voice, if a national one, was also one more and more constrained to the diminished sphere of poetic discourse. The republican Milton, Latin orator, strident pamphleteer, servant to the Commonwealth and poet of a stern and urgent Christian vision, became a literary figure of a milder sobriety, increasingly freed from the languages of faction and revelation.

[64] Shaftesbury, *Characteristicks*, 3 vols. (London, 1711), I, pp. 51–3, 358–61; III, pp. 228–9.

CHAPTER 13

Borrowed language: Milton, Jefferson, Mirabeau

Tony Davies

Is there something un-English about republicanism? A glance at the standard student textbooks on political science might seem to suggest so. The index to L. J. MacFarlane's *Modern Political Theory* (1970) contains no entry for 'republicanism'. Neither does Rodney Barker's *Political Ideas in Modern Britain* (1977). An Open University reader on *Politics and Ideology* (1986), sympathetic as it is to anti-establishment causes, finds no room for the topic. Even a professed anti-monarchist like Tom Nairn sees no role for republican ideas in his vision of *The Break-Up of Britain* (1977). To the English ear, at least, the word suggests either Bush and Reagan or, more vaguely, Ireland – something alien and disagreeable to do with the Provisional IRA. English republicans there have been, to be sure, some distinguished and courageous; but it is hard to resist the inference that as an active political cause, English republicanism died on the scaffold with Algernon Sidney, and was buried, in an unmarked grave, by the settlement of 1689.

Such, at any rate, is the implication of Zera Fink's account of the 'classical republicans'.[1] But Fink's title reminds us that, as ever, there is a problem with the word. His republicans were 'classical' in two senses: that their conceptions of the ideal polity, the *res publica*, were derived from Plato and Cicero, Thucydides and Livy; and that they had a programmatic clarity and coherence not often found in English political thinking. His attempt to demonstrate just such a purposeful and principled consistency running from *Of Reformation* through the *Tenure of Kings and Magistrates* to the *Readie and Easie Way* is resourceful; but the feeling remains that, though Milton's politics were certainly classical in the first sense, they were adaptable and pragmatic in the second, in accordance with his friend

---

[1] Zera S. Fink, *The Classical Republicans* (Evanston, 1945).

Marchamont Nedham's principle that 'it matters not what the forms be, so we attain the ends of government'. Furthermore, not all supporters of the Commonwealth were doctrinaire anti-monarchists, and republicanism, then and later, could accommodate a number of forms ranging from direct plebiscitary democracy through limited monarchy (which Milton in 1641 had called 'divinely and harmoniously tun'd ... equally ballanc'd as it were by the hand and scale of Justice'[2]) to the meritocratic oligarchy he later espoused and even to a proto-Bonapartist 'dictatorship of the just'. English republicanism, then, is a broader church than the designation 'classical' might suggest; and in this wider and more complex sense it can be seen to have survived the 1680s: at home, it is true, as a generally marginal theme in the political repertoire, but in America and continental Europe as a central influence upon the discourse of popular emancipation and revolution. That influence is the subject of this chapter.

But first, I want to suggest that 'influence' is too inert a concept for the energetic intertextualities and discursive transactions I am going to talk about. 'The words of a dead man', as Auden wrote of Yeats, 'are modified in the guts of the living'; and the intensely active and transformative appropriation of the lives and writings of the seventeenth-century English republicans by the ideologues of the Atlantic Revolutions, the strong misreadings to which they subjected them, must now be admitted to constitute part of the meaning and significance of those writings, and certainly a major reason for their survival. Milton and Locke would no doubt have survived anyway, even if Montesquieu and Mirabeau had not found them useful. But who can doubt that such interest as there continues to be in Sidney and Neville is due to the prestige they enjoyed in eighteenth- and nineteenth-century France and America, not to any native enthusiasm? And who knows whether even Milton would have survived the lethal combination of late Victorian reverence and Leavisian 'dislodgement', without the patience and heroic fortitude of French and North American Miltonists?

The 'borrowed language' of my title comes from another writer, once esteemed and feared, whose survival may now be in doubt. In *The Eighteenth Brumaire of Louis Bonaparte* Marx describes the English and French Revolutions as just such 'strong misreadings', dramatic

---

[2] *Of Reformation*, in *CPW*, I, 599.

misappropriations or travesties of the forms and rhetoric of an earlier epoch, their neoclassical theatricality impelled by an obsessive anxiety of influence:

> The tradition of the dead generations weighs like a nightmare on the minds of the living. And, just when they appear to be engaged in the revolutionary transformation of themselves and their material surroundings, in the creation of something which does not yet exist, precisely in such epochs of revolutionary crisis they timidly conjure up the spirits of the past to help them; they borrow their names, slogans and costumes so as to stage the new world-historical scene in this venerable disguise and borrowed language. Luther put on the mask of the apostle Paul; the Revolution of 1789–1814 draped itself alternately as the Roman republic and the Roman empire... Unheroic as bourgeois society is, it still required heroism, self-sacrifice, terror, civil war, and battles in which whole nations were engaged, to bring it into the world. And its gladiators found in the stern classical traditions of the Roman republic the ideals, art forms and self-deceptions they needed... A century earlier, in the same way but at a different stage of development, Cromwell and the English people had borrowed for their bourgeois revolution the language, passions and illusions of the Old Testament. When the actual goal had been reached, when the bourgeois transformation of English society had been accomplished, Locke drove out Habakkuk.[3]

This suggestive passage, arising from Marx's own reflections on the failures of 1848, affords an important insight: that social and political revolutions, if they are to succeed, must also be cultural revolutions; that as much as institutions and formal ideologies they require imagery, memory and forms of identity; and that those things can only be derived from a relationship with the past that must always be deeply ambivalent, at once admiring and evasive. Marx contrasts the iconography of the English and French Revolutions, the first biblical, the second classical, as different stages of development; but the relation between them can itself be understood, not as part of a linear 'development' from superstition to enlightened secularity, but as another example of ideological and semiotic expropriation, of 'world-historical necrophilia'. And Milton, who after all was a poet and rhetor, not a professional ideologue or political theorist, serves this purpose particularly well.

George F. Sensabaugh makes the same point when he notes that the infant American republic

---

[3] Karl Marx, *The Eighteenth Brumaire of Louis Bonaparte*, in *Surveys from Exile*, ed. David Fernbach (Harmondsworth, 1973), pp. 146, 148.

needed at this time not so much intellectual arguments for basic positions as emotional symbols ... Milton supplied both, but the strength of his imagery soon prevailed over the relevance of most of his principles. For *Paradise Lost* would soon become a main arsenal of propagandist devices, furnishing Americans with images and symbols which could rhetorically if not logically argue a cause.[4]

The uses made, the meanings attributed to those images and symbols could by no means be deduced from a coolly decontextualized reading of the texts, as some of Sensabaugh's examples show. As early as 1702, for instance, Cotton Mather was justifying the extermination of the American Indians by identifying them – 'devils in flesh' – with the rebel angels of *Paradise Lost*.[5] But this is no mere cynical rationalization: the Miltonic images, narratives, arguments are fully internalized, absorbing the contexts and meanings imposed on them by the historical crises and ideological impulsions into which they are plunged. Over a century later, the conservative Federalist Andrew Bigelow, in an Independence Day speech a fortnight after the battle of Waterloo, drew upon the same associations to conjure the figure of the fallen Bonaparte:

Amidst the universal dismay ... a gigantic form, mantled in every terror, arose on the bewildered view; and, like Milton's Satan, strode resistless along the flaming waste. Of boundless ambition, he grasped at universal empire: of daring impiety, proudly 'shook his hand against the mount of the Daughters of Zion'.[6]

And here is Jefferson, who had himself been attacked by his Federalist opponents for his 'obdurate pride' and 'steadfast hate', looking back in old age and pondering the experience of defeat in a letter to a friend:

The battle of Hastings, indeed, was lost, but the natural rights of the nation were not staked on the event of a single battle. Their wish to recover the Saxon constitution continued unabated, and was at bottom of all the unsuccessful insurrections which succeeded in subsequent times. The victors and vanquished continued in a state of living hostility, and the nation may say, after losing the battle of Hastings,

> What though the field is lost?
> All is not lost; the unconquerable will

[4] George F. Sensabaugh, *Milton in Early America* (Princeton, 1964), p. 146.
[5] Cotton Mather, *Magnalia Christi Americana* (1702); quoted in Sensabaugh, *Milton in Early America*, p. 39.
[6] Andrew Bigelow, *An Oration Delivered Before the Washington Benevolent Society at Cambridge, July 4th, 1815*; quoted in Sensabaugh, *Milton in Early America*, p. 261. Waterloo was on 18 June.

> And study of revenge, immortal hate,
> And courage never to submit or yield.[7]

The history of England from the conquest, read, in terms that would
have been familiar to any russet-coated captain in the 1640s, as a
series of struggles between the 'natural rights of the nation', embodied
in the 'Saxon constitution', and a usurping Norman tyranny, is then
itself pulled into focus through a Miltonic prism, so that each element
becomes a commentary on the others; and the whole complex is then
extrapolated and extended, through a curious quasi-pun ('the
unsuccessful insurrections which succeeded in subsequent times') and
a striking shift of tense ('the nation may say'), to the present and
beyond: 1776 succeeds (in both senses) to 1649 as that succeeded to
1066. The pattern unfolds continuously, and its key is *Paradise Lost*.
There is no forcing here, none of the sense of strain, of connections
made by ingenuity and conscious effort, that are so often found in the
English radical Miltonists of the same period. The almost casual ease
with which each element evokes and makes sense of all the others
denotes a mind, and a political culture, in which these articulations
have become habitual.

 For Jefferson, *Paradise Lost*, or rather that reading of the poem that
might be called *Satan Agonistes*, seems to have had a special partisan,
and perhaps a personal, significance. I have already noted that his
opponents in the constitutional struggles of the 1780s and 90s
deplored his Satanic obduracy and implacability; and the editor of
his *Literary Commonplace Book*, in which Milton entries outnumber all
other poets,[8] notes that the many passages he transcribed from the
poem lay significant stress on Satanic rebellion. Washington and
other conservative federalists drew freely on the first two books,
described by Sensabaugh as 'a main arsenal of propagandist devices',
to attack 'Citizen Genet' and the radical republicans; and the
collected papers of the leading insurrectionists, and their opponents,
provide plenty of evidence to support Sensabaugh's contention that

---

[7] Letter to G. W. Lewis, 25 October 1825, in *The Writings of Thomas Jefferson*, ed. Andrew A.
Lipscomb and Albert E. Burgh, 20 vols. (Washington, 1903–5), XVI, p. 127.

 [8] The young Jefferson's Miltonic enthusiasm should be compared with the computation by
Donald Lutz of citations from European authors in American political writing of the
revolutionary period, in which Milton stands in twenty-second place, the only poets to
upstage him being Shakespeare (nineteenth) and Pope (twenty-first). The majority of writers
in Lutz's table are of course political theorists such as Montesquieu, Locke, Hobbes and
Machiavelli. See Donald S. Lutz, 'The Relative Influence of European Writers on Late
Eighteenth-Century American Political Thought', *American Political Science Review*, 78 (1984),
189–97. David Armitage drew my attention to this article.

'at this particular moment in American history Milton played a role he could play nowhere else: he could and did become an inextricable part of a country seeking national identity'.[9] The conservative *Virginia Gazette* compared Jeffersonian republicanism to

> all monstrous, all prodigious things
> Abominable, unutterable, and worse
> Than fables yet have feign'd, or fear conceived
> Gorgons and hydras, and chimeras dire.[10]

'You will observe', John Adams wrote to James Warren about Thomas Gage, the hated Governor of Massachusetts who commanded the British troops at Lexington and Concord,

that The Arch Enemy, is at work again in his infernal Council at Boston. I never think of the Junto there, immured as they are, without recollecting, the infernal Spirits in Milton after they have recovered from their first astonishment arising from their fall from the Battlements of Heaven to the Sulphurous Lake – not subdued tho confounded – plotting a fresh assault upon the Skies.

> 'What tho the Field be lost?
> All is not lost; th' unconquerable Will
> and Study of Revenge, immortal Hate
> and Courage never to submit or yield &c.
>   Of this be sure,
> to do aught good never will be our Task,
> but ever to do ill our Sole Delight' &c

though he did add that he thought this 'rather too frolick some and triumphant for the Times, which are dull enough – and as bad as they can be'.[11] Fifteen months later, the same association between British colonial rule and Satanic pomp informs Adams's letter to Horatio Gates:

The Tories will have a pernicious Influence, and will be indefatigable in their Intrigues Insinuations and Cabals, in every Colony while any one of them, holds an office under a King. When 'Thrones, Dominations Princedoms, Powers', in the Language of Milton, are excluded from their Ideas of Government, Toryism will be disarmed of its Sting.[12]

And the habit of looking at the Revolution through the refracting prism of *Paradise Lost* is found, too, in a letter from his wife Abigail, in

---

[9] Sensabaugh, *Milton in Early America*, p. ix.
[10] *Virginia Gazette*, 12 April 1776. Quoted in Gordon S. Wood, *The Creation of the American Republic, 1776–1787* (Chapel Hill, 1969), p. 98.
[11] *The Papers of John Adams*, ed. Robert J. Taylor, 6 vols. (Cambridge, Mass., 1977–), II, p. 209 (3 January 1775).   [12] Adams, *Papers*, IV, p. 148 (27 April 1776).

August 1778, on the subject of the English commissioners:

I cannot help considering them in the Light of the fallen Angles in Milton
who meditating upon their own miserable State and lost Liberties are
desirous of involving this new World, this paradice of Freedom in the same
chains and thraldom with their own and thus coveting,

> 'Here perhaps some advantageous act may be achievd
> By sudden onset, or with tempting Bribe
> To waste this whole creation or possess all as our own
> and drive, as we are driven the puny habitants
> or if not drive, seduce them to our party,
> that their God may prove their foe
> And with repenting hand, abolish his own work.'

They too like the Grand Deceiver must be making use of the same
instruments to effect their diabolical plans by tempting a Modern Eve to
taste the forbidden Fruit.

That the allegory here is not merely mechanical or decorative is clear
from the next sentence, which shows how fully, and how critically, the
poem has been imaginatively internalized.

But tis with pleasure I find in the General and Statesman a more rigid virtue
and incorruptable Heart than our primitive parent discoverd, tho perhaps it
may be happy for the Gentleman that his own Eve was not imployd, and she
the only Female on Earth, or that unbounded knowledg was not the Bribe,
instead of the paltry Gold.[13]

But if *Paradise Lost* supplied some of the core mythology and
subjectivity of the revolutionary enterprise, its ideological substance
demanded also an engagement with the prose writings. Jefferson's
pamphlets, correspondence and commonplace book demonstrate at
key points a debate with Miltonic ideas. His *Summary View of the Rights
of British America* looks back to the 1630s and 40s, and rehearses
Buchananite arguments for tyrannicide in the language of the *Tenure*
and the *Defensio*:

A family of princes was then on the British throne, whose treasonable crimes
against their poor brought on them afterwards the exertion of those sacred
and sovereign rights of punishment reserved in the hands of the people for
cases of extreme necessity, and judged by the constitution unsafe to be
delegated to any other judicature.[14]

And drafting legislation for disestablishment in Virginia in 1776, he

---

[13] *The Adams Family Correspondence*, ed. L. H. Butterfield and Marc Friedlander, 6 vols.
(Cambridge, Mass., 1963–93), III, pp. 77–8 (19 August 1778).
[14] Thomas Jefferson, *A Summary View of the Rights of British America* (Williamsburg 1774), pp. 7–8.

drew on *Of Reformation* and *The Reason of Church Government*, as well as on Locke and Shaftesbury, for arguments and examples of universal clerisy and the accountability of pastors and bishops.[15] Miltonic sources for his most famous piece of writing, the *Declaration of Independence* which he drafted in the same year as the Virginia constitution, are harder to demonstrate; but its opening sentence, especially in its first draft ('We hold these truths to be sacred and undeniable; that all men are created equal and independent, that from that equal creation they derive rights inherent and inalienable . . .'), may owe something to *The Tenure of Kings and Magistrates* ('No man who knows ought, can be so stupid to deny that all men naturally were borne free, being the image and resemblance of God himself . . .').[16]

Again, Jefferson's practical interest in Milton's prose was matched by his friend and collaborator John Adams. Adams, says Russell Smith in his study of Harrington's influence in America and France,

gives two or three lists of the writers who were most read in his day and in his opinion influenced American judgement most. They belonged to the three periods of English history, the Reformation, the Interregnum, the Revolution of 1688. In the first came translations and criticisms of Machiavelli; in the second, Harrington, Milton, and the 'Vindiciae contra Tyrannos'; in the third, Sidney, Locke, Hoadley, Trenchard, Gordon, 'Plato Redivivus'.[17]

A familiar republican pantheon is forming here. Adams, who after reading Milton recorded in his diary that 'That mans Soul, it seems to me, was distended as wide as Creation. His Power over the human mind was absolute and unlimited',[18] located American revolutionary ideas squarely in the English republican tradition, a tradition largely ignored in its own country. His *Thoughts on Government* (1776) begins:

A man must be indifferent to the sneers of modern Englishmen to mention in their company the names of Sidney, Harrington, Locke, Milton, Nedham, Burnet, and Hoadley. No small fortitude is necessary to confess that one has read them. The wretched condition of this country, however, for ten or fifteen years past, has frequently reminded me of their principles and reasonings. They will convince any candid mind, that there is no good government but what is Republican,[19]

15 'Notes on Episcopacy', in *The Papers of Thomas Jefferson*, ed. Julian P. Boyd *et al.*, 24 vols. (Princeton, 1950–), I, pp. 551–3.
16 *The Declaration of Independence*, ed. Julian P. Boyd (Princeton, 1945); *The Tenure of Kings and Magistrates*, in *CPW*, III, 198–9.
17 H. F. Russell Smith, *Harrington and His Oceana* (Cambridge, 1914), p. 186.
18 *The Diary and Autobiography of John Adams*, ed. L. H. Butterfield, 4 vols. (Cambridge, Mass., 1961), I, p. 23 (30 April 1756).
19 Adams, *Papers*, IV, p. 87. The *Thoughts*, which were widely circulated in manuscript and reprinted several times, exist in a number of versions.

and ends, in one version at least, with the opening quatrain of the
sonnet on the reception of the divorce pamphlets, 'I did but prompt
the age to quit their clogs/By the known rules of ancient liberty.'[20]

Like Jefferson, Adams took from the anti-prelatical writings
axioms about religious liberty and the derivative authority of
bishops, readily extrapolated into secular affairs. In the *Tenure*
and the *Defences* he found a heroic historiography of popular
emancipation. But the hardest arguments of all, after the Revolution,
were those about forms of republican polity; and there, the key
text was *The Readie and Easie Way*. Adams's republicanism, though
susceptible to populist rhetoric, was, like Milton's, hierarchical
and elitist, grounded in a 'natural aristocracy' of ability and
virtue. But the same premises that drove Milton, in the constitutional crisis of 1659–60, to argue for a permanent single chamber
impelled Adams in his *Thoughts on Government* in the opposite,
Harringtonian direction, advocating a double chamber as a check
on the tendency of nature's aristocrats to exploit their intellectual
superiority and usurp tyrannical powers. The issues here drew
Adams into argument with Thomas Paine, who, he writes in his
Diary (April 1776),

soon after the Appearance of my Pamphlet [the *Thoughts on Government*]
hurried away to my Lodgings and spent an Evening with me. His Business
was to reprehend me for publishing my Pamphlet. Said he was afraid it
would do hurt, and that it was repugnant to the plan he had proposed in his
Common Sense. I told him it was true it was repugnant and for that reason, I
had written it and consented to the publication of it: for I was as much afraid
of his Work [as] he was of mine. His plan was so democratical, without any
restraint or even an Attempt at any Equilibrium or Counterpoise, that it
must produce confusion and every Evil Work. I told him further, that his
Reasoning from the Old Testament was ridiculous, and I could hardly think
him sincere. At this he laughed, and said he had taken his Ideas in that part
from Milton: and then expressed a Contempt of the Old Testament and
indeed of the Bible at large, which surprized me.[21]

Paine, less literary than Adams, or less inclined to display his
literariness, is nonetheless another who on occasion articulates and
animates his ideas in Miltonic terms. 'Reconciliation', he urged the
waverers of 1776, 'is now a fallacious dream ... For as Milton nicely
expresses, "Never can true reconcilement grow where wounds of
deadly hate have pierced so deep"';[22] and his gnomic condensation of

---

[20] Adams, *Papers*, IV, p. 93.   [21] Adams, *Diary and Autobiography*, III, p. 333.

social contract theory in the same pamphlet, though a commonplace of radical thinking, has a Miltonic resonance and pathos: 'Government, like dress, is the badge of lost innocence. The palaces of kings are built upon the ruins of the bowers of paradise.'[23]

Adams was the new republic's first ambassador in England, and there, through Richard Price and the London Corresponding Society, as well as in Paris, where, accompanied by Jefferson, he joined Benjamin Franklin as a commissioner, he encountered a resurgent European republicanism, which the American Revolution had done much to foster, at first hand. There, writes Russell Smith,

the old battle began again, and the arguments that had been used by Milton and Nedham or the supporters of the Long Parliament against Harrington or the Cromwellians were again repeated. Dr Price, whose pamphlets met with a wonderful popularity, was backed up by Turgot and Mirabeau in his eulogies of the concentration of power.[24]

In April 1778, he met the young Condorcet, 'a Philosopher with a face as pale and rather as white as a Sheet of paper, I suppose from hard study'. But Adams, though delighted to be told that his command of the language was much better than Franklin's, whose pronunciation was so bad that he was incomprehensible, was never so fully at home in French intellectual life as his fellow commissioner. Franklin, a radical who said of British colonial policy that it 'puts me in mind of Milton's Description of Chaos, where every Thing is inconsistent with, and contrary to every Thing',[25] and a freethinker who raised *Paradise Lost* to the status of holy writ by incorporating the 'morning hymn' from Book v, set to music by himself and illustrated with a diagram of the solar system, into his private liturgy,[26] is the real bridge (the word is his own) connecting the American with the French republicans.

'We see them for the first time, a great people delivered from all its chains.'[27] Condorcet's salute to the American Revolution, from his *Sketch for a Historical Picture of the Progress of the Human Mind*, is only one of the passages from that remarkable work, written on the run and under the shadow of the guillotine, in which it is tempting to find a

[22] Thomas Paine, *Common Sense* (1776), in *Political Writings*, ed. Bruce Kuklick (Cambridge, 1989), p. 22.   [23] Paine, *Political Writings*, p. 3.   [24] Russell Smith, *Harrington*, p. 196.

[25] Benjamin Franklin, *Papers*, gen., ed. Leonard Labaree, 28 vols. (New Haven, 1959–), pp. 54–5.

[26] Franklin, *Papers*, I, pp. 106–7.

[27] Marie Jean Antoine Nicolas de Caritat, marquis de Condorcet, *Sketch for a Historical Picture of the Progress of the Human Mind*, trans. Jane Barraclough (New York, 1955), p. 144.

Miltonic echo. That perhaps is too close to the generic rhetoric of Rousseauist radicalism to sustain the claim; but consider the following:

Yet, little by little, day breaks again; eyes long condemned to darkness catch a glimpse of the light and close again, then slowly become accustomed to it, and at last gaze on it without flinching... We have already seen reason lift her chains, shake herself free from some of them, and, all the time regaining strength, prepare for and advance the moment of her liberation.[28]

Here the reminiscence of England in 1644 'shaking her invincible locks' (does an inspired misreading connect 'locks' with 'chains'?) and 'as an Eagle muing her mighty youth, and kindling her undazl'd eyes at the full midday beam'[29] is given some support by the context, in which Condorcet is arguing for the revolutionary effects of printing and the impossibility of censorship:

The instruction that every man is free to receive from books in silence and solitude can never be completely corrupted... How with a multitude of different books, with the innumerable copies of each book, of reprints that can be made available at a moment's notice, how would it be possible to bolt every door, to seal every crevice through which truth aspires to enter? ... Has it not become impossible today when it would be necessary to maintain an absolutely ceaseless vigilance and an unresting activity?[30]

Nothing will persuade me that, in the rich intertext that has by the 1790s constellated around this topic, Milton's defence of the liberty of unlicensed printing does not contribute a major strand of argument and imagery. But the mathematician Condorcet, driven by a taxonomic fury and a dream of a society as clean and orderly as a theorem of Newton, was no Miltonist. His own version of the republican tradition, 'Althusius and Languet ... Nedham and Harrington',[31] makes no mention of the poet. I have no idea whether he was familiar with *Areopagitica*; but if he was, it will not have been through the translation most easily accessible to him, in which the passage I have referred to does not occur. This was the version by a contemporary Frenchman who certainly was an enthusiast for Milton, namely Mirabeau.

It would be interesting to speculate on the reasons behind the surprisingly small attention paid by the American revolutionaries to the work that might have been expected to supply the libertarian cause with some of its most eloquent and compelling arguments. The priority of political and (to a lesser extent) ecclesiastical imperatives,

---

[28] Condorcet, *Sketch*, p. 124.   [29] *Areopagitica*, in *CPW*, II, 558.
[30] Condorcet, *Sketch*, p. 102.   [31] Condorcet, *Sketch*, p. 111.

and the constitutionalism and anti-clericalism of the radical Whig tradition in and through which they read Milton, may explain the emphasis on the anti-prelatical writings, the *Tenure* and the *Readie and Easie Way*, and the corresponding neglect of *Areopagitica*. In pre-revolutionary France, the situation is altogether different. Here, a Protestant 'reforming of reformation' grounded in Luther, Zwingli, Calvin and Foxe's *Acts and Monuments* has little meaning; and open discussion of tyrannicide and the virtues of republicanism is scarcely feasible. Radical thought, in consequence, is displaced from questions of state and church to the marginally less perilous ground of private and civil liberty, constructing an alternative canon of the prose Milton: the *Doctrine and Discipline*, the *Defences*, above all *Areopagitica*.

Mirabeau's translation and abridgement of the last of these, entitled *Sur la liberté de la presse, imité de l'Anglois, de Milton*, was published, ostensibly 'à Londres' but actually in Paris, in 1788, on the eve of the summoning of the States General ('At the very moment when the King invites the entire French people to enlighten him on the justest and wisest way of summoning the nation … the freedom of the press is being persecuted, in the Monarch's name, more savagely and with a more energetic and deceitful inquisition than the most unbridled ministerial despotism has ever dared attempt'), and addressed to the well-intentioned but timid and misguided *honnêtes gens* who had persuaded themselves that the freedom of the press, espoused by radicals and *philosophes*, was a stalking-horse for atheism and revolution:

It is therefore to them above all that we must address ourselves: and, since I assume them to be people of good faith, even where their adversaries are concerned, I have thought it useful to bring to their attention a refutation of their views, pursued through all its moral implications, by a man imbued, on this subject at least, with their own principles. He wrote 150 years ago, in a deeply religious century when, though one might be discussing the great issues of this life, no less than those of the next, it was theological arguments that would be by far the most effective. No-one has ever accused this man of being a *philosophe*: and if in some of his writings Milton showed himself to be a violent republican, in this one, in which he addresses the parliament of Great Britain, he is nothing but a peaceable advocate.[32]

---

[32] Honoré Gabriel de Riquetti, marquis de Mirabeau, *Sur la liberté de la presse* (Paris, 1788), p. 8 (translations from Mirabeau are my own). Mirabeau's use of Milton has been discussed by D. M. Wolfe ('Milton and Mirabeau', *Publications of the Modern Languages Association of America*, 49 (1934), 1116–28), and more recently by the French Miltonist and translator of *Areopagitica*, Olivier Lutaud, to whom I am indebted for a copy of his paper 'Des révolutions d'Angleterre à la Révolution française: l'exemple de la liberté de la presse, ou comment Milton "ouvrit" les Etats Généraux'. See also the article on Mirabeau in William B. Hunter *et al.* (eds.), *Milton Encyclopedia* 9 vols. (Lewisburg, 1978–83), v, p. 148.

This prefatory salvo demonstrates two of the three difficulties confronting Mirabeau's attempt to conscript Milton to the cause of moderate constitutional monarchism, at a time when his formidable powers of diplomacy and political manoeuvre were principally employed in attempting to devise a French equivalent to the English settlement of 1689. First, in France as in America, the prose Milton was firmly associated with a tradition of regicide and republican radicalism. Second, the biblical and theodicean character of his writing, acceptable in poetry, was uncongenial to Parisian intellectual culture, deist and Catholic alike. And thirdly, the imperialistic Protestant nationalism, which his American admirers, who still thought of themselves as God's Englishmen, could appropriate as merely an earlier expression of their own providentially guided enterprise, was far more problematic in a country where even anglophiles were likely to look to British expansionist aims with distrust. Mirabeau's *Areopagitica*, therefore, is skilfully constructed to disguise these aspects of Milton's text, diluting its historical and chiliastic immediacy, its close engagement with the biblical commonplaces of Protestant polemic, in favour of secular and practical arguments addressed not to a parliament of saints but to a readership of *bien-pensant* bourgeois. The title page illustrates this manoeuvre. The quotation from Euripides' *Supplices* gives way to an epigraph from the text itself, an epigraph pruned of the theology that gives the original much of its contentious energy. Compare Mirabeau's 'to kill a man is to destroy a reasonable creature; but to smother a book is to kill reason itself' with Milton's 'who kills a Man kills a reasonable creature, God's Image; but hee who destroyes a good Booke, kills reason it selfe, kills the Image of God, as it were in the eye'.[33] Or later, the quiet secularization that turns 'Who knows not the Truth is strong next to the Almighty' into 'Who can doubt its eternal and invincible strength?'[34] Or, in one of the most intriguing adaptations, the substitution for Milton's resounding theodicy ('This justifies the high Providence of God, who though he commands us temperance, justice, continence, yet powrs out before us ev'n to a profuseness all desirable things') of an unattributed paraphrase of the deistic commonplaces of the *Essay on Man* ('We sail in all directions upon the vast ocean of life; reason is the compass, but passion is the

[33] Mirabeau, title page ('Tuer un homme, c'est détruire une créature raisonnable; mais étouffer un bon livre, c'est tuer la raison elle-même'); Milton, *CPW*, II, 492.
[34] *CPW*, II, 562–3; Mirabeau, p. 52 ('Qui peut douter de sa force éternelle & invincible?').

wind').[35] By the same logic, many of Milton's most characteristic illustrative figures are lost: the 'fugitive and cloister'd virtue', the perversion of the 'acute and distinct Arminius', the Talmudist with his 'marginall Keri' and 'textuall Chetiv'.[36] The translation jumps over the long Pauline discussion of the notion that 'books are as meats and viands are' with an impatient 'But taking our leave of learning, authorities, examples, and returning to the reality of things'.[37]

Some cuts, admittedly, look like concessions to bourgeois squeamishness. Claudius' prudent decision not to insist on the criminalization of flatulence is lost;[38] and what reader, confronted with the decorous reticence of Mirabeau's 'there was no more abortion of the intellect than of the womb', would suspect its derivation from one of the most memorable of Milton's masculine *accouchements* ('the issue of the brain was no more stifl'd than the issue of the womb: no envious Juno sate cros-leg'd over the nativity of any mans intellectuall off spring: but if it prov'd a Monster, who denies, but that it was justly burnt, or sunk into the Sea')?[39] But others seem dictated by political caution, a wariness of the text's implicit republicanism. 'Ancient and famous Commonwealths' becomes the neutral 'most renowned governments';[40] and it may be this, as much its nationalism, that prompted the omission of the boast that 'our English, the language of men ever famous, and formost in the atchievements of liberty, will not easily finde servile letters enow to spell such a dictatorie presumption' and the decision not to attempt the famous peroration, beginning 'Lords and Commons of England, consider what Nation it is wherof ye are, and wherof ye are the governors.'[41]

Mirabeau's translation was reprinted the following year in a curious compilation entitled *Théorie de la Royauté, d'après la doctrine de Milton*. Some copies apparently claim Mirabeau's authorship, but the British Library copy is anonymous, with a contemporary hand-written inscription under the title 'p[ar] mirabeau'. In addition to the *Areopagitica* translation, this contains extracts from the *Doctrine and Discipline of Divorce* and an abridged translation of the *Defensio*,

---

[35] *CPW*, II, 527–8; Mirabeau, pp. 37–8 ('Nous naviguons diversement sur le vaste océan de la vie: la raison en est la boussole, mais la passion en est le vent'): cf. Pope, *Essay on Man*, II, 107ff.

[36] *CPW*, II, 515, 519–20, 517.

[37] *CPW*, II, 512ff; Mirabeau, p. 24 ('Mais laissant-là l'érudition, les autorités, les exemples, & remontant à la nature des choses').   [38] *CPW*, II, 504 and note.

[39] Mirabeau, p. 22 ('on ne faisoit pas plus avorter l'esprit que les entrailles'); *CPW*, II, 505.

[40] *CPW*, II, 493; Mirabeau, p. 11 ('des gouvernements les plus célèbres').

[41] *CPW*, II, 505, 551ff.

with the surprising claim that 'although most of the principles it contains are now acknowledged and accepted, it required in Milton's day a truly extraordinary genius to perceive and elaborate them as he did'.[42] This determination to draw the sting of Milton's republicanism and present him as a moderate constitutional monarchist runs into trouble, unsurprisingly, with the *Tenure, Eikonoklastes* and the *Readie and Easie Way*, precisely the texts that, for Mirabeau's friend Franklin, constituted the essential canon of Milton's political value. The first is described innocuously, without quotation, as a riposte to Presbyterian hypocrisy. The other two are quoted briefly and cautiously characterized ('Milton published a work in which he sketched a plan for a republic'[43]), and the responsibility for their offensive republicanism is tactfully displaced onto the English people as a whole:

The great fault of the English was, not to punish a guilty king, but to outlaw kingship itself; as if it had been an accomplice in the outrages of the man who wore its robes! That is the crime of the English people: for however extensive the rights of nations, they cannot enjoy the privilege of injustice.[44]

However guarded its endorsement of Miltonic principles, the *Théorie* is nonetheless remarkably outspoken, given its moment of publication. In the circumstances of 1789 it is a bold if oblique gesture to say of Charles I that 'Everyone knows that he lost his life on a scaffold, but it is quite futile to attempt to represent as murder something that is fundamentally nothing but a great example of justice',[45] or to retort to Voltaire, who had a poor opinion of Milton's prose, that 'A poet, wit and gentleman of the chamber must surely be ill-equipped to judge the political writings of the republican.'[46] And for all Mirabeau's

---

[42] *Théorie de la royauté* (Paris, 1789), pp. ii–iii ('Je me suis attaché sur-tout à sa fameuse défense du peuple Anglois ... quoique la plupart des principes qu'elle contient, soient maintenant avoués & reconnus, il falloit, du temps de Milton, un génie bien extraordinaire pour les appercevoir & pour les développer comme il l'a fait'). The *Théorie* was apparently compiled by J.-B. Salaville, but the authorship of the introduction and translations (except for the *Areopagitica*) cannot conclusively be assigned to Mirabeau.

[43] *Théorie*, p. lxxiii ('Milton fit paraître un ouvrage dans lequel il traçoit un plan de République').

[44] *Théorie*, p. lvi ('La grande faute que commirent les Anglois, ne fut pas de punir un roi coupable, mais de proscrire la royauté; comme si elle eût été complice des attentats de celui qui en etait revêtu ... Voilà le crime des Anglois: car quelque étendus que soient les droits des nations, elles n'ont pas le privilège de l'injustice').

[45] *Théorie*, p. lvi ('Tout le monde sait qu'il perdit la vie sur un échaffaud, & c'est bien inutilement qu'on a voulu transformer en parricide, ce qui n'est au fond qu'un grand exemple de justice').

[46] *Théorie*, p. lxxviii ('Un poète, bel esprit & gentilhomme de la chambre, devoit etre peu propre sans doute à juger par lui-même les écrits politiques du républicain').

circumspection, the radical potential of the *Théorie* was not lost on the regicide Jacobins of the Drome département, who reissued the translation of the *Defensio* in 1792 ('year one' of the revolutionary calendar) with a preface explaining the origin of the text, and calling for the trial and punishment of the king and the establishment of a republic:

In 1649 Charles the first lost his head on the scaffold, in consequence of a judgement delivered against him by the English parliament. This act of national justice, unparalleled in modern history, laid the English open to the charge of murder. Saumaise, a pedant of French origin, but now the pensioner of a republic where he was a professor, attempted to exonerate Charles for the crimes of which he was accused, and did not flinch from putting a whole nation in the dock in a diatribe entitled Defensio regia, a defence of the king. Milton responded vigorously to this sorry production, demonstrating that he was as profound a political thinker as he was a great poet, with the work that we now reprint, and which appeared originally under the title Defensio pro populo anglicano, an apology for the English people.[47]

The decree authorizing the publication conjures the 'venerable disguise and borrowed language' of Milton in even more extravagantly reverential terms, asserting that the *Defensio*

grounds and elaborates the inalienable rights of sovereignty of all peoples with as much clarity as solidity; that the genius which produced it inflames all hearts with the sacred fire of liberty ... that it demonstrates to all adherents of the inviolability of kings that in all times and among all nations their crimes have been expiated on the scaffold; that it is the duty of the Administrators to form and nourish public opinion on the great question that occupies the National Convention concerning the judgement of Louis Capet [Louis XVI], which must be presented to the jurisdiction of the people; that the Administration is certain to accomplish this object by disseminating, in the country districts especially, the knowledge of a book which has become very rare, and through the reading of which every French republican will be able to grasp intelligently the relation and analogy between the conduct of Charles Stuart and that of Louis Capet.[48]

Olivier Lutaud, writing of Mirabeau's *Areopagitica* translation, remarks that Milton 'opened the States General' in 1788. The 1792 *Défense* suggests that his posthumous shadow also fell across the guillotine that executed Louis XVI five years later. As for the

---

[47] *Défense du peuple anglais, sur le jugement et condamnation de Charles premier roi d'Angleterre, Par Milton, Ouvrage propre à éclairer sur la circonstance actuelle où se trouve la France* (Valence, 1792), sig. A2$^{r\ v}$.   [48] *Défense*, p. 5.

Areopagitica translation itself, it had three editions between 1788 and 1792, the last of them also dated 'year one', by which time its Girondin project of a constitutional monarchy constrained by bourgeois institutions ('a judiciously qualified attachment to the ancient forms') was already running out of time. It was reprinted in England in 1819, the year of Peterloo and Shelley's *Mask of Anarchy*, as an appendix to Thomas Holt White's edition of *Areopagitica*. And something of its wider European circulation may be suggested by the publication in 1831 in Nauplion, the first capital of the newly liberated Hellenic republic, of a Greek translation, *Perí Típou*, 'after Mirabeau, who took his original from Milton'.[49] Thus the 'surly and acrimonious republican' who wrote *Areopagitica*, and who had once written that 'if ... I could call forth our army and navy to free Greece, land of eloquence, from the Ottoman tyrant ... truly there is nothing which I should rather or sooner do', did perhaps at last play some part not only in the American and the French but in the Greek emancipation too.[50] And it completes a curious historical symmetry that the Athenian to whom he wrote those words was himself an ambassador at the court of Louis XIV.

'In these revolutions ... the resurrection of the dead served to exalt the new struggles ... to exaggerate the given task in the imagination ... to reawaken the spirit of revolution.'[51] For Marx, these 'world-historical reminiscences' serve as an ideological alibi, a masquerade of the illustrious dead to disguise or inflate the limited class-content and political programme of the revolutionary party. Jefferson and Mirabeau use Milton as he himself used Samson, as a figure for a project not yet complete, a powerful parent to be loved, feared and at last rejected, or at least transcended. 'When the actual goal had been reached, when the bourgeois transformation of ... society had been accomplished, Locke drove out Habakkuk.'

But this, written at a time when social revolutions could still be thought of as swift and decisive, may be too schematic, with its Hegelian confidence in the inevitable passage from superstition to enlightenment. Which of us can confidently say, now, that the 'bourgeois transformation of society' is anywhere complete? The

---

[49] *Perí Típou* ['On the Press'] (Nauplion, 1831). There are good grounds for thinking that this pamphlet, dedicated to the excluded republican members of the Greek Senate, may be the work of the young poet and journalist Panayiotis Soutsos, who had studied in Paris and was an admirer of Mirabeau.   [50] Letter to Leonard Philaras, June 1652, in *CPW*, IV, 853.

[51] Marx, *Surveys from Exile*, p. 148.

Chinese politician Chou En Lai, asked what he thought the most significant legacy of the French Revolution, is reported to have replied that it was 'too early to judge'. Perhaps this may be true of Milton too. Reports of his 'dislodgement' were certainly premature;[52] and the recent resurgence of serious attention to his political ideas and the republican traditions that animate them, to which this volume is a welcome testimony, cannot, for all their absorbing historical interest and importance, be ascribed merely to what Marx called 'a superstitious veneration for the past'.

[52] F. R. Leavis claimed in 1952 that Milton had been conclusively 'dislodged' from his canonical eminence. In the same essay he pronounced it 'deplorable' that students should 'devote any large part of their time to the solemn study of Milton's "thought"': Leavis, *The Common Pursuit* (Harmondsworth, 1962), p. 23.

Index

Ideas in Context

Edited by Quentin Skinner (general editor),
Lorraine Daston, Wolf Lepenies, Richard Rorty and J. B. Schneewind

Titles marked with an asterisk are also available in paperback